The Language of Liberal Constitutionalism

The Language of Liberal Constitutionalism explores two basic questions regarding constitutional theory. First, given a commitment to democratic self-rule and widespread disagreement on questions of value, how is the creation of a legitimate constitutional regime possible? Second, what must be true about a constitution if the regime that it supports is to retain its claim to legitimacy?

Howard Schweber proposes answers to these questions in a theory of constitutional language that combines democratic theory with constitutional philosophy. He observes that the creation of a legitimate constitutional regime depends on a shared commitment to a particular and specialized form of language. Out of this simple observation, Schweber develops arguments about the characteristics of constitutional language, the relationship between constitutional language and the language of ordinary law or morality, and the authority of officials such as judges to engage in constitutional review of laws.

The Language of Liberal Constitutionalism will be read by professionals and students in public law, the philosophy and sociology of law, and democratic theory, as well as general readers interested in constitutional law and political theory.

HOWARD SCHWEBER is associate professor of political science at the University of Wisconsin-Madison. He is the author of *The Creation of American Common Law, 1850–1880; Speech, Conduct, and the First Amendment*; and book chapters and articles in journals such as *Law and History Review*, *Law and Society Review*, and *Studies in American Political Development*.

THE LANGUAGE OF LIBERAL CONSTITUTIONALISM

HOWARD SCHWEBER

University of Wisconsin-Madison

CAMBRIDGE
UNIVERSITY PRESS

CAMBRIDGE UNIVERSITY PRESS
Cambridge, New York, Melbourne, Madrid, Cape Town, Singapore, São Paulo

Cambridge University Press
32 Avenue of the Americas, New York, NY 10013-2473, USA

www.cambridge.org
Information on this title: www.cambridge.org/9780521861328

First published 2007

Printed in the United States of America

A catalogue record for this publication is available from the British Library.

Library of Congress Cataloging in Publication Data

Schweber, Howard H.
The language of liberal constitutionalism / Howard Schweber.
p. cm.
Includes bibliographical references and index.

ISBN-13: 978-0-521-86132-8 (hardback)
ISBN-10: 0-521-86132-2 (hardback)

1. Constitutional law. 2. Legitimacy of governments. 3. Law – Language.
4. Law – Philosophy. I. Title.
K3165.S39 2007
342.001′4 – dc22
2006102483

Contents

Introduction

This book is devoted to an exploration of two closely interrelated questions. First, under what conditions is the creation of a legitimate constitutional regime possible? Second, what must be true about a constitution if the regime that it grounds is to retain its claim to legitimacy?

The focus on legitimacy derives from the fact that a constitution is fundamentally an instrument of legitimation for a set of juridical practices. By the term "juridical" I mean the combination of legal, political, and administrative actions that are undertaken in terms of laws or law-like rules as elements of formal institutions of governance. A constitutional regime is one in which the claim to legitimacy of these juridical practices rests, at least in part, on a prior claim of legitimacy on behalf of a constitution. This is not to say that the constitutional and legal claims of authority are coextensional; the relationship between a constitution and ordinary law will be the subject of a great deal of discussion in later chapters. But describing a system as a "constitutional regime" implies that the system of institutional organization and a set of basic guiding norms are authoritatively contained in the constitutional "text," however conceived. As a result, I will conceive of a constitutional system as one that has two critical elements: institutionalized mechanisms for collective action, and a set of law-like rules supreme within their domain. For a constitutional regime to be legitimate, each of these elements requires an adequate justification.

The scope of this discussion is therefore narrowed to a particular kind of political system that confronts particular kinds of challenges in asserting a claim to legitimacy. In addition, the inquiry that is undertaken here is not a search for the conditions of possibility of any conceivable constitution, but rather takes place within the tradition of liberal constitutionalism, a tradition that assumes the inescapability of value pluralism and accepts the fundamental importance of basic democratic principles. The challenge for liberal constitutionalism, then, is that we cannot answer the questions that this book asks by referring to a necessary set of universally shared moral values or belief in a higher law external to the constitution itself, nor may we accept an explanation that depends on the coercion of the population by force. If liberal constitutionalism is to be made legitimate, the answers to the two questions that motivate this study have to be couched in terms that are consistent with value pluralism and democracy.

The first traditional step in trying to answering these questions derives from the nature of liberal constitutionalism itself. Liberal constitutionalism assumes the acceptance of basic democratic norms in addition to the social fact of value pluralism. Respect for fundamental democratic commitments to self-rule, in turn, implies that legitimation depends on some version of consent of the governed. In the context of a theory of liberal constitutionalism, the question "under what conditions is the creation of a legitimate constitutional regime possible?" becomes shortened to "Consent How?" And the question "what must be true about a constitution if the regime that it grounds is to retain its claim to legitimacy?" becomes, in its shortened version, "Consent to What?"

The argument of this book is extensive and in places complex, but the answers that I propose can be stated simply. Broadly stated, the argument of this book is that the necessary conditions of possibility for legitimate constitutional rule ultimately involve the creation and maintenance of a language of liberal constitutionalism. What is required for the creation of a legitimate constitutional regime is an initial shared commitment to the creation of a system of constitutional language in a manner consistent with the principle of justification by consent. And for a constitutional regime to retain its claim to legitimacy, the integrity of the system of constitutional language must be preserved, again in a manner consistent with justification by consent. In their third and final iteration, then, the questions to be answered will become "How is consent to a system of constitutional language possible?" and "What must be true about that system of constitutional language in order that consent to its creation and maintenance is sufficient to ground a liberal constitutional regime?"

Each of the formulations just mentioned raises further questions. It is all very well to say that the creation of a constitutional regime requires an initial commitment to language, but how can such a commitment be shown to exist? Thereafter, how can an initial commitment to language be legitimately understood to bind subsequent generations? The idea of a constitutional language system similarly raises further questions. What is the relationship between constitutional language and systems of language employed in legal and moral discourse? And what qualities of form and content is a system of constitutional language required to have if it is to do the work that is being asked of it here?

There are a number of ways to approach these inquiries: One might ask about the sociological conditions that enable a population to engage in a certain kind of collective action; one might investigate the conditions of historical and cultural development that are required to make the phrase "constitutional order" meaningful; or one might ask what juridical traditions and institutions are needed for a project of constitutional construction have a high likelihood of success. My goal in this book, however, is to gain some purchase on the two original questions from a theoretical perspective. That is, I am not attempting to identify a set of historical circumstances under which constitutional democracy is likely to arise, but rather to derive a persuasive argument about legitimacy. My approach in developing the argument is minimalist, in the sense that I am only trying to determine the conditions of possibility for legitimate constitutionalism, not the ideal conditions for the best form of constitutional rule. The further questions of what conditions are sufficient to *ensure* a *desirable* constitutional regime – which are arguably both more difficult and more important than the questions I ask here – are left for another day.

There is also a non-trivial argument that while a constitutional order legitimates juridical practices, that order either cannot or need not be legitimated itself. Such an argument might take the form of the proposition that the project of legitimating a constitutional order is a waste of time. The creation of a constitutional system, it may be said, is a brute historical fact that defines the scope of "legitimacy" for a particular system, and there is no external basis for challenging or affirming the legitimacy of the constitutional order itself. Moreover, one can imagine a society in which the vast majority of persons are perfectly willing to abide by a system of laws without any commitment to principles that recognize those laws as "legitimate" by virtue of the operation of any specifiable principle. Persons might be said to accept a particular set of such rules without any particular view about their legitimacy because they believe that there is a chance that at some point in the future their side will win. Alternatively, the argument might be that persons might simply feel that they are materially better off under the present set of rules than under available alternatives. All of these are arguments for the position that the search for grounding principles of legitimation is both futile and unnecessary.

On closer inspection, however, these turn out to be arguments about the grounds of legitimacy rather than the relevance of the concept. Even in the most interest-driven and instrumental description of a person's reasons for accepting a juridical order, there are implicit appeals to meta-rules, or rule-like norms; an adequate likelihood of ultimate success under existing rules; the equal or characterizable "fair" application of the rules to different parties; and some notion of sufficient reciprocal commitment to the rules on the part of other players and authorized enforcers. The reference to "authorized enforcers," in turn, names another layer of the lurking set of meta-rules that are always involved in any formalized situation of strategic competition.

It is also not the case that appeals to interests and strategic advantage are ever completely absent from a theory of juridical legitimacy. It is, frankly, difficult to imagine an argument for legitimacy that does not coincide with at least one of these instrumental justifications. But these are not persuasive arguments against the necessity for legitimacy. They are arguments about the terms of that discussion. The possibility that today's losers may be tomorrow's winners, the promise of better conditions, or an appeal to rules for the game that are sufficiently rule-like are all ways of invoking legitimating principles quite familiar in constitutional and philosophical debates. In the same way that the most altruistic act can be described as self-interested ("I have an interest in thinking of myself as a moral person"), the most self-interested motivation becomes the basis for a legitimating principle when it is translated into juridical institutions. This observation provides the basis for one of the fundamental tenets of liberalism, that meaningful arguments for the legitimacy of a political system may emerge even in the face of a genuine pluralism of interests and values.

Furthermore, legitimation is an essential condition of possibility for sustained collective action. The term "collective action" refers to a classic problem in political science: How do groups coordinate themselves to act in ways that individual members accept as binding despite disagreements about the desirability of the group decision? An institutionalized system of collective action is one in which it is possible to know when a decision has been reached, the decision-making process is understood to involve direct or indirect participation by the relevant community, and the decision that is reached is understood to apply to community members. In other words, a system of politics.

A system of politics is a necessary implication of any constitutional system. By contrast, imagine a situation of truly absolute monarchial rule. In such a situation, it would be both possible and plausible that a single ruler would issue contradictory mandates to two subordinates, then leave it to them to fight it out. It would also be possible for such a monarch to change his or her mind without notice, or to dictate actions that are entirely destructive of the welfare of those subject to their edicts. Such a system of decision making yields neither collective action nor institutionalization. Decisions by such a governing authority cannot be described as meaningfully "collective" insofar as they rest entirely within the unfettered discretion of an individual actor, and any "action" is obtained through the direct coercion of individuals (excepting members of the coercing organizations, such as an army personally loyal to its commander). And there are none of the elements of predictability, transparency, and rationalization that are required for institutionalization. Multiplying the number of rulers into an oligarchy obviously does nothing to change this equation from a perspective external to the ruling group.

Systems of government that do not satisfy the criteria for institutionalized collective action are neither impossible nor necessarily unstable, but they are not "constitutional" in any meaningful sense. Rather than being maintained by politics, such regimes can be maintained only by the exercise of force, leading inevitably to the question that has bedeviled every dictatorship in history, "Do we hold the army?" If the assumption of the discussion is that we are concerned with regimes that can be sensibly characterized as "constitutional," the necessity that constitutional systems be legitimated is a matter of definition.

The necessity of legitimation is also evident as a matter of sociolegal practice, a conclusion that can be demonstrated by consideration of the prosaic example of the adjudication of private disputes. If participants in a system of dispute resolution cease to accept the outcomes as legitimate, there is a danger that they will either ignore the system or ignore the outcome of its proceedings. At a certain point, in turn, the willingness or ability of the state to mobilize coercive authority to compel respect for the judicial process will be exhausted. At that point, the absence of legitimacy in the system of laws results in a failure of that system as an institution of collective action at all. The statement "there is no right without a remedy" recognizes the meaninglessness of a legitimating standard in the absence of effective institutions of collective action to enforce it; conversely, those institutions cannot be effective for long – or even, in the sense described earlier, remain "institutions" – unless they are themselves viewed as legitimate. To the extent that "constitutional system" is understood to mean "constitutional system stable over time," the need for legitimating arguments is inescapable. By the same token, any description of the conditions of constitutional adequacy is also simultaneously a description of the possibility of constitutional failure.

Recognizing that the question of legitimacy is inescapable has important consequences for the understanding of the term "constitution" even before any particular argument is considered. A "constitution" is often described as a charter for government that performs the dual functions of organizing and defining the limits of the exercise of power. But it will not do to define any system that includes a written charter that fits that description as "constitutional," nor to exclude systems that have no formal charter from the discussion. The former category, after all, would include such regimes as the Soviet Union, while the latter limitation would arguably exclude constitutional systems such as Great Britain, not to mention less clear cases such as Israel. What is missing is the recognition of the special role that a constitution plays in articulating the legitimating principles for the political regime. This is not an observation that depends on the adoption of some particular theory of constitutionalism. Whether one conceives of a constitution as an aspirational statement of highest political goals, or purely as a compact between autonomous entities, consistency with that conception becomes the litmus test for the legitimacy of subsequent juridical acts. Any theory of constitutional rule requires justification by an appeal to a legitimating principle.

As I noted earlier, throughout the discussion that follows I have employed a minimalist approach. That is, I have not attempted to describe the circumstances under which a constitutional order will be the "best" – most just, most moral, most egalitarian, or most free – only the circumstances under which we can speak of a legitimate constitutional order at all. Similarly, I have not attempted to derive everything that might or should follow from the fact of a constitutional system – the most developed possible set of rights, the most effective system of democratic participation, or the most virtuous juridical order – only those consequences that are *necessarily* required for a constitutional system to be able to assert a claim to legitimacy. Nonetheless, I will argue that there are substantial conclusions to be reached with regard to both questions.

With respect to the first motivating question of this book, "Under what conditions is the creation of a legitimate constitutional regime possible?" as I have already indicated, I intend to argue that the creation of a legitimate constitutional regime depends on a prior commitment to employ constitutional language, and that such a commitment is both the necessary and the sufficient condition for constitution making. I will also argue that this initial observation requires us to reconsider the nature and operation of popular sovereignty and the basis for the authority of juridical officials. In response to the second question, "What must be true about a constitution if the regime that it grounds is to retain its claim to legitimacy?" having refocused the inquiry toward the language of constitutional discourse I will argue that a specific set of characteristics described in terms of exclusivity, completeness, and substance, are the analytically necessary answers.

Throughout the discussion, I will argue that the unequal political burdens that these answers impose on democratic action are not only justified, but are actually the inevitable results of the commitment to constitutional self-government. Finally, I will argue that serious errors of modern constitutional practice appear in the failure to preserve the boundaries of constitutional language against a variety of competing forms of discourse, including the languages of religious morality and ordinary law. I will also argue that the analysis requires us to reject claims of emergencies that cannot be expressed in terms recognizable in constitutional discourse. To explain the path of the argument, however, a somewhat more detailed description of its elements is required.

Chapter 1 begins with an exploration of some of the early roots of liberal constitutionalism. In the earliest Western political writings, the solution to the problem of collective action and the need for legitimating principles led to the focus on law as both a legitimating and a legitimate set of organizing principles. Those principles, in turn, derived their legitimacy from some version of natural law principles. That is, laws, and political regimes generally, were legitimate (or "just," or "desirable," or "moral") insofar as they accorded with the natural order of things (as in Aristotle and Cicero), or with divine revelation (as in the Hebrew Bible and Augustine). There were also hints in early writings on the subject of a specific focus on universal human nature – characteristics unique to humans and unconnected to the ontology of the rest of the universe – as the test for legitimacy, leading Justinian to distinguish *jus naturae* (universal laws of nature), *jus gentium* (laws universal to human societies) and *jus civile* (laws specific to particular societies). The natural law tradition is far from absent in modern constitutionalism, where it takes the form of an appeal to substantive moral norms. It should be noted that, in terms of the form of the argument, it makes no difference whether these moral norms are asserted to be uniquely suited to a community, universal to humans, or grounded in metaphysical authority. The argument remains that law is legitimate insofar and to the degree that its content is morally sound.

In the Early Modern period of European history, a different approach to the legitimation of juridical regimes appeared in the form of the theory of sovereignty developed by, among others, Jean Bodin, Thomas Hobbes, and John Locke. The text that is thought of as the beginning of this theory of legitimate government is Bodin's *The Six Books of the Republic*. Bodin was motivated, in large part, by a desire to establish a basis for secular authority capable of withstanding the divisive forces of religious conflict. His solution was to turn away from the content of laws as the basis of their legitimacy, and to focus instead on the identity of the human lawmaker. Contrary to the tradition of medieval constitutionalism, in which a monarch's rule was understood to be constrained by customary norms, the scope of authority in Bodin's version of sovereignty was bounded only by the conditions of its creation. So long as laws emanated from a sovereign and did not contradict the basic nature of its rule, Bodin argued, their legitimacy did not depend on their agreement with other, established normative principles.

Hobbes, and then Locke, developed the idea of sovereignty further, pointing to the centrality of authority over language as an element of lawmaking authority. In the process, the meaning of sovereignty underwent a transformation. For both Bodin and Hobbes, sovereignty was a fundamentally other-directed phenomenon, in which the sovereign exercised authority over others. With Locke, sovereignty comes to be understood as a collective form of self-rule, a formulation that leads to the conclusion that legitimate rule requires consent. In the process, Locke makes the definition of a legitimate governing sovereign the basic test for legitimacy in liberal constitutionalism, characterized by the assertion of collective self-sovereignty, legitimation by consent, and the exercise of authority over language. At the end of Chapter 1, after reviewing these three writers' arguments, I propose that some version of Lockean constitutionalism remains the strongest analytical approach to the problem of defining the conditions of constitutional legitimacy.

Chapters 2 and 3 look beyond Locke's prescriptions to an understanding of the problem in its modern form. These chapters are devoted to exploring the question that was earlier phrased as "Consent How?" Modern challenges to the possibility of legitimate constitutional rule focus on the problems of defining conditions of genuine "consent," describing an understanding of collective action appropriate to the process of constitutional creation, and justifying the possibility of precommitment. Responding to these challenges requires a reconceptualization of popular self-sovereignty as the first necessary step in describing a legitimate constitutional regime. Older models such as those of Bodin and Hobbes depended on a characterization of collective self-rule in terms of an anthropomorphic metaphor of the state as an "artificial person." This metaphorical understanding of collective action, however, is inadequate to provide satisfactory justifications for liberal constitutionalism. Locke's description of a commonwealth began the process of moving away from an anthropomorphic metaphor to something more descriptive of a modern state. To develop a Lockean theory of modern constitutionalism, we must look more deeply into the idea of an initial commitment to linguistic practice that provides the basis for subsequent acts of political consent.

The simple observation that there can be no social contract without a common language in which to express that agreement is the first step toward a theory of constitutional language. Locke's recognition that the creation of language precedes moments of political consent resolves many of the difficulties in establishing conditions of legitimacy at the moment of constitutional creation. At the same time, recognition of the critical fact that constitutional authority operates in the first instance as authority over the creation of new forms of juridical language requires the possibility of forward-looking "consent" of a different kind. Here, the content of constitutional language comes into play. Grounding the legitimacy of a constitutional text in the creation by consent of language-generating authority parallels the approach to grounding the legitimacy of a legal system in facts of sociolegal practice, thus cementing the connection between legitimate and effective constitutional rule in the very terms of its possibility. To apply an argument of this kind to the question of constitutional legitimacy, however, requires a consideration of the differences between constitutional and ordinary law, and rethinking the effect that the creation of a constitutional regime must have on the relationship between language and legitimacy thereafter. The creation of a constitutional regime alters the terms in which claims to legitimacy are asserted, including claims to the legitimacy of the constitutional regime itself.

But this must not be allowed to become an exercise in avoiding the problem of consent by an appeal to an infinite regression to ever-earlier moments of agreement. Ultimately, the conclusion is unavoidable that at the moment of constitutional creation, refusal to consent to some initial commitment to constitutional language does indeed challenge the legitimacy of the creation of a constitutional regime. Similarly, past the point of constitutional establishment, a refusal to accept the regime's authority over language equally denies the legitimacy of its rule. Rather than denying that conclusion, I try to use it to illustrate the ways in which an argument based on a theory of constitutional language has the potential to reshape our understanding of both challenges to, and defenses of, constitutional legitimacy. To avoid an infinite regress, furthermore, it is impossible to ignore the fact that certain specifiable characteristics of a system of constitutional language are required. If a prior moment of consent to a system of constitutional language is the necessary condition for the creation of a constitutional regime, what must, necessarily, be true about that language if it is to provide a sufficient basis for constitutional rule?

Chapters 4 and 5 of this book are devoted to consideration of this second question, which was earlier rephrased as "Consent to What?" Even in light of the commitment to asking the minimalist question of necessary, rather than ideal, conditions for constitutional formation, the problem of establishing an adequate basis for constitutional rule requires consideration. "Legitimate," to be sure, does not equate with "successful," as there are myriad reasons why a legitimate constitutional regime might fail, just as illegitimate regimes frequently flourish. Instead, the term "legitimate" refers to something else: the circumstances under which a regime can be said to deserve to succeed. Nonetheless, if a constitution is to serve as the basis of legitimation for a political regime, it must be plausibly described as serving that function in practice, not merely to stand as an exemplar for a hypothetical state unrelated to the reasoning and actions of real juridical actors.

As a result, constitutionalism has both formal and a substantive elements: a constitutional regime is one that produces an *effective* institutionalized system of collective action, and a legitimate constitutional regime is one in which that effectiveness can be sustained over time by an adequate argument for the authority of juridical institutions of governance. A legitimate constitution requires a persuasive claim to be the exclusive legitimating mechanism for the exercise of political authority. Preserving the conditions of possibility for continued consent to a system of constitutional language therefore requires a consideration of the content of that language in light of what would be required for the claim to legitimacy to be plausibly maintained over time.

To get at an answer to these questions that arise out of the inquiry "Consent to What?" it is necessary to consider the relationship between a constitutional regime and the operation of the various kinds of "law" in practice. In liberal political societies, law plays a special role as the arbiter of disputes between other bases for social organization and action. "Law," in this sense, is the name of an institutionalized set of rules for collective action that establish fixed practices, modes of communication, and decision-making authority. Fixed practices, modes of communication, and decision-making authority, in turn, require justification, which in a constitutional system ultimately rests on accord with a legitimate constitutional regime. Constitutional principles thus function as background tests for legitimacy against which juridical practice occurs as a foreground. A crucial question is how to describe the norms or institutions that a constitutional system invokes in this legitimating role without falling into an entirely circular argument in which the legitimacy of the constitution is grounded in the legitimacy of the laws that it is called upon to test. What, in other words, is the relationship between the legitimation of a system of laws in general and the legitimation of a constitution, specifically? That the principles of legitimation in these two cases might not be identical follows from the relationship between constitutional law and ordinary public or private law.

Furthermore, the background/foreground metaphor must not be reified; in other contexts, the roles are reversed, as when a discussion of constitutional principles turns on outcomes for juridical practice. It follows that a question that was previously settled can become unsettled by a shift in the dominant constitutional understanding or by a shift in juridical practice. This process of unsettling is alarming and unnerving to some, exhilarating to others, but inevitable in any constitutional system. It also follows that the location of these points of connection between constitutional principles of legitimacy and juridical practice are themselves contested, as when debate occurs over the question of whether a particular juridical act "really" invokes a question of rights, or when there is disagreement about the "correct" significance of juridical outcomes in resolving questions of constitutional principle. These elements of uncertainty in the relationship between constitutional, legal, and social norms necessitate going beyond the question of constitutional form to the question of content. In a system of liberal constitutionalism, a legitimate constitutional regime requires both a minimum degree of autonomy and a minimum degree of grounding in the prevalent juridical culture, and the content of constitutional language must provide an adequate basis for both if the system is to remain "constitutional" in the sense that I have just described.

The content of constitutional language that is required for a regime that has the possibility of legitimacy in practice is analyzed in Chapters 4 and 5 in terms of three dimensions: exclusivity, completeness, and normative substance. To what degree does the possibility of a legitimate constitutional regime depend on the adoption of a system of constitutional language to the exclusion of other modes of discourse? To what extent is that system of constitutional language required to be sufficient to articulate all arguments that actors might wish to make, and what follows from the possibility of linguistic incompleteness? And to what extent does the claim to legitimacy of a constitutional regime inescapably rest on an appeal to shared substantive norms that originate outside the system of constitutional discourse?

The consideration of these three questions gets at the larger question of what kind of a system of constitutional language is required if consent to that language is to provide an adequate basis for a legitimate constitutional regime? Once again, the answer is not that this problem can be simply made to disappear, but rather that consideration of the requirements of exclusivity, completeness, and normative substance provide a different way of asking the question.

The argument, in brief, is that a constitutional language that is sufficient to provide the basis for a legitimate constitutional regime must combine an essentially absolute claim to linguistic exclusivity with a high level of incompleteness. The question of substance is then addressed from the perspective of such an exclusive but incomplete constitutional language, an approach that points to a reconciliation of the fact of value pluralism with the necessity for shared grounds of constitutional legitimation. What connects these various character-istics is the strict requirement of "translation," a requirement that I propose in the full recognition that it operates unequally with respect to differing voices and viewpoints, and with a clear appreciation of the exclusionary consequences that follow as a result.

The final chapter (Chapter 6) explores some of the implications of the arguments of the preceding chapters, with a particular focus on the implications of the requirement of translation. Ultimately, the conclusion is that the preservation of a legitimate constitutional system requires a willingness not only to adopt a system of con-stitutional language, but also a willingness to exclude forms of dis-course derived from other spheres. Religious and moral claims and non-constitutional law, in particular, are sources of extraconstitu-tional language that must be excluded from constitutional discourse. By "excluded" I mean here that propositions formulated in these languages must be required to undergo translation into constitu-tional language before they can become elements of a legitimate constitutional discussion.

The requirement of translation also provides an argument against the possibility of "emergency" exceptions to constitutional norms, if that idea is understood to imply the legitimacy of actions that cannot be legitimated in the language of the constitutional regime. This not to say that a constitution cannot, or even should not, contain provisions identifying situations such as wartime in which extraordinary rules come into play. What is rejected is the proposition that the commitment to constitutional rule itself can be set aside for the duration of an "emergency" defined by criteria that do not appear in the system of constitutional language. These conclusions identify a besetting weakness of modern constitutional practice, in the United States and elsewhere. The purely theoretical argument of this book, in other words, ultimately has specific and important consequences for our understanding of the practice as well as the philosophy of constitutionalism.

This introductory discussion would not be complete if I did not express my appreciation for the assistance that I have received in the course of writing this book, and also offer an apology. The apology is to those writers whose work has received less attention than it deserved and those writers who can very fairly complain that I have chosen to focus only on certain elements of their work. In both instances, the explanation is that I was trying to use others' work to develop my own arguments. There is far too much excellent, thoughtful, constitutional theory and related research available in the literature for me to engage more than the small portion that most directly relates to the particular points of my immediate concern.

As for appreciation, this book has benefited tremendously from criticisms as well as encouragement from Richard Boyd, Donald Downs, Mark Graber, Georgene Huang, Eric MacGilvray, and Patrick Riley, as well as enormously valuable comments from anonymous reviewers employed by Cambridge University Press. My thanks also go to Ronald Cohen, who ably shepherded the manuscript through the editing and production process.

Portions of the argument presented here were earlier shared at the University of Wisconsin's Political Theory colloquium, a splendid example of collective action in its own right, and one from which this project has benefited in important ways. I also want to thank the University of Wisconsin Department of Political Science for allowing me to teach seminars across a wide range of areas, a practice that has permitted me to use my teaching to explore the ideas presented in this book. Graduate, undergraduate, and law students in those seminars have contributed more than they may ever realize to this project in their discussions and papers.

As always, the greatest debt is owed to my wife and editor, Lynn Schweber. The errors that remain in this book are mine.

1

The Search for Sovereignty

Law, Language, and the Beginnings of Modern Constitutionalism

Liberal constitutionalism is a recent invention, but its historical roots lie deep in Renaissance and Early Modern thought. An examination of the problems and the arguments that gave rise to the concept of liberal constitutionalism goes a long way toward clarifying the special role that authority over language plays in establishing the legitimacy of a constitutional regime.

At the beginning of the modern era, the question of political legitimation became the search for the true source of sovereignty. The search for sovereignty arose from the desire for a basis for human political authority unmoored from assertions of theological orthodoxy. In the fifth century C.E., Augustine had proposed that the survival of a state depended on its being governed in accordance with Christian teachings, rather than on the republican virtues that had been emphasized by writers such as Aristotle and Polybius. As a consequence, Augustine concluded that a government owed a duty to its people to provide Christian governance by virtue of its duty to promote the state's existence. In the fifteenth century, Florentine republican writers, among whom Machiavelli was the leading figure, argued that Augustine had it wrong. Confronted by the record of a millennium of religious conflict, and inspired by the recent redis-covery of ancient texts of classical republicanism, Machiavelli pro-posed that the key to creating and preserving the state was either a restoration of republican virtue or else the tyrannical but effective rule of a Prince bereft of either republican or Christian virtue. Since it is difficult, at best, to guarantee the virtue of a populace, as a practical matter the alternative to an appeal to theology meant accepting the authority of a sovereign ruler.

But Machiavelli's answer raised a critical question: by what authority does a Prince rule in the first place, particularly in the face of challenges from religious authority figures? The attempt to answer this question became the basis for modern constitutional theory. In this chapter, the development of that theory will be traced through the arguments of Jean Bodin, Thomas Hobbes, and John Locke. These three were not by any means the only writers to contribute to arguments about political and legal legitimacy. Among many others, John of Salisbury, Samuel Pufendorf, and David Hume could be mentioned, while Rousseau's challenges to fundamental assumptions built into the model of liberal constitutionalism continue to resonate to this day. But through the arguments of Bodin, Hobbes, and Locke it is possible to trace the line of development that culminated in modern liberal constitutionalism, and in particular to see the central relationship between constitutionalism and language.

Bodin contributed the idea of sovereignty, a category of justification for political rule that departed from both Christian and classical republicanism models by its emphasis on secular authority exercised over unequal others. In Bodin's account, a true understanding of "sovereignty" would go beyond the task of explaining why the rule of a Prince might be desirable to explain why such a form of government could be made legitimate, a project that led him to discover that the authority of the sovereign was limited by constraints inherent in its very nature.

In Hobbes' telling, the authority of the sovereign became, if anything, more absolute, and was both rooted in and extended over the field of language. At the same time, however, Hobbes introduced the possibility of democratic theory by grounding sovereignty in a moment of consent justified by an appeal to reason. Hobbes shifted the focus of his analysis away from the nature of the world, finding a form of natural law rooted in the facts of human psychology and epistemology rather than in a divinely prescribed order of the world. In the discussion that follows, I will refer to the idea of laws derived from the universal facts of human nature as "human natural law," to distinguish it from the Thomistic idea of natural law contained in the order of creation writ large.

Locke, finally, completed the move from sovereignty to liberal constitutionalism. For Locke as for Hobbbes, the sovereign's authority extended over language and was grounded in consent, but in Locke's telling, sovereignty took the form of self-rule rather than rule over others, and consequently was limited by much more substantive constraints than any recognized by either Hobbes or Bodin before him. Equally important, Locke described the legitimate sovereign as the product of not one, but a series of moments of consent, a description that focused attention on the question of the conditions that would make each successive stage of development possible. This move, more than any other, set the stage for modern theories of liberal constitutionalism. An examination of the progression of the argument for sovereignty through the works of these three writers illuminates the intellectual roots of liberal constitutionalism, and in the process demonstrates the points of criticism to which that theory must respond if it is to remain persuasive today.

JEAN BODIN: SOVEREIGNTY OVER LAW

In 1576, Jean Bodin provided an answer to the question of authority with the word "sovereignty," the assertion of legitimate absolute and exclusive authority over lawmaking on the part of a secular political ruler.[1] The term "secular" is slippery, here. Bodin's theory of sovereignty was emphatically based on Thomistic natural law in the sense that he appealed for his ultimate ground to a divinely created, normatively charged ontology discoverable by reason. But the

---

[1] The date 1576 refers to the publication of the first French edition of *Six Livres de la République*. The book was revised and reissued in French in 1578, then issued in a drastically revised Latin edition in 1586. The Latin edition included an entire additional chapter on classes of citizenship, and numerous emendations to the earlier French text. In 1606, Richard Knowles (or "Knolles") authored an English translation of the Latin edition that incorporated elements of the earlier French. In the discussion that follows, the primary text is the 1606 English edition; this may not be the most accurate reflection of Bodin's original ideas, but it is the clearest articulation of a unified thesis, and, moreover, it is the version of Bodin's masterpiece that was most widely influential on the subsequent development of constitutional thought. (McCrae, 1962.)

sovereigns whose authority was so justified were political rulers whose authority was grounded in their secular role as the creators of laws, in distinct contrast to religious figures whose claim to authority was based on their privileged knowledge of the laws promulgated by God, either through the authoritative interpretation of scripture or the equally authoritative reading of laws embedded in the order of Creation. "Sovereignty" was the name for the secular, political basis for the authority of the ruler; the absolute authority of the sovereign was not a divine dictate. In Quentin Skinner's words, sovereignty was "an analytical implication of the concept of the state." (Skinner, 1978: 287.)[2]

The secular nature of sovereignty was evident from the manner in which the argument was presented. Bodin only rarely appealed to biblical texts or Christian teachings; by far the bulk of his illustrations were drawn from the history of political regimes, primarily those of the Romans and Greeks, but also those of the Tartars, Swiss, and every other imaginable nation. The lessons that he drew from these histories were practical. Like Machiavelli, Bodin looked to the lessons of history to find an alternative to religious civil war, the "poison to make empires and states mortal, which else would be immortal." (Bodin [1606], 1962: 91.)

As a result, Bodin simultaneously rejected a key element of both Christian providentialism and classical republicanism – the appeal to some version of "virtue" as the key to a state's success. Virtue was no guarantee of success, and consequently the right form of government did not guarantee a commonwealth's prosperity. "For a commonwealth may be right well governed, and yet nevertheless afflicted with poverty, forsaken of friends, besieged by enemies, and overwhelmed with many calamities." (Bodin [1606], 1962: 3.) The difficulty, moreover, was not only that virtue could not guarantee success, it was also that there was no consensus concerning the measure of success, either for individuals or for communities, because the interests of the individual and the interests of the community need not always coincide.

---

[2] As Quentin Skinner notes, "[a]lready the foundations are fully laid for Hobbes's later construction of 'that great Leviathan' as a 'mortal God' to whom 'we owe under the immortal God our peace and defence ....'" (Skinner, 1978: 287.)

But for as much as men of affairs, and princes, are not in this point agreed, every man measuring his good by the foot of his pleasures and content- ments; and that those which have had the same opinion of the chief felicity of a man in particular, have not always agreed, That a good man and a good citizen are not all one; neither that the felicity of one man, and of a whole commonwealth are both alike: this hath made that we have always had varieties of laws, customs, and decrees, according to the diverse humors and passions of princes and governors. (Bodin [1606], 1962: 4).[3]

These comments were more than an ironic rejection of republican utopianism. Bodin here also set forth the problem that he accused earlier writers of avoiding. Given a plurality of views concerning a good outcome, and given that adherence to moral law and perfor- mance of civic duty might not be coextensional, what general principles can be articulated and defended concerning the nature of legitimate political rule? This was arguably the first articulation in political theory of the problem of liberal constitutionalism: how is political rule justified in the face of a genuine pluralism of values?

To answer his question, Bodin began with a natural form of human organization, the family. Every form of state, he argued, begin with the combination of families into a "commonwealth," which is characterized by the common ownership of property and the identification of a ruling sovereign.[4] "[T]hree principal things especially [are] required in every commonwealth ... the family, the sovereignty, and those things which are common to a city, or com- monwealth." (Bodin [1606], 1962: 3.) The family unit was not only the material out of which a commonwealth is constructed, it was also the commonwealth in microcosm, "the true seminary and beginning

---

[3] Bodin was likely inspired by Aristotle's *Politics*, which contains the proposition that the virtues of citizenship and the virtues of private life are different for everyone except a ruler. "But will there be no case in which the excellence of the good citizen and the excellence of the good man coincide? To this we answer that the good ruler is a good and wise man, but the citizen need not be wise." (Aristotle, 2004: 66.)

[4] "A Commonwealth is a lawful government of many families," the books begin, "and of that which unto them in common belongeth, with a puissant sovereignty." (Bodin [1606], 1962: 1.) Although nominally a Catholic, Bodin was heavily influenced by Petrus Ramus and other Calvinist dialecticians, and their influence shows in his insistence on always proceeding by naming, definition, and characterization. He was also heavily influenced by Jewish philosophy, and for a time considered converting to Judaism.

of every commonwealth, as also a principal member thereof."
(Bodin, 1962 [1606]: 8).

The family – or rather, to use a more precise term, the household –
was to the state as "members" to "the body," an image that echoed
Aristotle's description of the relationship between a citizen and his
polis,[5] but did not yet reach the anthropomorphic metaphor of the
state as a "person" possessed of a "will" that is characteristic of later
writing.[6] But the sovereign prince was only analogically equivalent
to the natural authority of the head of a household. "[T]he
prince ... hath power over his subjects, the Magistrate over private
men, the Father over his children, the Master over his scholars, the
Captain over his soldiers, and the Lord over his slaves. But of all
these the right and power to command, is not by nature given to any
beside the Father, who is the true image of the great and almighty
God the Father of all things." (Bodin, 1962 [1606]: 20.)

The emphasis on the household rather than the family as the
natural unit of social order had important political consequences.
Even the natural sovereignty of a father over his children gave way
to a juridically defined relationship of subordination within a
household, by virtue of the fundamental political principle that
authority over lawmaking must settle on a single ruler. Thus, a slave
or an adult son living in the household would have no authority over
his wife; instead, all would be subject to the rule of the head of the
household. "The reason whereof is, for that a family should have but
one head, one master, and one lord: whereas otherwise it if should
have many heads, their commands would be contrary, one forbid-
ding what another commandeth, to the continual disturbance of the
whole family." (Bodin, 1962 [1606]: 15.) And even the authority of
the head of household could be superseded by the political
authority of the sovereign in an appropriate case. Magistrates were
authorized to interfere with the patriarchal management of the

---

[5] "Further, the state is by nature clearly prior to the family and to the individual, since
the whole is necessarily prior to the part; for example, if the whole body be
destroyed, there will be no foot or hand." (Aristotle, 2004: 14.)

[6] The analogy of the state to a human body, with different elements representing
different organs and bodily functions, appears in its earliest form in the writings of
John of Salisbury, a twelfth-century English Scholastic who studied in France and
Rome and served for a time as the bishop of Chartres. (Rubin, 2005: 45–7.)

household to protect "the private goods of orphans, of mad men, and of the prodigal .... As in like case the laws oftentimes forbiddeth a man to procure, to alienate, or to pawn his own goods or things, except upon certain conditions ... for that the preservation of every private mans goods in particular, is the preservation of the commonwealth in general." (Bodin, 1962 [1606]: 12–13).

In other words, having begun with an appeal to Thomistic natural law, Bodin quickly moved to a purely political argument. The justification for the subordination of the family to the sovereign was the same as the justification for a single ruler in the family: the need for order and the fundamental republican commitment to the idea that the good of the collective trumped the interests of the individual. And the need for order ran both ways. Just as a household relied upon a well-ordered state, the state relied upon well-ordered households. Bodin bemoaned the consequences of arguments that there were circumstances under which a son would be justified in resisting his father. "O what a number of fathers should be found enemies unto the commonwealth, if these resolutions should take place? And what father is there which in the time of civil war could escape the hands of his murderous child?" (Bodin, 1962 [1606]: 26.)

The reference to civil war is telling. Bodin's greatest fear was chaos, the greatest promise of the commonwealth, social order. A strong patriarchal family might survive the absence of a state intact, but anything less would fall into the general chaos of civil war; conversely, should the state fail to support order in the household, the claim on the loyalty of heads of household would be forfeit.[7] The

---

[7] Bodin later uses almost identical language in describing the risks of defining citizenship in a way likely to arouse discontent among the populace. Bodin rejects Aristotle's definition of a citizen as one who participates in government. "[I]t is better and more truly said of Plutarch, that they are to be called citizens that enjoy the rights and privileges of a city. Which is to be understood according to the condition and quality of every one; the nobles as nobles, the commoners as commoners; the women and children in like case .... For should the members of man's body complain of their estate? Should the foot say to the eye, Why am not I set aloft in the highest place of the body? or is the foot therefore not to be accounted amongst the members of the body? Now if Aristotle's definition of a citizen should take place, how many seditions, how many civil wars, what slaughters of citizens would arise even in the mildest of cities." (Bodin, 1962 [1606]: 53.) The constant theme, again, is a warning of chaos, and especially of civil war.

natural order of the household was thus justified by its political consequences, not the other way around.

The absolute priority that Bodin placed on order as the highest good led him to the conclusion that the power of the prince was greater than the power of the people whom he rules. "So we see the principal point of sovereign majesty, and absolute power, to consist principally in giving laws unto the subject in general, without their consent." (Bodin, 1962 [1606]: 98.) The sovereign was the sole authoritative source of human law as the head of the state, which was an entity separate from the people, despite their possible role in its creation, "except the king be captive, furious, or in his infancy, and so needeth to have a protector or lieutenant appointed him by the suffrages of the people." (Bodin, 1962 [1606]: 95.)[8]

Bodin's sovereignty was a form of rule over others, in which a prince ruled over a people from which he, himself, stood apart. At the same time, however, the analogy of households to parts of the body pointed toward the introduction of the anthropomorphic metaphor of the state as a vehicle for a collective "people" capable of acting as sovereign, a theme that appears in the reference to "the suffrages of the people" in the case of monarchial incapacity. This points to one of the most ambiguous elements in Bodin's theory. Although he had a great deal to say about the nature and characteristics of sovereignty, he said very little about the *source* of such absolute authority. At several points, Bodin stated that a prince occupies a throne by divine providence, but in numerous other places, he seemed to grant at least the possibility, in some political systems, that power is initially transferred from "the people." For example, where authority was given to rulers for a certain term, as in the case of non-hereditary monarchy, sovereignty remained with the people. "I say no sovereignty to be in [the rulers], but in the people, of whom they have a borrowed power, or power for a certain time, which once expired, they are bound to yield up their authority."

---

[8] "It is of course true that Bodin continues to speak of la Republique rather than l'Etat .... Nevertheless, it is clear from Bodin's analysis of the concept that he thinks of the State as a distinct apparatus of power .... [Bodin] thus arrives at a conceptualization of the State as a locus of power which can be institutionalized in a variety of ways, and which remains distinct from and superior to both its citizens and their magistrates." (Skinner, 1978, vol. 2: 355–56.)

The people are the true sovereigns because "the ... people themselves, in whom the sovereignty resteth, are to give account unto none, but to the immortal God." (Bodin, 1962 [1606]: 8, 86.)

Where "the people" were sovereign, as in a democracy, Bodin preserved sovereignty-over-others by drawing a sharp and critical distinction drawn between the sovereign collective "people" and individual persons, as in his discussion of oaths and the obligation to obey the law.

[A]ll the citizens particularly swore to the observation of the laws, but not all together; for that every one of them in particular was bound unto the power of them all in general. But an oath could not be given by them all: for why, the people in general is a certain universal body, in power and nature divided from every man in particular. Then again to say truly, an oath cannot be made but by the lesser to the greater, but in a popular estate nothing can be greater than the whole body of the people themselves. But in a monarchy it is otherwise, where every one in particular, and all the people in general, and (as it were) in one body, must swear to the observation of the laws, and their faithful allegiance to one sovereign monarch; who next unto God (of whom he holds his scepter and power) is bound to no man. (Bodin, 1962 [1606]: 99.)

In every political society, there could be only one sovereign, whose authority was second only to that of God, but God was not the direct source of sovereign authority.

Sovereignty, as noted earlier, was fundamentally the authority to make laws.[9] (Bodin, 1962 [1606]: 159) The very term "law," according to Bodin, contained a necessary reference to a sovereign lawgiver. "This word the Law, in the Latin importeth the commandment of him which hath the sovereignty." (Bodin, 1962 [1606]: 91.) From the implication that law implies a sovereign, Bodin concluded that lawmaking is a necessary and exclusive prerogative of a

---

[9] In an earlier text, *Methodus*, Bodin identified five fundamental powers of sovereignty, four of which are clearly related to the administration of a system of laws: "The first and most important is appointing magistrates and assigning each one's duties; another is ordaining and repealing laws; a third is declaring and terminating war; a fourth is the right of hearing appeals from all magistrates in last resort; and the last is the power of life and death where the law itself has made no provision for flexibility or clemency." (Quoted at Franklin, 2003: xvi.) The version of sovereignty that is presented in *Methodus*, however, is far less absolute than that which appears in the *Six Books of the Republic*. (Franklin, 2003: xxi-xxii.)

singular sovereign. (Bodin, 1962 [1606]: 156.) The fact of sovereign authority, in turn, defined the legitimacy of the law, without reference to any external standards. "The laws of a sovereign prince, although they be grounded upon good and lively reasons, depend nevertheless upon nothing but his mere and frank good will." (Bodin, 1962 [1606]: 92.) The idea of sovereign as lawmaker was sharply different from the earlier, quasi-constitutionalist idea of a monarch, familiar in both French and English writings, as one who is bound to uphold the laws of his realm.[10] As Skinner observes, the shift in the role of sovereign from the guardian of the law to lawmaker meant that the role of the monarch was no longer "upholding the sense of justice already embodied in the laws and customs of the commonwealth," (Skinner, 1978: 289), but rather to create norms by the positive exercise of will.

Nonetheless, the lawmaking authority of the sovereign remained subject to three sets of limitations.[11] First, sovereigns remain subject to the "laws of God and nature." "[A]s for the laws of God and nature, all princes and people of the world are unto them subject: neither is it in their power to impugn them, if will not be guilty of high treason to the divine majesty, making war against God." (Bodin, 1962 [1606]: 90, 92.) Remarkably, this led Bodin directly to the protection of private property. "Now then if a sovereign prince may not remove the bounds which almighty God (of whom he is the living and breathing image) hath prefined unto the everlasting laws of nature: neither may he take from another man that which is his,

---

[10] Medieval notions of monarchial authority limited by customary law were the basis for the arguments of Claude de Seyssel in 1519. (Franklin, 2003: xxi.) Something of this idea also appears in Fortescue's description of the authority of an English monarch. (Pocock, 1975.) Julian Franklin suggests that Bodin saw an inevitable, logical progression from the idea of a monarch bound by customary law and an ultimate claim to a right of resistance. "Bodin must thus have seen, at least intuitively, that binding restraints upon the ruler implied some sense in which the community was higher than the king, and that some right of resistance was inherent in its representatives." As a result, Franklin argues, Bodin concluded that absolute monarchial authority was required to forestall the assertion of right of revolution. (Franklin, 2003: xxiv.)

[11] Skinner identifies the three traditional checks on monarchial power as "*la police, la religion*, and *la justice*." Of the three, it is *la police*, the authority of customary law, that Bodin denies outright. "His own view is that law and custom must be distinguished so completely that the idea of a check of custom on the right to legislate is automatically ruled out." (Skinner, 1978: 298.)

without just cause, whether it be by buying, by exchange, by confiscation." (Bodin, 1962 [1606]: 109)[12]

The second limitation on sovereignty inhered in a distinction between public and private spheres that appeared in several forms, not always consistently.[13] The analogy of *pater familias* to sovereign prince applied only in those areas in which the sovereign dealt with property owned in common by the commonwealth. These were not insubstantial areas of activity, to be sure,[14] but "the master of a family hath the government of all domestical things, and so of his whole family with that which is unto it proper." Bodin presented this as an argument about the conditions that would be required to foster republican virtue, rather than as an outer bound to sovereign authority. "It is needful in a well-ordered commonweal to restore unto parents the power of life and death over their children," because "domestical justice and power of fathers [are] the most sure and firm foundations of laws, honor, virtue, piety, wherewith a commonweal ought to flourish." (Bodin, 1962 [1606]: 22–3.)

In this argument, the justification for the limitation on sovereign authority appears to be as much prudential as ontological, just as Bodin was at pains to ground the distinction between public and private property on an argument that private property owners could be counted on to care for their property, whereas property owned in

---

[12] It is desirable, however, that citizens willingly part with their property when it is needed for the safeguarding of the general good, as in a case of a peace treaty that involves ceding territory to another sovereign. "But forasmuch as the welfare of private men, and all the goods of the subjects are contained in the health of our country, it beseemeth private men without grudging to forgive unto the Commonwealth, not only their private displeasures, and injuries received from their enemies, but to yield also for the health of the Commonwealth, their goods." (Bodin, 1962 [1606]: 109.)

[13] Franklin describes Bodin as "evasive" on the subject of absolutism, and argues that his account "was ... the source of confusion that helped prepare the way for the theory of royal absolutism, for he was primarily responsible for introducing the seductive but erroneous notion that sovereignty is indivisible." (Franklin, 2003: xiii.)

[14] Common ownership, in a commonwealth, extends to "their markets, their churches, their walks, says, laws, decrees, judgments, voices, customs, theaters, walls, public buildings, common pastures, lands, and treasure." "[A]ll which I say are common unto all the citizens together, or by use and profit, or public for every man to use, or both together.... For otherwise a commonwealth cannot be so much as imagined, which hath in it nothing at all public or common." (Bodin, 1962 [1606]: 11.)

common was likely to become the subject of disputation.[15] This admixture of forms of argumentation – definitional, natural, and prudential – is characteristic of Bodin's writing throughout *The Six Books*, and leaves the question of the ultimate ground for the limitations on sovereign authority as unresolved as the question of the ultimate source for that authority. Sovereign authority is absolute within its sphere, but its sphere is limited; both of these propositions required justifications that Bodin was ultimately unable to provide.

Laws of God and divisions between public and private affairs were only two of three sets of constraints on the sovereign. The third was a set of "laws" that followed definitionally from the nature of "sovereignty," itself only analogically a phenomenon of the natural order. A sovereign was bound by laws establishing the legitimacy of his authority, such as the rule of male succession. "But touching the laws which concern the state of the realm, and the establishing thereof; forasmuch as they are annexed and united to the crown, the prince cannot derogate from them." (Bodin, 1962 [1606]: 95.)[16] In addition, a sovereign was bound by a duty of self-preservation such that he could never act in a way that threatened to diminish his own sovereignty. "Those royal rights cannot by the sovereign be yielded up, distracted, or any otherwise alienated; or by any tract of time be prescribed against. ... And if it chance a sovereign prince to communicate them with his subject, he shall make him of his servant, his

---

[15] "For that which thou shouldst dearly love must be thine own, and that also all thine: whereas community is of the Lawyers usually called of it self, the mother of contention and discord. Neither are they less deceived, which think greater care to be had of things that be common, than of things that be private; for we ordinarily see things in common and publick to be of every man smally regarded and neglected, except it be to draw some private and particular profit thereout of." (Bodin, 1962 [1606]: 12.)

[16] As Kenneth McRae wryly observes, Bodin's inclusion of the law of succession as a binding limitation on the authority of an absolute sovereign posed "a stiff exercise in logic for all later commentators on his theory." (McRae, 1962: A16.) McRae is perhaps overenthusiastic in the importance that he attaches to the limitations on sovereign authority when he proposes that Bodin "was being more sophisticated than Hobbes, more modern than John Austin. He was, in fact, developing a theory of sovereignty strikingly similar to those of the present time." (McRae, 1962: A19.) Nonetheless, it is clearly true that for all his language of absolute authority, Bodin worked the idea of structural constraints on the legitimate exercise of power into his definition of sovereignty, a move with clear resonances in later theories of constitutional rule.

companion in the empire: in which doing he shall loose his sovereignty, and be no more a sovereign: for that he only is a sovereign which hath none his superior or companion with himself in the same kingdom."[17] (Bodin, 1962 [1606]: 155.)

Despite these limitations,[18] the outstanding features of Bodin's version of sovereignty, to modern eyes, were the complete absence of any political basis for questioning the legitimacy of the sovereign's actions and the emphasis on the idea of sovereignty as rule over others. Restrictions on the exercise of sovereign authority might be instrumentally useful, but the only necessary restrictions were those that were analytically necessary elements of the definition of sovereignty itself or if they were voluntarily undertaken by the sovereign. Thus the sovereign could not be compelled by any outside power to limit the authority to which he was entitled, he could only be persuaded (by Bodin) to do so voluntarily, and the sovereign was never bound by his own rules but only followed them out of convenience (Holmes, 1995: 110, 113.) As a result, Bodin's argument appears essentially morally neutral. (McRae, 1962: A20–A21.) In Bodin's understanding, a sovereign who ran roughshod over the laws and customs of his people was a tyrant, but he remained a sovereign, and his subject did not have any right of resistance or revolt as a result of his actions. Where a sovereign acted contrary to the laws of nature – "makes war on God" – his

---

[17] Drawing on these and other passages, Stephen Holmes concludes that the prohibition on self-binding itself reflects a deeper prohibition on self-destruction by the sovereign of his power. "More profound than the self-binding taboo, and underlying it, therefore, is the self-destruction taboo. Self-binding is illicit when it entails a diminution of royal power. For the same reason, self-binding is permissible and even obligatory when it helps maintain or increase royal power." (Holmes, 1995: 113–14.)

[18] In addition to the limitations on the power of the sovereignty, it was also the case that a sovereign was bound by his commitments in the same manner as any other person. "We must not then confound the laws and the contracts of sovereign princes, for that the law dependeth of the will and pleasure of him that hath the sovereignty, who may bind all his subjects, but cannot bind himself: but the contract betwixt the prince and his subjects is mutual, which reciprocally bindeth both parties" (Bodin, 1962 [1606]: 93.) Even in the absence of an explicit commitment, duties between sovereign and subject were mutual, even if the basis for sovereignty itself was not. "As the subject oweth unto his lord all duty, aid, and obedience; so the prince also oweth unto his subject justice, guard, and protection: so that the subjects are no more bound to obey the prince, than is the prince to administer unto them justice" (Bodin, 1962 [1606]: 500.)

subjects were relieved of the duty of obedience, but remained bound to avoid resistance; judgment would be visited on the tyrant by God.

THOMAS HOBBES' *LEVIATHAN*: SOVEREIGNTY OVER LANGUAGE

Thomas Hobbes continued Bodin's project of defining the terms of political sovereignty, but he went much farther in defining the source of sovereignty and of its limitations. Hobbes shared Bodin's commitment to an ideal of a political sovereignty whose authority was both equally absolute and equally securely legitimated as that of religious authorities. But by Hobbes' time, the analogy to the natural order of the family had become the basis for the early modern doctrine of the divine right of kings.[19] For Hobbes, as for Bodin, such a claim was untenable, if only because of the inherent insecurity that was entailed. If political authority depended on religious doctrine, then the rejection of religions doctrine would lead directly to a rejection of secular authority, raising the familiar specter of religious civil war. Like Bodin, Hobbes sought a basis for political authority that would be immune to challenge on the basis of competing claims of religious orthodoxy.[20] Unlike Bodin's appeal to a natural order, however, Hobbes drew his grounding principles from

[19] Skinner identifies the source of the doctrine of the divine right of kings in a combination of Bodin's theory of sovereignty and Protestant theology. "They all begin by taking over Bodin's claim that an absolute form of legislative sovereignty needs by definition to be located at some determinate point in every state. To this they add the originally Protestant belief that all such powers are directly ordained of God, so that to offer any resistance to the king is strictly equivalent to resisting the will of God. With the union of these two arguments, the distinctive concept of the 'divine right of kings is finally articulated." (Skinner, 1978, vol. 2: 301.)

[20] A number of writers have found an implicit theological understanding at the basis of Hobbes' political ideas, particularly in terms of his commitment to natural equality. Joshua Mitchell argues that Hobbes' theory of sovereignty "should not be viewed as an absolutist *political* theory, but as a worldly extension of a theological insight." For Mitchell, Hobbes' politics is a worldly solution to the problem of pride, based on the anti-foundationalism of Hobbes' epistemology that treats the attempt to derive moral principles from reason as an example of vainglory. (Mitchell, 1993: 79, 81.) Mitchell concludes that the necessity for submission to a single sovereign "recapitulates aspects of Reformation theological speculation about the (prideful) priesthood of all believers under one sovereign (Christ)." While this is an interesting and plausible interpretation of Hobbes' project, it does not diminish the significance of the observation that Hobbes' arguments did not fit

the universal facts of human epistemology, locating both the source and the limitations on the authority of the sovereign in the nature of language.

The key move in separating political authority from its religious roots was a shift in focus in the meaning of "natural law." For Bodin, natural laws were the laws of God. For Hobbes, by contrast, "laws of nature"[21] were consequences of the universal facts of human psychology, and fundamentally of the desire for self-preservation.[22] In the preface to *On the Citizen*, Hobbes explained that his initial project was to explore "the faculties of human nature" in order to

---

into any orthodox Christian teachings of his day, an observation that leads Mitchell to describe Hobbes as a "perverse Christian." (Mitchell, 1993: 86, 84.)

[21] The use of the term "law" is tricky, here, as Hobbes declares that "dictates of reason, men used to call by the name of laws, but improperly; for they are but conclusions, or theorems concerning what conduceth to the conservation and defense of themselves; whereas law, properly is the word of him, that by right hath command over others." (Hobbes [1651], 1996: 90. See Gauthier, 1979: 551–52.) This positivistic definition of the word "law" is arguably in tension with Hobbes' occasional references to laws of God. One explanation is that God created Man to have a certain nature, including the desire for self-preservation, an understanding that fits well with the idea that is described here as "human natural law." Michael Oakeshott uses the distinction between a "law" and "conclusions, or theorems" to argue that Hobbes would have rejected the distinction that I have drawn between categories of "natural" law. "[N]o proper distinction can be maintained between a Natural or Rational and a Revealed law. All law is revealed in the sense that nothing is law until it is shown to be the command of God by being found in the Scriptures." (Oakeshott, 1991: 268–69.) English Calvinists, however, took a different view. "Thus there are two books from whence I collect my divinity," wrote Thomas Browne in 1643, "besides that written one of God, another of his servant Nature." (Browne, 1643: 1.) In 1639, William Ames went so far as to declare that "[a]ll the precepts of the moral law, are out of the Law of Nature, except the determination of the Sabbath day ... there is nothing in them, which is not so grounded upon right reason, but it may bee solidly defended and maintained by human discourse, nothing but what may bee well enjoined from clear reason." (Ames, 1639: 107.) Skinner points out that the mode of reasoning characteristic of this strain of Calvinist thinking, associated with the teachings of Petrus Ramus, is evident in Bodin's arguments. (Skinner, 1978: 291.)

[22] Gregory Kavka elucidates Hobbes' reliance on human natural law as follows: "[I]f some of our dominant shared ends, like survival, are unavoidable givens of our nature, rational beings with such natures will be unable to avoid pursuing what they perceive to be the necessary means to those ends. It follows that the requirements of any moral system capable of effectively guiding human action must be compatible with undertaking these means, that is, these means must be at least morally permissible. Here is a derivation of moral permissions, if not ought-judgments, from facts (about our natures) and the logic of the moral concept 'ought.'" (Kavka, 1986: 292.)

determine "whether [men] are born fit for society and for preserving themselves from each other's violence, and which faculty makes them so." From the conclusions reached in that regard, Hobbes proposed to "explain the policy which they had inevitably to adopt for that purpose ... which are simply the fundamental *laws of nature* under another name." (Hobbes [1642], 1998: 21.) Hobbes' "laws of nature" thus revealed aspects of what I have referred to as human, as opposed to divine, natural law – that is, laws grounded in specifically human nature. Hobbes did not deny the proposition that humans receive this nature from their divine Creator, but his immediate subject of concern was the set of universal human traits rather than their origin or their connection to a global normative order.

In *Leviathan*, Hobbes both began his study and ultimately relied for the verification of his findings on an introspective analysis of the psychology of human experience.[23] "[W]hen I have set down my own reading orderly, and perspicuously, the pains left another, will be only to consider, if he also find not the same in himself. For this kind of doctrine, admitteth no other demonstration." (Hobbes [1651], 1996: 11.) To the extent that analysis could be shown to be universal, and his political conclusions shown to follow necessarily from his psychological analysis, Hobbes would have created a universal theory of the conditions of possibility of political rule in human society. "I say the similitude of passions, which are the same in all men ... not the similitude of the objects of the passions, which are the things desired, feared, hoped, etc.: for these the constitution individual, and particular education do vary." Natural laws would reflect the goods than any person must rationally desire as the product of prudence, "a presumption of the future, contracted from the experience of time past" (Hobbes [1651], 1996: 10, 23.)

To establish universally desired goods, Hobbes began by constructing an epistemolgical theory of language. For Hobbes, thoughts began with perceptions. Borrowing from Galileo, Hobbes

---

[23] "Read thyself .... for the similitude of the thoughts, and Passions of one man, to the thoughts, and Passions of another, whosoever looketh into himself, and considereth what he doth, what he does think, opine, reason, hope, fear, &c., and upon what grounds; he shall thereby read and know, what are the thoughts, and Passions of all other men, upon the like occasions." (Hobbes [1651], 1996: 2.)

identified perception as the sensation produced by change, or motion.[24] But sense perceptions could not yield direct knowledge, only mediated observations indistinguishable from illusions or "fancy." The only certainty was the sensation of perception itself, a proposition with obvious connections to the Cartesian invocation of the *cogito*.[25] Consequently, the "thoughts of man," or "understanding," could not be certainly grounded in direct perception, but could only reflect the organization and recollection of sense-impressions that were themselves no more than "fancies" in response to external motions of objects.

To get from the sensation of perception to coherent thought, organization was required. The "train of thoughts ... that succession of one thought to another ... is called mental discourse." (Hobbes [1651], 1996: 20) By itself, however, the train of thoughts had no necessary logic. Thoughts became coherent when the train of imaginations was "regulated by some desire, and design." "From Desire, ariseth the Thought of some means we have seen produce the like of that which we aim at; and from the thought of that, the thought of means to that mean; and so continually, till we come to some beginning within our power." (Hobbes [1651], 1996: 20–21.)

[24] "If we should suppose a man to be made with clear eyes ... but endued with no other sense; and that he should look only upon one thing, which is always of the same colour and figure, without the least appearance of variety, he would seem to me ... to see, no more than I seem to myself to feel the bones of my own limbs by my organs of feeling." In another move that prefigures twentieth-century epistemology, Hobbes denied the existence of a "ghost in the machine," an observing "I" capable of recognizing the experience of perception. "[A]lthough someone may think that he was thinking (for this thought is simply an act of remembering), it is quite impossible for him to think that he is thinking, or to know that he is knowing. For then an infinite chain of questions would arise: 'how do you know that you know that you know....?'" (quoted in *Objections to Descarte's* Tuck, 2002: xvi–xvii, xix). Joshua Mitchell relies on this physical character of thought to draw a sharp distinction between truths knowable by reason and those that depend on metaphysical sources. (Mitchell, 1993: 80.) If one accepts the idea that Hobbes' natural law principles are grounded in human psychology, rather than derived from religious teachings, however, then the necessity for importing this distinction disappears.

[25] "[S]ense in all cases, is nothing else by original fancy, caused (as I have said) by the pressure, that is, by the motion, of external things upon our eyes, ears, and other organs thereunto ordained. "(Hobbes [1651], 1996: 14.) Richard Tuck comments that the emphasis on perceptions of motion was the dividing principle that separated Hobbes' epistemological system from that of Descartes. (Tuck, 2002: xvi.)

Because of our interests, we organize perceptions to reach conclusions about causal relationships, so that we will be able to act instrumentally in the future; this, for Hobbes, was the source of human reason. Natural self-interest thus appeared as the precondition for coherent thought, a relationship that could be extended to consideration either of causes or consequences, forward or back along causal connections. "In sum, the Discourse of the Mind, when it is governed by design, is nothing but Seeking, or the faculty of Invention." (Hobbes [1651], 1996: 21.)

The connection of interests to the generation of thought created a political epistemology. In the second step of his critique of reason, Hobbes turned the focus of that political epistemology directly to language, in a rigorous examination of the relationship between sense, word, and idea. Words, he argued, were nothing more than the names attached to ideas. As interests organize thoughts into coherent patterns, "the general use of speech, is to transfer our mental discourse into verbal; or the train of our thoughts, into a train of words." Language consists in the applications of names to mental experiences in the form of "marks" or "signs." These names served two fundamental functions: "[W]hereof one is, the registering of the consequences of our thoughts .... So that the first use of names, is to serve for marks, or notes of remembrance. Another is, when many use the same words, to signifie (by their connexion and order) one to another, what they conceive, or think of each matter .... And for this use they are called signs." (Hobbes [1651], 1996: 25.)

Language, for Hobbes, consisted of internal marks translated into external signs, organized into trains of words that conveyed a train of thoughts, whose coherence was based on the purposive pursuit of interests. Language was also the mechanism by means of which humans as interested organisms connect their perceptions into thoughts by the construction of causal inferences. What separated reason from the internal sensation of thought was the imposition of order and the translation of thoughts from "mental discourse" into spoken language.[26]

---

[26] For Hobbes, errors such as Descartes' reliance on innate ideas were at the root of wrong thinking. Inspired by his one-time employer, Francis Bacon, Hobbes believed that the first step in crafting a well-reasoned theory of human nature was the correction of erroneous assumptions that might cloud subsequent reasoning. The

By its very nature, language was a source of error as well as of communication. As a result, in the move from the state of nature into a state of discursive communication by language, new errors arose. "Natural sense and imagination, are not subject to absurdity. Nature itself cannot err; and as men abound in copiousness of language; so they become more wise, or more mad than ordinary. Nor is it possible without Letters for any man to become either excellently wise, or ... excellently foolish." (Hobbes [1651], 1996: 28.) The first fundamental error was the mistaking of the experience of perception for an experience of the thing itself, and the second consisted in errors of naming. These two errors conflated into the act of falsely naming as real what was only perceived by the imagination, an act specifically identified with moral philosophy. Language thus becomes the carrier of the first fundamental error, of mistaking perception for reality, by way of the second. Through his theory of language, Hobbes' skepticism about the possibility of direct knowledge of the world translated directly into skepticism about the reliability of moral and juridical claims of authority.

In reading Hobbes' account of language, it is important to distinguish between "error" and "absurdity." "Error" refererred simply to a mistake of fact, an erroneous description of perceptions. The term "absurdity," by contrast, refererred to words without meaning – that is, a form of language disconnected from its "natural" function of connecting a "train of words" with a "train of thoughts."

[E]rror is but a deception, in presuming that somewhat is past, or to come .... But when we make a general assertion, unless it be a true one, the possibility of it is inconceivable. And words whereby we conceive nothing but the sound, are those we call absurd, insignificant, and non-sense. And therefore if a man should talk to me of a round quadrangle, or accidents of bread in cheese, or immaterial substances; or of a free subject; a free-will; or any free, but free from being hindered by opposition, I should not say he

---

error of mistaking perception for reality is a constant theme. "It is implanted by nature in all animals that at first glance they think an image of something is the thing itself being seen .... And men definitely think that an image is the object itself (if we except the few who have corrected the judgement of their senses by reason." (*De Homine*, quoted and translated in Tuck, 2002: xxi.)

were in an error, but that his words were without meaning; that is to say, absurd. (Hobbes [1642], 1998: 34.)

This notion of "absurdity," a form of error unique to abstract propositions, emphasized the connection that language creates between sense impressions and philosophical propositions.[27]

Both claims of "absurdity" and claims of simple error appeared with explicitly juridical consequences, as the reference to "a free subject" suggests. Hobbes rejected, for example, the notion that political organization was itself an element of human nature, declaring that the idea that man is *zoon politikon* "proceeds from a superficial view of human nature." The tendency toward association "does not happen because by nature it could not be otherwise, but by chance." (Hobbes [1642], 1998: 22) "By nature," he writes, "we are not looking for friends but for honour or advantage from them .... [E]very voluntary encounter is a product either of mutual need or of the pursuit of glory." (Hobbes [1642], 1998: 22–3.)[28] But, while mutual need identified the true state of human affairs, the pursuit of glory was itself the result of an error. A person "supposing

[27] The connection between linguistic absurdity and philosophical error was emphasized in Hobbes' famous rejection of Robert Boyle's claim to have produced a vacuum on the *political* grounds that where there is a vacuum there can be no sovereignty. (Shapin, 1989.) At first glance, Hobbes in the unlikely position of a pre-Baconian traditionalist resisting the possibility of a separate category of ideas called "scientific." Hobbes' rejection of the vacuum pump makes more sense, however, when we remember that for Hobbes there was no direct observation of physical phenomena, only linguistic constructions of the experience of the perception of motion. Thus, Boyle's argument, translated into Hobbesian language, would be that his device (the vacuum pump) created motions whose effects would be experienced as a perception whose applicable sign would be the absence of anything. The sign of "vacuum" was thus a kind of oxymoron, a linguistic construction that denied its own grammatical logic. Such a proposition was not incorrect, it was "absurd," a "train of words" without meaning because they could not express any possible "train of thoughts" consistent with human natural laws.

[28] The tendency toward a pursuit of glory plays an important role in the argument. Glory-seeking represents a kind of appetite that is based on a false understanding. Augustine's treatment of glory-seeking was somewhat different. Albert Hirschman notes that Augustine described the desire for glory as a vice, but a useful vice that could be used to curb others. Through the medieval period, writers elevated the idea of glory in the context of Christian morality – that is, chivalric honor – until it reached the level of a prime virtue associated with piety and hence with moral rightness. Machiavelli and the Renaissance republicans, in turn, sounded the death knell for glory. (Hirschman, 1977: 9–12.)

himself superior to others, wants to be allowed everything, and demands more honour for himself than others have; that is the sign of an aggressive character. In his case, the will to do harm derives from vainglory ... and over-valuation of his own strength." (Hobbes [1642], 1998: 26.) The seeker of vainglory, guilty of the philosophical error of self-conceit, was the cause of violence. The pursuit of glory through violence was a vice based on errors of judgment that lay at the root of the misery of the natural condition. By contrast, a true understanding of the laws of human nature, leading to a recognition of mutual need, would demonstrate the necessity of submission to a sovereign.

Vainglory was merely an example of error; "absurdity" entailed a more profound abuse of language. As an example of absurdity in speech, Hobbes proposed the idea of an "unjust law." "But what is good law? By a good law, I mean not a just law: for no law can be unjust." (Hobbes [1651], 1996: 239.) Unpacking the assertion that "no law can be unjust" shows central elements of Hobbes' political theory that inform the question of constitutional legitimacy by connecting a theory of human natural law with a theory of language, and working from there to an understanding of sovereignty.

Hobbes relied heavily on an anthropomorphic metaphor (or homology) of the state. The sovereign in Hobbes' state was the commonwealth, an artificial person: "[O]ne person, of whose acts a great multitude, by mutual covenants one with another have made themselves every one the Author, to the end he may use the strength and means of them all, as he shall think expedient, for their peace and common defence." (Hobbes [1651], 1996: 121.)[29] As noted earlier, among natural persons the discovery of the meaning of abstract concepts such as "law" or "just" was not a matter of determining

[29] To conceive of the exercise of will by anything other than a singular sovereign is, to Hobbes, akin to adopting an unnatural conception of will. In a later discussion of this point, Hobbes invokes the idea of monstrosity: "To what disease in the Naturall Body of man I may exactly compare this irregularity of a Common-wealth, I know not. But I have seen a man, that had another man growing out of his side, with an head, armes, breast, and stomach, of his own: If he had had another man growing out of his other side, the comparison might then have been exact." (Hobbes [1651], 1996: 228.) The analogy is in line with Aristotle's account of monstrous births as deviations from the natural ends of creatures, but derives here from Hobbes' psychology rather than from an Aristotelian theory of essences.

essential truths established in the order of nature, but an exercise in discovering what meaning those names signified in thoughts that themselves achieved coherence only in response to our nature as instrumentally interested actors. The same was true of the discourse of the sovereign. The sovereign did not discover the meaning of "justice" by examining the beliefs and practices of its subjects; the sovereign *defined* justice and other moral signifiers in the exercise of its sovereignty. "Civil Law, is to every subject, those rules, which the commonwealth hath commanded him, by word, writing, or other sufficient sign of the will, to make use of, for the distinction of right, and wrong; that is to say, of what is contrary, and what is not contrary to the rule." (Hobbes [1651], 1996: 183.)

The authority of the sovereign consequently extended to determinations of moral judgment, because the first authority of the sovereign was to establish the meaning of critical terms such as "justice." The absence of universal agreement on such terms was Bodin's reason for requiring a sovereign in the first place. Hobbes picked up on the point to recognize that the creation of a sovereign solves the problem only if the sovereign's authority extends to the meaning of the terms of moral evaluation.[30] The surrender of authority to the sovereign was the surrender of authority over language in matters of the commonwealth.[31]

---

[30] Tuck, 1996: xxxi-xxxii. Michael Oakeshott concludes that Hobbes' sovereign must necessarily have had authority over religious questions as a result of his authority over the definition of moral terms. The fundamental teaching of Calvinism, and the basis for the rejection of the polity of the Catholic Church, was that each individual was equally able to interpret Scripture. The consequence of such teaching, Oakeshott suggests, is to add to the chaos of the state of nature. If the creation of the commonwealth is to alleviate the conditions of chaotic competition prevalent in the state of nature, "the natural right of each man to interpret Scripture and determine the law of God on his own behalf will be transferred with the rest of his natural rights." (Oakeshott, 1991: 271.) As a result, the sovereign's authority over matters temporal and spiritual are one and the same. "[A]s none but Abraham in his family, so none but the Sovereign in a Christian commonwealth can take notice what is, or what is not the word of God." (Hobbes [1651], 1996: 324.) This, argues Oakeshott, was Hobbes' resolution of the problem that remained after Bodin, that "every believer was subject to two laws – that of his *civitas* and that of his religion." (Oakeshott, 1991: 268.)

[31] As Kavka points out, the areas in which the prerogative of disagreement are surrendered to the sovereign are those involving "social states of affairs," where if citizens act on the basis of their own moral preferences the ability of the commonwealth to act is curtailed. "[U]nless individuals reach wide-ranging

The key point to recognize here is that for Hobbes, the issue of "justice" was subsumed into a question of reason, and consequently one of correct naming and avoiding absurdity. In the state of nature, individuals' "rights" were synonymous with the exercise of right reason. By the same token, the actions of the sovereign would be within the sovereign's rights – would have the quality of laws – insofar as they too comported with the dictates of right reason directed to the purpose of sovereignty, the preservation of the subjects' lives.[32] "And what is not contrary to right reason, all agree is done justly and of right. For precisely what is meant by the term right is the liberty each man has of using his natural faculties in accordance with right reason." (Hobbes [1642], 1998: 27.) The sovereign's authority over language simultaneously explains the absoluteness of its authority and points to the sole plausible limitation on the authority of Hobbes' sovereign. A statement that is irrational (that is, any edict that no rational person could commit

---

agreement on standards of evaluation or completely subordinate their judgments of goodness to those of public authorities, substantial sources of practical conflict will remain in the form of differing private values and standards of evaluation." (Kavka, 1986: 296, 297.) By contrast, there is no necessary surrender of authority outside the range of matters in which moral judgment is necessarily surrendered to the sovereign, disagreement is entirely permissible. "Outside civil society – and presumably within civil society in matters wherein public standards have not been laid down or agreed to – an individual is free to choose his own standards of evaluation and to treat objects or states of affairs as good or evil according to his preferences." (Kavka, 1986: 295.)

[32] Richard Tuck observes that limitations on the sovereign's legitimate powers, inhere in the requirement that the sovereign's acts be genuinely undertaken for the purpose of ensuring the self-preservation of the authorizing subjects. "[A] sovereign in his capacity as [the subjects'] representative was strictly entitled only to enforce on his subjects those things which he believed necessary for their preservation. He might, of course, go beyond this limit, and subjects would have to accept his judgment; but he would in fact have had no natural right to do so, and he would be breaking the law of nature . . . . In such a situation the sovereign would act without right in ordering something and the subject would act without right in resisting." (Tuck, 1996: xxxviii.) The result would be likely revolution, not by any claim of right but as the "natural punishment" for misrule. "And hereby it comes to pass, that intemperance, is naturally punished with diseases; rashness, with mischances; injustice, with the violence of enemies; pride, with ruin; cowardice, with oppression; negligent government of princes, with rebellion; and rebellion, with slaughter." (Hobbes [1651], 1996: pg. 254.) The requirement of sincerity adds an interesting dimension of uncertainty to the relation between sovereign and subject, particularly in light of Hobbes' epistemological skepticism.

herself* to obey) is "absurd"; it is a linguistic act unrelated to its referent. An act by a sovereign that could not rationally serve the subjects' collective interest in self-preservation would not have the quality of "law" in the first instance.[33] There could be no such thing as an unjust law, because the act of lawmaking defines justice, but an absurd definition has no force.

The idea that lawmaking is a discursive act is central to Hobbes' description of a "good" law, as opposed to one that is merely legitimate. Hobbes argued that the work of the commonwealth is to secure the peace by achieving the willing obedience of its subjects rather than by domination. As a result, in his conception the role of the sovereign lawmaker was to educate the populace to see the rational necessity of acknowledging their consent to be governed. A good law was therefore one which served this work by conveying the message of necessary consent – and hence the justification of the rule of the sovereign – by teaching right moral principles.

This somewhat circular rationale (laws exist to demonstrate that they should be obeyed) meant that a law was "good" insofar as it was directed toward the end of encouraging virtuous behavior and insofar as it was effective in securing obedience to law generally. This followed, ultimately, from the character of civil laws as commands of the sovereign, which "is Law only to those, that have the means to take notice of it." (Hobbes [1651], 1996: 187.) In other words, laws that are not of nature, and hence not imminently susceptible of reason, have to be made evident to subjects if they are to function as commands, just as orders must be delivered to be obeyed. "For the will of another, cannot be understood, but by his

---

* Throughout this book, where a generic pronoun is called for, I have alternated between masculine and feminine. No significance is intended by either choice at any point in the discussion that follows.

[33] The reference to a collective, rather than an individual, interest in self-preservation is the basis for David Gauthier's analysis of the problem that Hobbes' account does not obviously explain why a subject should not be a free rider – that is, why a subject should sacrifice his interests to actively participate in the maintenance of the system of laws. Gauthier proposes that the solution inheres in a problem, conceiving of the individual subject as calculating the likely deterrent effect on others of his (and his neighbors') willingness to participate in law enforcement. In this way, Gauthier is able to identify the fact of commitment, itself, as advantageous, rather than relying on the consequences of the performance of that commitment. (Gauthier, 1988: 78.)

own word, or act, or by conjecture taken from his scope and purpose; which in the person of the commonwealth, is to be supposed always consonant to equity and reason." (Hobbes [1651], 1996: 188–89.) Furthermore, in order for a law to fulfill its function of reinforcing the lessons of reason, it must be evident that it is the law of the sovereign. "Nor is it enough the law be written, and published; but also that there be manifest signs, that it proceedeth from the will of the sovereign . . . . there is therefore requisite not only a declaration of the law, but also sufficient signs of the author, and authority." (Hobbes [1651], 1996: 189).

Like Bodin's conclusion that the sovereign was bound by a duty to avoid destruction of his own authority, which Hobbes shared (see Kavka, 1986:391), for Hobbes the very fact of absolute sovereign authority created a duty binding on the sovereign to make the nature and purpose of the civil laws evident to his subjects. "I conclude, therefore, that in the instruction of the people in the essential rights (which are the natural, and the fundamental laws) of sovereignty, there is no difficulty, (whilst a sovereign has his power entire) but what proceeds from his own fault . . . it is his duty, to cause them so to be instructed; and not only his duty, but his benefit also, and security, against the danger that may arrive to himself in his natural person, from rebellion." (Hobbes [1651], 1996: 180.)

With the idea of the good law, the argument comes full circle. The truth of natural laws has been disguised by the bad teachings of Aristotelian doctrines of essence and religious superstitions. True teaching depends on recognizing the truth of natural forces, and the precise meaning of language. From the wisdom that is produced by true teaching, rational persons will recognize the necessity of their agreement to the covenant that creates the sovereign. (Hobbes [1651], 1996: 233–37.) Once created, the laws of the sovereign have as their essential function the reinforcement of the process of public education that ensured their acceptance in the first place. The theme of precise language is revisited, in this context, in the duties of judges to interpret ambiguous laws in a fashion consonant with their purposes. (Hobbes [1651], 1996: 194–95.) Repeating the very term with which he described his analysis of human nature at the outset, Hobbes describes a good law as, "Needful, for the good of the people, and withall <u>perspicuous</u>. This <u>perspicuity</u> consisteth not so much in the words of the law is self, as in a declaration of the causes, and motives, for which it was made." (Hobbes [1651], 1996: 240.)[34]

But the test for legitimacy is far less specific than the characterization of law as "good." The anthropomorphic metaphor extends to a test of the sovereign's legitimacy in the form of an implicit inquiry into the sovereign's own rationality. Extending the metaphor, the conclusion seems to be that nothing short of a kind of political insanity could exceed the bounds of legitimate sovereignty. In the process of formulating this argument, Hobbes drew on elements familiar from Bodin: the anthropomorphic metaphor already alluded to, the idea of legislation as a heuristic act designed to reenforce sovereign rule, and the combination of sovereign powers limited only by their nature with the wisdom of accepting a certain degree of additional restraint on the exercise of those powers.[35]

The test of absurdity that connects Hobbes' theories of language and politics appeared in yet a third iteration with the consideration of the direct translation of individual natural rights into political authority that creates the sovereign. The sovereign is not a party to the social contract, which is made between individuals, "the covenant of every man with every man." Instead, the sovereign is the product of the contract, while the subjects stand in the position of the "authors" of their rule.

This done, the multitude so united in one person, is called a commonwealth .... This is the generation of that great LEVIATHAN, or rather (to speak more reverently) of that mortal God, to which we owe under the immortal God, our peace and defense .... And in [the sovereign] consisteth the essence of the commonwealth; which (to define it) is one person, of whose acts a great multitude, by mutual covenants one with another, have

[34] Lest the point be lost, Hobbes returns to the institutions of society at the end of the chapter; the work of the Legislator requires help from England's universities. "[T]he instruction of the people, dependeth wholly, on the right teaching of youth in the universities." (Hobbes [1651], 1996: 183.)

[35] Gerald Mara suggests that *Leviathan* should be understood primarily as a text addressed to rulers, explaining how they might best keep the peace in their kingdoms, rather than as addressed to citizens of a commonwealth in order to instruct them to accept the sovereign's laws. In this reading, the text is fundamentally prudential in its concerns, so that the description of the absolute authority of the sovereign is only the preface to a set of recommendations for exercising self-restraint. (Mara, 1988.)

made themselves every one the author, to the end he may use the strength and means of them all, as he shall think expedient, for their peace and common defense."(Hobbes [1651], 1996: 119–120.)

The word "author" here refers not to the creator of a written text, but rather to one who authorizes the sovereign to act. (Gauthier, 1979; Pitkin, 1972.) "[E]very one, as well he that voted for it, as he that voted against it, shall authorize all the actions and judgements, of that man, or assembly of men, in the same manner, as if they were his own." (Hobbes [1651], 1996: 121.)

Authorization is not representation; Hobbes' sovereign emphatically remained one who rules over others.[36] The authors retained no control over the actions that they authorized; the authority, following the moment of the creation of the sovereign, flowed entirely in one direction, and the grant of authority was irrevocable. (Kavka, 1986: 388; Pitkin, 1972: 19–20.)[37] While the acts of the sovereign could go beyond the legitimate scope of his powers, such actions could not deprive the sovereign of his authority. Since the covenant that created that authority was not one to which the sovereign was a party in the first place, he could never be guilty of its violation. (Hobbes [1651], 1996: 122.) Thus no right of revolution existed even by consensus of the persons who inhabit the commonwealth.

By the same logic, the authority of the sovereign was greater than that of the people acting in combination, just as it had been for Bodin. And those who argued to the contrary were not merely mistaken; they were engaged in "absurdity." "For if by all together, they mean not the collective body as one person, then all together,

---

[36] As a textual matter, Tuck observes that the term "representation" entered Hobbes' text from its French translation. (Tuck, 1996: xxxvi, n. 50.)

[37] Kavka takes issue with Gauthier's argument that the idea of "authorization" is the key to the formation of an Hobbesian sovereign. The concept of authorization, says Kavka, does not "add anything of substance to the contract or its consequences that is not already implied in the transfer of the right of self-government or self-rule." (Kavka, 1986: 389.) Gauthier's argument, however, is that there is a distinction between transferring the right to govern and authorization. A transfer of the authority to govern might still carry with it the possibility of reevaluation by the subject, in the manner of a contract between subject and sovereign. By contrast, "[a]uthorizing the sovereign commits the subject to more than self-interestedly assisting him in his punishments and enforcement activities. It commits the subject to accept the sovereign's *judgment* in place of his own." (Gauthier, 1988: 77.)

and every one, signify the same; and the speech is absurd. But if by all together, they understand them as one person (which person the sovereign bears,) then the power of all together, is the same with the sovereign power; and so again the speech is absurd." (Hobbes [1651], 1996: 128.) The use of "absurd" takes us back into the territory of "round quadrangles" and other impossibilities. Here, the logical impossibility inheres in the fact that the "people" do not become a whole, capable of collective action, except by the creation of the sovereign. The collective identity of "the People" is lodged in the sovereign, and is forever separate from the mass of persons. Hobbes' sovereignty-over-others derived necessarily from the fact that his social contract was not a formula for self-rule, but essentially for mutual rule over one another by the constitution of a political community.

The reference to "absurdity" in the description of a People separate from its sovereign made standards of reasoned discourse into elements of juridical legitimacy. In its first appearance, the concept of absurdity pointed to the idea that an action of a sovereign could be illegitimate only insofar as it exceeded the bounds of "reason," the orderly naming of "signs" among which "sovereignty" took pride of place. In the second iteration, discursive standards of reason entered into the calculations of political legitimacy in the definitional standards of "justice," whereby a "law" could not be "unjust" because "[f]or all these words, he that in his actions observeth the laws of his country, make but one name, equivalent to this one word, just." (Hobbes [1651], 1996: 26.) Now, in the deployment of the term "absurd" to characterize an argument justifying rebellion, standards of discursive reason – not the "discourse of the mind," but the public discourse of speech – appear yet again. Those who attempt to justify rebellion are not mistaken as a matter of fact, nor morally corrupt; instead, they are guilty of adopting political positions that, articulated as semantic propositions, lack all definitional sense in the manner of the phrase "a round quadrangle." The first errors of speech derive from errors of naming, and the justification of rebellion errs by misnaming its subject.

Hobbes' account of the social contract did not present the creation of sovereignty as a way to satisfy other needs. It proclaimed that sovereignty itself is our first and most fundamental political need. By contrast, moral rules existed only in the context of a state, rather than as the external basis for the evaluation of either the legitimacy or the desirability of laws.[38] A telling example appears in the need to treat everyone as equals. Hobbes took it as given that differences in social status were purely the creation of human convention, reflecting no differences in the natures of the persons involved, as indeed he had to do in light of his theory of universal preferences embedded in human nature. At the same time, however, he did not rely on the metaphysical truth of this proposition, but was willing instead to say that it was necessary to act *as if* everyone were equal in order to achieve peace.[39] Like Bodin, Hobbes was willing to combine prudential and analytical arguments to overdetermine the validity of the rules that would guarantee political order.

Although Hobbes drew the connections between a theory of human nature/psychology and political order, his theories were not a basis for constitutional legitimacy in the modern sense of the phrase. Hobbes' theory was an explanation of the necessity of sovereignty as a phenomenon, not a set of background legitimating principles against which a regime or its actions could be tested, a limitation indicated by the line in *Leviathan* with which this part of the discussion began: "[T]here is no such thing as an unjust law."

On the other hand, Bodin's and Hobbes' theories of sovereignty pointed the way toward further developments. For one thing, both writers' versions of sovereign authority were far less absolute than they appeared at first glance. Crucially, both recognized that limitations on sovereign power inhere in the nature of sovereignty itself. Hobbes' innovation in this regard was to treat the purpose

---

[38] Gauthier describes the transformative effects of language and reason on morality as follows: "[Hobbes'] true moral theory is a dual conventionalism, in which a conventional reason, superseding natural reason, justifies a conventional morality, constraining natural behavior. And this dual conventionalism is Hobbes' enduring contribution to moral theory." (Gauthier, 1979: 547–48.)

[39] "I know that Aristotle in the first book of his Politics, for a foundation of his doctrine, maketh men by Nature, some more worthy to command ... others to serve ... as if master and servant were not introduced by consent of men, but by difference of wit: which is not only against reason; but also against experience. For there are very few so foolish, that had not rather govern themselves, than be governed by others .... If nature therefore have made men equal, or unequal; yet because men that think themselves equal, will not enter into conditions of Peace, but upon equal terms, such equality must be admitted. And therefore for the ninth law of Nature, I put this, That every man acknowledge other for his equal by nature. The breach of this precept is pride." (Hobbes [1651], 1996: 79–80.)

behind the creation of the sovereign as an integral element of its nature, and to connect that purpose to the construction of political language.

While both writers relied on a model of sovereignty-over-others, Hobbes opened the door to a theory of self-rule with his conflation of "the People" with the sovereign. If the two could be separated – that is, if a theoretically sound account could be given in which the moment of collective self-constitution as a People was prior to, and separate from, the moment of the creation of the sovereign – then a theory of sovereignty as self-rule would become possible. In addition, Hobbes' connection of epistemological and linguistic theory to a consideration of the conditions of possibility for sovereignty provided the ground in human nature that was necessary to separate political from metaphysical justification. Finally, and as a direct result of the elements mentioned thus far, Hobbes' arguments pointed to the possibility of situating the moment of consent at a point prior to the promulgation of laws, thus completing in a proto-democratic form the redirection of attention away from the content of laws to their source as the basis for legitimacy. These moves laid the groundwork for John Locke's creation of modern constitutionalism.

JOHN LOCKE: LANGUAGE, LAW, AND POPULAR SOVEREIGNTY

Locke's conception of sovereignty, and of the relations between sovereign and subjects, were very different from those that had come before. Unlike Hobbes, Locke did not speak of an "artificial person," nor very much about "sovereignty."[40] And while neither

---

[40] Ruth Grant argues that both legislators and executive officers are subordinated to the law, and "the chain of authority originates in the people who retain the supreme power to alter their legislative should it violate its trust." But the people themselves are not sovereign, either, inasmuch as they are not actively involved in the process of lawmaking. So long as political power operates, all members of the society owe obedience to the law as the expression of the public will that is supreme over the private will of each .... This is the effect of abandoning the concept of sovereignty as the grounds of the argument .... The law rules all members of the community because to consent to be a part of a political community means to obligate yourself to its laws. The people are supreme because all authority originates in their common consent." (Grant, 1987: 77–8.)

the anthropomorphic metaphor of the state nor the appeal to sovereignty were absent from Locke's reasoning, they were reconfigured in important ways.

For Locke, the success of a state depended less on the virtues of its citizens than on the strength of its case for their continuing loyalty.[41] The question of legitimacy thus became explicit, and its establishment depended on the possibility of a persuasive reasoned argument, not on an appeal to historical tradition or metaphysical necessity.[42] As a result, the commonwealth and its members occupied a far more dialogic relationship than the one between Hobbes' subjects and their sovereign. Sovereignty ceased to be the purpose for entering into the social contract, and became instead the name for the capacity to do so, while lawmaking came to include the capacity for self-rule as well as the capacity to rule others.

In addition, Locke extended the connections that Hobbes had drawn between epistemology, linguistics, and political authority, and in so doing laid the groundwork for liberal constitutionalism.[43]

---

[41] In this way, Locke is properly understood as an opponent of the republican tradition of the English Whigs that relied on the tradition of the "ancient Constitution." (Kramnick, 1968: 61–63; Pocock, 1975: 423–24.) Locke was a member of a circle led by Shaftesbury, including Bolingbroke and Priestly, that was concerned with reviving the republican tradition of the sixteenth-century "commonwealthmen" as the basis for asserting a radical alternative to both royalism and Whig traditionalism. Regarding Locke's radicalism vis-à-vis contemporaneous Whigs, compare Quentin Skinner's description (Skinner, 1978) with those of Richard Ashcraft (1980) and Peter Laslett (1956), both arguing forcefully that Locke's writings should be understood as a prospective justification for the revolution of 1688, rather than as a retrospective defense of the form of government that emerged from that event, a reading that emphasizes the revolutionary and quasi-utopian potential of Locke's arguments.

[42] It is noteworthy that nothing in the surviving text of the *Two Treatises on Government* talks about the English tradition of constitutionalism per se. In discussing the proposition that a monarch may lose the legitimate right to rule, Locke says "if there needed authority in a Case where reason is so plain, I could send my Reader to Bracton, Fortescue ... and others; Writers, who cannot be suspected to be ignorant of our Government." (Locke [1689], 1988: 426.)

[43] Locke was writing in large part in response to Filmer. The significance of Hobbes' arguments for Locke is unclear. In his general introduction to *Two Treatises*, Peter Laslett suggests that Locke's awareness of Hobbes' arguments exerted a "gravitational" influence, while the writings of Pufendorf, Grotius, and Filmer provided Locke's more immediate target. "When he wrote Two Treatises, then, Leviathan was an influence, a gravitational constant [sic] exercised by a large body though at a great distance." (Laslett, 1988: 74.)

To recognize and appreciate these connections, it is necessary to read Locke's political arguments through the lens of his earlier analysis of language and his ontological portrayal of law. What emerges from this reading is a unified description in which stages of linguistic, moral, and political development coincide in a progression that culminates in the creation of the commonwealth.[44] Specifically, the relationship between the use of language to name natural and conventional objects in the *Essay Concerning Human Understanding* ("*Human Understanding*") parallels the relationship between natural and conventional law that is introduced in the *Essay On the Laws of Nature* ("*Laws of Nature*") and the more developed discussion of the relationship between conventional law and political authority in the *Second Treatise on Government* ("*Second Treatise*").

In each text, Locke describes a progression between three stages of development. In *Human Understanding*, epistemological and linguistic development progresses from simple ideas captured in

---

[44] The idea that there is a direct relationship between Locke's epistemological and political doctrines is a matter of dispute. Jean Barbeyrac, who annotated editions of Grotius and Pufendorf and corresponded with Locke at length, argued that Locke's understanding of property, in particular, was directly grounded in his theory of moral knowledge outlined in the *Human Understanding*. (Tully, 1980: 6). Among modern writers, John Yolton most clearly echoes this argument (Yolton, 1958: 181–95), while William von Leyden argues that the discovery of the *Essays on the Law of Nature* provide the missing pieces, so that "it is now possible to recognize that Locke's two main bodies of doctrine, namely his political theory and his theory of knowledge, have a common ground and that this lies in his early doctrine of natural law." (Leyden, 1956: 3.) In a similar rein, Hans Aarsleff proposes that *Human Understanding* provides the theoretical basis for the more concrete and practical account of civil government in the Second Treatise. (Aarsleff, 1969: 99.) Peter Laslett goes the farthest in the opposite direction, asserting that there are no philosophical links between the *Essay* and the *Treatises* whatsover, based in part on the observation that Locke's treatment of natural law within the *Treatises* is itself not entirely consistent. For Laslett, this supports the implication is that the *Treatises* are "something very different from an extension into the political field of the general philosophy of the *Essay* [*Concerning Human Understanding*], and reminds us that Locke differed in the character of his thinking from Hobbes." (Locke [1689], 1988: 83.) James Tully takes an intermediate approach, suggesting that the projects of *Human Understanding* and the *Treatises* are connected, but by an intellectual "relationship ... much looser than formal logical demonstration." (Tully, 1980: 8.) I believe that Tully is correct in that the the "parallels" that I am describing are a matter of structural similarity rather than logical necessity, but conversely that the basic principles outlined in the *Essay* are consistent with the epistemological and linguistic principles alluded to in the *Essays Upon the Law of Nature* and the *Two Treatises on Government*.

names, to mixed modes that identify combinations of simple ideas, and finally to purely conventional complex concepts that have no referent outside themselves. In *Laws of Nature*, a similar progression appears as laws of nature are replaced by laws derived from the observation of social practices, and finally by positive legislation. And in the *Second Treatise*, between the state of nature and the eventual creation of the commonwealth, there occurs the creation of "society," in which people gather together and agree to live by rules of their own creation. Ultimately, Locke's argument sets the stage for modern liberal constitutionalism, but the progression of arguments requires careful attention to his theories of the development of language and law as well as his more famous theory of the state. The epistemological account of language precedes the political argument both analytically and chronologically; it is therefore appropriate to begin there.

HUMAN UNDERSTANDING: FROM SIMPLE IDEAS TO CONVENTIONAL MEANINGS

Like Hobbes, Locke was skeptical of the possibility of direct and unmediated perception of the world.[45] In *Human Understanding*, Locke argued that all knowledge begins with sense perceptions, which lead to "ideas" of the world that provide the subject of both thought and discourse. "Simple" ideas are the names given to the perception of natural objects. These objects of perception, however, are merely combinations of sense perceptions; it is the act of naming them and the creation of their idea that causes them to have a distinct identity. Initially, there is a world of perceivable characteristics, and the sense perceptions thereof. Upon the perception that

---

[45] In a much-quoted passage, Locke suggests that our inability to perceive the true essence of things derives from the limited capacities of our sense organs. "Had we senses acute enough to discern the minute particles of bodies, and the real constitution on which their sensible qualities depend, I doubt not but they would produce quite different ideas in us; and that which is now the yellow color of gold, would then disappear, and instead of it we should see an admirable texture of parts of certain size and figure. This microscopes plainly discover to us." These limitations, however, are elements of divine design and are suited to the divine purpose for human existence. (Locke [1689], 1982: 398.)

some set of characteristics frequently occurs together in nature, the perceiving mind imposes an idea in the form of a name.[46] Examples of simple ideas include "yellow, white, heat, cold, soft, hard, bitter, sweet," which occur when "external objects convey into the mind what produces there those perceptions." (Locke [1689], 1982: 105.)

There is also a second category of simple ideas–those that refer to the workings of our own mind and are obtained by "reflection." Examples of this latter type of simple ideas include "perception, thinking, doubting, believing, reasoning, knowing, willing ... which we being conscious of, and observing in our selves, do from these receive into our understandings, as distinct ideas, as we do from bodies affecting our senses." But our perceptions of the workings of our minds are no more direct than our perceptions of the external world. In both instances, our conscious minds have access only to the ideas of the things so perceived. "These two, I say, viz. external material things, as the objects of sensation; and the operations of our own minds within, as the objects of reflection, are, to me, the only originals, from whence all our ideas take their beginnings." (Locke [1689], 1982: 104.)[47]

[46] "The mind being, as I have declared, furnished with a great number of the simple ideas, conveyed in by the senses, as they are found in exterior things, or by reflection on its own operations, takes notice also, that a certain number of these simple ideas go constantly together; which being presumed to belong to one thing, and words being suited to common apprehensions ... are called so united in one subject, by one name; which by inadvertency we are apt afterward to talk of and consider as one simple idea, which indeed is a complication of man's ideas together." (Locke [1689], 1982: 295.)

[47] The description of Lockean reflection offered here is obviously problematic. At times, Locke treats reflection as an example of sense perception, while at other times reflection appears to be something closer to a Cartesian *cogito*. Thus Locke writes both "knowledge then seems to me nothing but the perception of the connection and agreement, or disagreement and repugnancy of any of our ideas" and "there can be nothing more certain, than that the idea we receive from an external object is in our minds; this is intuitive knowledge." (Locke [1689], 1982: 525, 537.) Douglas Odegard, among others, argues that Locke is best understood as presenting reflection as a form of intuitive knowledge rather than perception, if only in order to account for Locke's emphasis on sensation in the first instance. (Odegard, 1965: 2.) On the other hand, there are numerous places at which Locke employs the alternative description. Positing the workings of our minds as the subjects of sense perceptions sets up complex problems of defining the locus of consciousness and identity, and indeed *Human Understanding* contains a lengthy discussion of the problem of defining an individual's identity, leading Michael Zuckert to argue that the fundamental

Language, for Locke, begins with the naming of simple ideas, after which the reliance on names substitutes accessible "nominal essences," the objects of reference, for the unknowable essential substances that are the objects of perception. Like Hobbes' "marks" that organize perceptions into thoughts, Locke's nominal essences refer to an internal application of language through the act of naming as the beginning of reason. In the case of gold, for example, "it is the real constitution of its insensible parts, on which depend all those properties of color, weight, fusibility, fixedness, etc., which are to be found in it. Which constitution we know not; and so having no particular idea of, have no name that is the sign of it. But yet its color, weight ... etc. which makes it to be gold, or gives it a right to that name, which is therefore its nominal essence. Since nothing can be called gold, but what has a conformity of qualities to that abstract complex idea, to which that name is annexed." (Locke [1689], 1982: 419.)

The naming of objects is thus already doubly conventional even at the level of simple ideas. We give names to those objects we tend to encounter frequently, based on those characteristics we are able to perceive, and thereafter the set of characteristics identified by the name – the nominal essence – becomes the subject of our understanding. (Aarsleff, 1982: 63–4.) And what is true of gold is equally true of ourselves; the nature of humanity is no more subject to our perceptions than is the nature of anything else.[48] Significantly,

---

difference between Locke and Hobbes was the former's development of a more sophisticated model of the "self" that constitutes the rights-bearing subject. (Zuckert, 2002: 9–12.) I find that for purposes of this discussion, reflection is best understood as a form of sense perception, in order to focus attention on the sharp distinction between perception and reflection, on the one hand, and the construction of complex concepts or "mixed modes," which are not subject to intuitive knowledge, on the other.

[48] "There are creatures in the world, that have shapes like ours, but are hairy, and want language and reason .... If it be asked, whether these be all men, or no, all of human species; 'tis plain, the question refers only to the nominal essence: for those of them to whom the definition of the word man, or the complex idea signified by that name, agrees are men, and the other not. But if the inquiry be made concerning the supposed real essence, and whether the internal constitution and frame of these several creatures be specifically different, it is wholly impossible for us to answer." (Locke [1689], 1982: 450–51.) The point is reiterated in several places. (See Locke [1689], 1982: 440.)

Locke's skepticism about our capacity to directly perceive the workings of our own minds set his epistemological theory apart from that of Hobbes, who relied on introspection to determine universal human truths. For Locke, beyond simple sense perception there was only language.

Locke's argument did not imply that humans have no nature, nor that laws of human nature are unknowable, only that human nature is not accessible to *direct* perception and naming. There were other means of obtaining knowledge about the world, and providential guarantees that our simple ideas drawn from sense perceptions coincide with the true natures of objects in the world. "[S]imple ideas are not fictions of our fancies, but the natural and regular productions of things without us, really operating upon us; and so carry with them all the conformity which is intended; or which our state requires .... And this conformity between our simple ideas, and the existence of things, is sufficient for real knowledge." (Locke [1689], 1982: 563–64.) Divine design gives humans the ability to perceive at the level that is necessary for their lives; enough "to lead us to the knowledge of the Creator and the knowledge of our duty; and ... to provide for the conveniences of living." (Locke [1689], 1982: 302.)

This theological fallback is characteristic of the early stages of Locke's arguments in all three of the texts considered here. Faith in a benevolent Creator provided a secure base from which to proceed forward in the face of the challenge of Cartesian skepticism, while at the same time maintaining a connection to the theological traditions of English Calvinism.[49] But it nonetheless remains the case that human nature, or the nature of any other thing, is not the same as our description and understanding of that thing. And the possibility

---

[49] Zuckert describes Locke's approach as a "much modified Cartesian" theory of the self deeply influenced by "the experience of the Cartesian doubt." (Zuckert, 2002: 15–16.) Zuckert, expanding on Leo Strauss' obscurantist interpretation of Locke's writing, takes the position that appeals to Christian authority were essentially dishonest attempts to conceal his true intentions from potentially hostile audiences, so that Locke's frequent allusions to Hooker are meant merely "to cloak his doctrine of the state of nature in the respectability that judicious name provides." (Zuckert, 2002: 90; for a review of arguments on this point, see ibid, 90–95. For an analysis connecting Locke's epistemology to specific disputes within English Calvinist natural theology, see Lamprecht, 1927.)

of inconsistency between our understanding and the object of description becomes more acute when we attempt to combine descriptions of simple objects into categories. It is in this second stage, at the development of "mixed modes," that the problem of epistemological skepticism begins to have serious consequences.

Mixed modes are "the complex ideas," created by "several combinations of simple ideas of different kinds." (Locke [1689], 1982: 288.) "The mind often exercises an active power in the making [of] these several combinations. For it being once furnished with simple ideas, it can put them together in several compositions, and so make variety of complex ideas, without examining whether they exist so together in nature." (Locke [1689], 1982: 288.) The naming of a class of objects is an exercise in the taxonomical definition of species, which itself has no necessary connection to the natures of the objects being described. "[T]ake but away the abstract ideas, by which we sort individuals, and rank them under common names, and then the thought of any thing essential to any of them, instantly vanishes." (Locke [1689], 1982: 440.)

Furthermore, the selection of simple ideas on the basis of which to construct the idea of a species is always arbitrary. "[E]ndeavouring to make the signification of their specific names as clear, and as little cumbersome as they can, [humans] make their specific ideas of the sorts of substances, for the most part, of a few of those simple ideas which are to be found in them: But these having no original precedency, or right to be put in, and make the specific idea, more than others that are left out." (Locke [1689], 1982: 381.) And again, what is true of other objects of description is equally true of man. "[I]f several men were to be asked, concerning some oddly-shaped fetus, as soon as born, whether it were a man or no, 'tis past doubt, one should meet with different answers. Which could not happen, if the nominal essences, whereby we limit and distinguish the species of substances, were not made by man, with some liberty; but were exactly copied from precise boundaries set by nature." (Locke [1689], 1982: 454.)

As a result, the act of naming serves a very different function in the case of mixed modes than it does in the case of natural objects. The name of a simple idea identifies the cluster of characteristics that cause it to be so identified. Mixed modes, by contrast, take their meaning by convention, by the agreement to treat a set of simple ideas as a single idea that causes the named *concept* to exist. The name of a mixed mode identifies the collective, socially undertaken decision to treat that set of characteristics in a consistent way that is effected by the act of naming them. The only constraints on naming mixed modes are social ones; in a truly presocial state, the naming of complex ideas would be a purely arbitrary act. "[W]hat liberty Adam had at first to make any complex ideas of mixed modes, by no other pattern, but by his own thoughts, the same have all men ever since had .... but only with this difference, that in places, where men in society have already established a language among them, the signification of words are very warily and sparingly to be altered. Because men being furnished already with names for their ideas, and common use having appropriated known names to certain ideas, an affected misapplication of them cannot but be very ridiculous." (Locke [1689], 1982: 470–71.)

Mixed modes are the first example of complex ideas. But while Locke is not perfectly clear about the distinction, he also refers to a third stage of linguistic development characterized by complex ideas that have no external referents at all. These are complex ideas that are not formed by combining and arranging simple ideas, but rather by an act of creative imagination.

At this stage, language becomes generative, as naming, defining, and creation occur simultaneously by an act of linguistic construction. Once language is in place, the fact of communication itself becomes capable of generating subjective ideas without the necessity for any corresponding sense perception of the idea being communicated. "Indeed, now that languages are made, and abound with words standing for such combinations, an usual way of getting these complex ideas, is by the explication of those terms that stand for them .... Thus a man may come to have the idea of sacrilege, or murder, by enumerating to him the simple ideas that these words stand for, without ever seeing either of them committed." (Locke [1689], 1982:289.) The examples of sacrilege and murder point to the consequences of this theory of language for law. The possibility of using words to "enumerate" simple ideas that have no corresponding experience of perception means that communication through language is generative of "natural" as well as "conventional" laws.

To use another of Locke's terms, the real essence for an idea is called its "archetype." In the case of a simple idea, the name (nominal essence) describes the archetype (the set of experiences of perception that define the class of objects identified by the name.) In the case of mixed modes and purely conventional concepts, by contrast, the archetype and the nominal essence are one and the same. "For these abstract ideas, being the workmanship of the mind, and not referred to the real existence of things, there is no supposition of any thing more signified by that name, but barely that complex idea the mind itself has formed ... and so in these the real and nominal essence is the same." (Locke [1689], 1982: 436.)

Complex ideas of mixed modes and conventional archetypes are the only kind of knowledge with respect to which there can be certainty because there is no pretense that they name any object of reference outside of themselves. "All our complex ideas, except those of substances, being archetypes of the mind's own making, not intended to be the copies of any thing, nor referred to the existence of any thing, as to their originals, cannot want any conformity necessary to real knowledge .... So that we cannot but be infallibly certain, that all the knowledge we attain concerning these ideas is real, and reaches things themselves." (Locke [1689], 1982:564.) This leads Locke to the critical conclusion that the knowledge of moral matters can be certain not because it refers to real natural laws, but precisely because it contains no referent external to itself; such knowledge is purely a matter of human imagination and convention.[50]

Certainty in moral matters does not guarantee agreement, but it dictates against defining disagreement as *error*. Disagreement occurs by virtue of the fact of incommensurate conventions, not inconsistent realities. "When a man is thought to have a false idea of justice, or gratitude, or glory, it is for no other reason, but that his

---

[50] "The mathematician considers the truth and properties belonging to a rectangle, or circle, only as they are ideas in his own mind. For 'tis possible he never found either of them existing mathematically, i.e. precisely true, in his life. But yet the knowledge he has of any truths or properties belonging to a circle, or any other mathematical figure, are nonetheless true and certain, even of real things existing .... And hence it follows, that moral knowledge is as capable of real certainty, as mathematics." (Locke [1689], 1982: 565–66; see Tully, 1980: 21.)

agrees not with the ideas, which each of those names are the signs of in other men." (Locke [1689], 1982: 387.) The only apparent limitation, again, is the social constraint of wishing to avoid appearing "ridiculous," a close cousin to Hobbes' warning about absurdity. Both refer to the same danger – the use of words in ways that convey no meaning to others.

Locke's skepticism should not be overstated. Through all his discussion of conventional law, Locke never abandoned his particular version of natural law as a present element of the rules of human conduct. To begin with, he took as simply obvious the proposition that divine natural law must exist. "That God has given a rule whereby men should govern themselves, I think there is no body so brutish as to deny." The only question, then, was the source for knowledge of the content of that law. Here, things get more difficult. Locke appealed to a hedonistic theory, whereby the crucial evidence is the fact that some ways of acting tend to lead to lesser or greater happiness for the actor. "This is the only true touchstone of moral rectitude; and by comparing them to this law, it is, that men judge of the most considerable moral good or evil of their actions; that is, whether as duties, or sins, they are like to procure them happiness, or misery, from the hands of the Almighty." The difficulty lay in the fact that "happiness" was itself a complex idea. Since complex ideas are social constructions, there was no guarantee of the conceptual unity. "Hence naturally flows the great variety of opinions, concerning the moral rules, which are to be found amongst men, according to the different sorts of happiness, they have a prospect of, or propose to themselves." (Locke [1689], 1982: 352.)

The reference to happiness draws the connection between Locke's ontology and his politics that supplied his resolution to the danger of pure intellectualism. To say that "good" and "evil" are human terms that name complex concepts related to happiness, not dictates of God, invites moral skepticism.[51] To escape that danger,

---

[51] "Good and evil, as hath been shown ... are nothing but pleasure or pain, or that which occasions, or procures pleasure or pain to us. Morally good and evil, then, is only the conformity or disagreement of our voluntary actions to some law, whereby good or evil is drawn on us, from the will and power of the law-maker ... that we call reward and punishment." (Locke [1689], 1982: 351.) "These ideas, in turn, are connected to happiness. Therefore what has an aptness to produce pleasure in us,

Locke introduced the argument that God has so designed human nature that happiness coincides with obedience to natural law, just as in the case of simple ideas, God so designed human perception that it accurately reflects the essential nature of objects. Thus hedonism becomes "the means by which man is guided to the moral rules that pertain to the law of nature." (Aarsleff, 1969: 127.)

Locke made his argument for a connection between happiness and morality in the context of a demonstration that the fact that people tend in most cases to follow a rule does not prove it to be consonant with divine natural law. But the argument has the unexpected, and in Locke's writing unexplored, consequence that even those who do not acknowledge God's agency may nonetheless arrive at a correct understanding of natural laws of morality, merely by observing what leads to happiness.[52] This becomes the first move in Locke's separation of political from divine authority, as God is increasingly bracketed in the analysis, acknowledged as Creator but not the subject of study. Ultimately, it is neither the case that the study of God leads to insights about politics, nor that the accord between a political order and divine design can be measured in any direct way.

Part of the reason for leaving appeals to divine authority out of the discussion, for Locke, was his skepticism about the knowability of the laws of nature. Natural moral laws are self-evident in the sense that it would be unreasonable to believe that they do not exist, but that does not mean that knowledge of their content is available by introspection. For example, the fact that rules that are consonant with natural law are nonetheless frequently broken demonstrates

---

is that we call good, and what is apt to produce pain in us, we call evil, for no other reason, but for its aptness to produce pleasure and pain in us, wherein consists our happiness and misery." (Locke [1689], 1982: 258–59.)

[52] "I think it must be allowed, that several moral rules, may receive, from mankind, a very general approbation, without either knowing or admitting the true ground of morality; which can only be the will and law of a God.... For God, having by an inseparable connection, joined virtue and public happiness together; and made the practice thereof, necessary to the preservation of society, and visibly beneficial to all, with whom the virtuous man has to do, it is no wonder, that every one should, not only allow, but recommend and magnify those rules to others, from whose observance of them, he is sure to reap advantage to himself." (Locke [1689], 1982: 69.)

that knowledge of those rules is not innate. (Locke [1689], 1982: 74–5.) Instead, it is the study of human behavior and its consequences to adduce the universal rules of what yields "public happiness" that leads to knowledge of natural law.

In this way, Locke begins to blur the distinction between divinely inscribed natural law and the laws of human nature. Moreover, in a later section, Locke concludes that reason is not only a route toward the discovery of natural laws, it is superior to divine revelation.

"[N]othing, I think, can, under that title [of revelation], shake or over-rule plain knowledge; or rationally prevail with any man, to admit it for sure, in a direct contradiction to the clear evidence of his own understanding." (Locke [1689], 1982: 691.)[53] At the end of *Human Understanding*, it is the study of specifically human nature – principles adduced from the observation of human conduct and its consequences – that turns out to be the immediate basis for the knowledge of Locke's natural laws.[54]

---

[53] So, for example, revelation of miraculous occurrences must be treated skeptically because revelation, itself, ultimately rests on reason and perception. "Since the evidence, first, that we deceive not our selves in ascribing it to God; secondly, that we understand it right, can never be so great, as the evidence of our own intuitive knowledge ....And therefore, no proposition can be received for divine revelation, or obtain the assent due to all such, it if be contradictory to our clear intuitive knowledge." (Locke [1689], 1982: 692.) As for indirect revelation, by way of written scriptures or tradition, these are even less to be relied upon, since the divine source of the text itself requires confirmation. (Locke [1689], 1982: 693–94.) The consequences of this skepticism for Christian doctrine was to be a matter of considerable concern for subsequent writers, but for the moment it is sufficient to observe that by these formulations, Locke has entirely blurred the distinctions between divine, physical, and human natural law.

[54] Scriptural commandments are a supplement to human natural law; but it is the latter that provides the basis for political legitimation. Patrick Riley warns against overreading the famous passage in which Locke describes natural law as consisting of reason; as Riley rightly reminds us, it is always necessary to maintain the distinction between the source of natural law, its content, and the method by which it can be known by human minds. To demonstrate that a moral precept accords with natural law, one must "build his doctrine upon principles of reason, self-evident in themselves ... or he must show his commission from heaven, that he comes with authority from God, to deliver his will and commands to the world." (Riley, 1974: 444.) These dual sources appear to echo the standard Calvinist idea of "two books of revelation," without any clear resolution of the difficulty of squaring that theological ideal with the conventional elements of Locke's epistemological and linguistic theories.

There are significant elements of the argument in *Human Understanding* that remain unclear. It is difficult to connect the categories of ideas to a story of collective, societal development. Locke analogizes the progression between forms of ideas to successive stages of development in the consciousness of children. (Locke [1689], 1982: 411–12.) In other places there are ambiguous references to a kind of linguistic genealogy.[55] At still other points, Locke posits that complex ideas exist *prior to* the invention of language. "[I]t is evident, that in the beginning of languages and societies of men, several of those complex ideas, which were consequent to the constitutions established amongst them, must needs have been in the minds of men, before they existed any where else." (Locke [1689], 1982: 288.)

The reference to the existence of complex ideas prior to "the beginning of languages" points to something about the nature of language itself. For Locke, to be prelinguistic is to be presocial, but language is not essential to thought. Language in this formulation is purely a medium of interpersonal communication, while the processes of subjective idea-formation are left essentially mysterious.[56] In Locke's formulation, language appears as the public medium for the expression of private ideas, a division between public and private realms at the very bedrock of human identity.[57]

---

[55] "I doubt not, but if we could trace them to their sources, we should find, in all languages, the names, which stand for things that fall not under our senses, to have had their first rise from sensible ideas. By which we may give some kind of guess, what kind of notions they were, and whence derived, which filled their minds, who were the first beginners of languages." (Locke [1689], 1982: 403.)

[56] "This, therefore, being my purpose to enquire into the original, certainty, and extent of human knowledge; together, with the grounds and degrees of belief, opinion, and assent; I shall not at present meddle with the physical consideration of the mind; or trouble my self to examine, wherein its essence consists, or by what motions of our spirits, or alterations of our bodies, we come to have any sensation by our organs, or any ideas in our understandings; and whether those ideas do in their formation, any, or all of them, depend on matter, or no. These are speculations, which, however curious and entertaining, I shall decline." (Locke [1689], 1982: 43.)

[57] This is consistent with Locke's earlier identification of the essence of an object with its purposive ends, as the ends of language are decidedly social: "First, to make known one man's thoughts or ideas to another. Secondly, to do it with as much ease and quickness, as is possible; and thirdly, thereby to convey the knowledge of things. Language is either abused, or deficient, when it fails in any of these three." (Locke [1689], 1982: 504.) On the dangers of erroneous uses of language, the

The public aspect of language appears in Locke's description of the social event of naming as something inherent in the purposive nature of language itself. "[W]e shall find the end of it to be the end of language; which being to mark, or communicate men's thoughts to one another, with all the dispatch that may be, they usually make such collections of ideas into complex modes, and affix names to them, as they have frequent use of in their way of living and conversation, leaving others, which they have but seldom occasion to mention, loose and without names, that tie them together." (Locke [1689], 1982: 290.) In this passage, the public and private uses of language appear as distinct but complementary phenomena. One version of language is employed to group simple ideas into complex concepts in accordance with individual needs; thereafter, a second, public language is employed in communication with others to achieve shared agreement on the conventional meaning of words. As for what is required to make this process work, Locke presages the arguments of twentieth century Logical Positivists that care in definitions is the key to the construction of social language. (Locke [1689], 1982: 517.)[58] Locke's theory of the relationship between speech and moral reasoning, then, is as much a rule of social practice as a literal developmental account. The parallel with the ambiguously historical or mythical state of nature is inescapable, and points to the necessity of presuming a moment of linguistic consent prior to a political social contract.

Working out the relationship between Locke's account of linguistic and societal development provides the starting point for his political theory. Complex ideas such as "law" and "morals" are developed through the use of public language, bound solely by social convention. Already, these observations point toward the critical role of political authority over language; the authority of the sovereign to make laws becomes the authority to define "law" and the juridical concepts that law employs. To see the connections

---

importance of linguistic precision in Locke's thought, and connections between Locke and the "plain style" favored by the Royal Society, see Mulligan, et al., 1982. For a discussion of the public and private dimensions of language in Locke's theory, see Ashworth, 1984; Dawson, 2003.

[58] For an extended argument to the effect that Locke, himself, did not comply with his own linguistic prescriptions, see Zuckert, 2002.

between Locke's epistemology and his theory of law more fully, however, it is necessary to turn to his legal and political texts and consider how their arguments appear in the context of the theory of linguistic development. For this purpose, it is useful to begin with the *Essays On the Laws of Nature*, an earlier and less skeptical version of the argument than that found in the *Two Treatises*.

LAWS OF NATURE: FROM DIVINE WILL
TO HUMAN NATURE

For purposes of this discussion, *Laws of Nature* is primarily of interest as a bridge between *Human Understanding* and the *Second Treatise on Government*. It is important to recognize the progression between categories in Locke's account of natural law, however, because of the critical role that concept plays in the *Second Treatise*.

In his writings, Locke provided inconsistent accounts of the ultimate ground for his particular version of the laws of nature. One of Locke's contemporary critics, Thomas Barnet, challenged him on this very point in 1697. "[W]hat is the reason or ground of the divine law? Whether the arbitrary will of God, the good of men, or the intrinsic nature of the things themselves?" (Oakley and Urdang, 1966: 63.)[59] As in *Human Understanding*, Locke's response to this

[59] Barnet's question points toward the seventeenth-century debate between two models of divine natural law. The "voluntaristic" or "nominalist" view held that terms such as "right," "just," or "good" were simply names for the consequences of divine edicts, themselves grounded in nothing more than God's will, and consequently might be changed by, for example, a subsequent act of revelation demonstrating a new set of divine edicts. In this sense, to a voluntarist God stands in relation to "right" as the author of a complex concept; the meaning of the concept is defined by the act of its authoritative naming. An intellectualist theory, by contrast, was one according to which "right" had a meaning independent of God's will, and was thus in some sense binding on God's own acts. It was by no means a matter of coincidence that what God willed was right, but the meaning of "right" could be determined independently of an examination of God's will. Intellectualist theories of divine natural law opened the door for the introduction of elements of physical or human natural law by separating the source of natural law (God) from the source of knowledge of its contents (reason). Oakley and Urdang present a persuasive case that Locke's view should be conceived of as an intermediate alternative in which God could have devised any order of the world that pleased the divine will, but once that order was instituted, the moral laws of nature were necessarily implied by the order of the particular creation that had been undertaken. (Oakley and Urdang, 1966: 77.)

challenge was to bracket the role of God as the author of human nature, and to subsequently treat human nature itself – as opposed to either divine will or the order of the natural world – as the grounding constant at the base of natural law. "[S]ince man has been made such as he is ... there necessarily result from his inborn constitution some definite duties for him, which cannot be other than they are .... as it follows from the nature of a triangle that, if it is a triangle, its three angles are equal to two right angles." (Locke [circa 1664], 1997: 125.)[60] Like Hobbes, Locke drew on an analogy from geometry to describe the deductive analytic necessity of his grounding commitments, and – again, like Hobbes – for Locke the discovery of these commitments could occur without reference to theology.

In this way, through the course of *Laws of Nature*, Locke's theory progresses toward a conception of human natural law effectively unconnected to its theological roots (Soles, 1977), just as in *Human Understanding* Locke's theory of language involves a progression from natural to conventional modes of meaning construction. By the end of his discussion, Locke has effectively severed the legitimating basis for government from any necessary theological source, but to get to that point the argument has to go through a series of stages.

In *Laws of Nature*, Locke begins by drawing a connection between the natural order of creation and the "light of reason" in the familiar terms, shared by scholastics and Calvinists alike. God's existence is conclusively demonstrated by the simple observation (sense perception) of the "fixed course of nature." Since humanity is an element of divine creation, humanity, too, must bear the marks of God's design. "[I]t seems just therefore to inquire whether man alone has come into the world altogether exempt from any law applicable to himself, without a plan, rule, or any pattern of his life.

---

[60] James Byrne notes that the argument for natural law in the *Essays on the Law of Nature* is more voluntarist/nominalist than the later, more rationalist version that appears in the *Essay Concerning Human Understanding*. (Byrne, 1964.) It is noteworthy that the *Two Treatises* similarly reflect a more pronounced skepticism concerning the direct perception of the order of creation than is present in the *Essays on the Law of Nature*, which already display a position far too skeptical to permit Bodin's direct analogies between the natural and political order.

No one will easily believe this." (Locke [circa 1664], 1997: 81.)[61] But as in the discussion of the connection between happiness and morals in *Human Understanding*, knowledge of the existence of natural law is quite different from knowledge of its contents, a distinction identified in the different roles of human reason in "discovery" and "interpretation" of the laws of nature. "[R]eason does not so much establish and pronounce this law of nature as search for it and discover it as a law enacted by a superior power and implanted in our hearts. Neither is reason so much the maker of that law as its interpreter." (Locke [circa 1664], 1997: 82.)

At the stage of discovery, sense perception demonstrates the existence of natural laws in the first instance by the experience of beauty and regularity in the world. "[F]or it is surely undisputed that this could not have come together casually and by chance into so regular and in every respect so perfect and ingeniously prepared a structure. Hence it is undoubtedly inferred that there must be a powerful and wise creator of all these things." (Locke [circa 1664], 1997: 103–04.) At the stage of interpretation, however, "reason" appears in a distinct and different sense.

> By reason here we do not mean some moral principles or any propositions laid upon the mind such that, if the actions of our life fitly correspond to them, these are said to be in accordance with right reason; for right reason of this sort is nothing but the law of nature itself already known, not the manner whereby, or that light of nature whereby, natural law is known.... On the contrary, reason is here taken to mean the discursive faculty of the mind, which advances from things known to things unknown and argues from one thing to another in a definite and fixed order of propositions. It is this reason by means of which mankind arrives at the knowledge of natural law. (Locke [circa 1664], 1997: 100, 101.)

Just as God the Creator was gradually removed from the study of human nature, God the sovereign lawgiver is removed from the

---

[61] In another essay fragment, Locke connects reason, divine inspiration, and the idea of binding law in the form of a religious duty to act reasonably. "If he finds that God has made him and all other men in a state wherein they cannot subsist without society and has given them judgement to discern what is capable of preserving that society, can he but conclude that he is obliged and that God requires him to follow those rules which conduce to the preserving of society?" (Locke [circa 1664], 1997: 270.)

discussion with the abandonment of "right reason" in favor of a "discursive faculty of the mind."

In *Human Understanding*, divine providence provided a kind of ontological backstop that prevented skepticism from sliding into moral nihilism. In *Laws of Nature*, the same move is relied upon to rescue the fact of moral obligation from the implications of reliance on sense perceptions and language as the alternative possible sources of knowledge: "ultimately, all obligation leads back to God." (Locke [circa 1664], 1997: 117.) But this is not the same thing as involving the divine source of obligation in the interpretation of natural laws. The *discovery* of natural law can be achieved by sense impressions of the natural world, but the *interpretation* of natural law is to be determined by an examination of human faculties and experience, and reveals principles specifically applicable to human affairs, leaving the divine source of that nature in the background.[62] These examinations of human experience, not deduction from ontological premises, are the basis for Locke's conclusion that men have natural duties "to God, their neighbor, and themselves." (Locke [circa 1664], 1997: 105–06.) The content of natural law is determined by the observable facts of human nature, captured in complex ideas created by language.

The reference to reason as a "discursive faculty of the mind" points to the fact that sense perception is an interaction between a mind and an external world. Whereas in the seventeenth century, "discursive" meant merely ordered, here naming and the consequent creation of nominal essences appear quite literally as a discourse, an inquiry conducted by a human observer's interrogation of humanity to determine its essential nature. And whereas for Hobbes this act of interrogation was directed inward in the form of introspection, for Locke the questioner's inquiries are directed

---

[62] In part, this was a necessary implication of the term "law." For Locke, as for modern writers, "law" was by definition something knowable by virtue of publication. The laws of nature, therefore, had to be explained as knowable in order to be binding, since laws not knowable by reason would not have been propagated by their author, and hence would not be "laws" at all. Similarly, such laws can only apply to reasoning beings. "[N]o body can be under a law which is not promulgated to him; and this law being promulgated or made known by reason only, he that is not come to the use of his reason, cannot be said to be under this law." (Locke [1689], 1988: 305.)

outward toward past and present human society. Out of this process of interrogation the interpreter is able to derive the content of the laws of nature. A more precise term than "interpretation," in modern usage, might be "extrapolation." Humans are observed in their social state, and imagined in their natural state, and from those observations and the exercise of imagination the Lockean observer is able to extrapolate universally applicable laws of nature.

Reading *Human Understanding* and *Laws of Nature* together demonstrates a parallel progression in the relationship between knowledge of universal laws and God. In the first stage, humans have knowledge of the existence of laws of nature promulgated by God the sovereign. In the second stage, the interpretation of those laws, and their naming as rules of conduct, is achieved by the application of discursive reason. And in the final stage, the content of those rules is tested and combined to form human natural laws defined by "happiness," without any necessary direct connection to divine authorship at all, just as the complex ideas used to articulate these rules no longer have any necessary connection to an event of sense impression.[63] What remained to be explored was how the existence of human natural laws led to a prescription for the exercise of sovereignty.

SECOND TREATISE: LANGUAGE, LAW, AND POLITICAL AUTHORITY

In *Laws of Nature*, Locke proceeded from the discovery of laws through simple observation to their interpretation – or extrapolation – by the exercise of discursive reason. This same set of moves is reiterated in the *Second Treatise*, in a process that moves from the same knowable laws of nature to the extrapolation of political principles that runs from the state of nature, to society, and at last to

---

[63] Patrick Riley speaks of an "equilibrium" between competing models of natural law rather than a progression. (Riley, 1974). I believe that the difference is as much one of emphasis as of substantive interpretation. It is also the case that the characterization that one chooses to describe the tension between different elements of Locke's argument in different works reflects the purpose of examining those works. The imagery of progression and development is certainly frequently referred to in Locke's writing, and it is obviously suited to an attempt to situate Lockean ideas in the development of modern constitutionalist thought.

the creation of the commonwealth. The *Second Treatise* thus articulates a third iteration of the evolutionary scheme of progressive stages of understanding, but here, finally, all three versions of the the progression are combined in an argument specifically directed toward the derivation of political truths.

In addition, whereas particularly in *Human Understanding*, Locke was concerned with characterizing stages of development, in the *Second Treatise* his focus has shifted to moments of transition between those stages. The focus on moments of transition is the move that causes ideas of consent and political legitimacy become relevant in ways that they never were before. "Consent" does not provide reasons to accept the conditions that pertain at a given stage of development so much as it identifies the condition of legitimacy for the transition from one state to the next. This brings us directly to a consideration of the conditions for the creation of a constitutional regime, which occurs as the last of these moments of transition.

In the state of nature, sense perceptions and simple ideas combine to produce language and the discovery of natural laws. Sovereignty belongs solely to God, as there is no law other than that which exists as a direct consequence of human nature. As noted earlier, in the *Laws of Nature* Locke initially described laws of nature as directly perceived through sense perception – that is, through observation – and those laws were varied and extensive.[64] In the *Second Treatise*, however, Locke appears to recognize the problem inherent in squaring that description with his commitment to epistemological skepticism. If there can be no direct and unmediated perception of the world, there can be no direct and

---

[64] John W. Yolton comes up with the following partial list: "(1) Love and respect and worship God; (2) Obey your superiors; (3) Tell the truth and keep your promises; (4) Be mild and pure of character and friendly; (5) Do not offend or injure, without cause, any person's health, life, or possessions; (6) Be candid and friendly in talking about other people; (7) Do not kill or steal; (8) Love your neighbor and your parents; (9) Console a distressed neighbor; (10) Feed the hungry; (11) 'Whosoever sheddeth man's blood, by man shall his blood be shed'; (12) That property is mine which I have acquired through my labor so long as I can use it before it spoils; (13) Parents are to preserve, nourish, and educate their children." As Yolton observes, "It would seem a gross overstatement to argue that all of these concrete rules are derivable from a law of nature which is apprehended by the function of reason and sense." (Yolton, 1958: 23–4.)

unmediated perception of natural laws inscribed in its order, including those with which human nature is invested. Since our knowledge of other persons derives from sense perceptions, this knowledge, too, has the status of "ideas" or "nominal essences," so that what we know of the laws of nature is the result of the interpretation of an idea of humanity, and the discovery of laws within that idea.[65]

As a result, in the *Second Treatise*, Locke moves to a far more minimalist conception of the laws of human nature. Although these laws are undoubtedly familiar to most readers, it is worth taking a moment to review their contents to set the stage for a reconsideration of the relationship between political authority and language that is a necessary element of the Lockean social contract.

The first law is the law of equality, a proposition that is described as "evident in itself, and beyond all question."[66] The evident fact of equality, in turn, produces the natural law against harming others. " [B]eing furnished with like Faculties, sharing all in one Community of Nature, there cannot be supposed any such Subordination among us, that may Authorize us to destroy one another." (Locke [1689], 1988: 271.)

The next most important among Locke's laws of human nature, both in themselves and because of the role that they play in his later discussion, are those relating to property. In the natural state, property is initially entirely common. The natural right to property is entirely "inclusive," entitling all to make use of the commons for their benefit. Still within the law of nature, however, there is the

---

[65] In the context of a distinction between elements of divine and human natural law in Locke's argument, his skepticism takes on political significance in that it points away from Bodin's and Filmer's direct appeal to revealed truth in favor of something closer to Hobbes' introspection as the source for knowledge. It is also the case that epistemological skepticism militates in favor of an interpretation of Locke more in line with the rationalist than the nominalist/voluntarist tradition of divine natural law. Locke's argument that the laws of nature are discovered and interpreted by the application of reason to sense perceptions fits perfectly with his arguments elsewhere that human knowledge of the world – and, by extension, of humanity – consists in ideas expressed in language.

[66] It may be noteworthy that this "evident" truth requires no direct perception of real essences, but only of relations between ideas os such essences, a category of word Locke refers to as "particles." (Locke [1689], 1982: 471–73.)

possibility of creating property rights of "exclusion," in which an individual can claim ownership of property to himself and the authority to repel others by appropriating property out of common ownership.[67] This is accomplished by the addition of labor to property, which mixes a person's ownership in themselves with an external object to create private ownership.[68]

The familiar consequence of these two principles is that everyone is equally free to add his labor to some portion of the property and take it out of common ownership, thus making it his own. Crucially, this natural form of property ownership does not depend on the consent of any other persons. "He that is nourished by acorns he picked up under an oak, or the apples he has gathered from trees in the wood, has certainly appropriated them to himself.... And will any one say he has not right to those acorns or apples he thus appropriated, because he had not the consent of all mankind to make them his?" (Locke [1689], 1988: 288.) Instead, the limit to appropriation in the state of nature was the natural law against waste. To accumulate property that was not put to productive use "offended against the law of nature," and the same was true of someone who enclosed more land than he could productively work. (Locke [1689], 1988: 294–95.)

Locke did not have to appeal to an imaginary natural, presocial state to illustrate the idea of common property, as it was immediately evident to his readers in an observation of the conduct of fishermen on the ocean.

This original law of nature for the *beginning of property*, in what was before common, still takes place: and by virtue thereof, what fish any one catches in the ocean, that great and still remaining common of mankind; or what ambergris any one takes up here, is by the labor that removes it out of that common state nature left it in, made his property who takes that pains about

---

[67] "God, who hath given the world to men in common, hath also given them reason to make use of it ... as no body has originally a private dominion, exclusive of the rest of mankind, in any of them, as they are thus in their natural state: yet being given for the use of men, there must of necessity be a means to appropriate them some way or other before they can be of any use." (Locke [1689], 1988: 286.)

[68] "The labor of his body, and the work of his hands, we may say, are properly his. Whatsoever then he removes out of the state that nature hath provided, and left it in, he hath mixed his labor with, and joined to it something that is his own, and thereby makes it his property." (Locke [1689], 1988: 287–88.)

it. And even amongst us the hare that any one is hunting, is thought his who pursues here during the chase. For being a beast that is still looked up as common, and no man's private possession; whoever has employed so much labor about any of that kind, as to find and pursue her, has thereby removed her from the state of nature, wherein she was common, and hath *begun a property*. (Locke [1689], 1988: 289–90, emphasis in original.)

Locke's evocative phrases, "beginning of property" and "begun a property," point to the fact that with the transition between stages of political development, the meaning of "property" changes. Natural property is different from property as it exists in society, which in turn is different from property as it exists in an established commonwealth. Natural property is defined solely by the laws of nature, which are known by the application of discursive reason to the sense perceptions that give evidence for the existence of a divine plan in the construction of human nature. This is "property" as it appears in the commons of the ocean, and which was omnipresent in the state of nature.

With the formation of society – the second stage of political development – people begin to make rules governing their conduct. Initially, the rule governing property remains the same, that it is the addition of labor to common property that creates ownership. But this rule is now grounded in the covenential moment of societal creation that left that property common in the first place. "We see in commons, which remain so by compact, that 'tis the taking any part of what is common, and removing it out of the state nature leave it in, which *begins the property*; without which the common is of no use. And the taking of this or that part, does not depend on the express consent of all the commoners .... Though the water running in the fountain be every ones, yet who can doubt, but that in the pitcher is his only who drew it out?" (Locke [1689], 1988: 288–89, emphasis in the original.)

Again, the emphasis is suggestive. A fountain, as compared with the ocean, is an artificial object, the product of collective labor for common usage, for the collective good. But that usage is limited; the restriction of access to a fountain (or a well) to members of the tribe that dug it may be the oldest form of property ownership in the world. This second moment of property is different from the first. Property at the stage of society remains subject to the laws of nature, but only insofar as those laws have not been modified by an act of collective consent (the property "in commons ... remains so by compact"). The "compact" to which Locke refers is not merely an artifact of discursive reason, it is an act of actual discourse. Nonetheless, it remains the case at this second moment of development that property is merely "begun"; it is not yet completely defined.

Importantly, at the stage of society, when humans have left the state of nature but not yet formed a commonwealth, the agreement on rules already extends to language in the form of the creation of the complex concepts, which, as Locke explained in *Human Understanding*, are maintained by social custom. The creation of these complex concepts, in turn, is what opens the possibility for the replacement of the laws of nature by conventions. For example, both the possibility and the necessity for the creation of conventional forms of property result from the prior creation of "money," a critical act of linguistic meaning-generation. With the invention of money, "and the tacit agreement of men to put a value on it," it ceases to be the case that the accumulation of more property than a person could use results in spoilage. (Locke [1689], 1988: 293.) As a result, it becomes useful to own more property, including land, than a person can use. The tacit agreement to treat money as valuable displaces the natural law against excess accumulation, and even undoes the fundamental assumption of equality, with the ultimate result that the peace of the state of nature is broken and the laws of nature cease to apply.[69] "[S]ince Gold and Silver ... has its value only from the consent of men, whereof labor yet makes, in great part, the measure, it is plain, that men have agreed to disproportionate and unequal possession of the earth, they having by a tacit and voluntary consent found out a way, how a man may fairly possess more land than he himself can use the product of." (Locke [1689], 1988: 301–02.) In this form, property, which "began" with a

---

[69] Zuckert locates this development within the state of nature. "[C]ontrary to the initial claim, it turns out that human beings may lawfully harm each other, and in the state of nature they will do so to such an extent that Locke's state of nature, just like Hobbes's, is a state of war." (Zuckert, 2002: 192.) By contrast, I find that the discussion of complex concepts such as "money," the redefinition of "property," and the replacement of natural laws of harmony with unlimited competition clearly identifies "society" as a separate, intermediate stage of political development.

natural right, is defined in conventional terms, resulting in a near-
total displacement of the laws of nature. (Zuckert, 2002: 192.)

The convention establishing the value of money is one of only
three specific examples of tacit consent that Locke identifies (along
with accepting the authority of fathers in the state of nature and
choosing to reside in a foreign country) and the only one relevant to
indicating the shift from the state of nature to the state of political
society. As Ruth Grant notes, in all three cases "there must be some
voluntary individual action, that is, one that is not coerced, but it
need not be a spoken or written declaration, and its implications
need not be fully self-conscious." The result of this tacit consent is
the creation of society, a form of political organization that is not yet
a commonwealth, but rather implies only "government in the broad
sense." (Grant, 1987: 125, 109.)

The first, tacit moment of consent that results in the creation of
society is the acceptance of linguistic terms that describe socially
accepted juridical practices. It is important to note that this is
something more than the simple agreement to speak a certain
language and to accept the meanings of ordinary words. In one
sense, after all, the creation of names for simple ideas equally
requires tacit consent to become the basis for a working language.
But there is a critical difference between the two cases. In the case of
simple names, the only "consent" that is required is to the assignment of a particular sound to a particular object. Even in the case of
mixed modes, the only point of "consent" that is required is in the
assignment of names and the grouping of nominal essences to be
captured, taxonomically, by the use of those names. In the case of
purely conventional complex ideas, by contrast, consent is required
for the objects of reference to come into existence *at all*. This is why
the agreement to treat "money" as valuable is not merely a different
treatment of natural property; it entails the construction of a new
concept of "property," which names a set of socially accepted conventions, just as naming a species creates the idea of "species" out of
whole cloth. There is no claim of any reference to a natural object at
all, with the result that the principles governing the use of both old
and new forms of property are entirely reconceived. Locke's tacit
consent to language presages the acceptance of juridical authority
over language.

Society, the intermediate stage between nature and common-wealth, is the point at which the connections between linguistic, legal, and political developments that create the possibility of a legitimate commonwealth come into being. The conventional rules that govern society are not yet true laws, however, as there is no human authority capable of creating binding laws – that is, there is no sovereign. Instead, these rules are merely manifestations of unanimous tacit consent. In juridical terms, this is the stage of customary law, while in terms of linguistic usage this is the stage of informal social conventions.[70]

Similarly, the creation of juridical concepts at the stage of society is not yet the stage of pure linguistic convention. After all, although the "property" that is named in "money" has no natural existence, the social practice that is named exists prior to and independent of its naming, just as the creatures that are grouped together in a species have a real and independent existence prior to their naming. Society thus represents an intermediate stage of both linguistic and political development. The names of complex concepts group observed social practices into categories, thus representing mixed modes, while the laws that develop at this stage of political development are similarly drawn from observations of social practice, as in the cases of the fountain, the acorns, and the ocean. The tacit consent to language is the linguistic equivalent to a political consent to be ruled by consent, the move that makes the later moment of constitutional consent possible.

The third stage of linguistic and political development is reached with the creation of a system of civil law by which the commonwealth exercises sovereignty over the meaning of purely conventional juridical concepts. The complex juridical concepts that are generated by acts of lawmaking do not describe existing social practices; they define and prescribe juridical practices through the creation of a separate, juridical form of language coexisting with ordinary spoken language. It is important to recognize that the authority of the commonwealth is to generate juridical language in addition to

[70] In Grant's description, the crucial characteristic of society is that it is "the juridical unit with the right to constitute a government by delegating its political power to be exercised by the society's trustees for the preservation of the society." (Grant, 1987: 107.)

ordinary language, not to reinvent social patterns of speech. This observation gives rise to a whole range of questions that Locke does not himself explore, such as the relationship over time between the meaning of property as that critical term is defined in positive law and the meaning that the same term has in ordinary social discourse. But even without examining those kinds of issues, the "determining" of property in positive law following the move from society to commonwealth illuminates the relationship between those two stages of political development.

With the creation of the commonwealth, property becomes an entirely conventional complex idea, subject to redefinition as both an inclusionary and an exclusionary right by the act of a sovereign lawmaker. It is only at this stage, as a purely conventional complex idea, that property takes on a determinate meaning. "[T]hose who are counted the civilized part of mankind ... have made and multiplied positive laws to determine property." (Locke [1689], 1988: 289.) Even property that remains in common in a commonwealth is not the same as common property at either of the earlier stages. After the formation of a commonwealth, property in common takes on an exclusive as well as an inclusive character, as property remains common (until it is appropriated), only as to members of the commonwealth. "And though it be common, in respect of some men, it is not so to all mankind; but is the joint property of this country, or this parish." (Locke [1689], 1988: 292.) That is, an exclusionary right of ownership is established against outsiders, while members of the commonwealth remain in possession of their natural inclusionary rights. Thereafter, all common property is subject to appropriation on whatever terms the commonwealth devises by its civil laws, just as all previously appropriated property may be defeased in the same way.

With the promulgation of positive laws, the original natural meaning of property disappears entirely into the genealogical background of political language, replaced by a juridically constructed concept grounded solely in the sovereign authority of the commonwealth. James Tully goes so far as to argue that the creation of the commonwealth extinguishes all natural rights to property, reopening a kind of new state of nature, a second moment of possibility for appropriation from a state of communal ownership, this time by convention. (Tully, 1980: 164–65.) One need not accept Tully's argument for a complete division between the pre- and post-conventional state. It is not only possible, but arguably necessary for social stability, that the commonwealth receive complex concepts into its political definitions. Those concepts may then be either reaffirmed or redefined in the their instantiation in the civil laws. Furthermore, appeals to natural law retain normative force as claims that civil laws may be called upon to satisfy. But these points of continuity, while plausible, are not analytically necessary. Locke clearly speaks of two distinct forms of property – one before and one after the creation of the commonwealth – and the possibility of the creation of a conventional form of property is an illustration of the generative power of juridical language regardless of the extent to which that power is exercised in a particular case.

The point is made clear in Locke's description of enclosure and its aftermath. Following enclosure, "laws within themselves," not laws grounded in either divine or human nature, "settle" the bounds of property in the forms of deeds, bills of sale, testaments, and recording statutes. (Locke [1689], 1988: 295; see also Dunn, 1967: 163–64.) The law's act of "saying" is not merely a matter of assigning a name; it is the creation of a purely conventional complex concept. In the commonwealth, the law does not merely name "property," it defines its nominal essence by creating its archetype. Conventional property, then, is not the same thing as property in the state of nature or society at all; it is an entirely new entity, grounded in a different kind of archetype, brought into existence by the linguistic act of generation. For Locke, law is definitional in relation to property just as for Hobbes, law was definitional in relation to justice.

This observation resolves an obvious difficulty in one of the best-known propositions in Locke, the proposition that government is created to protect "property." In paragraph 123 of the *Second Treatise*, Locke famously explains that persons in the state of nature give up their natural freedom in order to gain security over their property. (Locke [1689], 1988: 350.) But "property" means more than goods; the term is repeatedly defined as "life, liberty, and estate," and in paragraph 138, "property" is identified as something created by an existing juridical system, "such a right to the goods which by the laws of the community are theirs." (Locke [1689],

1988: 350, 360.) That is, Locke is not saying that we agree to have laws to protect our property; he is saying that "our property" is defined as that which the law protects.[71]

Property at the stage of society is insecure because it is not subject to definition by law. A complex concept such as money exists as a form of property only by tacit consent to treat it so, a consent that can be withdrawn at any moment. Making property secure is accomplished by surrendering authority over its definition in practice to the authority of the lawmaker. As a result, it is the complex idea of "property" that is made secure, not a particular set of objects. Furthermore since only complex, purely conventional concepts have certain definitions, it is only when "property" is defined by law that we can have certain knowledge of its contents, and hence be secure in our understanding.

The commonwealth arrives with a conceptual apparatus for the description of legal and political rights in the form of prior linguistic conventions, but is not itself bound by those conventions. The creation of money and its effect on the meaning of property is an exemplar case, although far from the only one – family relations come to mind as another – of the creation of juridical categories by custom, which categories are subject to redefinition by positive acts of lawmaking following the creation of the commonwealth. As noted earlier, there is nothing that requires the commonwealth to use its lawmaking powers to confirm the conventional understandings that were developed through custom in prepolitical society. It is conceivable, to be sure, that the tacit agreement to define "money" and the subsequent redefinition of property, will be ratified by the sovereign's positive laws, which establish a specific form and value of coinage.[72] But it is equally the case that sovereignty's exercise may displace the definitions of the earlier period. The law of inheritance, after all, displaces the notion that private ownership derives from labor (Riley, 1974: 451),

---

[71] As Joshua Cohen points out, the fact that money and inequality of wealth precedes the state precludes any appeal to a veil of ignorance. The state of nature had been characterized by equality, freedom from political obligations, and rational pursuit of self-interest. In the creation of the commonwealth, Cohen argues, freedom and equality supply the form of the agreement while rationality, in the "civil interests" of the parties, defines its content. (Cohen, 1986: 314–18.)

[72] The specific value of coinage was a different matter, a point demonstrated as early as 1576 by Bodin in his "Reply to the Paradoxes of Malestroit."

the laws regulating coinage displace social customs concerning money, and laws of title and deed replace customary rules of land ownership with positive systems of formal laws. The creation of the legislature is the commonwealth's assertion of sovereignty over juridical language, the exclusive authority over the creation of juridical complex ideas through the enactment of positive laws.

Locke's legislature does not have the absolute authority of Hobbes' Leviathan. Instead, to a far greater degree than Bodin's sovereign, Locke's legislature is bound by the limitations inherent in the nature of its power. At the same time that the creation of the commonwealth generates a sovereign with authority over language, it also determines the mode in which that authority may be exercised. Consent to the creation of the commonwealth makes law the vocabulary in which the generation of complex juridical concepts must be phrased. This observation, finally, takes us to the point in Locke's political account at which modern liberal constitutionalism begins to appear.

LOCKEAN CONSTITUTIONALISM AND THE THEORY OF CONSTITUTIONAL LANGUAGE

To summarize, Locke describes a progression between stages of development in language, law, and political authority. In the state of nature, divine natural law is known by sense perception and expressed in the categories of simple ideas, and human political authority does not yet exist. "Property" at this stage names the natural phenomenon of appropriation by the addition of labor, actions that trigger natural rights that others are bound to respect. At the stage of society, complex concepts are created and accepted, by tacit consent, as the basis for customary laws. "Property," including its artificial forms exemplified by "money," now becomes the name for a set of social practices grounded in laws of human nature that displace the natural law against waste in favor of the tendency to gather wealth. And in the third stage, a new, human-generated sovereign is constituted in the commonwealth, which carries the authority to create or redefine complex concepts by the generation of purely conventional civil laws and thus create a distinct juridical language that defines legal rights. The formation of the commonwealth is less "a search for a person to obey" (Riley, 1974: 452) than a search for a person to *define* the language of political and legal discourse.

What, then, are the limitations on the authority of the common- wealth over language? Consider the importance of Locke's lingering reliance on an anthropomorphic metaphor. Despite his differences with Hobbes and Bodin, Locke's commonwealth remains not only greater than, but also different in kind from, the sum of its parts. In Bodin's argument, this was logically necessary to explain the possi- bility of sovereignty over others, but Locke's appeal to consent points toward a different understanding of sovereignty that does not depend on finding a source to replace the natural authority of fathers. Similarly, where Hobbes posited the creation of sovereignty external to the collective "people" who created it, for Locke sovereignty remains internal. Locke's sovereignty is a principle of self-rule grounded in consent, which accounts for the familiar principle that violation of the terms of consent deprives the commonwealth of the authority to command obedience from its members.

Nonetheless the anthropomorphic metaphor continues to play a role in Locke's theory. For one thing, in dealing with the outside world, the commonwealth is an single collective entity inhabiting an international state of nature. ""For though in a commonwealth the members of it are distinct persons still in reference to one another, and as such are governed by the laws of the society: yet in reference to the rest of mankind, they make one body, which is ... still in the state of nature with the rest of mankind." (Locke [1689], 1988: 365.)

Moreover, even within the commonwealth, the metaphor of a col- lectively constructed "person" persists in Locke's description of the legislature as the "soul" of the commonwealth. The choice of meta- phor is deeply informative. In *Human Understanding*, Locke had described the "soul" of a person is that which has the capacity for thought, "thinking is the action, and not the essence of the soul." (*Human Understanding*, 1982: 228.) In the *Second Treatise* [1689], 1988, he describes the legislature as that thinking soul. "['T]is in their leg- islative, that the members of a commonwealth are united, and com- bined together into one coherent living body. This is the soul that gives form, life, and unity to the commonwealth." (Locke [1689], 1988: 407).

The earlier established conventions of language are not binding on the commonwealth. A new, artificial entity has been created, with the authority of Adam that Locke described in *Human Under-standing*, "to make any complex ideas of mixed modes, by no other pattern, but by his own thoughts." (Locke [1689], 1982: 470.) But "thoughts" is a critical term, here. The capacity of the common-wealth to perceive and name objects and complex ideas – its "dis-cursive reason" – lies in its lawmaking authority, since it is by laws that concepts such as "property," "household," and "citizen" can be redefined. This is the point at which grant of exclusive authority carries its own inherent limitations. Locke's commonwealth has the authority to redefine "property" by the generation of meaning through lawmaking, but that act of redefinition could *only* take place through such a generative lawmaking act. To attempt to assert control over property without an appropriate act of redefinition would violate the terms of the creation of the commonwealth, and thus vitiate consent. A simple example that was mentioned earlier will serve to illustrate the point. In a commonwealth, the sovereign lawmaking entity undoubtedly has the authority to redefine the rules of inheritance, or even abolish inheritance altogether. But the same sovereign cannot, legitimately, declare that "the rules of inheritance will hereafter be ignored"; the *form* of the sovereign's meaning-generative statements must be that of law, a requirement imposed as a condition of the constitutional consent that created the sovereign in the first instance.

The requirement that the sovereign act by lawmaking is the point of connection to the lurking limitations on the authority of even Hobbes' absolute sovereign. In Hobbes' scheme, so long as indivi-dual parties to the social contract retained the ability to exercise their reason and determine that a pronouncement of the sovereign was "absurd," there remained the possibility of challenging the legitimacy of the sovereign's exercise of authority, at least as to those persons. Even in Hobbes' system, the creation of sovereignty by an act of language meant that the constraints inherent in relying on language – that is, on claims of justification amenable to reason – established an outer limit to the sovereign's authority. Locke's commonwealth is bound by the same premise, but much more strictly. Since the commonwealth speaks through legislation, its acts must satisfy the propositional requirements of that language even as it exercises authority over the creation of its terms.

The conclusion that the legislature's exercise of sovereignty over juridical language is bound by limitations inherent in that language is the first appearance of an idea that I will call "constitutional grammar." This is the idea that the rules governing the formulation of valid propositions in a juridical language impose constraints on state action even in the absence of any reference to the specific contents of that language. Locke's commonwealth is governed by an internal dialogue between citizens and state, which requires mutually comprehensible language. When a resolution is reached, the commonwealth will employ that language to speak in its collective voice through the legislature.

The reading of Locke presented here points toward an idea specific to modern constitutionalism: that consent to the creation of a juridical language is what calls a sovereign "people" into being in the first place. A people, after all, is a complex concept created by a consensual act of conventional naming. Since the archetype of this complex concept is identical to its description, the fact that a people is capable of exercising self-sovereignty is definitional, rather than descriptive, in just the same fashion that the legislature exercises authority over "property." Modern constitutionalism appears in Locke as the political consequence of the epistemological theory of language construction. Without consent to the meaning of complex terms, there is no language in terms of which political organization can be accomplished. Without consent to the project of political organization, there is no "people" to engage in self-government. And without consent to the operations of government, the commonwealth ceases to act as the artificial person embodying the collective will, reason, and voice of the people. A group of persons constitutes itself as a self-sovereign People by an act of political will exercised over the field of discourse. Authority over all other forms of social interaction follow in the wake of this initial, constitutive moment of consent.

This reading of Locke helps clarify a troubling element of ambiguity about the creation of the commonwealth and its consequences. At the moment at which the commonwealth is formed, the applicability of all earlier laws is in doubt, but it is not yet the case that positive laws have been created to replace them. There is thus a moment in which the customary law of society appears to have been suspended by virtue of the creation of a sovereign possessed of lawmaking authority. During that moment, what is the law, and by what authority does it bind the citizenry? Imagine a moment at which a commonwealth has been formed, a government established, but no laws yet enacted, or perhaps an executive has been created but no legislature yet assembled.[73] At that moment, it would seem to be the case that all property has reverted to a common state among the members of the commonwealth, all rights and obligations are subject to redefinition, and all rules and principles governing matters of social convention are suspended, awaiting resolution.

Such a moment of suspension is intolerable. It presents Locke with the same yawning chasm of nihilism that has always been a lurking presence at the margins of his epistemological, moral, and now juridical skepticism. Some mechanism must exist to rescue the members of Locke's commonwealth from epistemological chaos. In the first two instances, what rescued his readers from vertigo was the assurance of divine design. In the political case, that comforting assurance is provided by consent. Not the consent to the creation of the commonwealth, but an implied and entirely necessary prior consent to the creation of juridical language. At every stage, institutions require a suitable language in which the consent to their creation can be expressed. In other words, moments of political consent are necessarily preceded by moments of linguistic consent, consent to the generation of complex juridical concepts. What does consent of this kind look like?

At the stage of society, consent to the creation of conventional language is tacit, which means that it must be genuinely unanimous. Disagreement on the meaning of complex concepts implies a different discursive frame; persons who disagree on the meaning of

[73] Something like this moment appears at the end of the *Eumenides*, the last play in Aeschylus' *Oresteia* trilogy that describes the end of the sovereignty of the gods. Athena, having been called upon to judge between the Furies and Apollo's claims of authority to determine Orestes' fate, declares that henceforth neither gods nor Furies will judge the people of Athens. 'I will pick the finest men of Athens, return and decide the issue fairly, truly – bound to our oaths, our spirits bent on justice." And this is to be the new form of the law for Athens. "Now and forever more, for Aegeus' people this will be the court where judges reign." (Aeschylus, 1977: 253, 262.) But at the end of the play-cycle, the finest men of Athens have yet to issue a judgment or decree: even Orestes' trial ended in a draw. What, at that moment, is the state of the law?

"good" cannot achieve consent, since they differ on the basic purpose for their efforts, while persons who disagree on the meaning of "money" are mutually incomprehensible.[74] Therefore it must be assumed that all the citizens of the newly created commonwealth already agree on conventional understandings of juridical concepts that were generated in society. Consequently, it must be assumed that until that redefinition occurs, the consent to conventional language that marked the stage of society remains in force. From the very moment of the first act of legislation, then, there are not one but two systems of juridical language, one established by custom and accepted in social life, and a second, developing language crafted in the enactment of positive laws, which supercedes the other by the authority established in the legislature's status as the organ capable of expressing the collective mind of the commonwealth.

Locke's account of the development of language, law, and government provide the basis for liberal constitutionalism, but that is not to say that his theories can be simply applied wholesale in the modern context. At the stage of the creation of civil laws, Locke relies on the retention of moral and religious elements to a degree that appears incongruous in a discussion of modern liberal constitutionalism.[75] Moreover, for reasons that I will discuss in the next chapter, I believe that we are poorly served by continuing to rely on an anthropomorphic metaphor for the state, even in the limited form in which that metaphor appears in the *Second Treatise*. Nonetheless, Locke's fundamental insight that the capacity of juridical language to generate meaning creates the conditions of possibility for self-sovereignty is the crucial move that makes liberal constitutionalism a meaningful possibility, and provides the starting point for the rest of the discussion in this book.

---

[74] Such a disagreement comes close to implying inconsistent understandings of the meaning of interest, which casts doubt on the mutual rationality of the speakers. See Cohen, 1986: 314. For a discussion of Locke's arguments concerning the "natural" value of coinage and the impossibility of currency manipulation by governments, see Appleby, 1976.

[75] Jeremy Waldron goes so far as to conclude that Lockean liberalism requires a shared commitment to Judeo-Christian theology as the only possible basis for the necessary initial assumption that all individuals are fundamentally equal in some meaningful sense. (Waldron, 2002.) Waldron, himself, describes this as a commitment only to theism generally, but it is noteworthy that not all theistic traditions lend themselves to the assumption of equality of human individuals.

2

Consent How?

Challenges to Lockean Constitutionalism

Chapter 1 explored some of the history of modern ideas of sovereignty, consent, and political authority over the generation of juridical language in order to get to the Lockean model of constitutionalism. That model, of which Locke's own argument is only one possible version, relies on a series of moments of consent, beginning with the adoption of a shared juridical language and followed by the creation of authority over its subsequent development. As noted in that chapter, the focus on stages of consent requires a focus on the question of the conditions of consent; how, and under what circumstances, is it possible to posit the occurrence of the kind of consent that is required to move from one stage in the Lockean progression of development to another? The last of these moments is what I will refer to as "constitutional consent," the moment of creation of a constitutional regime legitimated by an appeal to democratic principles of popular self-sovereignty. The question that motivates this chapter and the next one, "Consent How?" asks what elements of Lockean constitutionalism need to be revised or expanded in order to explain the possibility of a regime legitimated by a moment of constitutional consent.

To get to an answer to the question "Consent How?" we must recognize that the account of constitutional development that appears in Locke's writings leaves many unanswered questions. For one thing, after the creation of the commonwealth and the generation of new meanings for complex juridical concepts, what is the relationship between this new language and the older, preexisting modes of discourse? In Locke's account, the two seemed to coexist, but is that a plausible outcome? Or is it the case that over time, the language of political authority must either displace older forms or itself become unstable? Locke's description of "money" is a perfect example. Today, the state asserts the authority to define that term, as in the legend "legal tender for all debts public and private" that adorns American currency. Nothing prevents private parties from accepting other forms of payment, but if a time were to come when they refused to accept state-issued currency, the authority of the state to define "money" would be thrown into question. In the event that private parties come to accept only barter, refusing all forms of artificial currency as tender for transactions, the concept of "money" itself would be thrown into doubt. This dissolution of authority over language is the sign of the dissolution of political authority writ large, but even without the threat of such dissolution, the interaction between juridical and ordinary language requires consideration.

Moving away from the question of the relationship between juridical and other forms of linguistic practice, how can we retrospectively describe the adoption of constitutional language, and the subsequent exercise of authority over that language, in a way that justifies a continuing obligation on the part of subsequent generations of citizens? This is the question of "Consent How?" that is the focus of this chapter and the next one. If consent is the precondition for constitutionalism, what are the conditions of possibility for that consent, and what makes it binding?

Locke himself did not tell us very much in answer to this question. One reason may be that he wrote from a perspective that took for granted the existence of an unbroken line of historical development reaching into the distant past. Locke was writing within the English tradition of common law authority, of which political as well as legal dimensions were captured in the motto *"salus populi suprema lex est"* ("the good of the people is the supreme law"), the dictum that had legitimated the exercise of regulatory authority by local government since long before the modern era. (Novak, 1996.) As a result, in common law practice, the legitimation of the system of laws and the legitimation of lawmaking authority – the moments of legal and constitutional consent – were essentially one and the same. Juridical institutions did not have a specific moment of origination prior to the promulgation of the system of laws; they were present as natural objects, elements of the landscape in which new institutions were being constructed.

The assumption that the system of laws and legal institutions predates the political order is obviously problematic if the goal is to devise a coherent account of the legitimacy of a constitutional regime. Nonetheless, to a considerable extent, constitutional theorists after Locke continued to rely on the assumption of a shared historical understanding expressed as unanimously accepted institutional norms. A brief consideration of two writers in the tradition of Lockean constitutionalism, James Wilson and A. B. Dicey, does a great deal to sharpen our focus on the points in Lockean constitutional theory that require further development if the project of describing the conditions of possibility for a legitimate constitutional regime in the modern world is to make sense. For both Wilson and Dicey, the question "Consent How?" will turn out to be centrally focused on the relationship between the legitimacy of the constitutional and legal orders, a relationship that has strong parallels with the realtionship between customary and positive legal definitions in Locke's own argument.

LOCKEAN CONSTITUTIONALISM: JAMES WILSON AND A. B. DICEY

The direct connection between constitutional and legal legitimation was a critical element in the reasoning of the leading legal theorist among the American Federalists, James Wilson.[1] Bodin and Hobbes

---

[1] No American legal writer of the generation that adopted the Constitution was more important than Wilson. Among his many other contributions, Wilson authored the Pennsylvania Constitution of 1790, was one of six men who signed both the Declaration of Independence and the Constitution of the United States, and was instrumental in securing ratification of the Constitution in Pennsylvania. Although Madison was undoubtedly the Federalists' leading political scientist, Hamilton the leading economist, and Jefferson the leading political philosopher, it was Wilson who more than anyone else devoted himself to developing a theory of constitutional legitimacy grounded in the combination of Lockean liberalism and the prevailing understanding of law. (McCloskey, 1967: 1–5; Stoner, 2003: 37.) Wilson's major work was the series of lectures on the American Constitution that he delivered at the College of Philadelphia in the winters of 1790–92 and 1791–92, a series that began

had moved the question of legitimation away from conformity with an externally established standard of right lawmaking to one of the authority of sovereign lawmakers. Locke, in turn, had transformed the idea of sovereignty from authority over others to a notion of autonomous self-rule, and called attention to the characteristics of a society that could produce a commonwealth through consent. Wilson, continuing that path of intellectual development, situated sovereignty itself at a preconstitutional moment, making sovereignty a characteristic of a society rather than of the political regime that it creates. Writing in the early 1790s, during the debates over the ratification of the American Constitution, Wilson also introduced an explicitly constitutional dimension to the idea of legitimate state formation, with specific reference to a written document, thus taking Lockean constitutionalism far beyond its source and into the modern era.

Wilson took it to be a matter of definition that sovereignty meant autonomy, rather than rule over others, and hence that government could be legitimated only by consent. "The dread and redoubtable sovereign, when traced to his ultimate and genuine source, has been found, as he ought to have been found, in the free and independent man." (Wilson, 1967: 81.)[2] This result led Wilson directly to the principle of justified revolt. "[There is] one great principle, the vital principle I may well call it ... which diffuses animation and vigour through all others. The principle I mean is this, that the supreme or

---

while the debates of ratification were in full swing. Thereafter, as a justice of the United States Supreme Court, Wilson articulated a conception of the role of the Constitution in American politics and, by extension, of the judiciary that was entirely consistent with the theoretical understanding that was expressed in his lectures. Wilson is probably best known today for his opinion in *Chisholm v. Georgia*, 2 U.S. 419 (1973); his statement of his argument in that case, in fact, is a remarkably succinct summary of his entire theory.

[2] This proposition, along with many others drawn from Locke (usually without attribution), had earlier been central to the writings of John Trenchard and Thomas Gordon in the 1720s, whose *Cato's Letters* were among the first statements of modern constitutional principles. "There is no government now upon earth, which owes its formation or beginning to the immediate revelation of God, or can derive its existence from such revelation.... Government therefore can have no power, but such as men can give, and such as they actually did give, or permit for their own sakes; Nor can any government be in fact framed but by consent, if not of every subject, yet of as many as can compel the rest." No. 60; Letter of Saturday, January 6, 1721. (Trenchard, 1995: 413.)

sovereign power of the society resides in the citizens at large; and that, therefore, they always retain the right of abolishing, altering, or amending their constitution, at whatever time, and in whatever manner, they shall deem expedient." (Wilson, 1967: 77, 79).

The revolution principle implied that sovereignty remained with the people after the creation of a constitutional order. "[T]he truth is, that sovereignty, dominion and power are the parents, not the offspring of government." (Wilson, 1967: 169, 171) The idea of a sovereign people broke the essential connection between sovereignty and the power of legislation. Since sovereignty inhered in the society from which the government emerged, rather than in the government, it was the autonomy of the society that defined collective self-sovereignty, a relationship that collapsed the distinction between society and state. "Every civil society, under whatever form it appears, whether governed merely by the natural laws of such a society, or by them and civil institutions superadded – every such society, not subordinate to another, is a sovereign state." (Wilson, 1967: 270.) The creation of political institutions, especially legislatures, was an act carried out by a sovereign, politically organized society, rather than the genesis of sovereign authority. The sovereignty of the society, in turn, derived from initial conditions of individual self-sovereignty, natural equality, and consent.[3]

Wilson's argument thus establishes a new version of the Lockean progression. The state of nature is peopled with sovereign and equal individuals who entered into not one, but a series of covenants.[4] They form society by a political covenant; in a subsequent covenant, the society forms a constitution, and thence a government. At the beginning of the entire process stand the familiar dictates of Lockean human natural law – derived from the facts of human nature without specific reference to other sources – which also explain the necessity of

---

[3] "Those who unite in society, lived, before their union, in a state of nature; a state of nature is a state of equality and liberty. That liberty and that equality, belonging to the individuals, before the union, belong, after the union, to the society, which those individuals compose.... Every state, therefore, composed of individuals, free and equal, is a state sovereign and independent. The aggregate body possesses all the rights of the individuals, of who it is formed." (Wilson, 1967: 270.)

[4] Wilson cites Puffendorf, among others, for earlier versions of this multiple covenant idea.

lawmaking.[5] "To be without law is not agreeable to our nature; because, if we were without law, we should find many of our talents and powers hanging upon us like useless incumbrances. Why should we be illuminated by reason, were we only made to obey the impulse of irrational instinct?" (Wilson, 1967: 124, 130) This originary law of the rule of law is a parallel to Locke's consent to rule by consent. Such an idea speaks to the problem of identifying an original grounding norm, a problem for which Wilson's (somewhat circular) solution is finally an appeal to human natural law in the form of the experienced facts of human psychology. "If I am asked a third time – how do you know that you ought to do that, of which your conscience enjoins the performance? I can only say, I feel that such is my duty. Here investigation must stop; reasoning can go no farther. The science of morals, as well as other sciences, is founded on truths, that cannot be discovered or proved by reasoning." (Wilson, 1967: 133.)[6]

Human natural law, for Wilson, translates into legitimating political principles by way of the anthropomorphic metaphor of the state, an analytical process exemplified in his explanation of the right of a state to defend itself. "Let us recur to what the law of nature dictates to an individual. Are there not duties which he owes to himself? Is he not obliged to consult and promote his preservation, his freedom, his reputation .... From the duties of states, as well as of individuals, to themselves, a number of corresponding rights will be found to arise." The metaphor is a limited one, however, constrained by the primacy of society over the state, and by

[5] Wilson's vocabulary is confusing here, as he occasionally refers to both divine and Aristotelean natural law. In the end, however, Wilson's focus is on the set of laws that are necessary consequents of specifically human nature. "As promulgated by reason and the moral sense, it has been called natural; as promulgated by the holy scriptures, it has been called revealed law. As addressed to men, it has been denominated the law of nature; as addressed to political societies, it has been denominated the law of nations .... Of that law, the following are maxims – that no injury should be done – that a lawful engagement, voluntarily made, should be faithfully fulfilled." (Wilson, 1967: 76, 124.)

[6] The alternative to reason, for Wilson, was an unexplained phenomenon of moral sentiments. "Reason may, indeed, instruct is in the pernicious or useful tendency of qualities and actions; but reason alone is not sufficient to produce any moral approbation or blame. It is requisite that *sentiment* should intervene, in order to give a preference to the useful above the pernicious tendencies." (Wilson, 1967: 141.)

the revolution principle. "By the voluntary act of the individuals forming the nation, the nation was called into existence: they who bind, can also untie." (Wilson, 1967: 154.)[7]

Like Locke, Wilson's epistemological understanding directly served his political commitments. Early in the discussion, he expressed a skeptical note of caution. "We are in danger of circumscribing nature within the bounds of our own notions." (Wilson, 1967: 99.) In the course of his argument, however, Wilson departed from this skeptical line of analysis, rejecting Locke's intermediate "ideas" in favor of a commitment to the reliability of direct experience of the external world. "Suffice it, at present, to observe, that the existence of the objects of our external senses, in the way and manner in which we perceive that existence, is a branch of intuitive knowledge, and a matter of absolute certainty; that the constitution of our nature determines us to believe in our senses; and that a contrary determination would finally lead to the total subversion of all human knowledge." (Wilson, 1967: 202)[8]

Wilson's assertion of the reliability of human perception has important political consequences for advancing beyond the versions of consent in Locke. Locke had grounded the legitimacy of consent as a means of producing governments on an underlying accord between the terms of consent and specified human natural laws such as self-preservation, or common law norms of *salus populi*. One implication of

---

[7] The anthropomorphic metaphor had greater and more direct force when applied to society directly. For Wilson, the person-society-state order of development indicated an heuristic function of law and, by extension, of juridical institutions generally. "Society ought to be preserved in peace; most unquestionably. But is this all? Ought it not to be improved as well as protected? Look at individuals: observe that from infancy to youth, from youth to manhood. Such is the order of Providence with regard to society. It is in a progressive state, moving on towards perfection." The mechanism of that progress was law. "To protect and to improve social life, is, as we have seen, the end of government and law" (Wilson, 1967: 84, 88.)

[8] Wilson cited Thomas Reid, the Scottish Common Sense philosopher, in support of the evident directness of perception. But the connection may be misleading. Reid and his fellows (notably Dugald Stewart) advanced their theory to counter the threat that skeptical empiricism seemed to pose for Calvinism, since if observations of the world were not reliable and universal, then the moral and religious lessons to be learned from those observations might be left similarly vulnerable. In Wilson's description quoted earlier, however, it is manifestly not the need for divine authority but the conditions of human nature – "the constitution of our nature" – that leads to the conclusion that perceptions, and judgments formed on the basis of those perceptions, are reliable.

that connection, in both instances, was that the grant or withdrawal of consent might be based on erroneous perceptions, and hence not a valid basis for action. Wilson's insistence on the reliability of human judgment may be understood as a move that makes the necessary first principle procedural rather than substantive. For Wilson, it appears, consent can be withdrawn without specific justification because it is the *fact* of rule by consent, rather than its consequences, that legitimates the system of governance. This, ultimately, was the significance of the Federalist focus on representation, that "liberty" was transformed from a description of the actions of government to a description of the source of government power. "In America," Gordon Wood observes, "a constitution had become ... a charter of power granted by liberty rather than, as in Europe, a charter of liberty granted by power." (Wood, 1969: 601.) The challenge for eighteenth-century constitutional theory was to work out what "consent" consisted of rather than to determine the laws that it ought to produce, an approach that points toward a distinctly modern proceduralist solution to the problem of legitimation.[9]

As noted earlier, Wilson's formulation focuses more clearly than Locke's on the question of the conditions of possible consent, rather than on the outcome of such an agreement. Fundamentally, constitutional consent for Wilson becomes possible when society has developed to a sufficient degree, which is demonstrated by the sophistication of the language of public discourse. Extending the anthropomorphic metaphor, Wilson proposed that the advancement of language in an intellectually maturing individual is

---

[9] Paul Kahn emphasizes the connections that Wilson draws between political organization and moral improvement in what he calls the "model of [constitution] making." "Wilson, then, draws the moral consequences from Publius's identification of psychological and political phenomena. Not only right theory and practical history constrain the act of political self-construction; anything less than self-government would represent a failure to make use of the opportunity for moral development that politics presents." (Kahn, 1995: 21.) For Kahn, this emphasis separates the "conceptual model" of the constitutional founding from later periods of constitutional maintenance, with the ultimate result that the project of constitutional legitimation over time fails because of the fundamental inconsistency between an appeal to consent in the model of a community of discourse and and an appeal to "the science of government" at the period of constitution making. (Kahn, 1995: 212–3, 218.) For a more traditional and more sympathetic recent reading of Wilson's theory of self-government as the basis for binding constitutional obligations, see Amar, 2005.

paralleled by the advancement of language in a politically maturing society. "The attention paid to language is one distinguishing mark of the progress of society toward its most refined period: as society improves, influence is acquired by the means of reasoning and discourse" (Wilson, 1967: 231.)

As for how consent can be made the basis for a commitment by a fully developed society, the answer, yet again, is an appeal to the anthropomorphic metaphor. "[I]f a man cannot bind himself, no human authority can bind him. ... If no human law can be made without a superiour; no human law can ever be made." The possibility of commitment is found in ordinary law, as in the case of a simple bond. "In that bond, there are these words written – *I bind myself*. This form of a bond has been known and used and approved in England since time immemorial." (Wilson, 1967: 189.)[10] The evidence of consent, finally, is the social fact of legal custom captured in the phrase "time immemorial," itself an explicit reference to English common law. "Now custom is, of itself, intrinsic evidence of consent. How was a custom introduced? By voluntary adoption. How did it become general? By the instances of voluntary adoption being increased." (Wilson, 1967: 122)

Taken together, the elements of Wilson's argument describe a developmental account that begins with naturally sociable persons forming a society that becomes the vessel of their collective self-sovereignty; that society develops over time in the direction of increasing virtue, demonstrated by the sophistication of its language; that language converts customary practices into consent-based law; the existence of that law, in turn, articulates the conditions of possibility for constitutionalism, the creation of legitimate government by consent of the people acting through their representatives. At each stage, the further progression in the articulation of self-sovereignty is accomplished by a refinement of language, and at each stage, the existence of a developed form of language is the necessary precondition for further progress. When persons' linguistic skills

[10] The phrase "time immemorial" was a reference to William Blackstone's explanation of the authority of English Common Law. "Whence it is that in our law the goodness of a custom depends upon it's having been used time out of mind; or, in the solemnity of the legal phrase, time whereof the memory of man runneth not to the contrary." (Blackstone, 1979, vol. 1: 67.)

have sufficiently developed, they become capable of thinking abstractly and entering into covenants; when the language of the society has developed sufficiently, the artificial person of the commonwealth is able to generate a state; when the state has learned to speak in juridical discourse, law legitimated by consent is possible; and where the law contains a way of expressing the principle of self-commitment, the formation of legitimate, binding governmental authority can occur. The adoption of a written constitution is one step in the continuing process of development that runs from persons, to society, to state, to law, to legitimate government, and, finally, to constitutional juridical text.

Wilson's argument was characteristically American. In his own view, Wilson and his Federalist colleagues were carrying the English experiment to the conclusion that the English themselves had failed to realize.[11] Above all, Wilson insisted that sovereignty remained with the people, a position that was necessary in order to provide a basis for the principle of justified revolution and that followed naturally from the description of sovereignty as the capacity for self-government rather than its exercise. In sharp contrast, even as late as 1908, the British constitutionalist A. B. Dicey proposed that the creation of a system of government constituted an *irrevocable* transfer of lawful sovereignty from the people to its political institutions.[12] The word "lawful" is critical; what Dicey was disputing was the idea that there could be any legal check on the lawmaking authority of

---

[11] It is only in America, finally, that the last step in the progression was to be seen. "I shall have the pleasure of presenting to my hearers," declared Wilson while the state conventions were in the midst of debating ratification, "what, as to the nations in the Transatlantick world, must be searched for in vain – an original compact of a society, on its first arrival in this section of the globe." (Wilson, 1967: 70.)

[12] Although the electors retain the authority to use their electoral powers to check the actions of a Parliament, it is apparent that they entirely lack the authority to revoke their acceptance of the existence of a legally sovereign Parliament in the first instance. Once a sovereign entity is created, its powers extend even to the reformulation of its constitution contrary to the original will of the people, a point illustrated in Dicey's discussion of the Treaty of Unity. "[T]he Parliaments both of England and of Scotland did, at the time of the Union, each transfer sovereign power to a new sovereign body, namely, the Parliament of Great Britain. This Parliament ... became in its turn a legally supreme or sovereign legislature, authorised therefore, though contrary perhaps to the intention of its creators, to modify or abrogate the Act of Union by which it was constituted." (Dicey, 1908: 66–7, n. 3.)

Parliament. The people retained "political" sovereignty, in the form of their ability to elect new members of Parliament, but in the classical British tradition of sovereignty, the idea that an act of government could be invalid by virtue of its contradiction of a source of law external to itself was unacceptable.

The distinction between legal and political sovereignty was central to Dicey's analysis. Legal sovereignty was the authority to make laws, which are rules enforceable by courts, hence legal sovereignty is the grounding norm of constitutional law as opposed to constitutional politics. Parliament's legal sovereignty bound the British courts to its laws. "A law may, for our present purpose, be defined as 'any rule which will be enforced by the Courts.' ... [so] Any Act of Parliament, or new part of an Act of Parliament, which makes a new law, or repeals or modifies an existing law, will be obeyed by the Courts." (Dicey, 1908: 38.) "Political sovereignty," in turn, referred to "conventions," expressed in terms of practical "maxims" that are understood by the relevant community of actors, whether that community comprises a set of institutional actors or the entire body of popular electors. "Some of these rules could not be violated without bringing to a stop the course of orderly and pacific government; others might be violated without any other consequence than that of exposing the minister or other person by whom they were broken to blame or unpopularity." (Dicey, 1908: 26, n. 1.)

Conventions are not laws, because courts will not enforce them. "The subject [of conventions] is not one of law but of politics" (Dicey, 1908: 30.) The special authority of courts thus appears as definitional: courts are the institutional guardians of legal discourse, identifying what does and does not quality as "law" by their identification of rules that they will or will not enforce. The substantive content of law, however, is solely the creation of sovereign authority, which resides exclusively in Parliament.[13] Dicey's courts do not

---

[13] Dicey emphatically denied the proposition that courts' common law authority over precedent gives them lawmaking powers, on the grounds that British courts cannot exercise judicial review over acts of legislation. "[T]he adhesion by our judges to precedent ... leads inevitably to the gradual formation by the Courts of fixed rules for decision, which are in effect laws. This judicial legislation might appear, at first sight, inconsistent with the supremacy of Parliament. But this is not so. English judges do not claim or exercise any power to repeal a Statute, whilst Acts of

share in legal sovereignty because they entirely lack lawmaking authority.[14] Neither moral standards nor royal prerogatives have any sway over the decisions of Parliament, hence there can be no judicial review over legislation. By the same token, there is no element of residual legal sovereignty that remains with the electors, and consequently there can be no basis for a challenge in law to the actions of the lawmakers. "The sole legal right of electors under the English constitution is to elect members of Parliament. Electors have no legal means of initiating, of sanctioning, or of repealing the legislation of Parliament. No Court will consider for a moment the argument that a law is invalid as being opposed to the opinion of the electorate" (Dicey, 1908: 57.)

This observation points to a crucial aspect to Parliamentary supremacy; one Parliament is not empowered to bind another by its actions, hence there is no possibility that legal sovereignty will supersede political sovereignty. In terms highly reminiscent of Bodin, Dicey explains this outcome as intrinsic to the meaning of legal sovereignty. "[A] sovereign power cannot, while retaining its sovereign character, restrict its own powers by any particular enactment. An Act, whatever its terms, passed by Parliament might be repealed in a subsequent, or indeed in the same, session, and there would be nothing to make the authority of the repealing Parliament less than the authority of the Parliament by which the statue, intended to be immutable, was enacted." (Dicey, 1908: 65–6.)

The result of the division between legal and political sovereignty, said Dicey, was to make Great Britain a more strictly democratic system than the United States. "As things now stand, the people of England can change any part of the law of the constitution with extreme rapidity. Theoretically, there is no check on the action of Parliament whatever . . . ." (Dicey, 1908: 71, n. 1.) Dicey argued that the British system was democratic because the-People-as-Parliament

---

Parliament may override and constantly do override the law of the judges." (Dicey, 1908: 58.)

[14] "The principle of Parliamentary sovereignty means neither more nor less than this, namely, that Parliament thus defined has, under the English constitution, the right to make or unmake any law whatever; and, further, that no person or body is recognized by the law of England as having a right to override or set aside the legislation of Parliament." (Dicey, 1908: 38.)

were not limited in their actions except, potentially, by actions of the-People-as-electors. Moreover, the power of elections was not the only limit on political sovereignty. Dicey identified two additional sets of limits – "external" and "internal" – paralleling the dualities of convention/law and political/legal sovereignty. External limits refer to the sociological facts of positivistic legitimacy. "The external limit to the real power of a sovereign consists in the possibility or certainty that his subjects, or a large number of them, will disobey or resist the laws" (Dicey, 1908: 74.) Internal limits, in turn, are imposed by the nature of the lawgiver, as an aspect of human psychology. "The internal limit to the exercise of sovereignty arises from the nature of the sovereign power itself. Even a despot exercises his powers in accordance with his character, which is itself moulded by the circumstances under which he lives, including under that head the moral feelings of the time and the society to which he belongs." (Dicey, 1908: 77.)

Dicey's discovery of the limits of sovereign power was not a deployment of the anthropomorphic metaphor applied to a state; it was an identification of specific actors as the bearers of sovereign authority in a system of representation. The anthropomorphic metaphor reappears, however, in the form of qualifications for the role of representative/sovereign. "[T]he essential property of representative government is to produce coincidence between the wishes of the sovereign and the wishes of the subjects; to make, in short, the two limitations on the exercise of sovereignty absolutely coincident." (Dicey, 1908: 81.)

The representatives, in other words, must share the "political ethics" of the electors, expressed in constitutional conventions. In this way, the acts of Parliament ultimately do rest on the consent of the self-sovereign people. "Our modern code of constitutional morality secures, though in a roundabout way, what is called abroad the 'sovereignty of the people.'" (Dicey, 1908: 425–26.) The result is that the political legitimation of a juridical act trumps its violation of legal sovereignty. George III acted "constitutionally" in dissolving Parliament in 1784 because "He believed that the nation did not approve of the policy pursued by the House of Commons. He was right in this belief. No modern constitutionalist will dispute that the authority of the House of Commons is derived from its representing the will of the nation, and that the chief object of a dissolution is to ascertain that the will of Parliament coincides with the will of the nation." (Dicey, 1908: 430.)

Dicey's division between legal and political sovereignty meant that his theory, no less than Wilson's, rested on the presumption of an underlying unity of agreement among the present, politically acting People. On the other hand, that consent remained irrevocable. Although the electors retain the authority to use their electoral powers to check the actions of a Parliament, it is apparent that they entirely lack the authority to revoke their acceptance of the existence of a legally sovereign Parliament in the first instance. There is no Wilsonian revolution principle at work here; once a sovereign governmental entity is created, its powers extend even to the reformulation of its constitution.[15] Unanimous consent was Dicey's description of British political practice, not a normative justification for its institutions, a fact that grounded the argument securely in historical examples at the cost of limiting the application of the theory to the British case. In the end, Dicey's account stands as a positivistic description of English practice, which by its terms precludes the possibility of normative justification.

In considering the problem of defining the conditions for legitimate constitutional rule today, we are confronted by both the continuing vitality of Lockean ideas of self-sovereignty and government by consent and, at the same time, by the evident inadequacy of

---

[15] Dicey's key illustration is the historical controversy over the Septennial Act. A 1694 Act had limited the duration of a given Parliament to three years. In 1716, the Septennial Act extended that term to seven years and, more important, extended the term of the then-current House of Commons accordingly, thus altering not only the terms of subsequent elections but also the consequences of the preceding one. In response, thirty-one members protested: "[I]t is agreed, that the House of Commons ... are truly the representatives of the people, which they cannot be so properly said to be, when continued for a longer time than that for which they were chosen." (Dicey, 1908: 44.) Dicey entirely accepts the challengers' characterization of the law, but turns it into a criticism of their understanding of the authority of "the people" with relation to Parliament. "That Act proves to demonstration that in a legal point of view Parliament is neither the agent of the electors nor in any sense a trustee for its constituents. It is legally the sovereign legislative power in the state" (Dicey, 1908: 45.) Once Parliament was created, in other words, no element of legal sovereignty remained in the people because there was no longer any legislative power in the electors; consequently the Septennial Act did not usurp any residual popular sovereignty, and hence it was entirely legitimate.

both Wilson's and Dicey's descriptions of the conditions under which those political outcomes can be achieved. Wilson's appeal to unanimous consent demonstrated by the fact of customary law is inappropriate in a modern, pluralistic society for precisely the same reasons that an appeal to the authoritative dictates of a religious tradition are inappropriate: There is no basis for the assumption that everyone shares the historical grounding in the customary practices in question. Far from being a matter of unanimous approval, in fact, the tradition of customary law is widely viewed today as inimical to the very political values of popular sovereignty that Wilson claimed for it. In addition, a long history of constitutional formation, amendment, and interpretation has demonstrated beyond peradventure that it is empirically and historically inaccurate to describe any constitutional system as the simple expression of tradition. Dicey's answer serves us no better. A challenge to the legitimacy of a commitment entered into at an early time cannot be answered by a brute assertion that the commitment occurred.

But without these problematic assumptions, can the moment of constitutional consent be considered legitimate? Put another way, how can a non-unanimous ratification of a constitutional text have binding force without either accepting Wilson appeal to the prior acceptance of a system of laws by custom or abandoning the project of normative justification altogether in favor of Dicey's constitutional positivism?

OBJECTIONS TO LOCKEAN CONSTITUTIONALISM

Wilson's appeal to legal custom raises the question of the relationship between constitutional and legal legitimation.[16] Modern constitutional theorists have long recognized that a constitutional order need not be coextensional with a legal order; conversely, legal positivists of a sociolegal bent draw a distinction – more or less

---

[16] The appeal to unwritten law as the legitimating basis for constitutionalism reverses the order of priority for those who conceive of a constitution as, itself, a higher positive law. This was the difference at stake between Wilson and his opponents in *Chisholm*. Should the nation's Constitution be understood in accordance with previously established legal norms, or were all positive laws now subject to validation or challenge by virtue of their accord with constitutional dictates?

explicit – between the basis for the authority of legal systems and the political commitments that legitimate government regimes. One can conceive of a constitutional text as occupying the center position in a nested series of circles, where the outermost and largest ring represents the normative commitments of a society, however conceived or debated, within which there is the ring that identifies the norms that inform that society's order, followed again by a still smaller circle of specifically constitutional principles. The legitimation of the constitutional principles contained in the innermost and smallest ring does not depend on the legitimacy of the legal system as a whole, and still less on the unanimous acceptance of the larger, maximum potential set of constitutionally relevant norms, despite the fact that juridical actors at all levels may be involved in the processes of constitutional governance.[17] As a result, where Wilson saw the customary acceptance of law as evidence of self-sovereignty, a modern writer asserting a connection between constitutional and legal legitimacy is more likely to argue something to the effect that the *nature* of the argument for constitutional legitimacy must be the same as that which applies to a system of legal rules, rather than that the two are coextensional.

---

[17] Lon Fuller described thousands of "systems of law" occurring at various levels of both formal and informal institutionalized interaction. (Fuller, 1969: 124–25.) An analysis of the different ways in which constitutional norms are experienced and practiced at different levels of legal "systems" is a sociolegal and historical study of great importance, but such a study requires a more empirical and case-specific approach than the one I am employing here. To mention one important example, norms derived from private law-based systems of adjudication often both display and contribute to constitutional understandings, an idea that I have explored to some extent in an earlier work (examining constructions of citizenship implicit in the formulation of novel private law doctrines in the mid-nineteenth century) and which has, in addition, been the subject of recent studies by James Stoner (examining common law roots of American constitutional conceptions of "liberty" in the eighteenth and nineteenth centuries), Linda Kerber (examining ways in which conceptions of the proper roles of women informed ideas of citizenship as a source of both legal prerogatives and obligations), Christopher Tomlins (examining the ways in which legal doctrines governing private employment informed American political thought in the eighteenth and nineteenth centuries), and Mark Tushnet (examining the ways in which the legal constructions of markets and the institution of slavery shaped nineteenth-century constitutionalism), among many others. (Schweber, 2004; Stoner, 2003; Kerber, 1999; Tomlins, 1983; Tushnet, 1981.)

Moreover, in the context of a society marked by value pluralism, the appeal to custom seems to beg the question. An appeal to custom as evidence of consent only compels us to ask whether there exists unanimous agreement that the custom that is consented to is actually desirable. That is, consent to custom can legitimate political authority if the acceptance of that custom demonstrates unanimous acceptance of its justifying *norms* rather than merely legal practices or institutional roles. The statement "that's not how we do things around here" is only an argument for legitimacy if it is backed by the addition of the phrase "and it's a good thing, too."

But that last part requires unanimous consent just as much as the first. Appeals to human nature, local history, and moral correctness all equally seem to require the possibility of an appeal to unanimously accepted norms. Since such unanimous acceptance of norms is precisely what is missing in a society described as "pluralistic," this leads to the conclusion that only the most homogeneous, conformist, illiberal communities imaginable – in short, a mythically republican *polis* of the kind that can never exist and most likely has never existed in history – are even theoretically capable of supporting legitimate constitutional rule. Whether such an imaginary society is described in terms of its unanimous acceptance of a system of laws, its unanimous agreement about human nature and its consequences, or the unanimous acceptance of a set of moral precepts makes very little difference.

The appeal to the existence of a system of customary law, then, both requires too much and proves too little to be useful. To be sure, constitutionalism and ordinary law cannot be entirely separated. A theory of constitutional rule must provide a basis for an institutionalized system of norms for the critique *of* legal practice. But whatever background consensus is required to support that critical framework will have to be found somewhere other than in the previously established system of laws. Constitutional theory is thus separated from legal theory by virtue of the extralegal, politically foundational dimensions of constitutionalist principles.[18]

---

[18] As Richard Bellamy puts the matter: "Once societies are no longer viewed as naturally constituted according to some moral order, then the norms that animate

The move of decoupling the project of constitutional legitimation from a reliance on a real or imagined history of legal practice, however, leads directly to the major objection to Lockean constitutionalism. This is the argument that there can be no legitimation of a system of law by consent because of the inescapability of disagreements and that, consequently, only present unanimous acceptance can legitimate a constitutional regime. This challenge to liberal constitutionalism can take one of two forms: an argument that only unanimous present consent can legitimate juridical authority, or the argument that legitimation of juridical authority by consent is simply impossible, so that each particular outcome must be tested for accordance with substantive moral norms, a test that is applied subjectively by each observer based on the prior moral commitments of each.

Taken to their logical conclusion, either of these claims spells the end of the project of liberal constitutionalism per se. There are only two obvious strategies for escaping this outcome. The first is to find a set of norms that can plausibly be described as both universal and compatible with value pluralism, and the second is to find a basis for consent in something other than universal acceptance of substantive legal or moral norms.

A successful argument for the existence of universal norms compatible with pluralism would provide the elusive basis for present, unanimous consent in a society marked by value pluralism. "We may disagree on many things," goes the argument, "but so long as we all agree on x, y, and z we have a sufficient basis for constitutional government by consent." This is the approach adopted by John Rawls in *Political Liberalism*. Rawls refers to the contents of the innermost and smallest circle of values, the ones to which consent is required for a constitutional regime to be viewed as legitimate, as the set of "constitutional essentials." "Our exercise of political power," he writes, "is proper and hence justifiable only when it is exercised in accordance with a constitution the essentials of which all citizens may reasonably be expected to endorse in the

---

and regulate human affairs have to be politically constructed and legitimated by those who are to submit to them . . . . On this view, constitutional government consists of a form of politics that strives to motivate law-making in the public interest and render it accountable to citizens." (Bellamy, 1996: 43–44.)

light of principles and ideals acceptable to them as reasonable and rational. This is the liberal principle of legitimacy." (Rawls, 1996: 217.)[19] Thus the locus of necessary "overlapping consensus" is limited to a finite set of substantive normative commitments, leaving room for rampant disagreement in the outer circles where legal and moral argumentation occur.[20]

Turning to the problem of defining the substantive content of "constitutional essentials," Rawls' inclusion of substantive normative ideals becomes the basis for a generous set of policy commitments: guarantees of health care and employment ("society as employer of last resort"); adequate education; "a decent distribution of income and wealth" and a guarantee of "the all-purpose means necessary ... to take intelligent and effective advantage of ... basic freedoms"; and public financing of elections "and ways of assuring the availability of public information on matters of policy." (Rawls, 1996: lviii-lvix.)[21]

---

[19] Indeed, in practice, the range of constitutional principles that are actually articulated in a formal, institutional setting is a smaller circle still. The idea of concentric layers of analysis is described by Lawrence Sager in terms of the distinction between the "adjudicated Constitution" and the potential "whole" meaning of the document. "[T]he adjudicated Constitution is reduced from the whole, and the whole of constitutional substance is reduced from all of political justice." (Sager, 2004: 1431.) Sager argues that the "underenforcement" of the American constitution is an artifact of the institutional reliance on judicial review. Arguments that institutional constraints on constitutional interpretation result from reliance on courts is also the basis for recent works by Larry Kramer (arguing for a restoration of a popular role in constitutional interpretation as a matter of democratic principles of popular sovereignty), Mark Tushnet (arguing that reliance on courts has resulted in insecure protections for rights as well as antidemocratic outcomes) and Louis Fisher (arguing that as a matter of historical practice, the freedom of religion has been protected in American history by extrajudicial institutions as much or more than by the judiciary). (Kramer, 2004; Tushnet, 2000; Fisher, 2002.)

[20] Rawls term "overlapping consensus" does not refer to points that happen to be elements of all competing ideologies represented in a society, but rather to a set of ideas acceptable to everyone, on the basis of which a "freestanding" political ideal of justice can be agreed upon. (Rawls, 1996: 10.) Rawls also considers the possibility of a narrower, more limited area of "constitutional consensus" in which "rather than supposing that the consensus reaches down to a political conception covering principles for the whole of the basic structure, a consensus may cover only certain fundamental procedural political principles for the constitution." (Rawls, 1996: 149.) The precise meanings of these terms are among the least well-developed elements of Rawls' arguments.

[21] This list, included in an Introduction added to the second edition of *Political Liberalism*, is in tension with Rawls' identification of ease of agreement as one of the

Rawls' substantive commitments are not presented as moral requirements derived from any particular "comprehensive doctrine" but as necessary conditions for the exercise of public reason. They depend, however, on a shared view of political justice, which is distinguished from philosophical views of justice by its scope, but whose "content is expressed in terms of certain fundamental ideas seen as implicit in the public political culture of a democratic society." (Rawls, 1996: 13). Conversely, Rawls' version of public reason imposes considerable duties upon citizens, to employ "public reason" when discussing questions that fall within the aegis of these constitutional essentials. (Rawls, 1996: 213–30). This may be taken to be nothing more than a requirement of what Habermas once referred to as a "will to reasonableness." (Habermas, 1972.) As Samuel Freeman points out, "[p]olitical liberalism aspires to discover a basis for social cooperation and the exercise of political authority that is freely acceptable to reasonable democratic citizens," a standard which presupposes an authoritative understanding of what it means to be free, reasonable, and an adequately responsible citizen. (Freeman, 2004: 2049.)

It is at the point where one is called upon to define constitutional essentials in concrete terms, however, that the presumed possibility of discovering an overlapping consensus becomes most doubtful.[22] From the perspective of politics, Rawls' list of constitutional essentials is far too generous to be useful; if constitutional legitimacy depends on the universal and unanimous acceptance of government-guaranteed employment, education, health care, and campaign financing, then constitutional legitimacy is a chimera. The basic idea of finding universally acceptable norms in the conditions of constitutional discourse, rather than in prior commitments to customary law or a philosophy of human nature, remains the most

---

criteria distinguishing constitutional essentials from ordinary political questions in the earlier version of the argument. "It is much easier to gain agreement about what the basic rights and liberties should be, not in every detail, but about the main outlines. These considerations explain why freedom of movement and free choice of occupation and a social minimum covering citizens' basic needs count as constitutional essentials while the principle of fair opportunity and the difference principle do not." (Rawls, 1996: 239.)

[22] In Michael Dorf's words: "Given profound disagreement, any foundational set of procedures or principles sufficiently abstract to secure consensus and thereby work its way into a popularly chosen constitution will be too abstract to resolve the most acute subsequently arising constitutional controversies." (Dorf, 2003: 884.)

important approach to answering the challenge of describing universal norms in a pluralistic society. Nonetheless, if the legitimation of a constitutional regime requires universal agreement that a specific set of material conditions suitable for participation must be established, the goal of a theory of constitutional legitimation seems distant, indeed. And to the extent that actual consent is not required, only the expression of a judgment that "citizens may reasonably be expected to endorse in the light of principles and ideals acceptable to them as reasonable and rational," then the question becomes "reasonably be expected by whom?" and the problem of legitimation is back to its starting point. For the moment, at least, Rawls' answer does not seem to provide an adequate response to the problem that unanimous present consent is impossible.

Randy Barnett presents a strict version of the argument that the legitimation of every juridical act depends on its accordance with moral principles. Barnett begins by arguing that legitimation of a lawmaking process by consent is impossible, because any such consent would have to be unanimous to be "actual." "Though 'the People' surely can be bound by their consent, this consent must be real, not fictional, and unanimous, not majoritarian. Any consent that is less than unanimous simply cannot bind nonconsenting persons." (Barnett, 2003: 137.) Since unanimous consent to policy outcomes is impossible to achieve in practice, the basis for constitutional legitimation must be found elsewhere. In Barnett's view, the alternative source of legitimacy is consistency with an external standard of substantive justice. Barnett quotes Lysander Spooner for the proposition that "[j]ustice is evidently the only principle that everybody can be presumed to agree to, in the formation of government." (Barnett, 2003: 137.)[23]

---

[23] "[I]f a constitution contains adequate procedures to assure that laws imposed on nonconsenting persons are just (or not unjust), it can be legitimate even if not consented to unanimously, whereas a constitution that lacks adequate procedures to ensure the justice of valid laws is illegitimate even if consented to by a majority. Indeed, only by realizing that the "consent of the governed" is a fiction can one appreciate the imperative that lawmakers respect the requirements of justice (whatever one believes those to be)." (Barnett, 2003: 113.)

Moreover, for Barnett the appeal to justice is not simply a practical necessity, it is an analytical implication of the theory of legitimation by consent itself. The very requirement of consent, for Barnett, demonstrates a tacit understanding that "first come rights, and then comes law," or "first come rights, then comes government," since otherwise the proposition that consent justifies lawmaking is ungrounded. That observation leads to the conclusion that consent is unnecessary and probably unhelpful as a measure of legitimacy. "The assumption that 'first come rights, then comes government' helps explain how lawmaking can be legitimate in the absence of consent." (Barnett, 2003: 115, 142.) Unanimous acceptance of moral principles contained in shared conceptions of rights is the sole basis for the legitimacy of government.

The problem, initially, lies in identifying the point in the lawmaking process at which agreement concerning Barnett's principles of "rights," or agreement as to the scope of Rawls' "constitutional essentials," is required to appear. When discussing the general moral obligation to obey the law, Barnett seems to argue that legitimation by consent is not possible unless there is unanimous acceptance of the outcome of each moment of lawmaking. In the specific context of constitution-making, Barnett seems to assume that what is required is consent to the text that is the product of the process. This was the problem that the Lockean model of a series of consents proceeding from an initial point of unanimity was intended to address. Like Barnett, Locke and Wilson each recognized the necessity of a moment of unanimity on which to ground subsequent claims of consent, but they attempted to push that moment back beyond the process of constitution-making to a moment of societal formation that takes place in the mist-shrouded realm of an imagined past.

Thus it is not clear that Barnett's insistence that consent, to be effective, must be "actual, not fictional" draws a simple distinction. It is also not clear on what basis Barnett, like Rawls, feels comfortable in asserting that the possibility of unanimous agreement concerning the meaning of "justice" is more readily obtainable than unanimous agreement concerning the legitimacy of laws. In a strong theory of legitimate sovereignty, indeed, the converse is presumed to be true. In the end, if the legitimation of a constitutional system cannot be made to reach beyond the subjective conclusion that it accords with a prior set of moral commitments, then, once again, the goal of constitutional legitimation is likely unattainable.

Other writers have made similar attempts to link the legitimacy of law or constitutionalism to a shared commitment to moral principles.[24] But the difficulties remain the same. Ascribing moral significance to constitutional principles might be descriptively interesting, but it cannot account for the necessary conditions of the existence of that ascription unless morality itself is externally grounded and universal. Thus the argument either becomes the impossible proposition that "only a constitution whose provisions are universally regarded as morally sound is legitimate," or else the banal proposition that "a constitution whose provisions comport with principles that are universally regarded as sound within a community is legitimate for that community," a return to the assumption of universal consent by something like an appeal to custom. Either proposition is equally unlikely to be satisfied under conditions of pluralism.[25]

As the preceding comments suggest, one interesting consequence of both the shift toward a focus on social practices and the appeal to substantive moral norms is that sovereignty becomes a nearly absent category in the discussion. This is not only an aspect of American critiques of the Lockean constitutionalist tradition. European writers

---

[24] John Finnis argues that moral considerations are inescapably an element of the analysis of any legal order as a matter of definition, not merely as a matter of justification. As an example of practical reason, Finnis argues, law exists in the first instance as a mechanism for the expression of shared moral concerns. Consequently, for Finnis, an authentic description of law requires an understanding of those concerns as a matter of taxonomical logic. (Finnis, 1980: 16.) As Brian Leiter acutely observes, Finnis arguably conflates moral and epistemic norms, thus conflating the idea of "law" with a specific standard of "just law." From a sociolegal perspective, the definitional norms that Finnis describes are epistemic norms that identify a socially constructed activity to its participants, not normative justifications for substantive outcomes. (Leiter, 2003: 33–34.)

[25] In the different but related context of judicial interpretation of constitutional provisions, Michael Dorf refers to arguments for legitimation based on moral principles "right answer" theories. "Upon inspection, however, the "right-answers" thesis, even if correct, does not respond to the indeterminacy problem .... The metaphysical claim that there is a right answer to this question does not help unless tied to some mechanism for finding that answer. ... The right-answers thesis simply does not address the fact of moral diversity." (Dorf, 2003: 898–99.)

confronted by the project of creating and securing the adoption of a European Constitution raise the same challenges to Lockean constitutionalism, often explicitly focusing their arguments on the proposition that sovereignty is a defunct and unnecessary concept.[26] Instead, legitimacy is said to derive from one of the sources identified above: either, first, from an appeal to universal values embodied in global institutional structures, so that "constitutionalism" occurs in a new kind of political space in which "sovereignty" is not a meaningful concept (the parallel to an appeal to subjectively held normative principles); or, second, from the fact of community, a form of consensus located in social practices rather than in moral priors (the parallel to an appeal to consent by custom within an historically defined community).[27]

The first argument takes the form of the proposition that sovereignty as it is traditionally understood is actually opposed to the development of constitutionalism generally, and to the emergence of global constitutionalism in particular. Drawing on Bodin's arguments that were described in Chapter 1, Luigi Ferrajoli argues that "[w]ithin constitutional democracies absolute and sovereign powers or subjects no longer exist. The very principle of popular sovereignty that is still included in many constitutions is no more than a verbal homage to the democratic-representative character of contemporary political systems." (Ferrajoli, 1997, 152.)

---

[26] Describing the European Union and its prospects for the adoption of a Constitution, for example, Neil MacCormack uses the term "commonwealth" to indicate a situation in which neither member states nor the EU have "sovereignty" in its traditional sense at all. Instead, MacCormick describes the working of European institutions as "polycentric, pluri-systemic, multi-state legal order." (MacCormick, 1999: 142, 155.) Ulrich Preuss similarly describes "horizontal" rather than "vertical" heirarchies of institutional authority as a modern challenge to the idea of sovereignty. "The characteristic of constitutionalism is a horizontal order of state authority, in which a system of careful coordination of the functionally specified powers produces a web of mutual and almost circular dependence . . . ." (Preuss, 1997: 17.) The problem of identifying the source of legitimacy for such an institutional arrangement, however, remains.

[27] European writers speak variously of a "democracy deficit" or a "legitimacy deficit" with respect to the European Union. These discussions, however, focus primarily on the problem of making a transnational European government system effective or politically acceptable rather than on the philosophical question of whether such a government requires a basis of legitimacy beyond the treaty obligations of already-existing sovereign states. (Erikson and Fossum, 2004; Verhoeven, 2003.)

What is analytically true of the nature of liberal democratic states, moreover, is said to be historically true of the world at large. At the international level, Ferrajoli argues that the equation of citizenship with possession of rights specified by a sovereign authority "collapsed" in the late twentieth-century, taking the concept of "citizenship" along with it. Instead, Ferrajoli finds that the basic concepts of sovereignty and citizenship have been displaced by "the global constitution in embryo which already exists in the United Nations Charter and the various international conventions and declarations of human rights. It involves viewing reality from the vantage point of a global constitutionalism that has already been formally established, even if it is still lacking any institutional guarantees." (Ferrajoli, 1997: 155.)[28]

Ulrich Preuss articulates a version of the argument from custom – that a constitutional regime may be legitimated by its authentic articulation of communal practices and norms – in his description of French constitutional thought.[29]

Unlike the United States, the creation of the constitution has not been the founding act for the French nation – rather the constitution is one of the emanations of the nation. The nation is antecedent to the constitution .... The essence of this concept of constitutionalism, then, is not embodied in the constitution itself; it is incarnated in the power of the nation to make and unmake a constitution at will and at any time. Constitutionalism, that is, consists of what one might call, 'constitution-creativity'; the power of the

---

[28] Ferrajoli's view is essentially optimistic, as he sees the promulgation of universal norms as strengthening the protection of individual rights. Other writers, similarly observing a decline in sovereignty and citizenship in the face of globalization, have arrived at the opposite, more pessimistic conclusion that the security of rights is being undermined along with the legitimacy of rights-securing institutions within states. (Weiler, 1999.)

[29] Whether Preuss' description accurately captures French constitutional theory – or whether there is a singular version of "French constitutional theory" to be captured – is a question I leave in abeyance. In this regard, a reader might consider the limitations of Preuss' description of American constitutional practice. "In the case of the U.S. it is the charisma of the founding act which is to be preserved over history in the text of the constitution and which makes this document a legacy, sometimes a burdensome legacy of the past which imposes itself on future generations. Knowing that this original compact of the Founding Fathers cannot be repeated, all its solemnity and pathos is 'invested' into the text of the constitution." (Preuss, 1997: 24–25.)

nation to constitute and reconstitute its sovereign power and give it its appropriate institutional shape at will. (Preuss, 1997: 23.)[30]

In Preuss' formulation, French constitutionalism looks not to a consenting "people" but, rather, to a consenting "nation," a distinctly different formulation. The question then becomes one more of accuracy, or authenticity, than legitimacy; does the constitution in question accurately capture social practices in the society at issue? "The nation," after all, cannot remake itself. It can only remake its constitution to more closely accord with the national character.

What all these arguments have in common is their rejection of a political category of sovereignty in favor of some version of an appeal to unanimously shared values. But as Boudin and Hobbes understood, where an appeal to moral consensus is either unavailable or inadequate to ground a system of democratic authority, the alternative is to appeal to some version of a principle of sovereignty. The focus on sovereignty shifted the focus away from the moral rightness of laws to the political authority of the lawmaker, conceived as one who rules over others, a move Bodin and Hobbes saw as necessary in order to escape the impossible search for moral consensus and the centuries of religious wars and oppressions that search had engendered. In its later Lockean formulation, sovereignty became the name for the capacity of the members of a democratic polity to engage in majoritarian self-rule based on the assumption of some prior moment of unanimity. The path of constitutional theoretical development from Locke to Wilson emphasized conditions or precedent events that are required in order for popular sovereignty to be created and exercised. The critical elements were a shared prejuridical language and beliefs as the precondition of political consent, multiple moments of consent, and the progressive emergence of a state whose actions are thereafter legitimized by a different, indirect version of consent.

All of these elements become gratuitous in the challenges to Lockean constitutionalism that eschew sovereignty as a category of

---

[30] Preuss' larger argument is that Britain, the United States, and France have fundamentally different constitutional orders resting on incommensurate legitimating claims. This is taken as a refutation of the premise that something like a social contract theory is universally required for legitimate constitutionalism. For a similar argument, see Venter, 1999: 11.

legitimation. Rawls' approach is particularly instructive in this regard. Modern liberalism has been built around a challenge to the presumption of shared values, most famously in Isaiah Berlin's description of a "pluralism of values," a phrase that captured both his belief in the irreducibility of conflict over fundamental moral choices and the impossibility of satisfying all "goods" simultaneously. (Berlin, 2002: 212–17.) As noted earlier, confronted by the prospect of disagreements at the level of the meaning of "good" in the form of "a well-ordered society," Rawls appealed to overlapping consensus and a commitment to articulate public positions in a language such that others could imagine agreeing with us.[31] This is a move not far removed from Locke's appeal to common notions of complex ideas, but with one very notable difference in practice. For Rawls, as for other modern liberals, the processes by which a commonwealth is formed and those by which it is governed are essentially indistinguishable. It is not clear, in other words, that the requirements of Rawlsian discourse change between the creation, adoption, and operation of a constitution, nor whether a specifically constitutional form of government is either necessary or useful for his model.[32] To put the matter in terms familiar from Chapter 1, it is not clear whether there is a moment at which sovereignty is established. Liberal democratic theory viewed in this way appears more as a process of social interaction than an eighteenth-century style exercise of self-rule.

There is much to be said in favor of the idea that a successful defense of constitutional legitimacy requires a move away from

---

[31] For Rawls, the possibility of a sphere of political discourse defined by overlapping consensus resides in the reasonableness of religious, philosophical, and other "comprehensive" worldviews. "History tells of a plurality of not unreasonable comprehensive doctrines. This makes an overlapping consensus possible, thus reducing the conflict between political and other values." (Rawls, 1996: 140.) The issues raised by the proposition that mutually "reasonable" comprehensive doctrines are either necessary or plausible as the basis for constitutional legitimation will be dealt with in Chapter 5.

[32] In contrast, Joseph Raz raises the possibility that old and new constitutions require different legitimating principles, not because the constitution at issue has changed with the passage of time, "but that the reasons for its validity did." (Raz, 2001: 169.) And an old constitution, argues Raz, cannot derive its legitimacy from the authority of its authors but must rather demonstrate consistency with prevalent moral norms.

anthropomorphic metaphors to a description of social behaviors. The difficulty is that the abandonment of sovereignty deprives constitutionalists of the traditional mechanism to resolve precisely the problem of pervasive and irreducible disagreement within the population that value pluralism presents for a theory of legitimation by consent. This problem becomes particularly acute when one recognizes the reality of pluralism concerning not only the content of moral rules but even their applicability to the evaluation of constitutional propositions in the first place. It does no good to insist that universal moral principles endorse a particular rule if your listener does not consider moral principles to be a relevant basis for rule-making. Similarly, it does no good to assert that a particular law was arrived at through a democratic process of decision-making if your listener does not think that democratic processes of decision-making guarantee legitimate outcomes. Just as unliquidated disagreement concerning processes of rule-formation precludes a simple proceduralist justification for the rules that are produced by the operation of those procedures,[33] unliquidated disagreement concerning the relevance of morality to constitutional legitimacy precludes any sensible appeal to morality as the basis of that legitimacy. At most, the presumed legitimacy of the moral sentiment can justify its forceful imposition over others, in which instance a constitution has the same functional "legitimacy" as a cannon; it is a useful weapon that can be pointed at the wrong citizens by the right citizens.

Ultimately, the arguments of writers such as Rawls, Barnett, and Ferrajoli prove too much to be useful for the project of identifying the necessary conditions of legitimate constitutions, just as the approaches of Wilson, Dicey, and Preuss proved too little. Wilson, Dicey, and Preuss prove too little because they provide a justification for a constitutional regime that requires no justification, whereas Rawls, Barnett, and Ferrajoli prove too much because

---

[33] See Barnett, 2003: 134–37. Jeremy Waldron makes this argument a central element of a case against the possibility of conceiving of binding precommitments as consistent with the principle of popular sovereignty. (Waldron, 2001.) This issue, and Waldron's argument, are discussed in Chapter 3.

their justifications require assumptions that cannot be satisfied in practice.

On the other hand, these arguments and others like them clearly identify two critical points that need to be addressed. First, the meaning of "legitimate" needs to be defined for this particular context, particularly since both "according with an externally grounded theory of moral obligation" and "according with established customary law" have been rejected as definitions. And, second, legitimation by consent does appear to rest on a moment of unanimous acceptance of some background principles at some point in the real-or-imagined historical chain of events. If, as I have suggested, an appeal to shared moral norms proves too much, what is the minimum content of that moment of unanimity?

In defining "legitimacy," the critical distinction is between that idea conceived as a description of a set of social facts and as a normative evaluation. For the purposes of this book, the former, socially descriptive sense of the term is the one that makes the most sense, but if the goal is to explain the requirements of a legitimate constitutional regime, that social acceptance must refer to a genuinely constitutional system of governance. That is, a "legitimate constitutional regime" is one that is perceived by relevant actors as authoritative on the basis of specifically constitutional principles. This is an idea that will be discussed more in the context of legal positivism and the idea of obligation, but a few observations are required here in order to set up the remainder of the discussion.

Characterizing "legitimacy" as a description of social attitudes rather than as a normative test does not by any means imply that the legal or constitutional system is itself morally neutral. It is perfectly plausible to describe a social practice of ascribing moral rightness to a system of constitutional norms,[34] or to describe a social practice of assigning binding authority to the authorial intent of the drafters of

---

[34] Brian Leiter refers to this as the "Soft Positivist" theory of law. "[I]t is still a conceptual possibility, on the Soft Positivist view, for there to be a Rule of Recognition, hence a legal system, in which morality is not a criterion of legal validity. That morality is a criterion of legal validity in some systems is just a contingent fact about the actual official practice in those systems, not a conceptual requirement of positivism's account of law." (Leiter, 2003: 25.) See discussion, Chapter 4.

a constitutional document.[35] What is avoided by this reliance on social description is the the necessity of relying on a normative choice *between* these differing bases for acceptance.

In addition, the characteristics that define a constitution's "legitimacy" may be argued to be different at different points in time. For example, even if some version of consent is accepted as the basis for legitimacy, the consent that makes the formation of a constitutional regime legitimate – what I have referred to as "the moment of constitutional consent" – may be different from what makes the continued operation of that constitutional regime legitimate over time. As Joseph Raz points out, at the moment of a constitution's founding the legitimacy of the instrument derives from popular acceptance of the authority of its authors. Thereafter, however, the basis for legitimacy becomes the existence of established social practice. "Constitutions, at least old ones, do not derive their authority from the authority of their authors. But there is no need to worry as to the source of their authority. They are self-validating. They are valid just because they are there, enshrined in the practices of their countries." (Raz, 2001: 173.) Francois Venter makes a similar argument, focusing specifically on juridical actors and practices as the locus of legitimation by social practice, resulting in what Venter calls "practical legitimacy."[36]

Raz adds an important caveat that connects his argument to the appeals to substantive moral principles described here. "*As long as they remain within the boundaries set by moral principles*, constitutions are self-validating.... It should be added that this conclusion follows *if*

[35] "But full knowledge of a social practice includes knowledge of how participants in the practice experience it, 'from the inside,' so to speak .... [and] does not preclude the practice's being one that has this as one of its features: that participants refer all questions about legal authority and validity to sets of standards to which ... they attribute the character of having been intentionally legislated." (Michelman, 2001: 73.)

[36] "It is submitted that the predominance of a constitution is maintained by the operation of the legitimately established devices of the constitution itself, which can remain effective only as long as the citizenry and the state's organs of authority which are governed by the constitution, continue to lend legitimacy to its institutions through the due employment of the mechanisms and procedures provided for by the constitution.... *It may thus be said that the force outside the constitution which ensures its primacy is its practical legitimacy*. Where the constitution gives reasonable and realistic expression to the principles and needs of the legal community which it serves, its legitimacy is not a frail thing." (Venter, 1999: 14.)

morality underdetermines the principles concerning the form of government and the content of individual rights enshrined in constitutions." (Raz, 2001: 173.) The idea of underdetermination is the idea that there can be unliquidated disagreement about questions of constitutional design despite agreement about basic moral norms.

Lawrence Sager makes a closely related point when he suggests that in practice, constitutions are "underenforced," meaning that constitutional rule-making does not extend to everything that might be argued to be elements of "constitutional justice." "Constitutional justice sits between all of political justice, on the one hand, and the much narrower substance of the adjudicated Constitution, on the other." (Sager, 1998: 244.) Constitutional norms not only do not directly necessitate specific outcomes, there is also room for debate about the extent to which constitutional norms should be pursued in constitutional practice at all, so long as the practice in question is understood as at least a partial realization of at least a subset of accepted constitutional norms and is consistent with the possibility of realizing the others. The result may not fit anyone's notion of an ideal outcome, but as Sager puts it, "[j]ustifying and constraining the disappointments and burdens of membership in a political community is the crucial project of constitutional justice." (Sager, 1998: 252.)

In Raz' and Sager's arguments, then, something like a more limited version of a Rawlsian overlapping moral consensus or Barnett's subjective moral certainty remains necessary if the legitimacy of an established constitutional regime is to be verified by the social practice of acceptance.[37] The point of unanimity occurs in a shared

---

[37] A somewhat extreme version of this argument that is commonly heard in European constitutional debates is what Judge G. F. Mancini (European Court of Justice) calls the "Volk" theory of constitutionalism, pointing to the "Maastricht *Urteil*" case in which the German Constitutional Court determined that the Treaty of Maastricht was incompatible with Article 20 of the German Basic Law guaranteeing democratic self-rule. *BVerfGE* of Oct. 12, 1993, 89, 155, 57 Common Market Law Reports (1994). (Mancini, 2000: 57.) Justice Dieter Grimm's case opinion asserted that the possibility of constitutional self-rule requires public political discourse, and that the conditions for public political discourse require, at a minimum, a common language. Mancini accuses Grimm and other Euro-skeptics of an attachment to a German Romantic notion of natural nationhood associated with Johann Herder. In response, Mancini asserts that there exist a "constellation of values informing [Europeans'] way of life," and "a heritage of values and

commitment to an underdeterminative set of moral norms, whereas majoritarian consent to constitutional outcomes consistent with those norms is justified by the shared interest in social and political stability. The combination of moral underdetermination and stability cause constitutional arrangements that are not themselves the subject of unanimous consent to nonetheless be understood by the relevant actors as legitimate. Raz' argument, which will be revisited in Chapter 5 ("The Question of Substance"), pushes the search for unanimous acceptance of grounding norms back from the moment of legislation to a prior moment of constitutional design in proper Lockean fashion.

Nonetheless, a difficulty remains. Regardless of where we locate the necessary moment of genuine, unanimous consent, or what its terms, the concept of "constitutional consent" is only useful if it is understood to include two characteristics: The consent is itself accepted as resulting in the creation of a legitimate political authority, and the fact of consent is accepted as legitimately binding. These elements of authority and bindingness are equally missing from the accounts of Rawls, Barnet, and Raz described earlier. We may universally share certain normative commitments, but how does that translate into an equally universal commitment to the proposition that those norms are a proper basis for government authority?

What is missing is the intermediate step that turns consensus on some set of principles into political authority capable of generating laws and institutional arrangements. In other words, what is missing is a locus for sovereignty. This is a flaw that makes it impossible to give an account of constitutionalism even if we grant the problematic assumptions of unanimous acceptance of legal custom, overlapping consensus, or shared subjective moral commitments. Every member of a community can share precisely the same moral

---

institutions shared by [the EU's] member states." (Mancini, 2000: 65.) Still a third European approach argues that a constitutional order does not require "a people" at all, but can instead be based on relationships between persons and institutions and between institutional frameworks. This argument takes the form of a Kantian "cosmopolitan" model, in which weak attachments permit broad and fluid forms of institutional attachment. (Eleftheriadis, 2001: 32). Jürgen Habermas argues for this third approach based on the insight that identities are formed in response to institutional arrangements as often as the converse. (Habermas, 1999: 161.)

commitments, so long as those commitments are under-determinative, but it remains the case that a separate commitment to accept the binding authority of some version of a "sovereign" is required for the creation of a legitimate constitutional regime. "Values" by themselves are slippery, monadic objects. The Lockean idea of a sovereign with authority over juridical language provided handles and glue: "handles" that make it possible to employ values in mutually comprehensible ways, move them around in discourse, and apply them to particular questions, and "glue" that holds constellations of values together in systems of positive law.

The point can be clarified if we revisit (not for the last time) the distinction between the legitimacy of a constitutional regime and the legitimacy of a legal regime. The existence of an identifiable "constitution" interposes a layer of decision making between the formation of a political society and the generation of laws. Subsequent to the adoption of a constitution, acts of legislation are tested against the terms of that instrument (or, in the unwritten case, against the set of constitutional conventions). But the creation of the political order, itself, requires legitimation.[38] This is the constitutional equivalent to the need for a norm that justifies the enforcement of shared values by government, or the necessity for a consent to legitimation by consent that was ascribed to Locke in Chapter 1. A specifically political commitment to the creation of juridical authority is required before the question of shared values even becomes relevant. The problem of legitimating a system of laws, then, is not the same as the problem of legitimating a constitutional regime. What makes the legitimation of a constitution problematic is precisely that it interrupts the direct relationship between the society and the generation of laws by formalizing the institutional arrangements of lawmaking. That gap must be filled by something like sovereignty.

None of the responses to challenges to Lockean constitutionalism suffices to get us away from the search for sovereignty if we are to

---

[38] In the case of the European Union, for example, this has been accomplished by the creation of treaty obligations, which are either explicitly authorized in state constitutions or (in a practice fraught with constitutional irony) are authorized by acts of ordinary legislation adopted by constituent member states. (Jyranki, 1999: 63–7.)

seriously address the question of how constitutional consent is possible. Ultimately, the question "Consent How?" is the question of how a moment of consent to language can be understood as sufficient to generate the kind of collective self-sovereignty that is required for the idea of a subsequent moment of binding constitutional consent to be sensible.

The legitimacy of the claim to a commitment to language itself continues to depend on an assertion of some version of consent, and for consent to create binding obligation requires sovereignty. On the other hand, it is not the case that in our search for a sensible account of constitutional consent we need to go as far as those writers who insist on actual subjective unanimity. When Wilson appealed to an "immemorial" custom of legal usage, he was pointing to a demonstration of consent by conduct, and the same kind of consent is at stake in identifying the social fact of linguistic usage in cases such as Locke's example of "money." These are examples of what I will call "as if" consent. For a system of laws to be treated as legitimate, it is not necessary that all participants in the legal system genuinely, subjectively find each legal rule to be desirable, only that they be sufficiently convinced of the validity of the body of laws to view the system as legitimate and to behave accordingly. Similarly, for a constitutional regime to be legitimate, it is not necessary that each act of lawmaking that is undertaken in the operation of the regime itself be considered legitimate, only that there be a sufficiently strong commitment to the regime itself that citizens are willing to act "as if" they viewed each act of lawmaking as an expression of self-sovereignty.

The observation that universal subjective agreement is not required for a system of laws to be legitimate is not the same as the observation that there will be persons who obey the law solely out of fear or in recognition of the possibility of advantage. A person who acts in that way is not making any statement about legitimacy; she is simply separating the problem of legitimacy from the question of her motivation for acting. Nor is this a restatement of the idea of tacit consent, in which a subjective mental state of genuine consent is imputed to actors in the absence of any particular conduct. What I am focusing on is the possibility that legitimation by consent, itself, may be demonstrated at a global or systemic level by acts indicating consent at the level of specific rules. A willingness to accept the legitimacy of laws as if one had directly consented to their promulgation is taken as a sufficient basis to conclude that a constitutional system is legitimized by Lockean consent. Applied to the idea of consent to language, the idea of "as if" consent becomes an argument that a demonstrated willingness to employ constitutional language, even in the absence of a specific subjective mental state of approval of its form or content, indicates consent sufficient to establish the legitimacy of the creation of that language.

Can consent to language ever be sufficient to establish sovereignty, or is a more direct claim of authority by consent to acts of positive lawmaking required? Put another way, is an account of even unanimous linguistic consent sufficient to legitimate a subsequent moment of majoritarian constitutional consent? An affirmative answer to these inquiries would go a long way toward answering the question "Consent How?" by shifting the focus away from the moment of lawmaking to a prior moment of social practice. The first obvious objection, which has already been discussed, is the problem of infinite regress. The response was to recognize the need for sovereignty and the necessity of some moment of actual, unanimous consent. This points to a critical observation: there are limits to the pluralism that can be made consistent with a constitutional regime. Nonetheless, the move from a focus on constitution consent to a prior moment of linguistic consent is an attempt to find a real, plausible starting point that is as least potentially consistent with value pluralism.

But the question remains unaddressed. Can consent to language be a sufficient basis for the creation of a sovereign people capable of constitutional consent? This represents an inversion of Locke's original formulation, making sovereignty a precondition for constitutionalism, and relocating the appearance of sovereignty away from the moment of political consent to the prior consensual agreement on language. I intend to propose that a unanimous "as if" consent to language can serve just this sovereignty-generating function, but to make that argument it is first necessary to develop a deeper understanding of what sovereignty looks like in the context of a theory of constitutional language.

SOVEREIGNTY AND LANGUAGE

Frank Michelman presents a straightforward and powerful argument that sovereignty can appear only at the moment of political consent, based on a traditional understanding with roots in Bodin of the sovereign as lawgiver. This is the reason, for Michelman, that sovereignty is a necessary element of any discussion of constitutional legitimacy. Since the fundamental purpose of self-organization into a constitutional commonwealth is the creation of a system of laws, it remains the case that the identification of an authoritative lawmaker is an irreducible element of the process. The perceived legitimacy of particular laws rests on the precedent moments of consent that created a lawmaking authority – that is, on the *sovereignty* of the lawmaker – not on acceptance of an earlier-established set of rules such as customary law, nor on a universally accepted set of pre-political moral or discursive norms. By the same token, the perceived legitimacy of a constitution relies on the sovereignty of its creators, which requires a separate and independent ground.

Michelman presents this argument in an essay entitled "Constitutional Authorship." Confronted with the problem of irreducible disagreement, Michelman argues that the search for sovereignty is indeed inescapable. At the same time, the possibility of self-sovereignty requires an area of shared agreement relating to the purpose and nature of the constitutional text. The fact of a constitutional text points to the idea of a moment of origin. What requires justification first is the act of creating the text; as a result, sovereignty is bound up with authorship in what Michelman calls the "author/authority" relationship. "[W]hen we regard a legal order as grounded we must – logically must – be positing a 'historically first constitution,' together with a socially prevailing 'basic norm' conferring on that first constitution's promulgators the authority to make it be the law" (Michelman, 2001: 73.)

"Consent," in this view, enters into the discussion in the fact of authorization, since a commitment to self-sovereignty requires that participants in the system conceive of that first constitution as their own creation. That conception, in turn, is only possible if the constitutional text displays a connection to the constitutional culture out of which the consent to self-government arose. People can perceive law as legitimate "only through the lawgivers' perceived or supposed participation in the same set of regulative ideas that they right now hold about what constitutions are for and are supposed to do." Thus Michaelman agrees with Wilson that there can never be a "clean slate" if one is committed to popular sovereignty; at the moment of constitutional origination there is already an implicit invocation of legitimate earlier commitment to a set of substantive legal norms. (Michelman, 2001: 81.)

Michelman's argument is an attempt to meld the idea of a law-giving sovereign with the idea of appealing to a limited but necessary set of universally shared present values. The metaphor of sovereignty as authorship nicely points up the act of discursive construction involved in the creation of a constitutional order, and the linguistic requirements for that act of construction to be possible. In the discussion of Locke's *Two Treatises* there was reference to a moment of suspension that occurs with the formation of the commonwealth, when the laws of nature are potentially in abeyance but new, positive, laws have not yet been made and the sovereign rules by prerogative. Here that moment of suspension reappears, when the collective author has been formed but has not yet written. The act of writing a constitution redefines the authority of the artificial person from sovereign ruler to sovereign author.

In some ways, Michelman's collectively constructed constitutional author remains bound by the tradition of the anthropomorphic metaphor. Consider the question of what earlier commitment(s) must be unanimously accepted in order for Michelman's act of sovereignty-by-consent to be possible. For Locke, the answer was the unanimous acceptance of certain complex ideas, such as "money," which defined the interests that would motivate individuals to consent to government, and in so doing created the conditions for the creation of the commonwealth. For Wilson, a thicker form of cultural understanding was required, one demonstrated by increasing sophistication of (juridical) language.

Michelman focuses explicitly on the idea on the acceptance of the anthropomorphic metaphor, itself, as the cultural precondition for the creation of a sovereign collective author. "What do we think this people-constituting, identity-fixing fact could possibly be? Must it not finally come down to an attitude of expectation or commitment shared by constituent members of the putative capital-P People?" This "constitutional-cultural notion" is the idea of continuity in the identity of the polity across time, an observation that draws a direct connection between the issue of sovereignty-formation and the possibility of binding commitments. (Michelman, 2001: 80.)[39]

The sovereign authority to engage in this form of writing remains self-sovereignty. Our acceptance of the authority of that author depends on our recognition that he shares our fundamental understanding of constitutional norms. "In other words, constitutional framers can be *our* framers – their history can be our history, their word can command observance from us now on popular-sovereignty grounds – only because and insofar as they, in our eyes now, were already on what we judge to be the track of true constitutional reason." (Michelman, 2001: 81.) We produce an author in order to stand as our constitutional authority, but since that authority is the result of agreement with our principles, it is equally the case that in regarding our constitution we take on the authorial role ourselves. The model of self-sovereignty, experienced through the act of collective consent to the production of a constitutional text, becomes a model of self-authorship.

But where did this process of collective self-definition begin? For Locke, committed as he was to providing a quasi-historical developmental account of self-government, that question had to be addressed in order to avoid the problem of infinite regress. Michelman views such explanations as illusory. "Where in history

[39] In another essay, Michelman suggested that to the extent that a constitution is conceived of as an identity-creating text, it depends on a correspondence between its terms and pre-existing social patterns. "While such an undertaking doubtless requires that attributions of constitutional-legal meanings satisfy, from occasion to occasion, certain experiential demands of comprehensibility and coherence, there is no reason why this satisfaction cannot – indeed, there seems every reason why it would have to – rest in part on a correspondence, achieved in part by interpretation, of law with prelegal form-of-life. An express amendment rule would doubtless be required to sustain such a venture in living-by-logos, and it could be more or less aptly designed to lead to better coherence." (Michelman, 2004: 1330–31, quoting a discussion of Harris, 1982.) This is essentially a functionalist argument that seeks to find the justification for rules restricting amendment procedures in their political utility rather than in any reference to a meta-legal standard of legitimation.

can this 'originary' constitutive moment – this founding act of citizen's authorship – ever be fixed or anchored? Surely what we have here is pure abstraction, a transcendental-logical deduction necessitated by the prior determination of a thinker to think something." That determination may be characterized in terms of either of the alternative theories of legitimation; that is, the "thinker" may be determined to think that the constitution is grounded in an earlier commitment to the authority of a sovereign-as-author, or that it is consistent with present "regulative ideas." In either instance, that prior commitment has to be accounted for if the problem of legitimacy is to be addressed seriously, leading Michelman to conclude that ultimately the authority for that original commitment becomes the basic event to be explained. This results inevitably, in a return, to the search for a sovereign emerging from a moment of consent, and hence to the requirement of an original constitutional author. "Either way, we produce an author because we have to." (Michelman, 2001: 91–2.)

Sovereignty, in this argument, is identified with authorship, and the authority of the author derives from our ability to collectively project our constitutional values into the products of that authorship. At the same time, however, there is a tension between Michelman's identification of "an attitude ... or commitment" shared by the "putative capital-P People" and his earlier reference to "lawgivers' perceived or supposed participation in the same set of regulative ideas that they right now hold about what constitutions are for and are supposed to do." The authority of the sovereign-as-author who creates the constitutional text guarantees the legitimacy of that act of creation; the continuing operation of the constitutional regime must be legitimated by reference to the shared constitutional norms of the postconstitutional sovereign people, norms that are themselves the product of the act of constitutional creation.[40] It may

---

[40] Ann Norton proposes that the act of creating a constitution itself exercises the transformative effect that causes the sovereign-as-constitutional-author to become the postconstitutional sovereign people. "The act of writing a constitution is an act of signification. In it men create a representation of their collective character. The representation, in the case of written constitutions, the text, of their nationality, is not subject to the vicissitudes that beset them in the flesh. It seems to secure constancy for their collective identity. Yet as we have seen, they are changed by the act itself. They will be changed again, as the Constitution makes a new sort of

be true that in both instances, "we create an author because we (analytically) have to," but it is far less clear that it is the *same* "author" in the two cases, a possibility that reopens the search for a ground from which to legitimate the creation of the sovereign-as-author in the first place. Again, the "consent how" question remains problematic. What, to repeat, is the relationship between the sovereign-as-author and the present sovereign lawgiver, and how does the moment of consent that calls the one form of sovereign into being secure the authority of the other?

In different ways, and with very different results, Bruce Ackerman and Keith Whittington have each directly confronted the question of the relationship between the authority of the sovereign-as-author at the moment of constitutional creation and the subsequent legitimation of the constitutional regime that is created as a result. Ackerman describes a theory of "dual constitutionalism," in which the American Constitution is understood as a mechanism to distinguish between extraordinary acts of political sovereignty and the ordinary exercise of political authority. (Ackerman, 1993: 3–33.) For Ackerman, popular sovereignty is a necessary precondition for the creation of a constitution, which thereafter defines self-imposed constraints on its subsequent exercise. Whittington's description of the relationship is more complex. In his view, the moment of constitutional creation calls the sovereign people into being by an act of self-creation.[41] Thereafter, the appropriate distinction is between "potential sovereignty" and popular sovereignty in action. During periods in which popular sovereignty is not being exercised, the constitutional system stands as a "placeholder for our own future expression of popular sovereignty." (Whittington, 1999a: 133.)[42]

---

citizenry, and again, as these newly constituted citizens become the authors of the Constitution they inherit." (Norton, 1988: 465.)

[41] "When the Constitution speaks in the name of 'We The People' and specifies that 'the people' will ratify the document through special conventions held in each of the states, it designates its own authority and creates the people itself.... The people did not exist until they constituted themselves through the action of forming a constitution." (Whittington, 1999a: 145.)

[42] Whittington also describes a phenomenon of "partial" sovereignty, in which political actors engage in gap-filling or other measures necessary to maintain the system during periods of potential sovereignty. (Whittington, 1999a: 157–58.)

Both authors sharpen our understanding of popular sovereignty as self-authorship by distinguishing between moments of authorship and periods of operation by appealing to an idea of historical moments at which "the people," possessed of sovereignty-in-reserve, periodically and temporarily become "the People," or popular-sovereignty-in-action. There are parallels between this idea and Dicey's distinction between legal and political sovereignty. Dicey had assumed that legal sovereignty was permanently relinquished to Parliament, but that the people as electors retained political sovereignty. By contrast, these American writers come closer to Wilson's earlier conception of sovereignty as both legal and political authority that is granted to the institutions of government but which can be recalled by the People when it is needed.[43]

The idea that Ackerman and Whittington propose is that popular sovereignty after the formation of a constitutional order should be understood in terms of potential, rather than active, authority. There are moments at which the people assert their sovereign authority, but in the periods between those moments, sovereignty remains vested in juridical institutional arrangements defined by a constitution and expressed in a system of representative government.[44] The distinction is between popular-sovereignty-in-reserve and popular-sovereignty-in-action. The reference to representation

---

[43] Alexander Hamilton comes very close to an argument of the kind proposed by Whittington in his description of the role of the independent judiciary in *Federalist* 78. "[R]epublican government ... admits the right of the people to alter or abolish the established Constitution, whenever they find it inconsistent with their happiness, yet it is not to be inferred from this principle, that the representatives of the people, whenever a momentary inclination happens to lay hold of a majority of their constituents .... Until the people have, by some solemn and authoritative act, annulled or changed the established form, it is binding upon themselves collectively, as well as individually; and no presumption, or even knowledge, of their sentiments, can warrant their representatives in a departure from it, prior to such an act." (Madison, et. al., 1987: 440.)

[44] As Larry Kramer observes, Ackerman's idea of extra-Article V moments of constitutional amendment does not result in any significant increase in popular, majoritarian control over ordinary law-making. "Ackerman argues that the theory of popular sovereignty makes room for an amendment process outside Article V, but the stringent rules of recognition he imposes on that process make clear that it is meant to be limited and to fend off popular authority in day-to-day administration. (Indeed, Article V amendments are considerably easier to obtain than Ackerman's informal amendments, which is why there have been so many more of them.)" (Kramer, 2004: 961.)

is significant. Popular sovereignty is never absent; it is merely institutionally channeled during periods of what might be called ordinary constitutional self-rule, whereas during moments of popular-sovereignty-in-action, popular authority is reclaimed and exercised directly.

This is an argument that helps to flesh out Michelman's description of self-sovereignty as self-authorship, particularly if we incorporate the idea of "as if" consent that was mentioned earlier. The reader approaching the constitutional text "as if" she were its author is understood collectively as the people approaching the constitutional text "as if" it were the People, precisely because it can take on that role at (collective) will.[45] What connects the people to the People, as it connects reader/subject to author/authority, is the fact of shared language. The point of similarity between the approaches of Ackerman and Whittington lies in the fact that they posit a continuity of understanding not only between people and People, but also between people and people, across moments of the exercise of popular sovereignty.

Returning to the formulation that was found to be implicit in Locke's analyses, at the initial moment of constitutional consent, the preconstitutional sovereign People share a language in which to engage in the act of constitutional authorship, an act that in turn defines the terms of juridical discourse for the people until the next moment of constitutional creation. For the formation of Locke's commonwealth to be possible, it was necessary that its future citizens share conventional understandings of complex ideas in order for them to be able to generate an authority capable of redefining those

---

[45] The "as if" principle described here is related to the an observation that Samuel Freeman makes about Rawls' public reason. "For public reason can accommodate the principles of justice of most any comprehensive liberal doctrine (including Raz', Rawls believed), so long as it does not insist on what must be a perfectionist requirement, namely ... that citizens accept liberal principles for the right reasons according to the true comprehensive doctrine." In Freeman's view, this is the response to critics such as Raz who have asserted that Rawls' formulation does not do enough to exclude "false" political conceptions of justice from the public discourse. (Freeman, 2004: 2040.) Similarly, perhaps, the project of defining the conditions for legitimate constitutionalism requires an assumption that the participants in the discussion are interested in a constitutional regime, but the "as if" principle precludes the necessity of assuming or requiring unanimity as to the reasons for preferring that form of governance.

ideas by the act of lawmaking. In just the same way, for Whittington and Ackerman it seems necessary that people – at least those who are parties to the consensual exercise of sovereignty – must share a commitment to a mutually intelligible political language in order to create a sovereign author, to ensure mutual intelligibility during moments of the exercise of sovereign authorship.

The sharpest difference between Ackerman and Whittington is that Ackerman sees the exercise of direct popular sovereignty in informal as well as formal processes, so that periods in which significant changes occur in the dominant understandings of political and constitutional meaning stand as moments of constitutional transformation.[46] By contrast, Whittington emphasizes the significance of a written text, so that only a formal process of textual amendment stands as a genuine (and legitimate) exercise of direct popular sovereignty. The moments of political realignment and popular reconceptualization that Ackerman identifies, are for Whittington either less than transformative or else represent usurpations rather than legitimate moments of popular-sovereignty-in-action.[47] Whittington's insistence on formal amendment

[46] Ackerman, for example, reads Article V of the United States Constitution as non-exclusive, based on implied background principles of popular sovereignty. (Ackerman, 1998: 268–74.) Whittington rejects the idea of legitimate extra-Article V amendment as a violation of implied background principles of textual interpretation inherent in the adoption of a written constitution. "[O]nly a fixed text can be adequately ratified, that is, legislated into fundamental law. In order to create law, the legislating body must be able to demonstrate its will and have an instrument that its members can examine and to which they can eventually give their assent." (Whittington, 1999a: 55.)

[47] In part, this becomes a question about the authority of a constitutional system to limit the process of its own amendment. Akhil Reed Amar argues that if a majority of the people of the United States demand a constitutional convention, one must be held despite the supermajority requirements of Article V, on the grounds that majoritarian democracy is the basic legitimating principle of the Constitution itself. "The majoritarian Preamble and Article VII – literally the original Constitution's textual and performative alpha and omega – stand on an analytically higher plane than 'countermajoritarian' provisions such as those in Article III." (Amar, 1995: 109.) Amar points out that Article V nowhere indicates that its provisions provide the exclusive mechanisms for amendment, and speculates that it might be understood to identify the mechanism by which the government can amend the constitution without direct appeal to "We the People." (Amar, 1995: 90.) What Amar argues against is the proposition that there can be identifiable commitments that legitimately bind "we the People" with regard to the process of constitutional amendment. This argument is discussed further in Chapter 3.

processes centers on the significance of a written text, whereas Ackerman's formulation is closer to Dicey's reliance on "conventions" as well as constitutional law.

Whittington's focus on writing connects the idea of a prior commitment to constitutional language with the exercise of popular sovereignty-as-authorship. Consider, once again, the distinction between self-sovereignty and external sovereign rule. Self-sovereignty requires discourse in the form of dialogue. That is, so long as self-sovereignty applies to a group of individuals, no one can know with certainty at the outset how that sovereign authority will be wielded. Dialogue is required, but dialogue is never simply a matter of ascertaining mental states or preferences. Dialogue, instead, is a form of discourse in which the participants themselves undergo alteration, even if this occurs only in the form of reinforcement of existing beliefs,[48] or in a changed understanding of the degree to which one's beliefs are shared by others. In the exercise of self-sovereignty, the members of a political community engage in a dialogue from which they may emerge with a different understanding of relevant political facts.

When popular sovereignty is exercised in the form of lawmaking, moreover, there is another moment of potentially mutually transformative dialogue. As opinion-formation becomes collective will-formation, new avenues for delegitimation appear. New juridical facts come into existence, the degree of consistency between an individual's beliefs and the system of governance is altered one way or the other, and the terms of interaction among citizens, government actors, and non-juridical institutional actors are altered. Since the fundamental assumption is that the citizens are, collectively, the sovereign author, this dialogic interaction results in a transformation in the nature *of the sovereign itself*; the author changes its voice. All of these potentially transformative elements of self-sovereignty-through-dialogue precede the creation of the written

---

[48] Reinforcement of existing views, rather than critical assessment and reevaluation of ideas, is characteristic of the phenomenon that Cass Sunstein calls "enclave deliberation" and demonstrates the fallacy of assuming that more talking necessarily equates with more critical thinking, a phenomenon that has been demonstrated to be widespread in political discourse. (Sunstein, 2001: 15–40; Walsh, 2003.) This point is discussed further in Chapter 4.

constitutional text, and hence must be taken account of in explaining the exercise of sovereignty as authorship. By contrast, none of these elements of dialogic discourse was present in the older model of sovereignty-over-others, in which the discourse that occurs at the moment of lawmaking is monodirectional and does nothing to alter the reasoning process or relevant political understanding of the sovereign.

The distinction between the People in a moment of popular-sovereignty-in-action and the people during periods of ordinary sovereignty-in-reserve describes the exercise of popular sovereignty as a dialogue. The renewed focus on sovereign authority thus leads once again to a consideration of language as juridically generative as well as the medium for the exercise of juridical authority. Both halves of the author/authority dyad are involved here, but in contrast to Michelman's insistence on the necessity of a persisting national identity, Whittington's description of a sovereign People acting at moments of constitutional authorship points us away from an overt reliance on the anthropomorphic metaphor in favor of an understanding of sovereign authorship as a description of a social event.

To draw out the connection between the ideas of self-sovereignty and self-authorship, the relationship between sovereignty-in-action and sovereignty-in-reserve needs to be developed further. One way to proceed is to consider the implications of "self-authorship" and the constitutional text. The creation of a constitutional text points toward an obvious analogy: the capital-P People engaged in sovereignty-as-authorship are the authors who produce a text, whereas the small-p people governed by the regime established in that text are its readers. That is, if the exercise of self-sovereignty can be described as a moment of self-authorship, then in relation to the text that is authored, "the people" occupy the dual roles of author and reader.

The relation between a text, its author, and its reader are central to Will Harris' understanding of constitutional legitimacy. To describe this set of relations, Harris distinguishes between a small-c constitution and a capitalized Constitution, which are effectively the Lockean stages of legal society and constitutional commonwealth. "A small 'c' constitution is the political order erected in the midst of the metaphorical Hobbesian-like chaos.... A large 'C' Constitution is the codex that gives meaning to that order." (Harris, 1993: 107.) Similarly, Harris distinguishes between two subsequent moments of popular sovereignty in terms familiar from Locke. "[T]he two stages of the people as sovereign makers of the Constitution and the people as self-governing citizens within the [post-constitutional] polity – where their collective authorship at the constitutional stage institutionalizes action at the governmental stage on the basis of something less than the impossible whole." This understanding imposes restrictions on popular sovereignty that again echo Locke's limitations on legitimate government. "[A] people cannot be interpreted to have constructed a project that would contradict the conditions through which this institutionalization of themselves was brought about." (Harris, 1993: 77.)

The phrase "gives meaning to that order" points, once again, to a connection between the constitutional text and a preceding legal order, but far from appealing in Wilsonian fashion to a theory of consent by legal custom, Harris intends to use the subsequent distinction between the collective authors of the constitutional text and the people subsequently governed thereby to get at the necessary implications of the original act of authorship. Harris distinguishes between pre- and postconstitutional acts of popular sovereignty by using the terms "popular sovereign" to indicate the actively sovereign People as they appear before or at the moment of constitutional foundation, and "Constitutional People" to refer to the People that exercise popular sovereignty thereafter, as in a moment of constitutional amendment. "The popular sovereign is a wild and natural people, a potentially new constitution maker outside the bounds of the constitutional order. There may always be fair questions about whether the whole popular sovereign has acted, since wholeness and deliberateness are the necessary criteria for its unlimited power. These criteria alone identify the popular sovereign as such. In this guise, however, the constitution-making people may freely remanifest and rearticulate its political character in the world." (Harris, 1993: 202.) This is the stage of action that requires unanimous consent and, in turn, opens up a moment of near-limitless possibility in the form of sovereignty created but not yet exercised when law is suspended. But Harris, too, relies on "wholeness and deliberateness," a moment of preconstitutional unanimous consent that is required to account for the sovereign authority of a constitutional author.

By contrast, the postconstitutional people display the transformative effects of their own actions. "The Constitutional people has been domesticated and civilized to the Constitution. As individuals in the constitutional order, the text runs through their minds; it supplies the political categories of their thought. Collectively, this People's identity is codified by the text; its sovereignty is a function of the Constitution, created by it for its own enactment and sustenance. This People may be the author of the text, but it is also a textually bounded creature of its own constituent act." (Harris, 1993: 202–03.) There is an element of Dicey's irrevocability here in the transformative effects of the initial moment of constitutional foundation. For Harris, as for Whittington and Ackerman, the people retains the ability to reassert its sovereignty through acts of amendment or interpretation, but the text as it stands "supplies the political categories of their thought." The popular sovereignty that at one time gave rise to the authority to create a constitution has been supplanted by a "sovereignty [that] is a function of the Constitution." In return for this loss of "wild" and total freedom comes the possibility of legitimate action "at the governmental stage on the basis of something less than the impossible whole."

In perfect Lockean fashion, in other words, there is a progression of more and more formal and conventional exercises of power requiring less and less unanimity for their justification. Creating a sovereign author requires some kind of unanimous consent; once that act of creation is adequately justified, its subsequent actions – beginning with the creation of a formal constitutional order – can be legitimated on the basis of something less. The creation of that constitutional order, in turn, transforms the sovereign that created it, thus creating new criteria for sovereignty-in-action.

Like Michelman, Harris conceives of the popular sovereign as author, poised to become a Constitutional People by the act of putting pen to paper. But for Harris, the relationship between authorship and authority takes on an added dimension by virtue of the complex relationship between author and reader. A written text requires interpretation, so that the act of reading becomes "a continual process in which the words of the document and the activity of the polity are aligned with one another through methods that reconfirm the conditions of popular authorship and readability which give the constitutional order its validity." Unlike a speaking sovereign, a written text "designs" rather than "commands," and its readers "interpret" rather than "obey" its commands. As a result, that Constitution's authority depends on its "public legibility." (Harris, 1993: 13–14.)

The result of thinking about a constitution as an interpretable text is to alter the relation between constitution and Constitution, pre- and postconstitutional People, viewed not only as sovereign author but also as what might be called sovereign *reader*. The constitutional text contains a description of "the ideal public audience as sovereign," in the form of a concrete demonstration of the transformative effects of the moment of constitutional dialogue that is recorded in the text. "The ideal reader is the one that the text constructs as its citizen. But the ideal reader of the Constitution is also its author ... living in the world created by the meanings that arise under ths particular document must also involve a willingness to join in its authorship. for, as I have suggested, this particular verbal-political construction sustains the conditions of its ongoing authority from the capacity of its citizens to find meaning from it." (Harris, 1993: 34, 100.) A constitution, in this sense, contains a normative description of "constitutional citizenship," which "entails a disposition to interpret the constitutional polity in a way that can be commended to fellow citizens." A constitutional text is a commitment to a "political grammar, an authoritative framework for how to talk about and how to carry on politics." This is the "linguistic transaction at the heart of political organization." (Harris, 1993: 166, 47, 54.) "Within constitutionalism," writes Harris, "the sovereign acts of will and reason become the constitutional practices of writing and reading." (Harris, 1993: x.)

The constitutional text, in this view, is not a set of instructions, but rather an exemplar of discourse. "The written form of the Constitution is not connected with a notion of exhaustive and intentionalist specificity but serves as a kind of intellectually enforcing metaphor for the laying out of limiting boundaries on power in advance of its use." (Harris, 1993: 25.) Whereas a written order issued by a human sovereign to a subject exists in order to convey the particular desires of that sovereign, a text that expresses the will of a self-governing collective sovereign takes the form of a dialogue.

In this view, the text becomes not merely a set of propositions, but a set of propositional *forms*, a recording of popular-sovereignty-in-action itself rather than merely the product of that action. "In this regard, the Constitution-as-fundamental-law can best be conceived of as the interpretive ground for authoritative meanings to be methodically constructed in public." (Harris, 1993: ix, 2.) Consequently, the fact of the constitutional project implies a grounding meta-norm of "intelligibility." "What distinguishes public authority is not so much that it can legitimately monopolize violence, in Max Weber's formulation, but that it issues out of a connection between the part and the whole – a connection of 'authorship' and 'readability.'" For Harris, constitutional consent is the agreement to be bound by a particular set of rules for thinking constitutionally. "In some central senses, an effective Constitution must be a *constitution of thought* – that is, a Constitution must effectively constrain and direct ways of thinking, such that its authentic citizens think and enforce *constitution-thoughts* when they reason politically." (Harris, 1993: 96, 207.)

Harris arguably goes farther than he needs to when he invokes the idea of constitutional thought. Like Michelman, Harris recognizes that it is not necessary to assume that this describes a moment in historical time; what is required only is that there be consensus to act *as if* such a moment had existed. "But this story of origins can be ratified, from inside the enterprise, by accepting the logical consequences of this working fiction for the processes of interpretation .... Deriving meaning from the Constitution that can be commended to the common understanding of the ideal constitutional reader is the internal means of achieving an ongoing popular ratification." (Harris, 1993: 111.) That is, there is no need to require that citizens think in ways that satisfy the legitimating standards of the constitutional model, only that in a particular context we agree to *act as if* we have undertaken such an engagement in the public discussion of constitutional issues. Similarly, there is no obvious necessity for an idealized constitutional reader, only an idealized constitutional interlocutor. The underlying commitment that is required to fill the role of Wilson's initial covenant by consensus is not Harris' "constitution of thought," but rather merely a willingness to be bound by a set of constraints on the manner of dialogue and deliberation in the specific context of public constitutional debate.

At this point, after this excursion through a variety of theoretical treatments of the problem, new and old, we are ready to answer the question "Consent How?" directly. Prior to the moment of constitutional consent there must already be a People in place capable of generating a text that satisfies the requirements of public intelligibility, describes a political grammar, and defines practices of writing and reading. A People capable of generating such a constitutional text requires sovereignty, which can be legitimately achieved only through consent. In short, before we can accept a constitutional text as the product of popular sovereignty-in-action engaged in an act of self-authorship, there must be indicia of a prior moment of consent sufficient to establish the conditions necessary for that act. That prior moment of consent establishes the language of constitutional self-authorship; in Lockean terms, it is not possible to have a social contract without first sharing a language for the expression of the juridical concepts that are its subjects.

The consent to language is not an agreement to employ an existing legal language but to create a *constitutional* language. The act of creating a constitution is not simply the authorship of a text, nor the delegation over future language formation, it is itself the authorship of a new and different language. This is the ultimate consequence of Locke's realization that the constitution of a legal sovereign creates an authority over language; the self-constitution of a people as a constitutional sovereign creates authority over the creation of constitutional language.

We need not posit such a unanimous consent as an historical event preceding the adoption of a written constitutional text. Like Harris and Michelman, we can conceive of this condition of prior unanimous consent as the analytically necessary assumption contained in the proposition of a legitimate constitutional regime. Or the matter can be put in more behavioristic terms by saying that what is required is not unanimous actual consent to the creation of a new form of language, but rather unanimous consent to act as if we had all agreed to create this new form of language. That is to say, the prerequisite for a people's capacity to act as a sovereign constitutional author is the willingness to employ the constitutional language that is created in the text in future constitutional discussions.

In Locke's scheme, an initial moment of agreement to language opened the space for the constitution of a sovereign authority with the power to subsequently redefine that language. As noted earlier, the case that I am describing is in some ways the converse. The adoption of a constitutional language, whether prospectively by unanimous "as if" consent or retrospectively as a matter of analytical necessity, alters the discourse, thinking, and political grammar of the authors. Whereas Locke saw language creating a sovereign with authority over language, this model is closer to positing a sovereign using language to create a new form of sovereignty, and the capacity to use language in that way as the defining characteristic of constitutional sovereignty. Sovereignty thus finally escapes the anthropomorphic metaphor. In this argument, sovereignty identifies a set of discursive commitments shared among members of a community, not an "artificial person" ruling over the community's discourse.

But the role of sovereignty as a governing concept, in the form of sovereign People as collective author and constitutional people as ideal readers, is not yet exhausted. The idea of writing ourselves into existence requires us to think carefully about the peculiar form of writing that we are talking about. Jeb Rubenfeld uses the term "demo-graphy" to describe the idea of a constitutional text as an act of collective writing that alters our self-understanding. (Rubenfeld, 2001b: 213.) The idea of a people writing itself into existence involves a consciously self-referential enterprise. An analogous and related phenomenon might be a collective decision to reinterpret our shared history. Constitutional revision is prospective, of course, but the analogy points out the element of usurpation that, for example, Whittington sees in Ackerman's description of informal amendments. A revisionist view of history is unsettling because of the sense of usurpation that results from the absence of any clear legitimating principle that gives some set of actors the authority to tell us that what we believed before is wrong.[49]

---

[49] There may be exceptions. In 1988, during the period of Perestroika, the Gorbachev government at one point canceled all secondary school history examinations on the grounds that the history of the Soviet Union had been so badly distorted by generations of revision that no reliable text could be ascertained. A

I propose a different metaphor, that of "inscription."[50] Inscription is a form of writing that alters the contours of the object written upon, such that subsequent ordinary writings must accommodate the effects of that inscription. What is "inscribed" in the creation of a written constitution is not a set of policy outcomes, however; these are the outcomes of ordinary writing, which can be erased or written over. What is inscribed in the terms of a constitutional text is the language of deliberation, a specialized language by means of which those outcomes may be legitimated or delegitimated, a language that is itself legitimated by the authority of the sovereign to engage in that act of inscription.

Constitutionally inscribed language does for the popular sovereign – the People – what Hobbes argued ordinary language does for the human mind. Language organizes our perceptions and interests into coherent trains of thought that can be expressed discursively in mutually comprehensible signs. The inscribed rules of constitutionalism organize the perceptions and interests of the self-sovereign people in just the same way, rendering them articulable in juridical language; the commitment to that form of articulation is the necessary precondition for constitutional consent. As we conceive of that act of collective self-authorship, the terms of that language are "inscribed" not only in the text, but in ourselves. Constitutionalism, after all, is not merely a mode of governance, it is a mode of thinking about governance.

In describing something called constitutional "language" I have in mind nothing more than a simple and formal understanding of

committee headed by Roy Medvedev was formed to create a new, authoritative and government-sanctioned version of Soviet historiography. In that peculiar case, to the extent that the government was recognized as legitimately sovereign – a question to which the answer was given not long thereafter – the New Soviet History might conceivably have had a claim to legitimate authority. The story was reported in an article by Esther Fein in the *New York Times* on May 31, 1988, A1.

[50] Ann Norton also uses the term "inscription," but with a somewhat different set of consequences. For Norton, the act of constitution-writing is "inscription" because of the actions of the authorial people upon the text, rather than vice versa. "In this use of the material, rather than the ideal, qualities of writing the people inscribe upon the text, and hence in their own nationality, an acknowledgment of the importance of writing to their constitution.... They include in the inscription a sign that they do so mindfully, in full recognition of the power of inscription to transform identity." (Norton, 1988: 459–60.)

the term. In Ferdinand de Saussure's classic formulation, a language is simply "a system of signs that express ideas," bound by a governing set of grammatical rules. (Saussure, 1966: 16, 134.) Like any other language, constitutional discourse requires both a grammar and a set of signs.[51] A grammar is a set of rules for the formulation of valid propositions, and a system of signs is the the set of elements that can be deployed in the process of that formulation. Together, a grammar and a set of signs make up a language. Applying these concepts to the argument thus far leads to the proposition that legitimate constitutional consent is initially made possible by the acceptance of a constitutional grammar.[52] The moment of popular-sovereignty-in-action is the moment of popular consent to be bound by the constraining rules of that constitutional grammar in the subsequent formulation of propositions out of the set of constitutional signs. Sovereignty is not authority over language; it is rather authority exercised *as* language, the creation of an artificial

[51] I use the term "constitutional grammar" here in a way that is different from Phillip Bobbitt's use of the same term. Bobbitt identifies six "modalities" of constitutional argument, which he characterizes as textual, historical, structural, doctrinal, prudential, and ethical. (Bobbitt, 1982: 12–22.) These modalities define "the grammar of law, that system of logical constraints that the practices of legal activities have developed in our particular culture." (Bobbitt, 1982: 24.) In H. Jefferson Powell's apt description, Bobbitt's rules of constitutional grammar are "second-order descriptions of how one goes about doing constitutional law, just as the rules of grammar are second-order descriptions of the way in which those competent in the language speak and write." (Powell, 1994: 1740.) The difference between Bobbitt's and my own use of the term "constitutional grammar" is that Bobbitt seeks to identify informal conventions of usage that have developed through practice, whereas I am attempting to identify structural features of the source text itself as the source of constraints on the formulation of valid constitutional propositions. In Saussurian terms, I am looking to the *langue* rather than the *parole* of constitutional discourse for the source of constitutional grammar. (See discussion, Chapter 3.)

[52] Bobbitt argues that the creation of the American Constitution entailed the imposition of a system of grammatical rules for the formulation of specifically constitutional arguments onto an existing language system of common law. (Bobbitt, 1991: 5.) The difficulty is that this leaves the legitimacy of the constitutional regime dependent on the successful legitimation of the earlier system of law. "[A]lthough a general theory of constitutional law may appear to establish the legitimacy of certain kinds of arguments ... it is in fact the other way round. It is because we are already committed to the force of an appeal to text that such an argument can be used in support of a court's role." (Bobbitt, 1982: 5.) In the terms that I have used here, Bobbitt's argument, and others like it, conflate the separate questions of "Consent How?" and "Consent to What?"

collective person who is both sovereign author and sovereign reader. The constitutional text demonstrates rather than articulates the rules of constitutional grammar. It stands as a foundational and exemplar text for a specialized mode of discourse.

In this chapter, I have presented an argument that a commitment to the creation of constitutional language provides the necessary conditions for the exercise of constitutional self-sovereignty. But to be an adequate description of the formation of a constitutional order by consent, the metaphor of inscription and the idea of constitutional language must not only identify conditions sufficient for constitutional consent, they must identify conditions sufficient for *binding* constitutional consent.

How can the self-sovereign People's commitment to constitutional language be made binding into its future? Even if a meaningful description of consent can be arrived at, how can that moment of consent create a "sovereign" capable of legitimately binding future actors who were not personal participants in the processes creating the sovereign entity in the first place, and who will not be direct participants in the process of lawmaking thereafter?[53] This last question becomes an inquiry into the possibility of reconciling democratic and constitutionalist principles. If the fundamental principle of democracy is self-sovereignty, how can a moment of constitutional creation be justified in light of the fact that the existence of a constitutional order limits the exercise of that sovereignty? The task of the next chapter is to explain how the creation of constitutional language can be understood to result in a set of legitimately binding precommitments to employ that language in subsequent constitutional discourse.

---

[53] In a federal system, such as that of the European Union, one solution is to treat the terms of the supranational constitution as part of a system of international law to which the member states have bound themselves by acts of their own, internal sovereignty. As a solution to the problem of defining conditions for constitutional legitimacy, however, the recommendation of a federalist system governed by norms of international law begs the relevant question. The legitimacy of the member states' actions in binding themselves and their citizens to membership in the federal entity requires explanation; insofar as these states are constitutional, the search for that explanation effectively reopens the entire discussion since the legitimacy of each member state's own constitutional regime must be independently demonstrated. (Verhoeven, 2003: 31–32.) The difficulty becomes particularly acute in cases where member states themselves are themselves already federations. (Kokott, 1999.)

3

Constitutional Language and the Possibility of Binding Commitments

At this point in the argument, we are presented with two fundamental propositions. First, that the initial commitment is to the creation of a language, and, second, that the commitment to constitutional language binds ourselves and future actors to employ that language for purposes of constitutional discourse. But the idea of a binding commitment to employ constitutional language raises the problem of precommitment. How can we justify asserting that a commitment entered into long ago continues to bind actors today facing situations that were not contemplated at the earlier time? To get at that question, some further reflections on the relationship between constitutional language and the constitutional text are required.

Chapter 2 considered various challenges to the basic model of Lockean constitutionalism, in particular the idea that constitutional legitimacy can be grounded in a demonstration of sovereignty created by consent. These objections were arrayed around a traditional understanding of the sovereign as lawgiver, based on the adoption of an anthropomorphic metaphor of the state, that continues to play a prominent role in modern discussions of sovereignty and its relationship to the problem of precommitment.[1] In response, an

[1] Among authors whose arguments will be addressed in this chapter, for example, Jon Elster finds the possibility of binding precommittments essentially by adopting a version of the eighteenth century anthropomorphic version of sovereignty; Jeremy Waldron denies the possibility of such a commitment on the grounds that he cannot

examination of the idea of constitutional authorship and its relation to self-sovereignty, suggested a more subtle description in which self-sovereignty emerged as the authority to engage in collective self-authorship. The question of under what conditions constitutional consent is possible ("Consent How?") therefore became the question of the conditions under which a people can exercise self-sovereignty as self-authorship. In the tradition of Lockean constitutionalism, this inquiry led to the question of what prior moments of consent must have occurred, and on what basis we can reasonably assert their existence.

The beginning of an answer was reached with the adoption of the metaphor of "inscription," describing a form of writing that permanently alters the surface on which subsequent, ordinary writing takes place. As for what was to be inscribed, this was described as the terms of a constitutional language, its grammar and its system of signs. The conclusion, then, was that the conditions that are required for the act of constitutional self-authorship are a prior commitment to the creation of a constitutional language. But a commitment to a constitutional language is only a sensible answer to the problem of defining self-sovereignty if the rules and elements of that language are not themselves subject to being overwritten by subsequent acts of collective decision making. This is the problem of precommitment applied to a theory of constitutional language.

There are some obvious qualifications that have to be added to the phrase "not themselves subject to being overwritten," especially in the context of a written constitutional text. Since the constitutional text has been described as the exemplar of a system of language, alterations to that text have the capacity to change the language of its writing. But texts may be amended. The phrase "not subject to being overwritten" therefore requires the addition of the

---

detect the presence of such a sovereign in action; and Frank Michelman and William Harris, in different ways, continue to assure us of the continuing validity of a written constitution by virtue of the location of sovereignty in the authority of the author. (Elster, 2000; Waldron, 2001; Michelman, 2001.) The anthropomorphic metaphor persists in European as well as in Anglo-American writing. Venter, for example, asserts that his theory of legitimation by ongoing practice "must not be understood to be a rationalised theory of popular sovereignty, but must be understood in terms of the nature of the state as a juristic person composed of all the citizens of the state." (Venter, 1999: 14.)

words "except insofar as the constitutional text itself establishes the possibility of its amendment." That move, however, merely pushes the question to a different level, as justifying a set of restrictive rules governing the process of textual amendment is a classic pre-commitment problem.[2] Where a supermajority is required to amend a constitutional text, for example, that requirement is itself a precommitment that limits the ability of future persons – whether conceived of as our future selves or future others (perhaps our children) – to determine the course of their society.

The issues raised by the existence of rules restricting the process of textual amendment are complicated by the fact that there may not be agreement as to when a change rises to the level of "amendment," and thus triggers the procedural mechanism out-lined in the constitutional text in the first place.[3] For example, a judicial interpretation that radically alters the understood meaning of the text may give rise to accusations of *de facto* amendment out-side the scope of the prescribed procedures, with the converse implication that the existence of amendment procedures creates a binding precommitment of judicial restraint.[4] By the same token,

---

[2] See, for example, David Dow, 1990, arguing that democracy and supermajority provisions are contrary principles, but that maintaining contrary principles is inherent in the nature of constitutional government; Elai Katz, 1996, arguing that supermajority requirements reflect commitments to higher values than those of democratic self-governance.

[3] This argument may be couched in terms of the meaning of "amendment," so that the use of that term in a constitutional text is taken to imply a substantive limitation on the scope of permissible alterations. Walter Murphy makes an argument of this form with respect to the German Constitution, distinguishing between "material change" and "supplementation" as his defining categories. (Murphy, 1980: 754–57.) Sotirios Barber makes the same argument in the American context, appealing to commonsense notions of the meaning of the terms involved. (Barber, 1984: 43.) Both of these arguments are quoted by Sanford Levinson in an essay proposing that the division between "amendment" and "interpretation" cannot be defined in terms of formal criteria, but insisting that the distinction between the two is necessary for the maintenance of a meaningful constitutional rhetoric. (Levinson, 1995: 33.)

[4] This was Robert Bork's argument in *The Tempting of America* with respect to the actions of the New Deal Supreme Court. (Bork, 1990: 215.) Despite his apparent belief that these (and other) decisions were illegitimate, however, Bork refrains from counseling their reversal on the grounds that the stability of the system of constitutional rules is a higher concern than the desire to restore the authority of Article V. It is somewhat difficult to make sense of this latter argument. As Sanford Levinson observes, "[u]nless we reduce Bork's argument to the rankest kind of

the determination that an act of ordinary lawmaking is unconstitutional can be understood either as the conclusion that lawmakers have stepped outside the realm of constitutional language or, alternatively, that such a law constitutes a *de facto* attempt by lawmakers to amend the constitutional text without meeting the appropriate procedural requirements.[5]

A different version of the same observation concerns the limitations of permissible substantive amendments, rather than the amendment procedure. The argument is sometimes made that certain kinds of changes to a constitutional system are so inconsistent with the previously established elements of that system as to be impermissible short of an outright replacement of the regime. In other words, without necessarily doubting the popular right of revolution, the argument is that so long as the existing constitutional regime is retained, "the people" are constrained from going too far in altering constitutional principles.[6] The result is a category

---

prudentialism ... it must be the case that he accepts, whatever his strong desires to do otherwise, the fundamentals of Ackerman's theory. These are (1) that there indeed have been constitutional amendments besides those comprising the numbered textual additions and (2) that there is a set of political practices, perhaps including sheer reliance, that can legitimate these non-Article V amendments...." (Levinson, 1995: 35–6).

[5] In a remarkable case in 1990, the California Supreme Court struck down a referendum proposition on the grounds that it constituted an effective amendment that had not been enacted in accordance with the procedural requirements of Article XVIII of the California Constitution, which provides that the state's constitution may be "amended" by initiative, but that a constitutional convention is required for "revision." The initiative proposition at issue would have altered section 24 of Article I of the California Constitution "to provide that certain enumerated criminal law rights ... shall not be construed to afford greater rights to criminal or juvenile defendants than afforded by the federal Constitution." "In effect," according to the court's ruling, "new article I, section 24, would substantially alter the substance and integrity of the state Constitution as a document of independent force and effect." As a result the provision of the initiative constituted a "revision" rather than an "amendment," and consequently could only be validly enacted by a constitutional convention. *Raven v. Deukmejian*, 52 Cal. 3d 336, 352–53 (1990).

[6] Referring to the possibility of constitutional amendments that effect a systematic transformation of the system of government, Walter Murphy asks, "*May* a people who accepted constitutional democracy democratically or constitutionally authorize such a political transformation?" (Murphy, 1995: 175.) Murphy proposes that amendments "must always be reasonably designed to protect the basic goals of constitutionalism" or else they go beyond the scope of permissible amendment. (Murphy, 1995: 179–80.)

of substantively unconstitutional constitutional amendment.[7] Insofar as a change, or at least a sufficiently radical change, in the constitutional text may be understood to have the consequence of altering the signs or even the grammar of constitutional language – the Fourteenth Amendment to the United States Constitution is a strong candidate for such a description – the possibility of amendment presents the possibility of undoing and remaking the moment of constitutional consent that the amendment process itself relies upon for its legitimacy.

And there is yet another complication that arises once one recognizes that possibility of amendment if one wishes to ground legitimacy in the content of a constitution as well as in the conditions of its making. To permit amendment is to concede the possibility of imperfection, and consequently the possibility that the current constitution is flawed, which in turn raises the possibility that those flaws are of a nature or extent that they threaten the claim to legitimacy of the constitutional regime. At a minimum, including the possibility of amendment in a constitutional text emphasizes the point that the legitimacy of that text must rest on some prior point of extratextual agreement, what was described earlier as "consent to consent" to constitutional self-rule, rather than solely on an evaluation of the constitutional text. Otherwise, there is no obvious way to avoid the invocation of an infinite progression toward an ever-receding vision of imagined future legitimacy, the flip side of the danger of an endless journey into the past in search of an originary moment of justification. Just as sovereignty was required to avoid falling into infinite regress, precommitment is required if legitimacy is ever to be assured in a moment of the living present.

The introduction of the text and the possibility of its amendment into the discussion requires a consideration of the critically important distinction between commitment to constitutional language and

---

[7] Dow presents an argument of this form to the effect that democratic majoritarianism must be understood to give way to commitments to moral principles. Dow argues that the assertion that precomittments that constrain the amendment process present a challenge to principles of democracy are based on a failure to recognize the constitutional regime as a system of "higher law." (Dow, 1995: 121, 130.) As noted earlier, for the purposes of this book's minimalist approach to the question of defining conditions of constitutional possibility, an appeal to higher law is highly problematic.

disputes over the correct or ideal mode of constitutional interpretation. Here, the model of a formal language system that has
already been employed provides some assistance. Saussure distinguished between *langue* and *parole* to capture the distinction
between the elements of an established language and the statements
into which those elements are combined in practice. *Langue* ("language") refers to a formal system of signs and rules of grammar,
while *parole* ("speech") refers to the ways in which that system is
employed in practice to formulate statements. As a result, *langue*
occurs at the level of social practice rather than individual behavior.
"For language is not complete in any speaker; it exists perfectly only
within a collectivity." The "execution" of language in *parole*, by
contrast, is individual. "[E]xecution is never carried out by the collectivity. Execution is always individual, and the individual is always
its master."(Saussure, 1966: 13–14.) The fit between *langue* and
parole is never more than approximate. *Parole* is ever-changing,
idiosyncratic, and inconsistent even within a given moment of time,
while *langue* changes only over time, and aspires to coherence,
consistency, and analytical rigor.

As a first cut at applying this distinction to constitutional language, we can conceive of a *langue* of constitutional discourse that
provides the materials and rules for the construction of constitutional arguments, and the *parole* of constitutional discourse as the set
of arguments that are articulated in that discourse, paralleling
Duncan Kennedy's use of *langue* and *parole* to describe the relation
between legal rules and legal arguments. (Kennedy: 2001, 1178.) In
a system that includes a written constitution, the text of that document comprises the *langue* of constitutional discourse, and modes of
constitutional argument concerning the meaning of that text constitute the system's *parole*. Modes of constitutional interpretation,
and arguments about different interpretive approaches, are properly elements of the *parole* rather than the *langue* of constitutional
discourse, different ways of speaking the same language rather than
entirely separate discourses.

Constitutional language thus begins with an act of differentiation
among forms of language, a move that presupposes the prior
existence of a shared juridical *parole* from which a constitutional
langue can be constructed. Thereafter, constitutional *parole* emerges

through the effort to apply the terms of constitutional discourse to new situations.

This account follows the Lockean developmental pattern, and connects the theory of constitutional language to a general understanding among linguistic and literary theorists that differentiation is the first step in the construction of meaning.[8] But the direct application of theories of language and literature to the study of constitutional language is problematic.[9] Constitutional language is the purely artificial product of a political act, which is why its legitimacy is an issue in the first place, and why sovereignty and precommitment are required if that legitimacy is to be maintained. None of this is true of ordinary language, or of literature (though whether similar observations can be made about other forms of discourse, such as the language of science, is an open question). The self-conscious fact of artifice carried out by an exercise of political authority backed by coercive force sets the situation of constitutional language apart from those other forms of discourse. In a discussion of constitutional language, therefore, the artificial simplicity that is involved in imposing a sharp distinction between *langue* and *parole* on the infinitely more complex experience of juridical discourse is

---

[8] As Jonathan Culler nicely puts it, "[i]f a cave man is successfully to inaugurate language by making a special grunt signify 'food,' we must suppose that the grunt is already distinguished from other grunts and that the world has already been divided into the categories 'food' and 'non-food.'" (Culler, 1982: 96.)

[9] The application of linguistic and literary theories to the study of law yields rich and important insights, as in James Boyd White's description of the task of a lawyer. "[I]n her conversations with her client, from the beginning, her task is to help him tell his story, both in his own language and in the languages into which she will translate it ... The client is thus led to learn something of the language of the law; at the same time, the lawyer must learn something of the language of the client." (White, 1990: 261.) White's description, like Culler's analysis, suggest that the sharp distinction between *langue* and *parole* is artificial, and fails to capture the nuances of what White calls "the literary view of language." (White, 1990: 81.) But there may be good reasons for hesitating to apply the lessons of ordinary language and literature to law, and *a fortiori* to constitutions. As numerous writers have pointed out, the presence of the coercive authority of the state, the inherently conflictual nature of legal discourse, and the need for reasonably clear rules of procedure all militate in favor of maintaining an artificially sharp differentiation between what I am calling constitutional *langue* and constitutional *parole*. (Kay, 2001: 28; Finn, 2001: 41.) As Robert Cover puts it, "constitutional law is ... more fundamentally connected to the war than it is to the poetry." (Cover, 1986: 816.)

justified if the maintenance of that distinction is shown to be a necessary element of the legitimacy of a constitutional regime.

Read as an argument from necessity, this observation answers the problem of precommitment by turning it around. "*If* we are committed to constitutional self-rule," one might argue, "then we *must* accept an artificial system of constitutional language as a matter of analytical necessity." But to provide an argument for sufficiency, as in the assertion that a commitment to constitutional language can be the basis for the subsequent legitimation of a constitutional regime, more is required. The characterization of constitutional language is not yet sufficient to demonstrate how a Lockean prior commitment to constitutional language secures the legitimacy of the system against the dangers of divisive disagreement over modes of interpretation. How, in other words, is the legitimacy of *langue* secured against the consequences of conflicting claims of legitimacy at the level of *parole*, particularly once we recognize the necessity of a shared juridical form of discourse as a prior condition for the creation of a constitutional language?

In deploying the Sassurian distinction between levels of language, Kennedy draws on the idea of a "language-within-a-language" found in the writings of Roland Barthes.[10] In the language of architecture, for example, a roof is an element of a valid "proposition" (a building), but in the language-within-a-language of architecture, a particular kind of roof indicates that the building in question is a pagoda or a hunting lodge, and in the process says something about the persons who occupy the building and the uses to which it will be put. (Kennedy, 2001: 1177–78.)[11] In the same way, debates over modes of interpreting constitutional language can

---

[10] "For example, to be 'dressed' (to make an utterance in the language of fashion), one must combine a set of elements into a costume according to set rules (like the rules for uttering a sentence). The costume then expresses, according to another set of rules, a meaning or set of meanings about the wearer in relation to other wearers.... We can do the same kind of analysis of architecture (a roof is a necessary element in the combination of materials called a house, but a particular roof may connote a hunting lodge and therefore that the owner is an aristocrat)." (Kennedy, 2001: 1177–78.)

[11] There is also the question of perspective. A curved roof identifies a pagoda only if we begin with the assumption that roofs are "normally" straight. (Li, 1993.) Working from this observation, in fact, it is possible to conceive of a "shape grammar" that defines the horizons of architectural "language" by delimiting the

be thought of as examples of the operations of competing languages-within-the-language of constitutional authority. Differences over the proper mode of interpretation need not imperil the legitimacy of the constitutional system so long as they do not reach the prior agreement to the employment of constitutional language.

This discussion of language and interpretation is a step removed from more traditional discussions of constitutional interpretation. Phillip Bobbitt, for example, identifies six modes of constitutional interpretation – textual, historical, doctrinal, prudential, structural, and ethical – and proposes that the legitimacy of a constitutional argument depends on the claim that it is phrased in one of these acceptable modes. (Bobbitt, 1991: 11–22.)[12] The pluralism of Bobbitt's approach to constitutional interpretation is attractive, as is his acknowledgment of what I will later refer to as the requirement of "exclusivity" (see discussion, Chapter 4). The difficulty at the initial stage remains grounding the commitment to those six modes of interpretation, and the exclusion of others, in the absence of a theoretical basis for asserting the legitimacy of the language on which those grammatical rules operate. This is the problem in response to which the Lockean move of grounding constitutional legitimacy in a prior commitment is required. The separation of constitutional language from the language-within-a-language of constitutional interpretation is necessary to avoid the danger that differences over *parole* will ultimately dissolve the authority of a common *langue*. The emphasis on law keeping language the same sets it apart from literature or speech, where language is molded to permit the author to articulate novel ideas or experiences. In law, by contrast, ideas and experiences are made to fit an existing system of juridical language.[13] And whereas ordinary legal language evolves

---

range of well-formed propositions in the same way that constitutional grammar is presented in relation to the discourse of constitutionalism. (Li, 2002.)

[12] "There is no constitutional legal argument outside these modalities. Outside these forms, a proposition about the US constitution can be a fact, or be elegant, or be amusing or even poetic, and although such assessments exist as legal statements in some possible legal world, they are not actualized in our legal world." (Bobbitt, 1991: 22.) Conversely, "[s]o long as a particular modality or modalities are adhered to – so long as the arguments are consistent with their premises, and they are not contradictory – the decision is legitimate" (Bobbitt, 1991: 114.)

[13] James Boyd White cites a speech in which Lysias argued before an Athenian Court that where the meanings of words used in laws have changed, it is the meanings

over time through legal practice, a constitutional text fixes a set of signs. It is in language that constitutionalism first demonstrates its inherently conservative and formalistic aspects.

These reflections on the character of constitutional language identify the precommitment that is required to ground a constitutional regime's claim to legitimacy. To reiterate, the condition that is necessary for the creation of a legitimate constitutional regime is a prior commitment to the creation of constitutional *langue* and the differentiation of that *langue* from the practices of constitutional *parole*. Or, to be more precise, a prior commitment to conduct ourselves *as if* we willingly shared that linguistic commitment. This prior commitment can be thought of either as an historical moment of consensus, or as an implication of the decision to engage in constitution making that is analytically necessary whether the participants in that decision are aware of that fact or not. Either way, locating the initial commitment at the level of the creation of a language means that the act of constitutional self-authorship defines the discursive parameters of the process of deliberation. Thereafter, the practice of deliberation according to the inscribed rules of constitutional grammar, employing the system of constitutional signs, must itself be accepted as capable of producing juridical authority.

The consideration of precommitment, then, comes back to the two distinct moments of consent that were identified at the outset. The consent to constitutional language involves precommitment to a set of discursive norms and a theory of self-government, and thereafter the moment of constitutional consent demonstrates the exercise of sovereignty over the deployment of juridical language.

A thought exercise demonstrates that this description is much simpler than it may appear. Consider two hypothetical cases in

---

that those words had when they were incorporated into laws that should govern their interpretation. "Lysias is here arguing that interpretation is a kind of translation.... And what Lysias claims for the Greeks is also true for us as well, that the law written at one time must be interpreted in another, when not only social and cultural circumstances but even more explicitly the language itself has undergone a change." (White, 1990: 240.) White is here using "translation" to describe the recovery of meaning across time; I use the same metaphor to refer to a present practice of converting propositions made in ordinary speech into legally or constitutionally cognizable statements.

which one or the other of the elements mentioned in the previous paragraph is lacking. A group of friends and I might get together and have a discussion about the ideal form of government, at the end of which we might agree on a set of fundamental principles for the formal institutionalization of collective action. Discursive grounding norms are not absent in such a situation; they may even be more developed than those described earlier as constitutional grammar, since as members of a community of like-minded persons we are free both to draw on vocabularies alien to public constitutionalism and to restrict the permissible scope of the utilization of that vocabulary more narrowly than would be acceptable in public deliberation. Such rules are likely to be informal, and enforced by social responses rather than recorded and administered in a pre-designed fashion. We might even engage in this mental exercise in a casual setting involving the consumption of beer, and have quasi-formal rules ("the first person who employs an argument that can be identified as having appeared in the writings of Hobbes must purchase the next pitcher"). Why not? It is well understood that we have no capability of producing juridical authority; there is no sense in which we conceive of our discussion as an exercise of sovereignty.[14]

Alternatively, imagine an attempt at consensual design of constitutional principles by a governing council that involves representatives of both the Taliban and the Society for Secular Humanism, backed by the full military might of a powerful state. Any agreement reached between persons speaking such entirely disparate languages can only be deemed "legitimate" in terms of each group's internal vocabulary; there is no conceivable common language of legitimation. As a result, any resultant constitutional order would not be grounded in any legitimacy, only a strategically advantageous outcome. Jürgen Habermas calls the deliberations that lead to such arrangements "bargaining," and suggests that in a discourse-theoretic sense they are not communicative at all.

---

[14] Frederick Schauer propounds a similar thought experiment concerning a group of friends who produce a document that they call "the Constitution of the United States." As Schauer writes, "[o]nly one of these 'Constitutions' would be the Constitution of the United States, because only one of these documents would have been accepted, socially and politically, by the people of the United States as their Constitution." (Schauer, 1994: 52.)

But to the extent that the bargaining process itself is conceived of by the participants as legitimate, an appeal to some underlying normative consensus is reintroduced into the equation. As Habermas observes, "the procedural conditions under which actual compromises enjoy the presumption of fairness must be justified in moral discourses." (Habermas, 1999: 167.) The implication of the second hypothetical case is not, therefore, that constitutional consent among persons who hold drastically different worldviews is impossible. In concrete terms, could Taliban representatives, consistent with their principles, accept as "legitimate" a constitutional order that did not make their particular version of Shari'ah binding law? If the answer is "yes," it must be on the basis of a separation between private/internal legitimating claims, such as religious faith, and a different set of public legitimating claims such as conditions of fair bargaining. In the case of the all-consuming ideology of the Taliban, such a principle of separation may be impossible, but the rest of us, to one degree or another, make this distinction between personal and political norms all the time. In other words, the necessary presupposition for legitimacy as a social fact in the face of irreducible value pluralism is a consensus on the normative scope of constitutional language. Value pluralism is consistent with legitimation by consent, but only insofar as it occurs against such a background consensus on *discursive* norms. Consensus concerning the scope of discursive grounding norms defines the scope of subsequent legitimate constitutional consent.

By way of contrast, consider the role that an appeal to "the public good" plays in Locke's discussion of executive power. Locke proposed that, in practice, the lawmaking authority of the legislature is supplemented by the executive's prerogative to act in the public good, "without the prescription of the law, and sometimes even against it." The prerogative power is exercised because "in some governments, the law-making power is not always in being," and because it is impossible to devise laws to deal with every situation that might arise. (Locke, 1988: 375.) Locke's appeal to the public good was simply a matter of employing the concepts with which he was familiar from the English tradition of common law,[15] but the

---

[15] *Salus populi suprema lex est* ("the good of the people is the supreme law") is one of the oldest and most basic propositions of common law. Since ancient times, this

source of this key organizing norm is less important than its consequences. For Locke, from the perspective of an evaluation of substantive political action, the relevant question was whether the public good was being served. From the discursive perspective of a theory of constitutional grammar and inscription, however, the issue is one of language, so that the relevant question becomes whether participants are articulating their positions *in terms of* an appeal to the public good.

The idea of a requirement that a particular form of constitutional language be employed when making constitutional arguments – the idea that *parole* is restricted by *langue* – is not far from Rawls' idea of "public reasons," but there are distinct differences. Rawls appeals to an assumed possibility of using the social process of dialogue and interaction to find reasons "in terms each could reasonably expect that others might endorse as consistent with their freedom and equality." (Rawls, 1996: 218.) The result is a "paradox of public reason," in that when citizens want to discuss the most important and far-reaching of all issues, they are simultaneously encouraged to limit the range of ideas or modes of expression that they bring to bear to the question. For Rawls, the resolution of that paradox lies in the assumption that within a liberal, pluralistic society, the differing worldviews of citizens will overlap at the points where fundamental values of tolerance, civility, and equality are located. In this situation, says Rawls, constitutional rule and the commitment to public reason become acceptable and plausible outcomes.[16] Rawls does not propose that such consensus must expand to all moral questions, nor that there be absolutely unanimity. What is required is overlapping consensus on "constitutional essentials," and a sufficient degree of consensus to ensure social stability. (Rawls, 1996: 137.)

---

principle has been employed to justify local regulation over the use of private property, along with a wide range of other regulations. (Novak, 1996; Stoner, 2003: 127–31.) For an examination of the development of this concept in American law in the mid-nineteenth century, see Schweber, 2004.

[16] "[W]hen the political conception is supported by an overlapping consensus of reasonable comprehensive doctrines, the paradox of public reason disappears.... citizens affirm the ideal of public reason, not as a result of political compromise, as in a modus vivendi, but from within their own reasonable doctrines." (Rawls, 1996: 218.)

A great deal of weight is placed, in Rawls' argument, on the evident truth that a given regime is "reasonable."[17] There is a double or triple remove here from actual consensus. Citizens are presumed to be willing to endorse constitutional principles on the sole ground that they are "reasonable and rational"; citizens are presumed to be universally willing to accept constitutional terms based on their accord with those principles. We do not care whether any group of citizens is in fact actually willing to endorse particular constitutional terms; it is only required that someone else (who? operating from what set of presumptions?) can reasonably expect that citizens might be expected to endorse a constitutional provision based on their presumed acceptance of the principle that reasonableness is the relevant criterion for acceptability. Finally, "our" exercise of power is presumed to be in accordance with the constitutional provisions at issue.[18]

This seems a remarkably and unnecessarily complex formulation, driven by the desire to prove that a certain constitutional order is the only possible reasonable outcome of rigorous philosophical analysis. By contrast, the theory that I am proposing has far more modest aims. In this argument, I have asserted only that a universal willingness to commit ourselves to the use of constitutional language is the condition of possibility for legitimate constitutional rule. (The question of whether such rule can itself be shown to be the *necessary* conclusion of any sufficiently rigorous exploration of political discourse is left to more philosophically adventurous writers.) Furthermore, there is no requirement for this theory that all speakers

[17] "[O]ur exercise of political power is proper and hence justifiable only when it is exercised in accordance with a constitution the essentials of which all citizens may reasonably be expected to endorse in the light of principles and ideals acceptable to them as reasonable and rational." (Rawls, 1996: 217.)

[18] A related problem is that of filling in the content of moral provisions that are identified in this "overlapping consensus." In *Justice as Fairness: A Restatement*, published in 2001, Rawls reiterates the primacy of equal liberties, but then makes "fair equality of opportunity" a shared norm superior to fairness in the distribution of wealth, thus moving further toward a proceduralist conception of legitimacy. The problem becomes reconciling fair equality of opportunity with the "difference principle," the principle that any institutionalized inequality must redound to the benefit of the least privileged members of society in order to be legitimate. Faced with the possibility – not to say inevitability – of conflict between these two principles, it is not clear that enough overlapping consensus survives to secure legitimacy for the constitutional order. (Rawls, 2001: 61–80.)

find certain substantive positions to be consistent with their desire for equal freedom and equality, nor even that all citizens be assumed to share that desire. What is required is a common willingness, on the basis of whatever subjective motivations, to translate private thoughts and opinions into an appropriate, artificial language of constitutional discourse.

Does this imply, as Bobbitt's argument might suggest, that any statement that has been translated into constitutional language is therefore a legitimate basis for constitutional rule? Not necessarily. The question of the limits and requirements of the substantive content of constitutional language will be addressed later (see Chapter 5). For the moment, it suffices to observe that for a constitutional proposition to be legitimate, it is minimally necessary that it be translated into the appropriate constitutional language, with the obvious consequence that statements that cannot be articulated in that language can never be the basis for a legitimate constitutional argument, let alone a constitutional rule. A proposition that cannot be composed out of the elements of a system of constitutional signs in accordance with that system's rules of constitutional grammar can never be an element of constitutional discourse.

Having identified the nature of the precommitment to constitutional language, we can now return to the question of how that commitment can be understood as binding. Even if we accept the legitimacy of the idea that a group of actors can commit themselves to employ constitutional language in the act of constitution-making, how can that commitment legitimately legitimately bind those same actors at a later time, or future actors – perhaps of generations yet unborn – to continue to do so?

It should be noted that a constitutional precommitment need not take the form of a concrete norm enforceable by the exercise of coercive authority. The existence of a textual precommitment provides a powerful rhetorical device to counter arguments in favor of a contrary practice.[19] Insofar as such a strategy is sufficiently effective

---

[19] For an argument of this form with regard to the rules of presidential succession, see Amar, 1995b. Gregory Magarian cites Amar's argument as an example of precommitment that extends to the effects of certain classes of federal legislation, exemplified by the Religious Freedom Restoration Act. (Magarian, 2001: 1919, n. 66.)

to be considered a case of precommitment at all,[20] however, it requires justification in precisely the same manner as an enforceable constitutional provision if the nexus between modes of discourse and constitutional legitimation is to be maintained at all.

To make an argument in favor of precommitments, we need to be able to establish two things: identity between our present and future collective selves, and a justification for the idea of binding commitments *per se*. These may be thought of as the minimum necessary conditions of possibility for the exercise of self-sovereignty. In the absence of such sovereignty, there is no obvious basis by which consent can legitimate constraints on *future* action, even if we accept a nearly metaphysical unity of collective identity across time or embrace a full-fledged version of the anthropomorphic metaphor. Extending a collective commitment past the next moment of time involves the assertion of sovereignty over persons in the future. The metaphor of inscription was intended to demonstrate that those future persons are our future selves, rather than others, in order to preserve the notion of self-sovereignty rather than reverting to a model of sovereignty-over-others. But this only reformulates the question. Why do our present selves have authority to bind our future selves? or, alternatively, why should we presently conceive of ourselves as bound by commitments entered into in the past?

THE PROBLEM OF PRECOMMITMENT

In trying to answer the question of how we might conceive of constitutional precommitments as legitimately binding on a democratic self-sovereign people, one obvious question is why a democratic self-sovereign people might *want* such binding precommitments to

---

[20] In his 1984 text, Elster listed five criteria for "precommitment." First, the precommitment must "bind oneself … to carry out a certain decision at time t_1 in order to increase the probability that one will carry out another decision at time t_2." Second, "if the act at the earlier time has the effect of inducing a change in the set of options that will be available at the later time, then this does not count as binding oneself if the new feasible set includes the old one." Third, "the effect of carrying out the decision at t_1 must be to set up some causal process in the external world." Fourth, "the resistance against carrying out the decision in t_1 must be smaller than the resistance that would have opposed the carrying out of the decision at t_2 had the decision at t_1 not intervened." Finally, "the act of binding oneself must be an act of commission, not of omission." (Elster, 1984: 39–46.)

exist. After all, if that question can be answered, then the argument of legitimation by consent comes into play.

The usual response to the question is that constraints on future decision making are a function of present calculation of interest. Arguments in favor of precommitment, in fact, often focus on the idea that it is a desirable and useful form of decision making that gives effect to the democratic process.[21] The question remains whether there is a version of our understanding of sovereignty that is capable of supplying legitimating principles for binding commitments that extend across time, and especially across generations. Even if an appeal to consent can justify precommitment as a form of democratic decision making in the present, after all, something more than simple present consent is required to explain how constitutional constraints that extend to future generations are consistent with democratic principles. Nonetheless, the arguments in favor of binding constitutional precommitments ordinarily begin with an argument to the effect that there are good reasons to want them to be there.

Arguments against the practice of precommitment focus more clearly on the question of legitimacy by arguing that if the purpose of precommitments is to make democratic self-rule effective, then the principles that justify the means are incommensurate with those that legitimate the stated end. In the American context, these arguments most often arise in the context of debates about the proper role of the judiciary in relation to that of the legislatures, exemplified by Larry Kramer's appeal to principles of "popular constitutionalism." (Kramer, 2004.) This institutional division, however, is grounded in the deeper problem of justifying the idea of

---

[21] Magarian summarizes the prudential arguments in favor of precommitments nicely: "As a methodology for protecting high-priority societal values, precommitment has several advantages. First, by definition, precommitment increases the likelihood that a normative preference expressed at t1 will be honored at t2. Second, precommitment reduces the unpredictability and instability of legal rules and regimes, because it gives the people some assurance that the entrenched policy goal will survive some measure of variation in other governing priorities. Third, precommitment decreases the costs of legislative decisionmaking by answering in one motion a question that might recur in a variety of societal controversies." (Magarian, 2001: 1919.)

constitutional precommitment in the first instance.[22] The authority of "the people" to create binding precommitments depends, ultimately, on either an appeal to moral certainties – which is, itself, essentially antidemocratic – or else a theoretical explanation for the idea of popular sovereignty extending across time.

One of the earliest theories explaining the legitimacy of constitutional precommitment appears in Alexander Hamilton's argument in favor of an independent judiciary in *Federalist* 78. "This independence of the judges is equally requisite to guard the Constitution and the rights of individuals from the effects of those ill humors, which the arts of designing men, or the influence of particular conjunctures, sometimes disseminate among the people themselves, and which ... occasion dangerous innovations in the government, and serious oppressions of the minor party in the community." (Madison, et al., 1987: 440.) In 1893, Supreme Court Justice David Brewer described a constitution as "rules proscribed by Philip sober to control Philip drunk" (Brewer, 1893: 428), a characterization that was picked by Charles McIlwain in 1940. "We must leave open the possibility of an appeal from the people drunk to the people sober, if individual and minority rights are to be protected in the periods of excitement and hysteria from which we unfortunately are not immune." (McIlwain, 1940: 22.)[23] Friedrich Hayek

---

[22] Michael Klarman presents a strongly worded version of this argument in his description of transgenerational precommitments as "inconsistent with the democratic principle that present majorities rule themselves. " (Klarman, 1997: 507–08.) Klarman asserts that judicial constitutional review can be justified in majoritarian terms only if the process is guided by a norm of anti-entrenchment in response to the recognition that legislatures, left alone, are prone to engage in anti-majoritarian strategies of their own. In this way, the division between legislatures and courts ceases to reflect a distinction between constitutional and ordinary law, and rather becomes a division of responsibilities within a system of majoritarian decision making. "The task of courts in this context would be to mimic what the legislature would have done had its decisionmaking not been distorted by entrenchment motives." (Klarman, 1997: 530.)

[23] The reference to an appeal from the people drunk to the people sober has its roots in a traditional story about Philip of Macedon. In 1844, Ralph Waldo Emerson used the story to make a general point about the variability of human judgment. "I resist the skepticism of our education, and of our educated men. I do not believe that the differences of opinion and character in men are organic. I do not recognize, beside the class of the good and the wise, a permanent class of skeptics, or a class of conservatives, or of malignants, or of materialists. I do not believe in two classes. You remember the story of the poor woman who importuned King

made the same point when he observed that "all men are apt...to violate rules of conduct which they would nevertheless wish to see generally observed." (Hayek, 1978: 179.)[24]

The idea of a self-aware moral lapse, like self-induced drunkenness, explains the decision to engage in collective precommitments that constrain future decision making as an act of prudential self-restraint. Another famous version of the metaphor is that of Ulysses ordering his men to bind him to the mast lest he fall prey to the song of the Sirens. Jon Elster has argued that decision making of that kind is basic to ordering human conduct, so much so that he has coined the term "constraint theory" to identify a study of this particular model of decision-making. (Elster, 1984.)

Jeremy Waldron, however, argues that both the metaphors of Ulysses bound to the mast and "the People drunk/ the People sober" are inapposite to a discussion of constitution-making. Waldron challenges the idea that binding constitutional precommittment can be explained by these analogies on the grounds that each of these involves an assumption that the decision maker at the moment of self-constraint is more rational – literally better in possession of his or her powers of reason – than the same decision-maker at a foreseeable future date. This is precisely correct. Writers such as McIlwain and Hayek applaud the conservative influence of constitutional rules that prevent the passions of a moment, inspired by the proverbial madness of crowds, from altering a system of rules that are conceived of as the product of long, careful, and calm deliberation, while Elster assumes that the imposition of constraints

---

Philip of Macedon to grant her justice, which Philip refused: the woman exclaimed, 'I appeal': the king, astonished, asked to whom she appealed: the woman replied, 'from Philip drunk to Philip sober.'" The written text of Emerson's address is in the public domain, and is available on the World Wide Web at: http://rwe.org/works/Essays-2nd_Series_9_New_England_Reformers.htm.

[24] Hayek argues that the model went further than a simple concern for the state of one's own future sobriety. "The problem is not merely one of giving time for passions to cool, though this on occasion may be very important, as that of taking into account man's general inability to consider explicitly all the probable effects of a particular measure." For Hayek, both the recognition of our own inability to see the long term and the element of mutuality ensure that individual self-interest can be made to serve the cause of preserving constitutional precommitments. "It need hardly be pointed out that a constitutional system does not involve an absolute limitation of the will of the people but merely a subordination of immediate objectives to long-term ones." (Hayek, 1978: 180.)

is justified by an estimation that in the long run this will result in outcomes that we will find more desirable. But, Waldron asks, what is the basis for that assumption? Particularly, what is the basis for the assumption that the "passions" of a later time are less reliable than the foresight of the present?[25]

In place of the figure of Ulysses, Waldron proposes "Bridget." Bridget is a person who, in a moment of religious fervor, locks sacrilegious texts into her library and asks a friend to hold the key. Like Ulysses or Peter, Bridget urges her friend not to return the key, no matter how earnestly she may request it. Later, Bridget's religious beliefs undergo a change, and she no longer views the texts in the library as spiritually unwholesome, so she requests the return of the library key. Should her friend continue to refuse to return the key? The answer, obviously, is "no." The new Bridget, after all, is not a less rational, less self-controlled version of the previous Bridget; the new Bridget is a perfectly reasonable person who happens to feel differently than the old Bridget on an important question.

A key element of the Bridget scenario is the observation that "Bridget" at time 1 is different from "Bridget" at time 2 ("Bridget 1" and "Bridget 2.") To refuse to release the key to the library to Bridget 2 cannot be justified in terms of what Bridget 1 "really" wanted. It can only be a statement on our own part of what we think Bridget 2 ought to want.[26] Like the sailors confronted by Ulysses

---

[25] Elster argues that Waldron mistakes the nature of the argument by failing to consider a broader range of reasons for desiring precommitments. "[A]mong motives for precommitment he [Waldron] considers only the need to preempt passion, thus neglecting the desire to overcome partisan interest and time-inconsistency as well as the desire to promote efficiency. I imagine that Waldron, too, would be sympathetic to the propositions that incumbent government should not easily be able to change the rules of the political game in their favor, and that stability of the political framework is desirable ...." (Elster, 2000: 92, n. 8.) The latter example, of government officials changing the rules of politics in their favor, turns out upon examination to involve two different premises: that officials are changing the rules during their tenure, and that the new rules are less fairly competitive than the old ones. The appeal to an underlying norm of fairness, however, can be explained in terms of substantive moral principles rather than procedural precommitments, an argument with which Waldron would presumably be perfectly in sympathy.

[26] The distinction between what we think we want and what we believe we ought to want – or what we believe others ought to want – echoes Isaiah Berlin's famous

pleading to be released, "there is nothing we can do but make our own decision about whether or not to blindfold [sic] him." The problem, from a democratic perspective, is squaring this situation with an idea of self-rule. "At that stage we should stop justifying our decision by calling it a consummation of Ulysses' autonomy; the best we can now say on autonomy grounds is that we are acting, paternalistically, as Ulysses would have acted had he been lucid and in possession of full information." (Waldron, 2001: 281.) In other words, the enforcement of constitutional provisions limiting or burdening the processes of democratic decision making are nothing more than the imposition of constraints by one group against another achieved by force. Any perception that such constraints, or the exercise of such force, is legitimate is a matter of false consciousness on the part of those who are being paternalistically controlled.[27]

In practice, moreover, the force must be not merely potential, but immediate. Turning away from metaphors and to the actual subject of constitutional government, Waldron points out that the processes of decision making will always take place against a background of unliquidated disagreement between intrinsically reasonable positions. Thus it is a majority of a people, over objections, who make a Constitution; a majority of the members of a legislative body who, over objections, enact a law; and a majority of a court who, often

---

distinction between positive and negative liberty. (Berlin, 2002.) Berlin's solution of value pluralism sits uneasily with the idea of constitutional commitments, a point explored by Stanley Fish in an essay called "Liberalism Does Not Exist." (Fish, 1994: 134–40.)

[27] Akhil Reed Amar similarly concludes that principles of self-sovereignty preclude the legitimacy of precommitments that limit the amendment process, specifically including the supermajority requirements of Article V of the United States Constitution. "What does the act of constituting say and do – for it does by saying and says by doing – about the legal right of We the People to alter or abolish what We have legally ordained and established?" (Amar, 1995a: 92.) In an earlier article, however, Amar himself concedes that "not even popular sovereignty can avoid all forms of entrenchment," pointing to the prohibition on infringing the freedom of speech, requirements of deliberative decision-making as examples of provisions properly secured against alteration by the majority. In addition, Amar recognizes the need to "entrench" an entity capable of exercising sovereignty. "[T]he People in one generation must unavoidably entrench some definition of itself – for example, 'the sovereign People of Massachusetts' or 'the sovereign People of America.'" (Amar, 1988: 1074, 1076.) As Brett King observes, "[I]f these areas of the political process can be entrenched, why not others?" (King, 2000: 636–67.)

over objections, uphold the law or strike it down upon review. "I cannot restrain myself from saying that anyone who thinks a narrative like this is appropriately modeled by the story of Ulysses and the Sirens is an idiot. Ulysses is sure that he wants to listen but not respond to the Sirens' song; the people in our example are torn . . . . In the constitutional case we are almost always dealing with a society whose members disagree in principle and in detail, even in their 'calm' or 'lucid' moments, about what rights they have, how those rights are to be conceived of, and what weight they are to be given in relation to other values." (Waldron, 2001: 283.)[28]

The absence of unanimity, for Waldron, precludes consideration of constitutional constraints as anything other than the forcible coercion of minorities by a majority. Bridget was not more rational when she chose to lock the library door than she was later, when she desired to re-open it. She simply changed her mind. The same is true of a collective people whose views of what is desirable legislation may change over time. "A constitutional 'precommitment' in these circumstances is therefore not the triumph of preemptive rationality that it appears to be in the cases of Ulysses and the smoker and the drinker. It is rather the artificially sustained ascendancy of one view in the polity over other views while the complex moral issues between them remain unresolved." (Waldron, 2001: 283–84.)

Waldron's conclusion is that precommitment to decision-making processes that limit or burden changes to constitutional rules cannot

---

[28] Stephen Griffin makes the point that such unliquidated disagreements between reasonable positions will inevitably include disagreements about whether or not a particular proposed change triggers the prescribed amendment process. To the extent that the legitimacy of a constitution is presumed to rest on a unanimous understanding of its meaning – what Griffin calls "rule of law constitutionalism" – this means that in every case, the decision must be in favor of textual amendment. "Those who oppose any important policy change argue that it requires an amendment. Even if they are only a small minority, their demands must be satisfied. If it is not, the minority claims that the Constitution is being improperly amended through a controversial interpretation that has no legitimacy. This destroys rule-of-law constitutionalism because the point of the doctrine is to guarantee that everyone has the same understanding of what the Constitution means." Conversely, including every policy change in an amendment to the text means that the constitution "would increasingly resemble ordinary legislation and would simply reproduce the conflicts of day-to-day politics rather than restructure them." (Griffin, 1995: 43.)

be justified as an element of democratic self-rule. (Waldron, 2001: 287.) Others, making similar arguments against the legitimacy of precommitment, have pointed out that "the democratic objection" becomes even more forceful when we consider the possibility that a constitutional provision enforces an evil outcome on a majority that would otherwise be motivated to act in a morally superior way. The assumption, after all, that the mass of the people, acting democratically, would necessarily arrive at outcomes "worse" than those enshrined in a constitutional text is more often asserted as an axiom than defended as an empirical proposition. (Kramer, 2004; Tushnet, 2000.)[29] As Jack Balkin puts the question, "If the Constitution, or parts of it, permits or even requires great evils, why does it deserve our fidelity?" (Balkin, 1997: 1707.) Moreover, it is not only the contents of the text as a formal document that require justification, but the set of practices that have grown up around it.[30]

At this point, moral judgments such as those to which Balkin alludes become inextricable from the problem of legitimacy. Accepting that premise, Frank Michelman proposes that the

[29] As Larry Kramer points out, the phenomenon of mistrust is bipartisan. "From the right we get public choice, positive political theory, and law and economics: all centrally dedicated to explaining why democratic institutions are irrational and inefficient. Better the invisible hand of a market – decentralized, unselfconscious, uncoordinated – than a body in which deliberate choices about how to govern are made. From the left, we get 'deliberative democracy,' a philosophical school that emphasizes preconditions for legitimate rule, and that turns out to be mostly about deliberation and hardly at all about democracy. Popular rule is legitimate, we are told, only if certain stringent prerequisites are satisfied: prerequisites that it just so happens can be met only by small bodies far removed from direct popular control." (Kramer, 2004: 1004–05.) Kramer could also have pointed to attempts to use constitutional constraints to preserve or enforce moral standards on a presumptively immoral public, exemplified in support for a constitutional amendment prohibiting same-sex marriages.

[30] Balkin observes that the usual response to the problem of "constitutional evil" is to deny its possibility by asserting that only "incorrect" interpretations of the text lead to bad results. The problem with this argument, he asserts, is that it ignores the fact that constitutionalism is a description of a set of practices, and of ideas developed through practice, as well as a credal statement of abstract principles. "We cannot simply dismiss the argument that the Constitution does not deserve our respect because there is an ideal Constitution that does deserve it. That is because even though we can imagine ideal Constitutions, we are not in control of what the Constitution means.... The meaning of the Constitution is determined in large part by the social institutions and actors who create social meanings, including the judges who create doctrinal glosses." (Balkin, 1997: 1714.)

problem of legitimation is miscast. Rather than focus on principles of collective agreement to constitutional precommitment mechanisms, Michelman suggests, we ought to consider the idea of legitimacy in terms of the "moral warrant for collaboration in your country's networks of legal compulsion," a warrant he finds in each individual's independent conclusion that the system of laws in question is "respect-worthy." The determination of respect-worthiness requires an evaluation of "the government totality," "the entire aggregate of concrete political and legal institutions, practices, laws, and legal interpretations currently in force or occurrent in the country" (Michelman, 2003: 347), rather than the dominant theoretical ideas that are espoused in the process.

The process of evaluation begins with the Hobbesian recognition that unity is a desirable outcome. In Michelman's formulation, this observation is not a trump that silences moral consideration of governmental actions in an Hobbesian fashion. It only means that all things being equal we should want to find an existing governmental system to be legitimate rather than illegitimate. Thereafter, the question of legitimacy can be framed in terms of an individual's analysis of the respect-worthiness of the juridical system. "[O]ne would judge whether the total performance is good enough, on the whole, to be accepted considering the practical, imaginable alternatives. If one judged that it would be, say, foolhardy to answer this question with a 'no,' then, keeping Hobbes' thesis in mind, one might judge the governmental totality to be respect-worthy. Consequently, everyone would be justified in collaborating in the country's networks of inducement and, where needed, compulsion, of universal compliance with every law that issues from the system." (Michelman, 2003: 347–48.)

Michelman's formulation of the problem relocates the moral content of the assertion of legitimacy. In what he calls "Ida's way" (as opposed to those of Ulysses or Bridget), legitimacy requires neither a Rawlsian consensus on the identification of a list of substantive "constitutional essentials," nor unanimous acceptance of any particular principle. Instead, so long as each "Ida" is able to arrive at the conclusion that the governmental system is respect-worthy, there is a moral mandate for participation in the enforcement of the system of laws, regardless of whether different Idas have the same basis for their conclusion.[31]

To use the language that I have employed previously, "legitimate" in Michelman's argument means "there are sufficiently good reasons to act *as if* one agreed with the aggregate of the actions of the governmental system over a period of time." But for Michelman, that legitimacy applies to the "government totality" rather than to a constitutional text or set of legal principles. Along with a plurality of moral priors, Michelman argues that recognition of a plurality of focii – law, policy outcomes, constitutional principles – as the subject matters of moral judgment is a condition for plausibly persuasive theories of legitimation. This is the basis for distinguishing Ida's way from a Rawlsian "overlapping consensus." Rawls' focus on a legal/constitutional form of legitimating consensus implies the imposition of a level of precommitment to the meta-proposition that contractual, legalistic obligation is the basis for political legitimation in the first instance.[32] "Inevitably, reasonable disagreement is going to reach its tentacles into the system-constructions arrived at by sundry Idas all acting in the best of faith." (Michelman, 2003: 363.) "Obdurate disagreement" at the level of system construction, not merely policy outcomes, threatens the framework of the understanding on which the consensus would have to be based.

As a result, Michelman concludes that appeals to constitutionalism provide a weak response to Waldron's problem of unliquidated reasonable disagreement. Ida's focus on the totality of government action, by contrast, provides a broader basis for discussion.

---

[31] "Since their moral priors will differ, so will the systemic reconstructions they arrive at. And this is a political-moral advantage, not a disadvantage! The plurality of the reconstructions the Idas arrive at will be precisely geared to a convergence across their number of favorable judgments of respect-worthiness of their country's political "procedure" – which is exactly what political liberals are driving at." (Michelman, 2003: 364.)

[32] "In Rawls' principle ... the constitutional essentials serve as a kind of a political contract – the adequately described terms of which, one fears, will be either too thick or too thin to carry the weight of a political-liberal legitimation project." (Michelman, 2003: 364.)

The existent practice we call the governmental totality is real, no doubt, and so it is, on some level of possible description, the same for all participants. But there is no reason why every single participant cannot or should not perceive it differently and describe it differently and thereby accommodate the pull each reasonable participant will feel, for good reason, toward finding it respect-worthy. Chartres can be reported beautiful unanimously, by numerous, competent critics, all regarding it partially from their several, differing angles of view. And the case also quite possibly could be that Chartres truly is beautiful, although no one ever will see it "whole." (Michelman, 2003: 364–65.)[33]

Since recognition of the phenomenon of obdurate disagreement is what drives the project of liberal political legitimation in the first place, the move away from a constitutionalist justification for government is a step toward a plausible theory of legitimation sufficient to encompass participation in coercion.

The difficulty lies in translating Ida's justification for her participation in the system into a justification for the system's creation in the first place, and from there into a justification for the enactment of laws binding on Ida as well as on others. There may be an argument here for Ida's participation in the enforcement of laws, but is there an argument for why she, herself, should obey them? In the specific context of a constitutional regime, this is the point at which the problem of justifying precommitments becomes inescapable. At any given moment a group of Idas may find the government totality of their society to be sufficiently advantageous to justify their participation in its operations, but it is not easy to see how that translates into an obligation on their part to respect limitations on the process of altering their government should they reach a different conclusion. In a sense, Michelman's focus on the totality of government action puts too much weight on the question of legitimacy by removing the layer of constitutional mediation between moral principle and government practice, so that Ida's alternatives are either to accept the current government as legitimate or to reject it entirely.

---

[33] This is very similar to Cass Sunstein's idea of "incompletely theorized" constitutional decision making, discussed in Chapter 4, "a process by which people agree practicalities, on outcomes, despite disagreement or uncertainty about fundamental issues." (Sunstein, 2001:9.)

What is missing is the possibility of a morally critical standpoint within the system that does not require lawlessness as the only integral expression of obdurate, reasonable disagreement. To return to the terms developed in the discussion of Locke, what is missing is the possibility of layers of non-unanimous consent legitimated by a precedent consensus. The focus on individual moral judgments, in other words, neither extends to legitimate the practice of constitutional precommitment nor shields constitutional discourse from the corrosive effects of raw moralism. If the legitimation of collective action rests on nothing more than the coincidental agreement of individuals' preferences at a given moment in time, without any commitment to a theoretical connection between those separate approving attitudes, then there is nothing that binds the collectivity and no basis for the assertion that political legitimacy continues from one moment to the next.

In the absence of an articulable claim of obligation, in other words, there is nothing that prevents or that should even discourage Ida from withdrawing her participation in the system of legal rules at any moment, or withdrawing and returning as it suits her. There may be a moral argument for Ida's participation in the exercise of coercive authority over others, but there is no moral argument – not simply no persuasive argument, no argument at all – to justify that exercise to those upon whom it is being exercised, nor to an outside or future observer, nor to any two Idas who happen to be in a room at the same time. "Legitimacy" has become a purely subjective mental state that can, if one is so inclined, be taken to provide a moral argument for obeying the law. The inclination to translate satisfaction with the totality of government action into a moral argument to obey the law is itself entirely inexplicable.

Furthermore, even as a description of a purely subjective mental state, Michelman's description of Ida ignores her awareness of her nation's constitution, assuming it has one. Ida's evaluation of the society's juridical institutions as respect-worthy or not implicates her understanding of her constitution. As Ann Norton points out, consideration of institutions and practices, in a constitutional setting, necessarily points toward a critical evaluation of the degree to which the totality of governmental action accords with the dictates of the text, and from there to an evaluation of the text itself. "The realization of the text in the lives of the people – the establishment of the institutions it describes, accordance (and evasion) of the procedures it sets forth, the assimilation of its vision of the nation's ends as well as its design by the people and their posterity – reveals much that was hidden in the text .... The establishment, the realization in the material world, of each institution and set of procedures that the Constitution describes, gives each a certain independence. They can be observed apart from the text in which they remain embedded. The text's construction of the people, the nation, the government, is thus its own deconstruction." (Norton, 1988: 464.)[34]

From a constitutional perspective, then, we are compelled to return to the problem of precommitment and the focus on processes of decision making rather than policy outcomes. Waldron is absolutely right that any approach that focuses on decision-making processes leaves disagreements over complex moral issues unresolved, just as Balkin is clearly correct that there is something profoundly inadequate about an assumption that under any "correct" interpretation of the constitutional text, precommitments guarantee outcomes morally superior to those that would be obtained by the democratic process. Leaving complex moral issues unresolved and avoiding appeals to moral superiority were, of course, the point of adopting a minimalist approach in this discussion, to see whether it is possible to describe conditions for legitimate constitutional rule without assuming unanimity (on the part of others) or moral certainty (for ourselves) at the stage of considering substantive outcomes.

This was necessitated in the first instance, it will be remembered, by the fact that today we cannot rely on a Lockean moral certainty about the content of natural law. There is, in other words, no good answer to Balkin's objection unless one can find a basis to legitimate a constitutional regime somewhere other than moral preference. In

[34] Norton proposes that a constitution and the people to whom it belongs occupy a dialectical relationship of mutual construction, grounded in the privileged authority that is granted to writing in modern culture. "The dialectic of mutual construction that marks politics in constitutional regimes provides a text, or rather, two texts, of its own. It comprises two linked commentaries: the commentary on the text which may be read in the people that the text constructs, and the commentary on the people that may be read (though, I would argue, no more easily) in the text that they construct." (Norton, 1988: 464.)

that context, however, Waldron's argument takes on disturbing dimensions. Read strictly, the Bridget, story seems nearly nihilistic in its implications for political organization.[35] in the absence of moral consensus. In that situation, the story implies, no one can ever be held to any commitment of any kind except by force; therefore any discussion of autonomy, democracy, or self-rule is based on delusion.

Waldron's argument, indeed, seems to spell the end for any project of legitimate democratic rule, or even of law itself, unless one of two conditions pertains: (1) the citizens of the state in question never disagree about anything important, or (2) the law is conceived of in its most brutally positivistic form, so that there is no need for binding commitment, only the base fact of violence. Under the latter approach, the law is that which a sufficient number of persons with a sufficient number of weapons agree to impose on others. "Legitimacy," in this view, cannot survive the Bridget metaphor as a coherent concept, since at any moment one of those armed individuals might similarly change his or her mind about wanting to continue to enforce the "laws." At that point, the sole basis for the existence of a system of laws is presumably fear of the others; a Hobbesian view, indeed.

THE CASE FOR PRECOMMITMENT

Aside from the fact that the Bridget story seems to undercut the possibility of a legitimate constitutional regime in any but the most

---

[35] In fact, Waldron is willing to posit what he calls "cosmopolitan" universal moral principles. "I am not a relativist, I am a cosmopolitan. I believe some human rights standards can be arrived at and ought to be upheld and enforced everywhere in the world; but, just because relativism holds in general, we are not entitled to assume the right to enforce whatever tentative conclusions happen to have emerged from our particular inbred set of debates about politics or welfare or free speech or autonomy. Until those debates are enriched in the cosmopolitan way, with an awareness of what is to be said about them and around them and against them from the variety of cultural, religious, and ethical perspectives that there are in the world, they remain parochial." Waldron, 1999: 137–38.) This is an eloquent and compelling description of a grand project, but as the basis for legitimate constitution-making it runs into the problems described earlier: if constitutions cannot be made without agreement to universal moral principles, they will never exist. The minimalist approach of this study is an attempt to get out of the bind imposed by the invocation of moral certitude as the basis for legitimacy.

homogeneous societies, there are a few analytical problems with this argument. For one thing, the comparison between Bridget and Ulysses is inapt. Ulysses was able to order his sailors to bind him to the mast by virtue of the prior recognition of his legitimate authority as captain. In Bridget's case, by contrast, the two decisions are entirely personal and individual. Thus Ulysses' order, like Locke's moment of constitutional consent, takes place against a background of legitimating principles that apply to his action in giving the order in the first place. In this sense, the Ulysses story is considerably more applicable to a consideration of constitutional questions than is the story of Bridget.

Ultimately, in fact, it is unclear why the Bridget metaphor leads to different conclusions than does the Ulysses metaphor. In both cases, what Waldron finds missing is a way to decide whether at a given moment the individual speaker is in his "right mind," other than our own paternalistic notions of what we think he should want. To the extent that this objection defeats the metaphor, it applies equally to both. Waldron, indeed, warns against the dangers of metaphors based on individual decision making. "Clearly there are dangers in any simplistic analogy between the rational autonomy of individuals and the democratic governance of a community. The idea of a society binding itself against certain legislative acts in the future is problematic in cases where members disagree with one another about the need for such bonds." (Waldron, 2001: 285.) Ulysses and Bridget must have had mixed feelings about binding themselves by enlisting others to restrain them, and the conflict arises when they have changed their minds. In both cases, unless we have some basis for distinguishing between the consequences of different expressions of their will, there is no basis for explaining our reaction.

But is it really the case that we have no basis for distinguishing between our collective mental states at different times? That is, is it really the case that we can never distinguish ourselves drunk from ourselves sober? The library scenario involved in Bridget's story is arguably a distraction, since the equation of decision-making constraints with censorship is calculated to appeal to the very constitutional impulses that cause us to embrace the Ulysses metaphor in the first instance; locking libraries, after all, is precisely one of the steps that binding constitutional constraints are commonly designed to prevent. Liberal constitutional constraints such as rules against censorship may be viewed as compelling a degree of decisional autonomy from which it would be more comfortable to shrink. By contrast, it is presumably a matter of well-documented historical fact that at times of great turmoil, even democratic governments are prone to actions that are later viewed as excessive, and would have been viewed as excessive prior to the moment of crisis.[36] It is the retrospective judgment of our own excesses that leads us to adopt prospective constraints.[37]

What is missing from Waldron's description is the possibility of reflection over time. Bridget exists at time A and at time B; but in between, Bridget may reach conclusions about the trustworthiness or reasonableness of her own decision-making process. Indeed, even the library example is not unambiguous. Suppose that before ever giving the key to her library to a friend, Bridget may have found that reading certain books caused her to become suicidally depressed or psychotically enraged. Should schizophrenics whose condition is under control by the use of drugs be asked whether they want to continue taking those drugs? Rather than evidence of paternalism, what may be at work here is the inescapable necessity of a consensus about certain aspects of human nature as the precondition for legitimate constitutionalism. That is, the experience of history may persuade us at time 1 that our judgment in moments of crisis or arousal is not as trustworthy as our judgment in moments of calm reflection.[38] When such a moment of crisis arises, we may

---

[36] It is not clear that Waldron, in fact, accepts this historical judgment. See Waldron, 2001: 293, denying that minority groups have "reason to fear that any legislative consideration of the rules about free speech and loyal opposition would be a way of crushing or silencing dissent."

[37] Stephen Croly describes the majoritarian difficulty that arises when judges are elected. "The majoritarian difficulty asks not how unelected/unaccountable judges can be justified in a regime committed to democracy, but rather how elected/accountable judges can be justified in a regime committed to constitutionalism. For constitutionalism entails, among other important things, protection of the individual and of minorities from democratic governance over certain spheres. When those charged with checking the majority are themselves answerable to, and thus influenced by, the majority, the question arises how individual and minority protection is secured." (Croly, 1995: 694.)

[38] As Michael Dorf observes, "egregious affronts to democracy tend to be recognized as such only in retrospect." (Dorf, 2003: 895.) As a result, Dorf concludes that

regret the substantive outcome that is dictated by our prior commitment, but *still accept the assessment of our political capacities*.

Furthermore, this may be a conclusion that is reached not only on the basis of our self-perceived history, but also on our underlying notions of human nature, or simply on an understanding of the fact that political processes of decision making are by their nature predisposed to give more weight to some considerations than others. Echoing a classic argument of Alexander Bickel's, Frederick Schauer describes constitutional rules in terms of the difference between long- and short-term conceptions of collective welfare. Procedurally constraining precommitments, by this reasoning, "are about entrenching those long-term values – not necessarily the most important of our values – that are especially likely to be vulnerable in the short term. Constitutional entrenchment, therefore, creates second-order constraints on wise and well-meaning first-order decisions. Recognizing that good people doing good things often produce bad collective long-term consequences, or that good people doing good things often neglect nonconsequentialist values, the negative Constitution establishes a series of restrictions targeting good decisions as well as evil ones and functions as a check on even the most well-meaning democratic decision making." (Schauer, 2004: 1055; Bickel, 1986: 24.)

There need be no particular moral commitment to constitutional values over those favored by the system of majoritarian decision making, only a recognition that some values are better protected by the mechanism of precommitment than by being left to the democratic processes of government. "[T]he rights, values, and procedures protected by the negative Constitution are best understood not necessarily as the most important of our rights, and certainly not as a comprehensive statement of our most fundamental hopes and

---

constitutional process theories – those that focus solely on procedural norms – cannot adequately respond to the problem of indeterminacy. "Democratic procedures cannot be used to determine the ground rules for democracy because this only raises the question of how to validate the democratic procedures for determining the ground rules, and so on ad infinitum. But at the same time, extra-majoritarian mechanisms for setting the ground rules also cannot validate themselves; they will invariably rely on just the sort of controversial moral judgments (about democracy) that process theory is meant to avoid." (Dorf, 2003: 896.)

ideals, but as the interests that appear to be in the greatest jeopardy from strict first-order decision making." (Schauer, 2004: 1055–56.) So long as at time 2 we continue to share the belief that was prevalent at time 1 as to the relative fragility of values protected in our constitution, we have good reasons, unrelated to claims of moral superiority or inferior qualities of reason, to accept constitutional precommitments as legitimately binding.

A classic conundrum for social scientists (among whom I include historians) is whether the actions of a society or system in moments of crisis reveals the "true" nature of that society, or whether behavior in those moments constitute aberrations, a pair of positions associated with Antonio Gramsci and Max Weber, respectively.[39] Regardless of where we come down on that question, we might want to think that our true nature is revealed by our acts of reflection, and we may continue to hold that preference later, during moments of crisis, even when we bridle at the consequences. Thus we arrive once again at the proposition that substantive precommitments may be justifiable, both intra- and intergenerationally, if at any given moment of challenge we are able to identify a persistent commitment to a prior moment of consent.

In addition, as discussed earlier, in any constitutional system that allows for a process of amendment, constitutional precommitments would never absolutely preclude the kind of decision that either Ulysses or Bridget seeks to make (except in the most philosophical sense that a sufficiently drastic alteration might be argued to imply a "revision" rather than a mere "amendment"). Leaving aside questions of interpretation, at most an amendable constitution imposes procedural limitations that burden the decision-making process. Thus, rather than a preference for the judgment of an earlier generation, a precommitment to a supermajority requirement may be taken as a preference for extended deliberation where a certain class of questions is concerned. That preference seems more easily justifiable in terms of appeals to our understanding of our historical experience and human nature.

---

[39] The idea that a society reveals its true nature in moments of crisis is most famously associated with Antonio Gramsci. By contrast, the idea that the norms of a system are most clearly discerned from its ordinary operation is a basic element of the Weberian approach to sociological studies.

But a requirement of extended deliberation is not neutral as to outcome. Procedural burdens alter the costs of success and thus shift the fulcrum of decision making in the direction of conserving existing constitutional arrangements. Thus, whether or not super-majority requirements are ascribed to a desire to protect the status quo, their justification requires an adequate account both of the extra procedural burdens that are imposed and the diminished likelihood of change that they produce. How can each of these elements be illuminated by the analogies with which we have been working thus far?

The answer is, "not very well." The problem is that "Ulysses" and "Bridget" are both anthropomorphic metaphors that impose an artificial singularity of consciousness onto a process of group decision making. With regard to a requirement of extended deliberation, an analogy to burdensome amendment procedures would be if Ulysses said to his sailors, "do not release me from the mast unless I present a written statement of my reasons for changing my mind," or if Bridget told her friend, "do not return this key to me unless I bring you a certificate of religious conversion." But these analogies still apply only weakly because of the missing element of self-rule. Ulysses and Bridget each appear in the role of a ruler who exercises sovereignty over others; there is no obvious analogy to a self-sovereign people in either of their actions.

Moreover, both anecdotes employ a model of individual decision making that is arguably inadequate, in addition to the problems in the model of group decision making that is involved. Waldron's sharp contrast between majoritarian group decision making and individual preferences seems to imply that Ulysses and Bridget are each immune from the need to impose decisions over contrary reasonable arguments. But this is an extraordinarily thin psychological model. Whether our individual is Bridget or Ulysses, that person is likely to have conflicting desires inside his or her own head at any given moment. Part of Ulysses must fear hearing the Sirens' song, and part of Bridget is certainly tempted to read the forbidden books. The exercise of self-control, in any but the most rudimentary imaginable psychological model, involves leaving complex moral issues unresolved in a way that is not unrelated to the processes of collective action. Locke's commonwealth has a mind of its own – its legislative "soul" – with all the burdens of uncertainty and the necessity for decision making that that entails.

Waldron's argument, in other words, points to a problem inherent in reliance on the anthropomorphic metaphor itself, not only to a particular utilization of that metaphor. To make the analogy work, we would have to treat individual preference-formation as the product of an internal dialogue. Perhaps we might have Bridget say something on the order of "do not return the key to the library to me unless I can present a neural scan that demonstrates that I really, truly, deeply want it back." That is, a supermajority requirement means that a constitutional amendment reflects a majority will that is more widely held than that which is ordinarily involved in democratic decision making, the equivalent of a more strongly held preference in an individual. Viewed this way, the case of Bridget supports the case for precommitment. In the American Constitution, at least, supermajorities were required for the creation of constitutional obligations, whether originally or by amendment, as well as for their relaxation (as in the case of the Eighteenth and Twenty-First Amendments enacting and repealing Prohibition). What is being required, in other words, is that Bridget's decision to change her mind must be as heartfelt as her original decision was. This requirement is nothing more than a psychological way of describing sovereignty-in-action.

A different approach is to challenge the idea that rules such as supermajority requirements for constitutional amendments are properly understood as "constraints" on democracy at all. Stephen Holmes proposes that constitutional rules, which may make limit the scope of subsequent rule-making or make the amendment process laborious, should be understood as "constitutive" rather than as constraining. "While *regulative* rules (for instance, 'no smoking') govern preexistent activities, *constitutive* rules (for instance, 'bishops move diagonally') make a practice possible for the first time." A key element of Holmes' argument on this score is the suggestion that such rules should not be understood in comparison with an imagined less-restrictive alternative, but rather in comparison with the absence of any rule-bound mechanism for change at all. Holmes argues that this is particularly true of rules that define a mode of discourse. "Far from simply handcuffing people, linguistic rules allow interlocutors to do many things they would not otherwise have been able to do or even have thought of doing." (Holmes, 1995: 162.)

In part, it is recognition of the fact that actors in a system of decision making operate interact in complicated ways that motivated Holmes' suggestion that constitutional rules of decision making should be viewed as constitutive. "When a constituent assembly establishes a decision procedure, rather than restricting a preexistent will, it actually creates a framework in which the nation can for the first time, have a will." (Holmes, 1995: 164.) These discursive rules thus set the conditions for collective action, which is the basis for the existence of a communal identity as "a people."

This is a different kind of argument from the straightforward application of the Ulysses metaphor, as Waldron recognizes. In response to Holmes' argument, Waldron proposes not that the argument is senseless, but that it is unnecessary and unrealistic.

It is an attractive argument. And I believe it would amount to a compelling case for the enactment of constitutional constraints immune to subsequent legislative revision if either of two conditions were met. It would be compelling if the people were constant and unanimous in their conception of majority decision and of the conditions necessary for its effective realization. Or – even if they did not agree about those issues – it would be a compelling argument for constitutional constraints if minorities had reason to fear that any legislative consideration of the rules about free speech and loyal opposition would be a way of crushing or silencing dissent. In fact, neither condition is satisfied. (Waldron, 2001: 293.)

The first of these two possible conditions, "if the people were constant and unanimous in their conception of majority decision," may be taken as a description of the conditions under which the anthropomorphic metaphor is likely to have significant purchase.[40] The second, in turn, may be taken to be a description of the

---

[40] In an earlier version of his argument, Waldron took essentially the opposite tack, arguing that precisely because collective decision making is not analogous to individual reasoning, groups might be able to engage in binding precommitments so long as there is genuine agreement as to what counts as "drunk" or "sober" forms of reasoning. "However, if we find that their disagreement extends even to the question of what counts as panic or pathology in decision making – as it surely does in many areas of political controversy – then the precommitment model ... has to be put to one side." (Waldron, 1999: 561–62.)

possibility that Philip sober might need to watch out for Philip drunk. As noted earlier, the lessons of history suggest that this possibility is a real one.

But historical evidence aside, rules of discursive practice need not depend on either of the conditions that Waldron identifies unless they are accompanied by a commitment to the anthropomorphic metaphor of the state. The shift to discursive rather than substantive constraints implies a group decision-making process that already casts doubts on the direct application of analogies to either Ulysses or Bridget. Ulysses had the help of his sailors, to be sure, and Bridget's friend is the agent of enforcement, but they each form their decisions entirely alone.

By contrast, collective political action takes place communally, through a process of formally structured discourse. In the original story, it is only because Ulysses is the sovereign over others that we are trapped in the problem of describing his actions in terms of an anthropomorphic metaphor of self-rule. What if Ulysses and his sailors agree among themselves that it would be best if he were lashed to the mast? Perhaps they even agree first, unanimously, to decide the question by majority vote and then vote on the question. In that situation, there is no difficulty in understanding why the sailors need not heed Ulysses' pleas to be freed to join the Sirens, and there is no need to appeal to the sailors' presumed knowledge of Ulysses' impaired mental state. The strongest implication of Waldron's challenge to the Ulysses story may not be the desirability of adopting the nearly nihilistic implications of the Bridget story, but rather the need to move beyond reliance on an anthropomorphic metaphor of binding political commitment altogether.

In subsequent treatments of the question, Jon Elster has revised his argument as it applies to constitutional systems. The reason is that he has lost confidence in the anthropomorphic metaphor of the state. "As in many cases," he writes, "the transfer of concepts used to study individuals to the behavior of collectives, as if these were individuals writ large, can be very misleading." Referring to constitutions, specifically, rather than a model of an act of self-binding commitment by an individual, Elster points out that the applicable description often involves binding others; as a result, he concludes, "constitutions may not have the power to bind in the first place."

(Elster, 2000: 92.) "The individual who wants to bind himself can entrust his will to external institutions or forces, outside his control, that prevent him from changing his mind. But *there is nothing external to society*." (Elster, 2000: 95.)[41]

On the other hand, Elster remains willing to recognize some forms of precomittment.

> In a few cases, we may talk about self-binding in a literal sense, for instance if a constituent parliament unanimously decides to give up some of its powers to another branch of government. The idea also makes fairly literal sense if the majority in the constituent assembly also expects to be the majority in the first legislature .... Creating a constitution that binds future generations may also, in a looser sense, be seen as an act of self-binding, namely, if future political agents are expected to have the same reasons for wanting to be restricted as the founding generation. (Elster, 2000: 96.)

Each of these three examples of possible self-binding deserves consideration. It is not at all clear why a branch of government or parliament needs to unanimously agree to give up some of its powers, so long as there was a prior unanimous agreement to be bound by the acts of the majority. That is, throughout the discussion we have seen the necessity of locating unanimity – or a unanimous commitment to acting as if there were unanimity – at some point along the decision-making path. In Elster's term, this prior unanimous agreement provides the "upstream authority" (Elster, 2000: 106), that constrains subsequent decision-making, *if* a self-binding commitment is possible in the first place. In other words, if precommitments are possible at all, there is no obvious reason why unanimity should be required at a point as far "downstream" as parliamentary decision making.

---

[41] Elster does acknowledge the obvious exception: "international institutions with powers of enforcement such as the International Monetary Fund or the World Bank. And even these cannot make it impossible to act against a precommitment, only make it more costly to do so." (Elster, 2000: 95, emphasis in original.) As was noted in the previous chapter, however, the structure of an argument legitimating a constitutional regime is analytically closely related to the structure of an argument doing the same thing for a system of international law. As Joseph Weiler puts it: "The classical model of international law is a replication at the international level of a liberal theory of the state. The state is implicitly treated as the analogue, on the international level, to the individual within a domestic situation."(Weiler, 1999: 342.)

The second example was the one in which a current majority expects to be the majority in a future decision-making body. The idea, presumably, is that in that situation each individual member of the current assembly is capable of individual self-binding, and the identity between the members of the current and future majorities give those individual commitments the effect of a collective commitment in practice. It would be, in other words, *as if* there were such a thing as a collective precommittment, although in fact the mechanism of obligation would take the form of individually self-imposed constraints.

The third example involves continuity of principle. This is another version of Michelman's proposal in a 2001 essay (which is somewhat different from the argument in "Ida's Way," discussed earlier), that the current generation finds an earlier generation's principles to be consonant with its own, in an implicit process of evaluation that yields the result "yes, this seems to me to be a good idea, I will continue to be bound by this obligation." While Michelman did not dwell on the difference between individual and collective decision making, his description of a "prior determination of a thinker to think something" and his reliance on a psychological state of affirmation both imply an individual committed, in his words, "to thinking something." (Michelman, 2001: 91–2; see discussion, Chapter 2.) In practice, the last two alternatives would likely appear identical. That is, the assumption that continuity in personnel matters makes sense only if we assume that a certain critical number of those persons will retain the ideas they held earlier. And the sense of identification with the values and principles of an earlier generation of writers must not be different in kind from the sense of identity we have with our own earlier selves if we are to assume the possibility of a continuity in thought and norm between generations.

In each of these instances, what is required is the capacity for individuals to enter into precommitments, but the translation of that capacity to a form of constitutional commitment is disengaged from a reliance on the anthropomorphic metaphor of the state. The same is true of two other versions of effective precommitment that Elster identifies. One is the enlistment of others to bind us, as in the instance of Ulysses and his sailors. "[R]ather than throwing away the key an addict might entrust it to another person, who has the right and preferably the duty not to accede to requests to hand it back." Another is mutual self-binding. "Alcoholics Anonymous is based on the idea that the members help each other to abstain .... In collective improvisation, each musician constrains the contributions of the other. More generally, artistic conventions may be viewed in this perspective. It is because each artist expects others to respect the conventional laws of a genre that he is motivated to do so himself." (Elster, 2000: 276–77.) The reference to "conventions" is an allusion to an important distinction that we have seen earlier, between textual precommitments and binding norms that emerge from practice.[42] For Elster, the distinction between constraint and convention is one of time. "Constraints" are voluntarily undertaken, or imposed, at a given moment of decision making, whereas "convention" refers to "a set of expectations that the agent simply finds in existence." (Elster, 2000: 273.)

In practice, the cases of mutual self-binding and the enlistment of others converge. Consider the famous case of the Church of the Holy Sepulcher in Jerusalem. Authority over the church grounds is divided between four Christian churches – the Roman Catholic, Greek Orthodox, Armenian Orthodox, and Russian Orthodox – so the keys to the church, by common agreement, are entrusted to a local prominent Muslim family (the Nuseibeh family), who are presumed to have no ties to any of the four groups in particular. This example points out something important about both mutual self-binding and enlistment of others. First, the "others" who are enlisted are selected by virtue of some quality that we believe makes them more competent to carry out our wish to be constrained than we, ourselves, are likely to be. This may be assumed to be true by virtue of a device, such as the wax in the ears of Ulysses' sailors, or by virtue of the character of the person involved. The latter possibility

---

[42] Dicey identified, "constitutional conventions" as the highest order of law. Similarly, Frederick Schauer has argued that the fundamental norms of a constitutional system may inhere in a set of practices, rather than in a text, so that the test for the legitimacy of a textual provision is the degree to which it accords with an established practice. (Schauer, 1993.) This argument is closely akin to James Wilson's idea that the social acceptance of common-law practice provided the background of unanimity that made legitimate constitutional creation possible.

makes a second point: the subject matter of mutually binding conventions may be, precisely, the enlistment of other decision makers. The distinction between mutually binding constraints and enlistment of others becomes especially blurry when we consider the fact that the "others" who are enlisted are likely to be drawn from among the ranks of ourselves, defined along some other axis of identification such as fellow residents of Jerusalem, fellow persons of good will, fellow members of our social circle, or fellow citizens.

Read this way, Elster's argument supplies a plausible response to Waldron. Waldron's analogy of Bridget rather than Ulysses is sensible and even persuasive at the level of individual decision making, but Waldron seems here to be assuming that we are bound to base our constitutional order on a direct transferral of that model of individual decision making to an anthropomorphic model of government. Elster, instead, argues that the possibility of individual self-binding can result in a practice of collective self-binding without the necessity of an intervening collective agent. So Bridget might indeed change her mind about many things, but if she changes her mind about participation in the collective and mutual commitment to employ a certain model of decision making, she will cease to be recognizable to her fellows. She will have become the Lockean criminal. At that point, she has two choices: to enter into a state of war with her erstwhile fellow citizens, or to continue to act in accordance with her commitment to behave as if she still accepts the constraints to which she once agreed. In a constitutional system, unlike the case of car keys at a party, part of that constraint includes enabling mechanisms for raising the question of whether the content of constraints should be changed. Again, it is the commitment to constitutionalism, not to a constitutional outcome, that is required for constitutional consent. If there are enough Bridgets, to be sure, they may initiate rebellion or a war of secession, but at that point they have taken themselves out of the constitutional system, so the conditions of its constitutional foundation are no longer a relevant matter for their concern.

But as a response to the problem raised by Waldron, this argument remains incomplete. The remaining difficulty, as noted at the beginning of this chapter, is that neither Elster nor Waldron can find a "sovereign" in action. This is a problem, since up to this point the argument for constitutional legitimacy has relied on the idea of a self-sovereign people. We therefore need to return once more to a consideration of sovereignty and determine whether a different understanding of the concept that was proposed in Chapter 2 might be more helpful in explaining the possibility of binding pre-comittments by a self-sovereign people.

SOVEREIGNTY, COMMITMENT, AND CONSTRAINT

Expanding on the idea of constitutive rules, Stephen Holmes points out that the idea of a self-constraining sovereign has its roots in Bodin's description of effective exercise of authority. Bodin explicitly denied that a sovereign can ever be bound by any constraints, including those of his own devising, but he also suggested that sovereigns would find it useful to accept constraints voluntarily. As a result, constitutional rules that appear as limitations on the exercise of authority might better be understood as mechanisms for the effective exercise of power. "By allowing his power to be restricted in certain specific ways, a sovereign increases the likelihood of social compliance with his wishes. This bargain explains how he can become a sovereign in fact as well as in law. But how can the wielder of the highest authority be *compelled* to compel himself? . . . . [Bodin's] solution was to redescribe traditional limits on royal power as conditions for the successful exercise of royal power. Successful does not mean just, or right, or in accord with God's law, but simply capable of preventing civil war and keeping domestic peace . . . . Bodin sought to reconceptualize traditional restraints as *instruments* of princely authority." (Holmes, 1995: 110.)

Bodin's sovereign is strengthened, for example, by displacing judicial authority onto another branch of government. Such man-euvers become not merely desirable but necessary if one incorporates a kind of political natural law principle that all systems seek their own stability. In other words, in order to answer the question of why a sovereign should want to accept constraints on his power, Bodin turns to the point of agreement between Augustine and Machiavelli: Sovereigns seek conditions under which their states will survive the turning wheel of history. A desire for survival, it is implied, is hard-wired into the fact of social organization. By this reasoning, if an argument can be made that precommitments are *necessary* for the survival of a constitutional order, they may be adequately justified as an element of that order, an institutional expression of the discursive constraints of constitutional grammar. "Illicit when it involves a diminution of the crown's authority, monarchial self-binding is possible, permissible, and even obligatory when it maintains and increases royal power. If the king can retain and extend his authority only by tying his own hands, then tie his hands he must." (Holmes, 1995: 114.) This, says Holmes, was Madison's insight about a formal constitution: that it could become "an instrument of, not an obstacle to, government." "An inherited constitution can institutionalize as well as stabilize democracy.... Precommitment is justified because it does not enslave but rather enfranchises future generations." (Holmes, 1995: 152–3.)

Applied to a case of self-sovereignty, however, Bodin's arguments appear more as policy prescriptions, or even as a matter of political necessity, than as binding obligations, since there is no one standing outside the People to whom an obligation to preserve authority can be owed. What makes a precommitment obligatory, rather than merely desirable? Something more is required to explain why constraints on the exercise of popular sovereignty are consistent with democracy than the observation that they may be useful to preserve the stability of the political process.

Holmes attempts to supply that something more in two ways. First, he invokes Locke's argument of tacit consent by the acceptance of benefits. Applied across generations, this becomes an argument about inheritance, an argument that works only insofar as inheritance is widespread. "[I]f bequests alone justify the obedience of successor generations, inheritable property must become widely diffused as quickly as possible," since the claim to legitimacy by government, in Locke's words, "necessarily supposes and requires, that the People should have property, without which they must be suppos'd to lose that by entering into society, which was the end for which they entered into it." (Holmes, 1995: 149, 150; Locke, 1988: 360.)

Stabilization of procedural rules – or grammatical principles – is a bequest that yields multiple benefits. For example, an investment-driven capitalist economy depends on stable political expectations.

"[G]eneral uncertainty [will] discourage every useful effort of steady industry pursued under the sanction of existing laws." (*Federalist* 43.) Other benefits include avoiding distractions. In response to Jefferson's fear of "the dead hand of the past," Holmes observes, Madison invoked the necessity for stable political institutions in order that private parties might be able to pursue their interests. "If the ground rules were placed beyond easy reach, by contrast, aggrieved parties would be encouraged to husband their resources. Citizens would benefit from having their hands tied in this regard: by avoiding a wasteful struggle over abstract rules, they could achieve more of their concrete aims." (Holmes, 1995: 154.) In a system in which the people have the capacity to alter the rules, the choice not to do so constitutes tacit consent to the receipt of the benefit of stability, and hence to the prior commitments that make those benefits possible.

A second source for the obligatory force of precommitment is simply the inescapability of constraint. This is as true of someone engaged in creating a constitution as it is true of everyone. "A constitutional framer can never be an unbound binder, any more than a sovereign can be an uncommanded commander .... To influence a situation, an actual power wielder must adapt himself to preexistent patterns of force and unevenly distributed possibilities for change." The constitutional text, then, does no more than capture and specify the set of constraints that will be operative. "Present decisions set in motion irreversible processes which, in turn, necessarily box in future generations. This is true whether we embody our decisions in 'irrevocable' charters or not." (Holmes, 1995: 160, 159.) Eschewing the constraints that are included by design in a constitutional text, says Holmes, merely means allowing ourselves to be controlled by constraints that we may be unable to identify even as they act upon us.

In Holmes' reading, the act of constitutional consent, is the selection and formal institutionalization of constraints that are inherent in any political system, with the advantage of being able to select and design the kinds of constitutive constraints that enhance the possibility of collective action. "Precommittment is justified because, rather than merely foreclosing options, it holds open possibilities that would otherwise lie beyond reach .... Far from simply handcuffing people, linguistic rules allow interlocutors to do many things they would not otherwise have been able to do or even have thought of doing." (Holmes, 1995: 162–63.) The abandonment of linguistic precommitments would thus constitute the abandonment of the project of collective decision making in its entirety, a collective surrender to passivity in the face of dimly recognized social forces.

Holmes' argument is both insightful and provocative, but it is ultimately insufficient as a response to the concerns raised by Waldron and Michelman. The reason, once again, is the difficulty of bridging the gap between showing that precommitments are desirable in a democracy and demonstrating that precommitments are democratically legitimate. Holmes is trying to move from the proposition that the People ought not to abandon their precommitments to the proposition that the People cannot do so. But he gets only halfway there: He provides a powerful argument that the People ought not to want to make such a move because it would entail a loss of important benefits and because a move away from one set of constraints is merely a move to another.

Beyond the observation that the central question is not yet resolved, there are problems with each of Holmes' arguments. The first argument, the persuasive case that maintaining an earlier commitment is desirable, has to be made anew every time a question arises, and has to be established to the satisfaction of every individual, a return to Michelman's "Ida." In any given case, a conclusion that the benefits that derive from the precommitment are insufficient dissolves the commitment. In other words, we need a response to the person who says, "The heck with the constitution, we are at war." What basis is there for asserting an obligation on the part of that person to remain committed to constitutional rule, given that he is perfectly willing to sacrifice the benefits of constitutionalism?

The second argument – to the effect that constraints are inevitable, so choosing those that are created by design is superior to relying on those we do not recognize – raises an even more fundamental problem of the same type. The fact that a sovereign People want to employ a particular mechanism for self-governance does not release them from the obligations that inhere in the form of their sovereignty, any more than Bodin's monarch was free to dissolve his kingdom. Recall Whittington's useful distinction between moments of sovereignty-in-action and periods of ordinary self-governance. During these periods of ordinary democratic rule, why is it not the case that the People stand accused of abdicating its role? Imagine a monarch who cedes all of his powers to a regent. The source of the regent's power is clear, but has the king violated the limitations on his actions that inhere in the fact of his sovereignty?

Nor is the situation helped by turning away from the anthropomorphic metaphor of the state. Describing "sovereignty" as the capacity for discourse determined by an act of self-inscription does not explain why a subsequent act of inscription should be required to alter the terms of that discourse. Let us expand on Holmes' description of the constitutive rules of chess. If the majority of the participants in a chess tournament want to move bishops in the manner of knights, what justifies holding them to a prior agreement to play by the standard rules? In the case of a real chess tournament, the most likely answer would be that use of the standard rules of chess is required for the results of the tournament to be accepted by the International Chess Federation. But that is where the analogy to constitutional discourse breaks down; again, there is no external authority to which the People can be called to answer consistent with basic democratic principles. To justify enforcement of the rules of chess in this imaginary tournament, we need to find a binding commitment to stick to previously agreed-upon rules.

One answer might be that sticking to the rules that were agreed to at the outset is inherent in the terms "chess" and "tournament." Christopher Eisgruber makes an argument of this kind. Much of Eisgruber's argument echoes points that were raised by Elster and Holmes about the desirability of enabling constraints. For Eisgruber, stable constitutional arrangements are enhancements to democratic self-rule in much the same way that voluntarily adopted constraints, in Holmes' interpretation, enhanced Bodin's systematic description of the exercise of sovereignty. Like Holmes, Eisgruber argues that the existence of stable institutions aids in democratic self-government in numerous ways, not least among which is that they provide an environment in which collective action can be carried out without repeating the initial investment of effort to create channels of communication and organization each time a group wants to influence policy outcomes. "One purpose of constitutional institutions in general, and supermajoritarian amendment rules in particular, is to enable democratic citizens to coordinate their behavior more effectively." (Eisgruber, 2001: 14.) But whereas Holmes, in particular, focuses on a reconsideration of "constraint," Eisgruber's argument centers on a reconsideration of the meaning of "democracy."

Eisgruber begins by distinguishing "the people" from "the will of the majority." "[A] majority is by definition merely a fraction of the people. It seems impossible to quarrel with the proposition that the people should govern themselves, but it is easy to deny that the majority should be able to dictate terms to minorities." This distinction separates majoritarian democracy from popular sovereignty in a way that requires a reconsideration of the conditions of self-rule. "Popular sovereignty is an attractive idea only if we interpret 'the people' to refer to 'the whole people,' and not just a majority .... It demands a government that is inclusive enough so that all people (and not merely the majority) can associate themselves with the project of self-government." (Eisgruber, 2001: 18–19, 19.) Self-rule by the whole people appears in government actions that display "impartiality," responsiveness "to the interests and opinions of all the people, rather than merely ... the majority, or some fraction of the people." Toward this end, Eisgruber points to the decision "to set up a variety of institutions with differing constituencies and responsibilities." (Eisgruber, 2001, 19.) American courts, in this view, serve the goal of impartiality precisely by virtue of the fact that they are non-majoritarian institutions, in contrast to legislatures.

The result of this approach is to reframe the argument over constraints in a way that challenges the received notion of democratic legislatures constrained by non-democratic courts. As Eisgruber points out – again echoing the arguments of Elster and Holmes – all institutional designs are constraining on future choices. A system of voting, for example, requires persons to act as voters, which is itself an institutionally defined role. "People may behave very differently when they take on the office of 'voter' than when they take on the office of 'juror' or when they testify at a public hearing." Consequently, legislatures are only more "democratic" than other governmental institutions to the extent that they are structured in a way that produces outcomes more accurately reflective of popular will. "[T]hose who believe that the legislature is entitled to speak for the people must defend that claim by analyzing the incentives that structure the behavior of legislators and voters; claims for legislative supremacy cannot be sustained on the basis of any intrinsic connection between direct elections and democracy." (Eisgruber, 2001: 50–51, 52.) The focus on incentives makes the important point that constitutional reform takes place against a non-neutral set of initial conditions.

In order for a norm of impartiality to legitimate an initial set of constitutional arrangements, then, impartiality must be situated prior to the constraining effects of institutional design; that is, in the realm of preconstitutional discourse. For Eisgruber, this outcome is achieved by thinking of constitutional discourse as fundamentally moral. Eisgruber insists that as a matter of human psychology, it is simply not the case that calculations of interest exhaust the vocabulary of political thinking. Instead, he insists that real-life persons are also possessed of moral commitments. Furthermore, people recognize that their moral commitments and their immediate interests do not always coincide. "To speak on behalf of the people, a democratic government must respect the distinction (which the people themselves make) between those issues that are matters of principle and those that are not." (Eisgruber, 2001: 53.) The idea of juridical institutions as those that speak for the whole People rather than for the majority is the idea of political institutions specifically called into existence in order to grant the agency of collective action a moral voice.

Thus Eisgruber conceives of the Constitution as "a practical device that launches and maintains a sophisticated set of institutions which ... [are] well-shaped to speak on behalf of the people about questions of moral and political principle." (Eisgruber, 2001: 3.) This rule implies constraints on the form and content of the dialogue between competing groups and the government. "The government must ... resolve moral issues on the basis of the right kind of reasons – reasons of principle rather than self-interest. The losing side must have some confidence that its views were rejected on the basis of an honest disagreement about the merits of the moral issue." (Eisgruber, 2001: 56)

Applied to the question of justifying constraining procedural requirements for amendment, the idea of a constitution as the moral voice of the collective points toward the need for institutionalized forms of interaction to preserve the dialogic nature of democratic juridical practice. The first requirement for a constitutional order is that it produce or preserve an environment in which Harris' "Constitutional People" are able to consider their role. " 'The people' cannot act except through institutions. If amendment is easy, then it is hard to see what institutional device would allow 'the people' to stand back from the amendment process and decide whether to debate another round of constitutional reforms." (Eisgruber, 2001: 13, 14.)

The decision whether to debate plays the same role in constitutional practice that the Lockean moment of 'consent to consent' plays in constitutional creation. Both recognize the necessity of a space separating the People in its role as collective sovereign from the ordinary processes of lawmaking and adjudication that are carried out by juridical actors, including political representatives, competing parties, and government officials. A constitution provides an environment for the former just as the set of political institutions that it authorizes provides an environment for the latter. Rules governing the process of constitutional amendment, then, are enabling constraints that permit the People to engage in a dialogue about the constitution itself, just as rights-guaranteeing provisions in a constitution permit the possibility of dialogue about laws.

What Eisgruber does not say, but what emerges directly from his argument, is that the role of a constitution as an institutional device for engaging in the dialogue of self-sovereignty implies that constitutional discourse is constrained in another way. The "moral" principles to which he refers are expressed in constitutional terms; this is the necessary implication of the suggestion that institutions devoted to constitutional interpretation exist in order to give voice to the moral beliefs of "the whole people." The principles that explain constitutionalism as a form of specialized democratic expression necessarily entail a requirement that moral principles be articulated in constitutional terms, so that such principles must be translated into constitutional propositions.

There is a powerful insight here: constitutions create rhetorical as well as institutional spaces for the dialogue of collective sovereignty, and both require enabling constraints. Returning to the analogy of the chess tournament, I suggested earlier that Eisgruber's argument would take the form of the assertion that the word "chess" implies a set of rules and that the word "tournament" implies that those rules will remain unchanged until the completion of the competition. What was required was a prior agreement to come together and hold a tournament, and an agreement to settle on its rules. Thereafter, the act of conducting the tournament and the individual matches in accordance with those rules declares the participants' willingness to be bound just as if they had subjectively consented to the outcome. If a discussion about modifications to those rules occurs, it will take place in the idiom of chess and chess tournaments, and the decision whether to debate alterations to the rules will call on each participant to decide whether the principles involved – of fair competition, or of how the game should be played – are adequately reflected in the present arrangements, or whether holding a meeting to discuss alternatives is warranted. But even the possibility of such a meeting depends on all the participants' acceptance that the conduct and outcome of the discussion would satisfy the conditions for a fair dialogue and that the outcome would be determined for "the right kind of reasons." Once again, in other words, we come back to questions of language, and of precommitment to discursive norms.

In many ways, in fact, the analogy to a chess tournament is more appropriate than some others that have been discussed. Unlike either Ulysses or Bridget in the earlier analogies, but like participants in constitutional discourse, the chess players are potentially repeat players. Also unlike Ulysses or Bridget, but again like participants in constitutional discourse, the chess players have an affirmative purpose in mind, not merely the avoidance of a bad outcome.

Watching children experiment with a game's rules demonstrates the point. Often, as they experiment, children will get to the point where they are proposing new rules at every player's turn. Eventually they become frustrated, and agree to leave one set of rules in place until the completion of a contest and then to revisit the issue again afterward as the only way to make the experience of play sufficiently coherent to be meaningful. By the same token, a speaker needs memory to construct a sentence, and rules of grammar known to others, if communication is to be achieved.

In each case, the limitation on changes in governing rules is supplied by the purpose of the enterprise: to engage in competition, or to communicate meaning. Even Ulysses' authority depended on his acting in a way that did not endanger the survival of the ship; otherwise the sailors would be justified in mutinying by his failure to live up to his commitments as the ship's commander. Democratic government similarly exists for a purpose. At a minimum, democracy has the purpose of permitting a people to rule itself, a purpose that includes the creation of institutions capable of expressing moral principles and of providing an adequately impartial forum for their debate.

Eisgruber's argument, in other words, is not so much a defense of constraint as a displacement of the democratic challenge. There is no particular problem of bridging the gap between the desirability of institutional arrangements and the justification of a binding commitment to their maintenance. If precommitments to stable rules of juridical discourse are necessary elements of democratic self-rule just as fixed rules of a game recognizable as "chess" are necessary for the duration of a tournament, then the democratic challenge to precommitment disappears. Nothing short of a rejection of democracy itself will suffice to undo the consent that gives the constitutional regime its legitimacy.

Eisgruber's description of the amendment process also answers the fear that the self-sovereign People will abdicate its authority during periods of ordinary governance. The "decision whether to debate" represents a reenactment of the moment of popular pre-constitutional discourse by the sovereign People. Occurring in the context of an established constitutional order, the act of discussing the adequacy of inherited institutions becomes a performative process of dialogue that comprises the very process that it contemplates. So long as that process continues to be bound by meta-constitutional discursive norms – so long as the standards for the adequacy of inherited institutions are consistent with the norms that justified their creation in the first place – the discussion remains one carried out by the Constitutional People. The possibility of amendment is itself always an element of political consciousness, so that in a constitutional regime, a critical evaluation of the institutional mechanisms of self-rule is built into the fact of their employment.

Conceived of in the terms of Harris' argument, the description of a decision whether to debate amendments to a constitution is the product of an ongoing conversation between the sovereign People and the constitutional People; in Ackerman's and Whittington's arguments, it is a dialogue concerning the desirability of summoning the sovereign People to action. An argument to replace a constitutional order outright asserts a degree of dissonance between the understandings of the self-governing people and its earlier incarnation so great that the constitutional arrangements have ceased to serve self-government. But aside from this extreme situation, the effectiveness of constitutional arrangements as mechanisms for self-government legitimates their continuation. The continued agreement to employ constitutional language is the necessary element that permits a continued discussion among the Constitutional People to continue without raising the possibility of summoning the Sovereign People to action. In linguistic terms, a continuing commitment to the stability of constitutional *langue* is what permits the possibility of a continuing debate over the terms of constitutional *parole* without abandoning the institutionalized previous expressions of popular sovereignty.

But the democratic challenge to precommitment is not yet exhausted. In the context of a theory of constitutional language, the challenge to precommitment on democratic grounds can be read in a different way. These are arguments that move beyond the anthropomorphic metaphor of the state, and instead ask whether the description of self-sovereignty as a set of discursive conditions is an adequate answer to the democratic challenge. In addition to containing an argument that precommitment cannot be justified, the democratic challenge implicitly also contains an argument that sovereignty and precommitment can never be a *sufficient* basis for legitimation in the absence of Michelman's "constitutional culture." Why is it not necessary to posit the existence of a thick set of norms contained in a dominant political culture, in addition to the minimalist commitments contained in a discursive understanding of self-sovereignty? The inquiry quickly becomes an argument by exhaustion. On the one hand, if we posit the existence of a prevalent social attitude that treats the commitment to constitutional language as legitimately binding, why do we need the discussion of pre-commitment at all? Conversely, if we cannot assume the existence of such a prevalent social attitude, how does an independent conception of legitimate sovereignty rescue a constitutional regime from dissolution? In either case, the creation of elaborate arguments to explain the legitimacy of constitutional precommitments is revealed to be a meaningless exercise, either fruitless or redundant.

Jeremy Waldron makes an argument of this kind in order to account for the particular authority that is attached to legislative discourse as opposed to mere discussion.[43] Waldron treats the existence of such a language as an aspect of a political culture of "good faith," in which political debates result from disagreement among "men and women of high spirits ... motivated in their disagreement not by what's in it for them but by a desire to get it right," which in turn acts as a guarantor of fundamental principles without either the necessity or the possibility of constitutional commitments. (Waldron, 1999: 305.) Richard Bellamy proposes something similar when he says of constitutional government generally that it "brings the various groups and interests within society into dialogue with each other and ensures that the making of law reflects mutual concern and respect and a desire to promote the common welfare." (Bellamy, 1996: 44.)

Writing in the same vein, Eisgruber appeals to something akin to Rawls' idea of overlapping consensus. "Americans on both sides of ... [a moral issue] might agree that they should have moral reasons to back up their moral positions. They might also believe that good faith moral discussion tends, over the long haul, to improve the quality of the moral reasons and moral positions

---

[43] Waldron makes a similar point in the context of legislation. "There is a constant temptation in modern discourse-jurisprudence to take as an implicit procedural ideal the model of an informal intimate conversation among friends ... I want to focus on the formal characteristics that make what happens in the legislature more like proceedings than like conversation, and the results of legislative proceedings more like canon than consensus." (Waldron, 1999: 70.)

which people adopt. Of course, people might believe none of this. They might believe that moral positions are nothing more than tastes which people happen to have .... Or they might believe that moral truth is ascertainable only through silent communion with the One True God .... But I think that most Americans do, in fact, believe that one should have moral reasons for taking moral positions, and that it is productive to discuss these reasons." (Eisgruber, 2001: 55.)

Although Eisgruber asserts that his description fits modern America, it is unclear whether for Waldron and Bellamy the existence of such a political culture is posited as an empirical description of democratic practice, or as a necessary and sufficient condition for "true" democracy. If the latter is the case, if self-government both requires and is ensured by the existence of a population of persons of good will, then the absence of pre-commitments to self-constraint poses no danger to democratic values. But this argument proves too much. One might reasonably feel hard-pressed to identify any system on the planet in which such a cooperative version of self-government is likely to be possible. And even if the former is the case, even if we assume despite evidence to the contrary that political debates are ordinarily undertaken in "good faith," with a commitment to "mutual concern and respect," and with something beyond our present interests driving the formulation of our arguments, we may nonetheless be sufficiently self-reflective to know that we do not always act on our best impulses, and systematic enough to contrive a mechanism for privileging our own better impulses. Alternatively, we may simply recognize that "good faith" is not sufficient to solve the problem of irreducible disagreements on questions of value such as the definition of "common welfare." Any of these is a sufficient reason to create binding commitments to institutional mechanisms of collective decision making, which brings us back to explaining the capacity of that mechanism to bind our subsequent acts, and hence to the search for the conditions of self-sovereignty and the possibility of precommitment.

Eisgruber's formulation, in particular, has a further problem. His assumptions about the American polity are not unattractive, but they risk becoming far too exclusionary. The appeal to improvement of moral reasons, itself, appeals to some universally accepted external standard for better or worse moral reasons, which is a necessary antecedent commitment to the rejection of divine guidance through "silent communion with the One True God." The problem is grounding that predecessor set of metamoral standards. In Eisgruber's description of moral argumentation – and, less obviously, in Waldron's "to get it right" and Bellamy's – "common welfare" – the problem of constitutional legitimation has been shifted to a problem of moral legitimation in a way that excludes a great range of actual moral thought as well as a great deal of the practice of constitutional politics. It may be taken as given that any theory that leads to the conclusion that persons of devout religious faith are unfit for constitutional citizenship is somehow flawed. The writers quoted earlier argue no such thing, of course; the difficulty is that they focus on substantive rather than discursive norms, and that they focus on personal beliefs of individuals rather than public discursive conduct. Once again, the appeal to a necessary and sufficient condition of a culture of good faith moral discourse proves too much, extending the necessary conditions for a legitimate and stable constitutional regime into the realm of human thought.

An alternative, analytically rather circular, solution is to attempt to employ the authority of sovereignty to mandate a constitutional culture by specifying a requirement of "good faith" in the constitutional text itself, so that commitment to the text, standing alone, is taken to be sufficient to guarantee a constitutional culture of good faith deliberation. The result would be that a successful defense of a precommitment to a particular constitution entails a simultaneous commitment to a thick set of political cultural norms contained within the four corners of the text. Something like this idea is at work in Article I-5(2) of the draft European Constitution of 2005:

Pursuant to the principle of sincere cooperation, the Union and the Member States shall, in full mutual respect, assist each other in carrying out tasks which flow from the Constitution. The Member States shall take any appropriate measure, general or particular, to ensure fulfilment of the obligations arising out of the Constitution or resulting from the acts of the institutions of the Union. The Member States shall facilitate the achievement of the Union's tasks and refrain from any measure which could jeopardize the attainment of the Union's objectives.

This "principle of loyalty," according to commentators, "embodies a pervasive duty to co-operate in good faith." (Verhoeven, 2003: 305).[44]

The problem here, of course, is that if the duty of loyalty is imposed by an external sovereign, then the authority of that sovereign must be grounded in the first place. And if the duty is imposed as an exercise of self-sovereignty, the argument creates a classic situation of infinite regress, as in the case of a promise to keep one's promises. This is very different from a requirement of good faith as an element of enforceablility in contract law, for example. In the latter situation, the sovereign political authority stands outside the contract and determines whether or not to bring its authority to bear to enforce the contract's terms as between the parties. Where "good faith" is made an element of constitutional order, however, the choice between infinite regress or neoPlatonic idealism seems inescapable. This is not to suggest that the inclusion of these words in the European Constitution are meaningless. They may be expressive of a prior commitment rather than presumed to create an obligation, akin to the closing phrase of the American Declaration of Independence in which the members of the Continental Congress pledged "our lives, our fortunes, and our sacred honor" to the revolutionary cause. Such a pledge was entirely unnecessary; with regard to lives and property, at least, the British military authorities were more than willing to enforce the commitment without any specific statement by the signers of the Declaration.[45] The question is what authority there would have been to enforce that pledge in the absence of British troops.

---

[44] The European Court of Justice, applying a similar provision contained in Article 5 of the EEC Treaty, has held that the principle of loyalty defines a "rule imposing on Member states and the Community institutions mutual duties of sincere cooperation." *Luxembourg v. European Parliament* (1983) E. C. R. 255, 287.

[45] A more theoretically interesting interpretation is that the referenced clause is an exercise in what is sometimes called "expressive" or "expressivist" jurisprudence, in which legal statements are understood to be exercises in attempting to influence the social construction of norms, either negatively (by sanction) or positively (by example). Challenges to this mode of understanding center around the difficulty of ascribing an expressive intent to a collective entity and the related difficulty of establishing a non-subjective meaning for the resulting expression. (Adler, 2000: 1390; see also Smith, 2001.) In response, Elizabeth Anderson and Richard Pildes argue that the criticism rests on a false distinction, as communication is always and

We thus come back to the problem of sovereignty that the theory of constitutional language was formulated to answer in the first place. In place of a culture of shared moral commitment and the exclusion of dissenters, I have argued that a legitimate constitutional regime can be grounded in the much thinner commitment to a constitutional language, and that the moment of that linguistic commitment is the first moment of sovereignty by consent. Such a commitment requires both more and less than "good faith." On the one hand, no subjective agreement is required – an "as if" commitment to the use of constitutional language is sufficient – and, on the other, the commitment to constitutional language provides a mechanism for dealing with problems that are not resolved by the fact of faith, and with those whose good faith we doubt. I do not need to be persuaded that my political opponent is speaking with subjective good faith, only that his argument is one that can be addressed in constitutional language, and that that language provides a basis for the construction of arrangements that bridge the gaps between heartfelt but incommensurate "good faith" beliefs drawn from other areas.

Similarly, it is not necessary for a stable constitutional system that all participants eschew moral principles derived from extra-constitutional sources, only that they accept the commitment to behave "as if" their constitution exhausted their moral precepts when engaged in a particular form of behavior. This was the way out of reliance on the anthropomorphic metaphor. The artificial person of the collective sovereign turns out to be nothing more than the ordinary human citizens who have accepted a commitment to act in an artificial way during moments of popular-sovereignty-in-action.

---

necessarily a collective act. "Communication establishes a public space of meanings and shared understandings between the speaker and addressee.... Both the speaker and addressee are held accountable to public meanings." (Anderson and Pildes, 2000: 1573–74.) From this perspective, Article I-5 of the European Constitution brings the idea of a duty of loyalty into public discourse, such that the debate turns to one about the meaning and consequences of that duty rather than its existence. One way to understand my argument in this chapter and Chapter 4 is that such a potentially "performative" (Culler, 1982: 112–14) effect on public discourse is possible only if there is a presumption of exclusivity that attaches to constitutional language, and that a commitment to act "as if" there is such a thing as a collective intent to communicate is precisely what is at stake in the self-sovereign act of constitutional consent.

But although the commitment to constitutional language is in some ways thinner than a hypothetical commitment to good faith in constitutional deliberations, it is no less absolute. If a commitment to constitutional language is the first necessary moment in the construction of a legitimate constitutional regime, the failure of that linguistic commitment spells the regime's end. A sufficiently widespread decline in that "as if" commitment, reflecting a rejection of the claims to legitimacy by a system of constitutional language, will rapidly render it ineffective.

The focus on rules of discourse as the basis for sovereignty in action provides a response to Waldron's objections to precommitment without going as far as Elster in abandoning the idea of collective action. The conditions for legitimate binding constraints are the existence of legitimate self-sovereignty by "the People," not merely a majority of persons. But such a popular sovereign cannot be bound by the limits of an anthropomorphic metaphor of will. Instead, popular-sovereignty-in-action occurs with the inscription of discursive rules of constitutional language that are binding because they are, in Holmes' terms, constitutive rather than regulative democratic principles, what Eisgruber calls "practical, procedural devices" for self-rule. (Eisgruber, 2001: 11.) The dialogue between the People and the people is a dialogue about the discursive rules that will govern future moments of popular-sovereignty-in-action at moments of constitutional revision. Revisions to those rules by the People are genuine acts of sovereignty only when they are formalized, in order that they can function as standards for the legitimacy of acts of the people, which can occur only in a form that defines ascertainable rules of constitutional grammar.

In examining the conditions that are required in order to make sense of a legitimate binding precommitment undertaken by a self-sovereign People, we have continually returned to the point at which something like consensus is required. What is required is not a standardization of the souls of citizens, only a willingness to speak constitutionally. That commitment is legitimately binding across the multiple levels of dialogic interaction because it is an essential element of democratic self-rule. Juridical institutions exist, and the grant of authority to juridical institutional actors is justified by their necessary role in preserving constitutional language. The underlying commitment throughout is to the survival of self-sovereignty, the same logical constraint on the exercise of sovereign authority that Bodin identified.

But the appeal to a necessary level of consensus cannot imply an appeal to unanimity in the formation of a constitutional order. That is, to the question "Consent to What?" the answer cannot be "that about which there is unanimous consent." Such a requirement of consent is essentially an artifact of the anthropomorphic metaphor. If we recognize that the Sovereign People is nothing more than individual citizens acting in a certain way, then we necessarily also recognize that persistent and unresolved disagreement is a necessary element of social existence. Unless a society is to engage in a permanent civil war, exiling or suppressing all those who disagree in a constant reperforming of the hypothetical moment of constitutional covenant, there has to be a way in which the formulation of the idea of preconstitutional consent makes the moment of constitutional creation plausibly legitimate even in the face of disagreement. Holmes' and Eisgruber's arguments are persuasive refutations of Waldron's implicit proposition that constitutionalism and democratic theory are incommensurate, but only if an acceptable basis can be found to explain the translation (a crucial metaphor!) of preconstitutional commitments into constitutional consent. The argument of this last discussion has been that the fact that participants in political discussions are possessed of "good faith" does little to preserve the integrity of the constitutional regime if those participants are unwilling – or cannot be compelled – to translate their positions into constitutional language. The unanimous and continuing "as if" commitment to constitutional language is the irreducibly necessary element of consensus that is required for a self-sovereign constitutional regime to be possible.

CONCLUSION – FROM "CONSENT HOW?" TO "CONSENT TO WHAT?"

It is now possible to articulate a complete answer to the first of the two questions with which this book began: "Under what conditions is the creation of a legitimate constitutional regime possible?" The answer is that a legitimate constitutional regime depends on the existence of a self-sovereign People capable of constitutional consent. The capacity for constitutional consent, in turn, requires a prior, unanimous, "as if" consent to the construction of a constitutional language, and the subsequent promulgation of the constitutional text creates the exemplar of that constitutional language. In response to the further question of how the initial commitment to the creation of constitutional language can be conceived of as binding over time, the answer is that in light of the reconception of self-sovereignty as a description of discursive capacity, precommitment to a system of constitutional language is an analytically necessary element of continuing democratic self-rule.

This description of constitutional legitimacy resting on a prior commitment to language has important consequences. For one thing, it is a short step from the argument presented thus far to a defense of the role of institutional juridical actors engaging in something like judicial review of ordinary legislation. The basic argument can be made quite simply: Courts, or similar institutions, are necessary to protect constitutional *langue* from the corrosive effects of disagreements at the level of constitutional *parole*. This implication of the present argument will be pursued further in the next chapter, in the context of discussing the relationship between the disparate languages of constitutional, legal, and moral discourse.

The same move that goes from a focus on consent to language to an argument in favor of the legitimate authority of juridical institutional actors also defines their fundamental duties. First and foremost, a grounding norm of consent to constitutional language implies a duty of translation for participants in constitutional discourse. "Translation" here refers to the necessity of articulating moral, legal, or political in terms of constitutional language when engaging in constitutional discourse, a variation of the event that occurs when ordinary life experiences are expressed in the form of legal claims. Translation is not a transparent process, to be sure. In the extreme case, propositions that are readily expressed in one language are semantically absurd or grammatically improper in another. When a statement is translated from one language to another, something of the flavor of a statement is always lost, while new layers of meaning and reference are always added.[46] If the text or statement is sufficiently important, the attempt at translation may be viewed as a threat to its meaning, as in the belief held by many traditional Muslims that the Qur'an cannot be translated into languages other than Arabic. (Ayoub, 1986.)

In the case of constitutional language, the costs of translation will be directly proportional to the "thickness" of that language. The greater the level of substantive normative commitment contained in the terms of constitutional language, the more difficult it may be to translate propositions drawn from other realms of experience into legitimate constitutional arguments. Norms are the building blocks of constitutional narrative. If a constitution is written in individualistic terms, it will be difficult to construct a narrative that captures the collective experience of a tightly integrated community. If a constitution's terms are arrayed around a central norm of freedom to pursue interests, it may be difficult to construct a constitutional narrative that contains a sense of social duty. And if a constitution's terms are expressed as the realization of a utopian vision of perfectly harmonious order, it will be difficult, if not impossible, while speaking that constitutional language, to express a contrary conception of self-fulfillment that would call existing political arrangements into question.

These last observations raise the question that motivates the second half of this book: "Consent to What?" In the chapters that follow, I will argue that the claim that propositions must undergo the process of translation into constitutional language to be proper elements of constitutional discourse points to a claim that constitutional language is "exclusive." The range of arguments that are capable of expression, and consequently the frequency with which translation will be required in practice, depends on the "completeness" of the constitutional language. And the degree to which the imposition of a requirement of translation will burden the articulation of arguments drawn from non-constitutional sources

---

[46] "In the law," writes White, "and to some degree in other translations as well, there is always conflict and always loss.... Neither story, neither language, is the sole source of authority; at some point choices will have to be made that favor one over the other. And both must yield, in much if not in all, to a third force, the language of the law that governs the process as a whole." (White, 1990: 262.)

will depend on the extent to which the constitutional language contains normative "substance" that is contrary to that contained in the language of the argument's original formulation. These three characteristics – exclusivity, completeness, and substance – provide the terms for the discussion of the nature of constitutional language in the chapters that follow.

4

Consent to What?

Exclusivity and Completeness in Constitutional and Legal Language

Chapters 2 and 3 concluded with the proposition that the conditions of possibility for constitutional consent involve a collective willingness to create a language in which to engage in an act of sovereign self-authorship, and that sovereignty and precommitment to language are a sufficient basis for a constitutional regime's claim to legitimacy. But that is only a partial answer, since it cannot be equally the case that any and every hypothetical system of constitutional language is equally appropriate to the task of legitimation.

This chapter begins to explore the content that a system of constitutional language must contain if precommitment to that language is to serve the central role in establishing the legitimacy of a regime that has been suggested here. In terms of the descriptions employed in these chapters, this is the move from the question "Consent How?" to the question "Consent to What?" Accepting the proposition that a binding commitment to a constitutional language is the necessary condition for constitutional consent, what are the necessary characteristics of that language for it to be a *sufficient* basis for the creation of a legitimate constitutional regime?

There are three basic dimensions along which this inquiry will be pursued: exclusivity, completeness, and substance. Identifying these essential categories of description for a system of constitutional language provides the specific inquiries that motivate this chapter and the next. First, to what degree must the constitutional language be exclusive, such that propositions that fail to comply with the rules of constitutional grammar, or cannot be constructed out of the system of constitutional signs, are necessarily excluded from constitutional discourse? In the terms borrowed from Saussure in the previous chapter, to what extent must constitutional *langue* constrain constitutional *parole*? Second, to what extent must the constitutional language provide a complete system of rules and signs, such that all the important norms involved in the operation of the juridical regime are provided without importing additional elements from other sources? And third, to what extent must a constitutional language include substantive normative commitments, such that the claim to legitimacy remains grounded in prior shared normative judgments? This chapter explores the first two questions, those concerning exclusivity and completeness, while the question of substance is the subject of the next chapter.

As the discussion thus far already demonstrates, it is impossible to treat exclusivity, completeness, and substance as perfectly separate categories of description. Similarly, the more a constitutional language is treated as exclusive, the less plausible it is to describe that language as complete. The possibility of completeness would best be achieved if the language of constitutional discourse is open to the addition of new elements any time a speaker finds them useful. Exclusivity, by contrast, carries the element of a limiting precommitment that will at times preclude a speaker from articulating a proposition in constitutional terms at all.

In Chapter 3, the focus was on the moment of consent to the creation of a constitutional language, a consent that, in proper Lockean fashion, was found to be necessary prior to the subsequent moment of constitutional consent. The first moment of consent creates the commitment to the fact of constitutionalism, not to its particulars. The initial agreement to employ constitutional language does not require specific agreement as to particular rules of constitutional grammar, or the content of specific terms in the system of constitutional signs. The content of a specific constitutional language is produced at the second, constitutional moment of consent.

This can most easily be seen in practice. Consider the fact that across the broad range of interpretive strategies that are proposed for applying the American Constitution, it is almost never the case that anyone begins anywhere other than with the (written) text.[1] Moving away from that starting point, there is room for a vast array of interpretive strategies, of course, but from the perspective of fundamental requirements for constitutional rule, the only "good faith" that is required is a commitment to what Jack Balkin has called the ideal of "constitutional fidelity." As Balkin observes, fidelity is "not a virtue but a precondition" of constitutional discourse. "To claim to interpret the Constitution is already to claim to be faithful to it. Conversely, insisting that one does not care about fidelity does not simply put one at a severe disadvantage in convincing others to one's point of view; it takes one outside of the language game of constitutional interpretation. It is to announce that one is doing something else . . . . When we say that fidelity is not important to us, we are no longer interpreting the Constitution, we are criticizing it." (Balkin, 1997: 1705.)

"Constitutional fidelity" is an ideal that, as Balkin warns, not only does not require more substantive normative commitments but may actually direct our attention away from their implications. There may be a temptation to find anything that we think to be an element of "justice" in the constitutional text, or we may alter our ideas of justice to suit what the text offers, a process Balkin calls "interpretive cooptation." And there is a third, more subtle danger. "Finally, the practice of constitutional fidelity can affect us in a third way. Immersing ourselves in this practice makes it seem natural for us to talk and think about justice in terms of the concepts and categories of our constitutional tradition. In this way, the practice of constitutional interpretation can actually skew and limit our understandings about

---

[1] A startling exception to this general rule appeared in the Rehnquist Court's treatment of states' sovereign immunity. In this context, almost uniquely, the majority of the Court's members have demonstrated a willingness to abandon the written text entirely in favor of a "background principle." See, for example, *Seminote Tribe of Florida, 517 U.S. 44, 72 (1995, Rehnquist, C.J.)*. This argument appeals to a preconstitutional understanding of state sovereignty and applies it to limit an explicit textual provision of the written constitution (Article III's grant of jurisdiction) in the name of an interpretive theory of originalism. (For a discussion of this line of cases and its implications for American constitutional design, see Noonan, 2002: chs. 2–6.) Accusing a judge of reaching beyond the constitutional text has been a staple of criticism of judicial actions since time immemorial; what is extraordinary about the cases concerning sovereign immunity is the *avowal* of an extratextual source of constitutional principle.

justice, because not all claims are equally easy to state in the language of that tradition." (Balkin, 1997: 1704.)

Balkin's last point, in particular, is a telling criticism of the focus on language as the ground for constitutional legitimation. In trying to justify a theory of constitutional language, we must not ignore the inevitable fact that such a language will express some notions of "justice" more easily than others; to defend a constitutional regime as legitimate, therefore, we are required to find a way to justify the imposition of that unequal that discursive cost.

These observations return us to a consideration of the character of constitutional language, couched in terms of the qualities of exclusivity, completeness, and substance that I previously identified. Exclusivity appears in the idea of Balkin's "fidelity" that excludes "doing something else"; completeness is raised in the question of what degree of agreement is required for "fidelity" to be meaningful, and across what range of political, legal, or constitutional discourse that agreement must extend; and "substance" appears in the question of whether there is some point at which the commitment to constitutional language may become intolerable.

The issue of substance points to what Balkin, along with Mark Graber, calls the problem of "constitutional evil," the possibility that a constitutional regime not only permits but actually requires the toleration of practices that one believes to be fundamentally morally wrong. The classic example, explored by Graber, would be an argument that although slavery is morally wrong, the U.S. Supreme Court's decision in *Dred Scott* was nonetheless "correct" as an interpretation of the Constitution as it then existed. Most tellingly, Graber identifies the near-universal vilification of Chief Justice Roger Taney's opinion in *Dred* as the result of a general acceptance of Robert Cover's conclusion that "many federal justices who protected slavery and declared free blacks to be non-citizens constitutionally defended those evils because they 'shared a jurisprudence that fostered imprecise thinking about the nature of the choices open to them.'" (Graber, 2006: 28–29, quoting Cover, 1975: 257.) Graber, however, argues that Cover's description of the problem is overstated. In a lengthy and persuasive reevaluation of the Dred Scott case, he demonstrates that the usual criticisms of Taney's majority opinion are poorly supported by the record.

Why, then, have so many writers from every possible political and constitutional perspective held the case up as the epitome of poor constitutional judging? The answer, for Graber, is an ahistorical tendency toward the "right answer" thesis, the belief that the problem of constitutional evils is obviated when the "correct" understanding of the constitution is found.

> The better lesson *Dred Scott* teaches is that constitutional theory cannot mitigate or eradicate constitutional evil.... [S]uch evils as slavery are not abolished when a plausible constitutional argument exists that the constitution is antislavery. Constitutional evils are eliminated by a constitutional politics that persuades or a non-constitutional politics that compels crucial political actors to abandon an evil practice.... Constitutional law is almost always structurally incapable of generating the clear right answer that might resolve hotly disputed constitutional questions. When a relatively enduring constitutional controversy divides a society, every position that enjoys substantial political support has plausible constitutional foundations. (Graber, 2006: 29–30.)

Furthermore, Graber warns, the search for the "right" constitutional answer can have deleterious effects on the very politics that we must rely upon if unjust practices that have previous been accommodated are to be reformed. "The 'right answer' thesis subverts the constitutional politics necessary for regime maintenance and the triumph of justice.... Constitutional theories that emphasize textual exegesis at the expense of political negotiations aggravate constitutional controversies by creating an environment in which all parties to the dispute are less likely to compromise because they believe the constitution previously settled the matter in their favor." (Graber, 2006: 31.)

Graber's argument is undoubtedly correct as far as it goes. Certainly, the problem of constitutional evils can never be escaped entirely, either by drafting a perfectly designed document or by discovering the one true mode of interpretation that will yield the "right answer." On the other hand, it is not by any means the case that all constitutions are equally amenable to permitting or requiring evils, nor that any particular constitution allows all categories of evil to be exercised equally. Whatever its limitations, for example, the thirteenth Amendment ensured that slavery as a formal institution would no longer be an element of American life; hence the post-thirteenth Amendment Constitution is quite different from the earlier version of the text with respect to this particular constitutional evil. At the same time, the case of American slavery is almost too powerful a vehicle for the message. As Mark Brandon points out, the constitutional divide prior to the Civil War was no mere difference of interpretation, but rather represented an outright failure of constitutional discourse. (Brandon, 1998.) Conceding that in less-extreme circumstances, any constitutional text will be amenable to interpretations that yield what one observer or another thinks of as "evil," is there a minimum of normative content of the kind contained in the thirteenth Amendment that is required if a constitutional regime is to be conceived of as legitimate?

In addition, constitutions not only require or permit evil practices, they also provide weapons that can be deployed to criticize and combat those practices. Graber is surely correct that constitutions cannot ensure a good outcome without a supporting political environment, but that does not render the constitutional text irrelevant to the outcome. Here, again, exclusivity appears to exacerbate the problem of constitutional evil; to the degree that constitutional language limits what can be said, it is increasingly difficult to use constitutional mechanisms to address evils that exist. Therefore the initial conclusion from the observation of constitutional evils is that exclusivity in constitutional language is to be avoided.

A related set of arguments imply that constitutional language should be complete. A lack of completeness contributes to indeterminacy, again opening the door to constitutional evils as well as weakening the claims of constitutional language in the face of the democratic challenges discussed earlier. Michael Klarman, responding to Balkin's essay, proposes that "the principal problem of constitutional fidelity" is not bad content but indeterminacy, "the nonexistence of any viable middle ground between the deadhand problem of originalist constitutional interpretation and the judicial subjectivity problem of nonoriginalist interpretation." (Klarman, 1997: 1739.) Klarman rejects both the perfectly deterministic assertion of a commitment to a complete system and the radically indeterminate consequences of a system so incomplete that it leaves constitutional interpreters free to incorporate any elements that suit them as additional elements of the discussion. A lack of normative substance does not necessarily lead to either of these problems but leaves open the possibility of both, and raises other concerns as well.

The challenges to fidelity identified by Balkin and Klarman imply that we should look for a system of constitutional language that is non-exclusive, complete, and substantively normative. In fact, however, I am going to argue in this chapter that precisely the opposite is the case. My argument will be that these are fine criteria for a legitimate system of laws, but that constitutional language is required to be both entirely *exclusive* and significantly *incomplete* (leaving the question of substantive normative commitments for discussion in the next chapter), and that these conclusions follow from the fact that constitutional language is not coextensional with "law." As a result, the discussion of the characteristics of exclusivity and completeness in constitutional language is bound up in a discussion of the relationship between a theory of constitutional legitimacy and a general theory of law.

THE ARGUMENT FOR EXCLUSIVITY

The adoption of an exclusive constitutional language has a negative or exclusionary effect on some set of propositions that might have been more readily expressed in a different constitutional regime.[2] It is therefore self-evidently true that exclusivity in constitutional language results in the exclusion of substantive normative

---

[2] The recognition that the creation of a language of discourse excludes others is a fundamental truth of philosophy. Feminist writers' explorations of the model of gender- and family-relations inherent in Lockean liberalism is one example. (Pateman, 1988; Hirschmann and DiStefano, 1996.) Applied to a discussion of constitutional language, this observation opens up the possibility of a broad range of normative critique exemplified in Robin West's provocative inquiry: "What might a liberal state look like, if it employed positive and relational rights, as well as negative and individualist rights, and conceived of those rights, furthermore as directed toward the protection of capabilities and autonomy both?" (West, 2003: 92.) Where a critique of this kind reaches the underlying conditions of putative consent, the problem for legitimacy becomes more fundamental. Pateman, for example, in particular, explicitly challenges the idea of "consent" on the grounds that the unit of consent – the constructed "citizen" of the Lockean commonwealth – incorporates an understanding of the experience of male heads of households that excludes the alternative experience of women, among others. Challenges at this level take us back to the very beginning of the conversation, to the discussion of the conditions that are necessary for there to be the possibility of consent.

commitments, or at a minimum a relative disadvantaging of certain
normative claims in comparison with others. This observation is no
different from – and, indeed, is closely related to – the recognition
of the relative burdening of certain classes of constitutional critique
that results from the adoption of a formal amendment process.
(Levinson, 1996: 123; Griffin, 1995: 172).[3] In both instances, the
relative discursive inequalities that are created must be justified if a
precommitment to exclusivity, in language or in formal amendment
processes, is itself to be justified.

Exclusivity in some sense is fundamental to any system of signs. A
linguistic system that excludes nothing enables nothing; this basic
insight of structural linguistics has crucial consequences for law in
general, and for constitution-making in particular. What Jacques
Derrida has called the "discursive violence" of excluding meanings
from a sign's referents in the moment of attaching others becomes
both visible and critically important when it occurs in the context of
law. (Derrida, 1990.)

In employing this term, Derrida defines "violence" in a simple
and common-sense understanding as the exertion of one person's
will to control that of another.[4] From this simple definition, Derrida
argues that any construction of meaning is "violent" in its exclusion
of other possible constructions. Such an event can be seen in the act

---

[3] In response to Griffin's assertion that "the Framers forced a significant amount of
constitutional change off the books and thus limited the ability of the Constitution
to structure political outcomes," Brandon Denning responds that "such change is
present in our constitutional regime and must be accounted for." (Denning, 1997:
159, quoting Griffin, 1995: 172.) Denning relies on a distinction between change in
interpretation and outright amendment, suggesting that informal changes in
understanding are often desirable as mechanisms to express Sunstein's incompletely theorized agreements, as in the example of a constitutional requirement of
gender equity. "[E]nough people were reluctant to constitutionalize equality of the
sexes as an abstract ideal and the amendment was never ratified. At the same time,
the Supreme Court, through a series of cases based upon its reading of the Fifth and
Fourteenth Amendments, has warned that gender-based classifications will be
regarded as suspect by the Court.... Public acceptance of these decisions reflects the
notion that through an incompletely theorized agreement, the Court has been able
to protect and facilitate the 'emerging consensus' that gender-based classifications
should receive a careful look." (Denning, 1997: 234–35.)
[4] The term "violence" is arguably inapposite by virtue of its negative connotations.
Derrida was working with the term expressed by the German word *Gewalt*, which, as
he points out, is closer to "force" than "violence: "*Gewalt* also signifies, for Germans,
legitimate power, authority, public force." (Derrida, 1990: 339.)

of one person's naming another, as any appellation that is not self-created has the consequence of diminishing one's nomological autonomy. The phenomenon of slave owners' inventing Western names for African slaves is an extreme example, but even the benign act of naming a child constrains the range of possibilities for that child's self-definition.[5]

For Hobbes, the assignment of names to thoughts ("marks") was an internal process that represented the first step in the creation of communicable language ("signs"). In Derrida's terms, Hobbes' act of naming appears as a form of self-enacted violence undertaken by the interest-driven self in domination of the perceiving mind.[6] The organization of "a train of thoughts" is described as an instrumental act organized around the pursuit of goals; other goals would yield other forms of organization. The selection of goals thus delimits the range of meaning contained in a system of language, as the significance of, and relation between, thoughts depends on the way in which uncoordinated thoughts become organized by being first named and then ordered, while thoughts not suitable for the "train" are treated as "absurd."[7] What Derrida calls "arche-violence," "the violence of difference, of classification, and of the system of appellations" (Derrida, 1974: 110), is Hobbes' prediscursive moment of naming that transforms marks into communicable signs.

[5] It is a matter of pure speculation, but it seems likely that John Marshall Harlan II, Dweezel Zappa, Willard Van Orman Quine, Thelonious Sphere Monk, and Sacvan Berkovitch may all have found the course of their lives dictated in part by the names their parents chose for them. I intend, of course, no disrespect to any of these extraordinarily accomplished public figures. Leaving aside these unusual examples, anyone who has ever named a child has contemplated the possible constraining or enabling consequences of his or her decision.

[6] There is an obvious problem of the construction of the subject, here; who is the "I" who attaches marks to "my" perceptions that might have been otherwise? This is an area of inquiry that has potential political consequences if the model of constitutional legitimation is made dependent on the adoption of an anthropomorphic metaphor. The theory of constitutional language avoids the necessity for resolving this intractable problem by defining a basis for legitimation that does not depend on the creation of an artificial collective person to stand in the role of Sovereign.

[7] The act of assigning names was the first task of Adam on earth in one of the two creation stories contained in the Book of Genesis. Interestingly, rabbinic interpreters of that passage have proposed that the names that Adam gave to the animals were miraculously the "correct" ones rather than those of his own inventions.

Once the system of language is in place as the basis for social interaction, moreover, those initial choices are concretized. As Locke observed, none of us since Adam has had complete freedom to give objects the names that seem to us most suitable; in its least coercive form, the very possibility of language rests on the existence of at least some social pressure to conform to norms of linguistic usage. (Locke, 1982: 470.) (In Lewis Carroll's telling of the story, Humpty Dumpty tried to challenge this principle, but his attempt did not last long.)[8]

Moving away from the relatively obvious instance of naming persons, the assignment of a relationship between words and referents in general carries with it the dimension of arche-violence. Again, there is nothing metaphysical or arcane about this observation. An example that is politically as well as epistemologically significant is the use of gendered language in descriptions of natural scientific phenomena. (Keller, ed., 1999.) The putative "objectivity" of the description makes the choice of language appear necessary, inevitable, and "natural," with the result that the language shapes our thinking without our being aware of its influence.[9]

Naturalistic metaphors are among the clearest instances of discursive violence, made all the more acute by the employment of a language that hides that violence in a veil of inevitability. The imposition of a metaphor of naturalness over a topic acts as a barrier to inquiry. Where such a metaphor is widely accepted, as in the

---

[8] "'Must a name mean something?' Alice asked doubtfully. 'Of course it must,' Humpty Dumpty said with a short laugh: '*my* name means the shape I am – and a good handsome shape it is, too. With a name like yours, you might be any shape, almost.'" Later in the conversation, Humpty Dumpty seems to propose that he, uniquely, is unbound by social conventions of naming. "'When I use a word,' Humpty Dumpty said in rather a scornful tone, 'it means just what I choose it to mean – neither more nor less.' 'The question is,' said Alice, 'whether you can make words mean so many different things.' 'The question is,' said Humpty Dumpty, 'which is to be master – that's all.'" (Carroll, 1984: 115–16, 124.) Humpty Dumpty's pronouncements draw a direct connection between sovereignty and authority over language, and provide a cautionary tale about the instability of one in the absence of the other.

[9] Duncan Kennedy makes precisely the same point about the vocabulary of juridical legitimation: "The particular set of hierarchies that constitute our social arrangements look more natural, more necessary, and more just than they 'really' are." (Kennedy, 1998: 236.) Another classic example is the assumption of "natural"-ness that attaches to traditional family arrangements. (Fineman, 2000: 21.)

historical cases of "natural" market conditions, "natural" gender roles, or "natural law," the result is to burden or advantage particular viewpoints and consequently to effectuate the imposition of certain wills over other, contrary wills. Discursive violence is thus reflected in the unique capacity of language to distort as well as to illuminate by the manipulation of signs. As Hobbes observed, the capacity for the construction of meaning by speech includes the capacity for self-deception: "[O]n account of the ease of speech, the man who truly doth not think, speaks, and what he says, he believes to be true, and he can deceive himself; a beast cannot deceive itself." (Hobbes, 1998: xx.) There is thus a warning in the discussion of language to be critically aware of the possibility of violence in our speech even in what seems to us our most benevolent moments.

Applied to law, Derrida's insight into the necessary exclusions of alternatives that accompany the construction of meaning becomes a statement about an originary moment of discursive violence that lies at the beginning of any series of legitimating juridical norms. Such violence is "discursive" in its subject matter, which does not mean that it may not be backed up by the threat of more concretely physical coercion, particularly in the case of a relationship between juridical and political authority. Law, after all, is something that is enforced. "The word 'enforceability' reminds us that there is no such thing as law (*droit*) that doesn't imply in itself, a priori, in the analytic structure of its concept, the possibility of being 'enforced,' applied by force." (Derrida, 1990: 338.) The argument is not that discursive violence is "just the same" as physical violence – there is a great gulf of distance between renaming and lynching – but the problem of justification is nonetheless a serious one.[10]

This formulation of the problem of violence inherent in law, is quite different from Robert Cover's arguments on the same

---

[10] Cover's call for a legal understanding that minimizes the violence of exclusion is echoed in James Boyd White's description of the "ethic" of translation. "The practice of translation, and interpretation too, demands an excellence, fully attainable by no one, that is ethical as well as intellectual in character.... In the law, the practical effect of such a consciousness, if we could attain it, would be the perpetual erosion of the force and authority of the merely bureaucratic." (White, 1990: 267.)

topic. For Cover, true normative accounts, and hence true narratives of experience, are created in autonomous communities separated from the state. The formal act of political lawmaking, then, is not the creation of "law" at all, but rather the selective destruction of the law-like normative orders that have emerged from these autonomous communities by the assertion of exclusivity, a process he calls "jurispathy." "To state, as I have done, that the problem is one of too much law is to acknowledge the nomic integrity of each of the communities that have generated principles and precepts. It is to posit that each 'community of interpretation' that has achieved 'law' has its own nomos – narratives, experiences, and visions to which the norm articulated is the right response." (Cover, 1983: 41–2.) The state's version of lawmaking is capable of jurispathy because it is accompanied by violence, not only Derrida's violence of language but also concrete, physical coercion, and everything in between. "[J]udges deal pain and death. That is not all that they do. Perhaps that is not what they usually do. But they do deal death, and pain. . . . In this they are different from poets, from critics, from artists." (Cover, 1986: 1609.)

For Cover, the violence of jurispathy (and hence exclusivity) is something to be resisted. "Legal meaning is a challenging enrichment of social life, a potential restraint on arbitrary power and violence. We ought to stop circumscribing the nomos; we ought to invite new worlds." (Cover, 1983: 68.) Let me reiterate Cover's call for a legal understanding that minimizes the violence of exclusion as echoed in James Boyd White's description of the "ethic" of translation. "The practice of translation, and interpretation too, demands an excellence, fully attainable by no one, that is ethical as well as intellectual in character . . . . In the law, the practical effect of such a consciousness, if we could attain it, would be the perpetual erosion of the force and authority of the merely bureaucratic." (White, 1990: 267.) By contrast, Derrida's emphasis on the inevitability of violence, even at the level of language, points to the necessity of justifying some level of violence that we necessarily embrace as an element of our constitutional order. Cover's implicit critique of exclusivity in constitutional language is telling, and it requires a response, but the necessity of exclusivity to a system of legitimating constitutional language is not thereby diminished. Instead, Cover's concerns point to the importance of separating the treatment of exclusivity as a quality of constitutional language from its appearance in the language of ordinary law. In addition, the less complete a constitutional language can be, the less the requirement of exclusivity at the constitutional level necessitates jurispathy at lower levels of lawmaking and adjudication.

Furthermore, while the point that the availability of a resort to force is implied in the form of law is undoubtedly correct, it is worth recalling that the exercise of that force depends on the acceptance by the state's agents of coercion of the legitimacy of the authority structure ordering its use. As was observed earlier, the ultimate indication of a political regime that has lost its legitimacy is the plaintive question, "do we hold the army?" The legitimacy of a constitutional order, presumably, is called into question long before that particular point is reached.[11] Even after the Civil War, Bruce Ackerman describes the question of the availability of forcible mechanisms of coercion as a central element in the consideration of the fourteenth Amendment. "Only one thing was clear: the Army's sustained support would be crucial in pushing the process despite the resistance of the established governments." (Ackerman, 1992: 208.)

The fact that the creation of law is necessarily accompanied by some form of violence does not mean that law lacks legitimacy. The justification for the violence contained in the imposition of the Fourteenth Amendment onto unwilling Southerners may simply be the necessity of preventing greater violence in the continuation of the legacies of slavery. Nor is the argument that "all violence is (equally) bad"; on the contrary, the recognition that some element of violence is omnipresent requires us precisely to articulate a basis for distinguishing just and unjust instances of its application. "How are we to distinguish between this force of the law ... and the violence that one always deems unjust? What difference is there between, on the

---

[11] Mark Brandon, in his study of antebellum America as an exemplar of constitutional failure, identifies four distinct dimensions of constitutional failure: failure of constitutionalism, failure of a particular constitution, failure of constitutional order, and failure of constitutional discourse. By "failure of constitutional discourse," however, Brandon means something closer to the problem of indeterminacy than a refusal in constitutional arguments to employ constitutional language. Thus, in Brandon's view, the capacity of both pro- and anti-slavery forces to craft serious arguments based on the U. S. Constitution represented a failure of constitutional discourse. (Brandon, 1998.)

one hand, the force that can be just, or in any case deemed legitimate, not only an instrument in the service of law but the practice and even the realization, the essence of droit, and on the other hand the violence that one always deems unjust?"[12] (Derrida, 1990: 339.)

Applied to constitutionalism, the problem of "justice" is the question of legitimacy. In the case of juridical language generally, the authority over the generation of meaning that was identified as the essential aspect of sovereignty produces an explicitly violent – that is, exclusionary – form of discursive construction. This is particularly true in the case of constitutional language, in which the violence of exclusion is both more obvious and more directly the result of conscious artifice than in the case of longstanding systems of legal rules. The creation of a constitutional language is the act of identifying a small subset of the signs recognized in an existing language and granting them a new, privileged role. In fact, I will argue that constitutional language necessarily represents only a small fraction even of the coexistent system of juridical language, itself a highly constrained subset of the language of the community at large. Hence the creation of a constitutional language possessed of exclusivity requires the enforcement of a particularly violent act of linguistic exclusion. Recognition of this inescapable fact makes the question of exclusivity in constitutional language central to the question of legitimacy.

Earlier, the idea of a constitutional language was discussed in terms of a set of rules of grammar and a system of signs. The term "signs" is familiar from Hobbes, as well as from modern theories of language, but in this instance I intend only to convey the idea of a vocabulary that comprises specific words, sets of words, textual and historical references, and other forms of discursive signification.[13]

---

[12] This inquiry leads Derrida to the most famous line in the essay: "Deconstruction is justice," by which he means that it is only through a process of deconstructing the language of law to discover the excluded alternative meanings that its justice can be evaluated. (Derrida, 1990: 343). For the narrower purposes of this discussion, we can substitute "constitutional legitimacy" for "justice."

[13] Will Harris, drawing on the classical Peircean semiotic definition of a sign as "the union of signifier and signified," describes the American Constitution as "a grand illusion of words, which shelters our political lucidity: an elaborate ruse when it decoys the constitutional understandings of would-be interpreters who read all their politics from the printed page, a working fiction when it symbolizes both the possibility and the need for intellectual access to the larger text. . . . That there is

This is not to deny the importance of the distinction between a written and unwritten text, particularly in light of the weight that was placed on the metaphor of inscription in earlier discussions. But the institutionalization of a constitutional language can be achieved through any number of different mechanisms, just as a system of legal rules can be sufficiently defined to maintain its coherence regardless of whether it depends on a system of codification or common-law precedent.[14] Conversely, of course, either system can produce a set of rules that are insufficiently well-defined to serve the social and political functions that are implied in the term "law," giving rise to the problem of indeterminacy.[15] The content of

---

such a relation between constitutional signifier and signified promises that the underlying structure of the polity is legible." (Harris, 1982: 36.)

[14] The English common law system of precedents grew out the tradition of "historical jurisprudence" promulgated by writers such as Coke, Hale, Selden and Blackstone, in which customary law became formalized through the institutional actions of courts. (Berman, 1994.) David Strauss argues that the common-law system of precedent has a direct analogy in the accretion of precedents interpreting the U. S. Constitution, such that no direct reliance on the written text is either meaningful or necessary. (Strauss, 1996.) In response, Barak Cohen argues that the such an argument can only be appropriate in a situation in which there is a long-established tradition on which to draw. Cohen proposes that experiences from emerging constitutional democracies (specifically Israel) demonstrate that "judges' formal commitment to text as a source of normative authority may prove critical in the early development of empowered constitutionalism." (Cohen, 2003: 588–89.) In this chapter, my argument is that it is not the form of written-ness that is essential, nor the existence of a single written text rather than a collection of written constitutional analyses (judicial or otherwise), but rather the characteristics of exclusivity and completeness.

[15] Michael Dorf finds that the problem of indeterminacy is presented any time a constitutional text requires interpretation. Dorf proposes that the solution lies in reconceptualizing institutional roles, making courts one set of participants among many others in the process of democratic deliberation, which he believes will resolve the conflicts and resentments that accrue in a system of judicial constitutional review. (Dorf, 2003: 887–88.) In contrast, Jules Coleman and Brian Leiter insist that the debate is more properly one about claims to objectivity than about any assertion of determinism. "[L]iberalism," they write, "is not committed to determinacy in the sense of uniquely warranted outcomes." (Coleman and Leiter, 1993: 594.) Instead, what is at stake in liberal political theories of jurisprudence is a commitment to "modest objectivity," defined as the proposition that "what seems right under 'ideal epistemic conditions' determines what is right." (Coleman and Leiter, 1993: 620.) In this chapter, the problem of describing a minimum degree of determinacy or objectivity that a constitutional text requires is approached in this argument as a byproduct of the requirements of exclusivity, completeness, and substance. That is, as I will argue in the next chapter, if a constitutional text satisfies these requirements, then it will have the

constitutional language is the set of signs that are identified as proper for employment in constitutional discourse, whether that identification takes the form of a written document or the conventions of a constitutional regime.

The distinction between the rules of constitutional grammar and the system of constitutional signs is the distinction between validity and correctness. The grammatical rules of constitutional language identify the inscribed terms of a constitutional text as a set of rules for the formulation of valid propositions, and for this purpose they must begin with a requirement of exclusivity. To see why, consider the connection between validity and legitimacy. A legitimate constitutional proposition must be valid according to the terms of constitutional grammar. Within that system, an invalid proposition is not merely incorrect, it is meaningless; in Hobbesian terms, it is "absurd." An example would be an argument that attempted to define "freedom of speech" as "the authority of the government to declare any and all speech impermissible at any time." Such an interpretation is impermissible because it violates the rule of constitutional grammar that states that words in the constitutional text are to be understood in a way that is sensible to its readers, who otherwise would be incapable of also acting as its authors. This is not a requirement that is specific to some "language within a language"; it is an analytically necessary element of speaking of "language" at all. So guarantees of "freedom" are to be understood as referring to the ability of persons to act, (whether this is defined in terms of negative or positive conditions of liberty), not the ability of government to engage in coercion. An attempt to make an invalid proposition the basis for a conclusion is thus either trivial or disastrous. Such a proposition is either safely ignored as mere noise, or else it threatens the continued stability of the system of rules in which the proposition is phrased.

Exclusivity is the first principle of constitutional grammar, the metarule that says that that a valid constitutional proposition must be constructed in accordance with the other rules of constitutional grammar and out of the elements contained in the system of

---

qualities necessary to serve its political function of providing an adequately determined and objective basis for juridical action to be viewed as legitimate.

constitutional signs. In addition, a legitimate constitutional proposition must be constructed in a way that is *meaningful*; that is, it must accord with some articulable interpretation that assigns meaning to the constitutional signs that it employed, in addition to being formulated in terms identified as elements of the system of constitutional language. Locke's criminal was simultaneously a revolutionary because he threatened the organizing premises of the political order. Similarly, an attempt to employ propositions that violate the rules of constitutional grammar or that exceed the bounds of the systems of constitutional signs is an act of usurpation of the authority of the collective sovereign because it challenges the logic that makes the language of constitutional order intelligible.

To provide an example to which I will return later, a conclusion that a law violates the Due Process Clause of the Fourteenth Amendment on the grounds that it is "immoral" is not a legitimate constitutional proposition because it incorporates a term that is not an element in the American system of constitutional signs. Principles of morality may be important guides to the interpretation of constitutional signs, but only so long as that process is undertaken within the rules of American constitutional grammar, as in an argument that any interpretation of the Due Process Clause that yields a substantively immoral result is a bad one for independent, specifically constitutional reasons. But principles of morality cannot be the subject of a *direct* appeal as the basis for determining a constitutional question in the American system; they must be translated into constitutionally valid propositions. The same goes for an appeal to an irrelevant source of authority, as if an American constitutional judge were to declare a law unconstitutional on the grounds that it conflicted with the Democratic Party platform, the Sermon on the Mount, or the principles of sportsmanship described by the Marquis of Queensbury. Such an argument violates the principle of exclusivity, and hence the rules of constitutional grammar, by employing elements not contained in the system of constitutional signs. Any of these might be relevant sources of inspiration in interpreting the constitutional text, or in filling gaps in the system of constitutional rules, but a direct appeal to these sources as authority for a proposition of constitutional law is "absurd."

It is not only sources of authority but also particular forms of argument that are excluded from a bounded constitutional language. The Fourteenth Amendment forthrightly declares that anyone born in the United States is an American citizen, a definition that excludes a whole range of republican philosophies that since ancient times have described "citizenship" – including the prerogatives of participating in political decisions and the right to the protection of private interests by the operations of law – to be conditional on a demonstration of virtue. Article 1 of the German Constitution describes the government's duty to preserve dignity; no such argument is available in American constitutional discourse because no such concept is included in the American system of constitutional signs.[16] And the very form of a written constitution asserts a claim to exclusivity that precludes appeals to the older, pre-Bodin constitutional idea of a "sovereign" bound by ancient custom that define the limits of lawmaking.

An additional level of exclusion occurs when there is an identified institutional actor with authority to conclusively determine the correct interpretation of constitutional terms. In a system that contains a robust system of judicial constitutional review, for example, the assignment of institutional roles privileges speakers as well as speech. As a result, it is not only the selection of terms but also their authoritative interpretation that results in exclusions. Examples are easy to come by: the U.S. Supreme Court's 1868 determination that constitutional rights apply only to limit state action, rather than to protect individuals from one another; the Court's 1886 declaration (with neither analysis nor argument) that a corporation is a "person" for purposes of applying the Fourteenth Amendment[17]; and the conclusion in 1976 that the Due Process Clause of the Fourteenth Amendment applies only to deprivations of a liberty or property "interest" that is separately defined either

---

[16] Article 1 of the German Constitution begins: "(1) Human dignity is inviolable. To respect and protect it is the duty of all state authority...."

[17] "Before argument MR. CHIEF JUSTICE WAITE said: The court does not wish to hear argument on the question whether the provision in the Fourteenth Amendment to the Constitution, which forbids a State to deny to any person within its jurisdiction the equal protection of the laws, applies to these corporations. We are all of opinion that it does." *Santa Clara County v. Southern Pacific Railroad Company*, 118 U. S. 394 (1886).

elsewhere in the Constitution, by federal law, or by the laws of the state in which the acts complained of occurred.[18] Each of these acts of linguistic construction preempt and exclude a range of arguments from being made in the context of constitutional adjudication, including arguments that had previously been accepted as valid, by virtue of the institutional authority of their authors, which itself rests on the exclusivity of constitutional language. To those who might feel deeply that these excluded propositions are essential to the articulation of their position, the fact of exclusion is experienced as forcible compulsion to either abandon their claims unless they can be translated into constitutional language. An exclusive constitutional language is violent because it not only determines what arguments can win, it determines what arguments can be made at all. It is therefore not surprising that where the exclusive effect of constitutional language is the result of an act of interpretation, that interpretation may be controversial.

Nonetheless, the "as if" commitment to employ constitutional language, with all the exclusions that are implied in that commitment, is the necessary precondition to a legitimate constitutional regime, keeping in mind that at the outset the word "legitimate" was understood to indicate elements of stability and efficacy.[19] The distinction between propositions that can be asserted in constitutional discourse and others that may be appealed to indirectly is

---

[18] *Paul v. Davis*, 424 U.S. 693 (1976). The latter argument has the strange result that the meaning of constitutional terms is defined by a body of extraconstitutional laws, which casts doubt on the exclusivity of constitutional language and consequently on the supremacy of constitutional law as the substantive basis for judicial review.

[19] Mark Graber points out that something very close to this analysis can be seen in Lincoln's political rhetoric. "Lincoln during the months before Fort Sumter treated the status of slavery in the territories as a contested constitutional question. '*May* Congress prohibit slavery in the territories,' his first inaugural address asked. 'The Constitution does not expressly say.' '*Must* Congress protect slavery in the territories,' Lincoln continued. 'The Constitution does not expressly say'.... The first inaugural elaborated a theory about the constitutional authority necessary to settle contested constitutional questions.... The same shared commitments to majority rule, past constitutional compromises, and valued constitutional relationships that obligated free state citizens to accommodate much perceived constitutional evil, Lincoln maintained, obligated slave state citizens to acquiesce in Republican rule when Republicans gained constitutional majorities playing by the constitutional rules." (Graber, 2006: 344.)

precisely the distinction between constitutional language and ordinary, or non-constitutional, discourse. The violence of exclusion is inescapable if the constitutional text is to have meaning; otherwise the system truly becomes radically indeterminate.

Without exclusivity, the authority of the constitutional text no longer rests on the authority of sovereignty; instead, the only possible claim to authority is grounded in the appeal to substantive right. Moreover, the appeal to substantive right is not so much a replacement for an exclusive language as a displacement of exclusivity from the constitutional text onto some other source of authority. The absence of an exclusive source for "right," after all, was precisely the problem of value pluralism that led us to reject a straightforward appeal to moral norms as the basis for legitimation in the first instance. But that does nothing to resolve the difficulty, because some set of moral norms will be included in any institutionalized system of rules, while others will not be so included. If a constitutional regime is legitimated by appeal to external norms, then those who do not share those norms will experience the same compulsion to abandon or reformulate their positions that was described as "violent" in the description of an exclusive constitutional language.[20] At any given moment in the operation of a political regime, then, the language of constitutional discourse must be constrained to an exclusive system of constitutional language if that regime is to be considered simultaneously "constitutional" and legitimate.

The requirement of exclusivity fills in some of the missing elements in Rawls' ideal of public reason. Samuel Freeman points out that Rawls' appeal to an overlapping consensus is vulnerable to the criticism that, in practice, such an overlap may be precluded by the depth of unliquidated disagreements on questions of value. As a result, Freeman suggests, a Rawlsian theory might be compelled to give up its foundational ideal of a "well-ordered society" in favor of

---

[20] As Robert Post observes in response to the arguments of Robert Cover, "I do not fully understand the emphasis that Cover places on the jurispathic nature of courts. All nomoi ... are jurispathic, because all construct their narratives by excluding and suppressing other possible narratives. The problem with courts is not that they are jurispathic, but rather that they are violent." (Post, 2005:13–14.)

a merely workable liberal polity.[21] Whether such an outcome is feasible in practice is an open question; insofar as the question before us is the possibility of a constitutional polity, however, the requirement of well-orderedness is adequately satisfied by the "as if" commitment to an exclusive constitutional language. The exclusivity of constitutional discourse, grounded in the binding discursive commitments of a self-sovereign people, is a mechanism for rescuing the ideal of a well-ordered society from to the challenge of value pluralism.

The references to judicial interpretations of the constitutional text point to the fact that even an entirely exclusive system of constitutional signs is not closed as to its meaning, only bounded. "Limited" is not the same thing as "closed." As suggested earlier, any number of sources can be brought to bear on the act of *reading* a constitutional text; it is in the act of constitutional *writing* and *speaking* that limitations become significant.[22] The institution of a constitutional system can be seen as serving the same role for political culture that constitutional language serves for political language; it isolates and delimits the scope of the necessary commitment to the smallest necessary area of discourse, and at the same time secures that commitment by an institutional structure. We need

---

[21] "In conceding that even under the best of conditions, where justice as fairness itself is in effect, there will be a pluralism, not just of reasonable comprehensive doctrines, but of liberal political conceptions of justice, Rawls appears to concede that a well-ordered society of justice as fairness is not feasible, at least not as originally conceived .... The most that we can expect is a society where there is general acceptance by all reasonable people of one or another liberal and democratic political view (justice as fairness being among them)." (Freeman, 2004: 2072.) The difficulty that remains, of course, is the weight that is put on the qualifier "reasonable."

[22] James Madigan proposes an "exclusive view of public reason," by which he means that "only reasons grounded in political values should be introduced when debating constitutional essentials and matters of basic justice such as fundamental rights." (Madigan, 2002: 720.) Madigan claims two advantages for an exclusive version of "public reason" that connect to the ideal of deliberative democracy. "The first advantage of an exclusive view is that it best enables the educative role of public reason. A debate relying exclusively on public reasons cannot help but educate its participants about the family of political conceptions of justice.... But the educative role for public reason is not just in citizens' passive voyeurism of public debate. Because the exclusive view of public reason operates solely within shared political values, it will (and ought to) spark questions about what has been left out." (Madigan, 2002: 752–53.)

neither assume that humans are angels, capable of extremely broad commitments without the requirement of any institutional reinforcement, nor that commitment can be imposed by an act of external sovereign authority. Instead, we can conceive of a limited locus of commitment that is specifically oriented toward the creation of an active popular sovereign by the generation of constitutional language.

This observation draws a connection between the property of exclusivity and the property of completeness. A system of constitutional language must be exclusive as far as it goes; but how far must it go? That is, how "complete" must a constitutional language be in order to be adequate to the task of supporting a legitimate constitutional regime? There are two different elements to this inquiry. First, how complete does the constitutional language need in terms of its content – the system of constitutional signs – to be in order to perform its political task? And, second, how much of that constitutional language has to be contained in an identifiable text?

THE ARGUMENT FOR INCOMPLETENESS

Samuel Freeman addresses the first question in considering objections to Rawls' ideal of public reason that it is "not sufficiently deep to deal with all the political issues it needs to if it is to serve as a basis for constitutional argument." As a result, according to critics such as Kent Greenawalt, "inevitably officials and citizens will have to appeal to comprehensive views to interpret the scope of basic constitutional liberties and other abstract liberal principles they all agree on." (Freeman, 2004: 2054.) In response, Freeman proposes that Rawlsian public reason can carry more freight than its critics assume. "My own view is that, because Rawls recognizes a family of political conceptions providing content to public reason, there has to be more than one politically reasonable answer to this issue. That is, far from being incomplete, public reason is overdetermined insofar as it provides more than one politically reasonable answer to many constitutional issues." (Freeman, 2004: 2055–56.)

As for the possibility that "there are some reasonable people who cannot accept the political resolution of [an] issue in terms of public reason," this does indeed raise the specter of political instability, but this possibility does not diminish the adequacy of the Rawlsian account of public reason. The existence in the polity of such persons is only problematic "if, as a result of their inability to accept the political resolution by public reason for one or more constitutional issues (e.g. regarding abortion), they are led to reject public reason itself in all other cases. Then those citizens and their comprehensive doctrine can no longer endorse a political conception of justice in an overlapping consensus with other reasonable comprehensive doctrines. Depending on how many citizens and how many reasonable comprehensive doctrines are in this position, it raises questions regarding the stability of the family of liberal political conceptions." (Freeman, 2004: 2056–57.)

Freeman's concern is not with describing the degree of completeness that a system of public reason would be required to have to serve the political function of legitimation, only whether a particular (Rawlsian) description of that concept is adequate to the task. But examining his argument points us in the direction of an answer to the question before us. First, Freeman, like Rawls, is careful to distinguish political reasons from political arguments.[23] That is, there is no suggestion that the requirements of public reason apply to motivations or personal norms, only to the manner in which those norms are translated into constitutional argument. As a result, what is presented as a problem of incompleteness is more properly understood as a problem of exclusivity; if it is the case that the construction of public reason is such that it excludes any possibility of a valid argument that articulates a speaker's beliefs, then that speaker will be compelled to choose between reaching outside the language of public reason or forgoing expression of her beliefs. An insufficiently complete but exclusive constitutional language makes it impossible for citizens to articulate critical arguments.

[23] Kent Greenawalt, considering the implications of the First Amendment's Establishment Clause for political debate, proposes what he calls an "intermediate" position of exclusivity. Legislation must be justified in terms of secular objectives, but when people reasonably think that rational analysis and an acceptable rational secular morality cannot resolve critical questions of fact, fundamental questions of value, or the weighing of competing harms, they do appropriately rely on religious convictions that help them answer these questions.... Though reliance on religious convictions is appropriate in these settings, argument in religious terms is often an inapt form of public dialogue." (Greenawalt, 1985: 356–57.)

The second point is that no exclusive constitutional language can ever be "complete" in the sense of fully capturing all the belief-systems that citizens in a pluralistic society will want to bring to bear on public discourse. There will, inevitably, be genuinely excluded arguments; this is the inescapable element of violence inherent in the construction of a juridical discourse. Freeman observes that this is only a "problem" if the level of frustration rises to the point of threatening the stability of the political arrangement. In the context of a discussion of constitutional language, we can restate this in a somewhat more precise way: a constitutional regime that is to function in the face of unliquidated disagreement over questions of values requires a constitutional language that permits the articulation of a sufficiently wide range of principles that the level of frustration experienced by those whose arguments are excluded does not become politically destabilizing. That is, such a language must be sufficiently complete to permit its broad acceptance as legitimate, not by virtue of its accord with differing values but by virtue of its capacity to provide for their articulation in constitutional discourse.

The problem remains, however, that there will be excluded propositions, and for some individuals this fact will preclude their granting legitimacy to the constitutional regime. But the problem of completeness need not be presented as a single inquiry. An alternative approach is one that recognizes the possibility of a constitutional language that is complete in some areas and incomplete in others. Such a langauge would be required to be exclusive only insofar as it is complete, and might leave open the possibility of employing other forms of discourse to fill the gaps. Keith Whittington appeals to something like this idea with his treatment of the distinction between "interpretation" and "construction." In Whittington's terms, "interpretation" is the act of eliciting meaning from a text, whereas "construction" is the act of filling gaps. "Constructions do not pursue a preexisting if deeply hidden meaning in the founding document; rather, they elucidate the text in the interstices of discoverable, interpretive meaning, where the text is so broad or so underdetermined as to be incapable of faithful but exhaustive reduction to legal rules." (Whittington, 1999b: 5.)

Whittington is primarily concerned with the historical case of the United States, and his description of construction in action concerns the role of non-judicial political actors in the creation of a constitutional tradition, but a series of important, broader theoretical points appear in the course of the discussion. For one thing, Whittington's description of constitutional construction raises the possibility that incompleteness may be a legal defect (because of the problem of indeterminacy) but a political asset. Constitutional construction entails the consideration of fundamental principles that structure a mode of political action, occurring at a moment of unsettled understanding (a criterion necessary to preserve the supremacy of the interpretable text). The result is that constitutional constructions operate in terms highly reminiscent of Stephen Holmes' discussion of enabling rules. "In this context, the Constitution is often understood less as a set of binding rules than as a source of authoritative norms of political behavior and as the foundation of governing institutions .... The Constitution not only constrains, it empowers." (Whittington, 1999b: 1, 4, 8.)

To serve its political function, Whittington's constitutional construction must reach beyond the text, and consequently beyond the limitations of any exclusive constitutional language. "In order to render constitutional values concrete, the text must be supplemented by something outside itself.... Constructions constantly add a denser web of values, institutions, procedures, and rights to the general framework established by the constitutional text and made clear by interpretation. The abilities to shape public understandings, to build institutions, and to achieve compliance without the force of law are critical to the success of constructions." (Whittington, 1999b: 208)

Moreover, the constraints of public reason do not apply to the process of construction in the manner that they apply to the act of textual interpretation. "Given that constructions are not grounded in discoverable meaning and are not concerned primarily with the formulation of legal rules, there are genuine limits to the ability of rational argument to fulfill the needs of construction .... Constructions are made by explicit advocates, not by disinterested arbiters." (Whittington, 1999b: 210.) Whittington argues that the existence of a political/constructed dimension to the U.S. Constitution has permitted the system to remain stable in the face of profound disagreements and complex institutional tensions in ways that a reliance on a purely legal/interpreted constitutional text would not.[24]

The argument is a strong one, and certainly one can easily recognize a danger in a constitutional text that is so complete as to limit the ability of the constitutionally established government to make institutional adaptations necessary for effective policy implementation. At the same time, there is a telling observation here about the rhetoric of constitutional construction as it is practiced in American politics. Like judges insisting that their discovery of constitutional rules follows from the implications of the text, political actors engaging in constitutional construction invariably legitimate their actions by claiming to be engaged in interpretation. "Very few of the individuals who entered into the debates over these several constructions contended forthrightly that the Constitution was indeterminate.... Whether defending an existing construction or advocating its replacement with a new one, those engaging in constructions sought to identify themselves with the true and required meaning of the Constitution." (Whittington, 1999b: 213.) This is an unsettling observation; if the constitutional regime depends on a practice that cannot, itself, be legitimated in the terms of that regime's constitutional language, what happens to the regime's claim to legitimacy?

Whittington's approach calls for a bifurcation between the written and unwritten portions of a constitutional text. The written text is treated as radically incomplete, but exclusive, while the range of extraconstitutional materials that may be employed to fill gaps in the text is potentially infinite. So long as the supremacy of the written text is acknowledged in cases of conflict – so long, that is, as gap-filling does not become usurpation – the constitutional regime

---

[24] For example, Whittington argues that a constructed resolution to the constitutional question of a President's authority to impound funds produced a workable set of institutional arrangements that might have been unavailable through the application of a traditionally judiciary-driven, legalistic model of constitutional interpretation. "[Congress] did not wish to reconstruct the budget powers on rigid, legal terms. Rather, congressional reformers sought to institutionalize a partnership between the branches.... The extent of the executive power and its hold over the power of the purse depended on the existence of a viable alternative far more than it did on a formal division of powers." (Whittington, 1999b: 170.)

remains intact despite any level of vigorous disagreement between arguments grounded in conflicting extraconstitutional sources. Taken as a whole, then, the system of constitutional language is complete and non-exclusive; the portion of that language that is contained in a written text is incomplete and weakly exclusive. Where Freeman attempted to rescue Rawls' public reason from the implications of exclusivity by appealing to its capacity for completeness, in other words, Whittington confronts the problem of exclusivity head-on and seeks a resolution by curtailing the claims of completeness.

To a great extent, and despite other areas of disagreement, Whittington's and Freeman's approaches echo that of Cass Sunstein. Like Freeman, Sunstein adopts the Rawlsian ideal of public reason to argue that the focus of democratic constitutionalism should be on the conditions of deliberation, and like Whittington he appeals to the benefits of incompleteness, in the form of "incompletely theorized agreements," to respond to the problem of unliquidated disagreement. Sunstein's resolution of the problem of relating exclusivity to completeness, however, offers a third alternative to those of Whittington and Freeman.

Sunstein's memorable term to characterize the American system of democratic constitutionalism is "a republic of reasons." "[T]he Americans insisted, in direct opposition to their English inheritance, that 'culture' was 'man-made.' In America, social outcomes had to be justified not by reference to nature or to traditional practices, but instead on the basis of reasons." (Sunstein, 1993: 19.) Sunstein identifies the necessity of public justification as the condition of legitimacy in a democratic system of collective action. "At the heart of the liberal tradition and its opposition to authoritarianism lies a requirement of justification by reference to public-regarding explanations that are intelligible to all citizens." The requirement for legitimation is what separates constitutionalism from simple interest-group pluralism. (Sunstein, 1993: 24–5.) His analysis, therefore, is devoted to attempting to describe the ways in which a constitutional order contributes to the conditions under which deliberative democracy can be maintained. "Constitutionalism can thus guarantee the preconditions for democracy

by limiting the power of majorities to eliminate those preconditions." (Sunstein, 1993: 142.)[25]

Much of Sunstein's discussion is devoted to a consideration of
theories of constitutional interpretation and the role of the judiciary, and is therefore tangential to this discussion. In the course of
his discussion, however, Sunstein draws a distinction between
"substantive" and "semantic" principles that, in important ways,
parallels the distinction between rules of constitutional grammar
and a system of constitutional signs.[26] The consequences of the
distinction for the moment of constitutional consent, however, are
almost the opposite of Sunstein's conclusions concerning the subsequent possibilities for a stable constitutional order.

In a nutshell, Sunstein argues for strict exclusivity with minimal
completeness. What is outside the range of the constitutional text's
completeness, however, is treated not as an alternative basis for the
creation of constitutional meaning, but rather as a background level
of non-constitutional discourse. The advantage that Sunstein sees is
that a focus on the conditions of deliberation enables a constitutional system to function even in the face of unliquidated disagreements over substantive principles. A complete system of
constitutional signs would imply a real or artificial consensus on all
issues of constitutional meaning. But even if such consensus were
plausible, Sunstein argues, it is not clear that it would yield the best
outcomes. The danger of relying on consensus is the tendency
toward group polarization, a tendency that is exacerbated by the fact

---

[25] Like Holmes and Harris, Sunstein dismisses the objection to constitutional rule as
undemocratic on the grounds that democracy involves more than simple
majoritarian decision-making. "Many rights are indispensable to democracy and
to democratic deliberation. If we protect such rights through the Constitution, we
do not compromise self-government at all. On the contrary, self-government
depends for its existence on firmly protected democratic rights." (Sunstein, 1993:
125.)

[26] "Semantic principles are those whose acceptance counts as part of what it means to
speak the relevant language in a simple, dictionary sense. People who reject
semantic principles reveal that they just do not understand what certain words
mean. ... Substantive principles are different. Such principles require not a
language lesson or a dictionary, but a substantive political justification. The idea
that the original understanding is (or is not) binding falls within the category of
substantive principles. So too with the idea that constitutional provisions should
always be read to promote the functioning of democratic processes." (Sunstein,
1993: 102.)

that the processes of opinion-formation often feature "enclave deliberation" (dialogue only among like-minded persons), "cascade effects" (the tendency to tailor one's opinions to fit those of dominant group members), and "rhetorical asymmetry" (the observation that the most extreme form of a position is often the easiest to articulate effectively). (Sunstein, 2001: 15–16, 31.) As an example of this last phenomenon, Sunstein points to debates over criminal sentencing. "Legislative judgments about criminal punishment may, for example, involve an asymmetry of exactly this kind; those favoring greater punishment for drug-related offenses appear to have a systematic advantage over those favoring lesser punishment." (Sunstein, 2001: 31.) Empirical studies have confirmed that this kind of self-reinforcing deliberation is a common feature of ordinary American political discourse. (Walsh, 2003.)

On the other hand, an imaginary system that ensures that all constitutional discourse takes place in large, heterogenous settings is not necessarily an improvement. "[T]here is a point more supportive of enclave deliberation: Participants in heterogenous groups tend to give least weight to the views of low-status members – in some times and places, women, African Americans, less educated people. Hence enclave deliberation might be the only way to ensure that those views are developed and eventually heard." (Sunstein, 2001: 16; see also pp. 44–45.) What is needed, therefore, is to devise a system that simultaneously permits enclave deliberation at the stage of opinion formation and ensures that it does not translate directly into collective will-formation.

For Sunstein, the condition of possibility for such an arrangement is consent grounded in "incompletely theorized" agreements. "[P]eople can agree that a certain practice is constitutional or is not constitutional, even when the theories that underlie their judgments sharply diverge," by engaging in a "conceptual descent" to a "lower level of abstraction." (Sunstein, 2001: 9.) In an extreme case, there can be disagreement about the correct outcome of a specific controversy even in the complete absence of agreement concerning the theoretical justifications for that outcome, a situation Sunstein calls "full particularity." Incompletely theorized agreement resolves the issue of persistent substantive disagreement by achieving "a major goal of a heterogenous society: *to make it possible to obtain agreement where agreement is necessary and to make it unnecessary to obtain agreement where agreement is impossible.*" (Sunstein, 2001: 50–51, emphasis in original.) So, for example, it might be possible to agree on the applicability of the clear and present danger test for protected speech (an example of a mid-level principle) without agreeing on the meaning of "free speech" in general, or to agree on a rule banning false police reports without agreeing on the acceptability of the clear and present danger test. (Sunstein, 2001: 53, 57.)

Sunstein is primarily concerned with the operation of a constitutional system, rather than with the conditions of its establishment, and at points his argument does not map easily onto the present discussion. In some sense, the "as if" commitment to a constitutional language can be thought of as an example of a necessary but incompletely theorized agreement. Certainly, identifying points where it is "unnecessary to obtain agreement" is a key element of the minimalist approach that informs this effort.

It is also the case that the shift in the focus of the initial commitment away from an anthropomorphic metaphor of sovereign identity toward a discursive principle of popular-sovereignty-in-action is a response to many of the same concerns that Sunstein tries to address. Thereafter, the system of constitutional signs would identify the limited areas in which something like complete theorization is required. A separate, specific system of rules for constitutional discourse insulates constitutional claims from the effects of rhetorical asymmetry, and the use of a separate, artificial set of discursive rules similarly insulates constitutional deliberation from the polarizing effects of enclave deliberation. The necessity of translating enclave-specific arguments into a common constitutional language moderates the dangers of legitimating extreme positions.

There is another benefit that Sunstein claims for incompletely theorized agreements that resonates with the argument for the model of constitutional language that is presented here. Sunstein suggests that incomplete theorization opens the space for civility that Rawls sought in the ideal of public reason. "[I]ncompletely theorized agreements allow people to show each other a high degree of mutual respect, or civility, or reciprocity." This is not only desirable as a matter of social organization or ensuring effective democratic deliberation, it is a direct requirement of democratic constitutionalism. "If reciprocity and mutual respect are desirable, it follows that public officials or judges, perhaps even more than ordinary people, should not challenge their fellow citizens' deepest and most defining commitments, at least if those commitments are reasonable and if there is no need for them to do so." (Sunstein, 2001: 53.)

The argument for avoiding challenges to the "deepest and most defining commitments" of citizens is both the strongest point of agreement and the clearest point of departure between Sunstein's theory of deliberative democracy and my own theory of constitutional language. The theory of constitutional language that is presented here is in part an argument that semantic principles precede and underlie a discussion of substantive principles. This is an observation that requires consideration of the relationship between different levels of theoretical justifications. Consensus on semantic principles – or a willingness to act "as if" there is such a consensus – is required for there to be a mutually intelligible discussion about the adequacy or desirability of substantive principles. Consensus on semantic principles is presented as an alternative to positing consensus on substantive principles.

But my concern in this discussion has not been merely to shield "citizens' deepest and most defining commitments" from government actors' disrespect, it has been to identify the level of semantic commitment required for the formation of a constitutional order of government in the face of citizens' differing commitments. From that perspective, the move that is required is precisely the opposite of the one prescribed by Sunstein. To avoid implicating citizens' differing fundamental beliefs, the level of consensus must be moved to a *higher* level of abstraction, first from substantive to semantic principles, and then from semantic to syntactic principles, the linguistic equivalent of the constitutive rules of a formal game situation.

This is not so much a point of sharp disagreement as the identification of a necessary precondition for Sunstein's argument. The exclusivity of constitutional language is what is required to make reliance on incompletely theorized agreement possible, by providing a set of discursive rules for the translation of incommensurate substantive principles into a commonly accessible vocabulary of rulemaking and rule legitimation. If constitutional language is to function in the face of such fundamental substantive disagreements, it may be necessary to insist on some degree of "incompleteness" at the semantic level, in addition to an openness to different substantive conclusions in the form of constitutional rules. The question of completeness, then, points toward three, rather than two, levels of theorization: the metalinguistic syntactical principles of constitutional grammar, the semantic system of constitutional signs, and the (as-yet-unexplored) substantive normative commitments that are necessary, rather than merely desirable, elements of constitutional discourse.

This engagement with the arguments of Freeman, Whittington, and Sunstein is not yet a complete argument for the degrees of exclusivity and incompleteness that are minimally required for a working constitutional language. To begin with, there is not yet a good answer to the question, "minimally required for a working constitutional language" to do what, exactly? Is the "adequacy" of a constitutional language measured against a set of existing political arrangements that it purports to describe, or a set of normative commitments for future conduct that it claims to articulate?

To get at these questions, it is useful to situate a theory of constitutional language in the larger context of theories of law generally, and ultimately to consider the extent to which the language of law is the appropriate model for the language of constitutional discourse.[27] Legal theory, like constitutional theory, wrestles with questions of exclusivity, completeness, and substance. These arguments frequently turn to specific consideration of constitutions and constitution

---

[27] Christopher Eisgruber argues forthrightly that the deployment of legal discourse to defend the institution of judicial constitutional review in the United States has had deleterious effects on Americans' constitutional understanding. "By treating the Constitution mainly as a set of legal restraints rather than an instrument enabling self-government, the Court has made more plausible the idea that constitutional interpretation is exclusively the province of lawyers – a professional elite who may have no special insight into justice or politics but who are expert at the manipulation of fine-grained rules." (Eisgruber, 2001b: 70–71.) John Finn, in an essay in the same volume, proposes a vision of "civic" rather than "juridic" constitutionalism, which "emphasizes not the legal character, but rather the political character of the basic charter, its status not as supreme law but as political creed. It envisions a political order in which constitutional questions, although partly questions of law, are fundamentally and first questions about politics, about the broad principles and normative commitments that comprise our commitment to shared community." (Finn, 2001: 42.)

making, and even when the subject-matter of the discussion is ordinary law, or an undifferentiated reference to "law" *tout court*, the analyses that result offer powerful insights for the present discussion. In the next section, therefore, I will ask what light is shed by arguments about the ground for the legitimation of legal systems generally on the specific question of what levels of exclusivity and completeness are required of a constitutional language.

CONSTITUTIONAL AND LEGAL LEGITIMACY: GROUNDING NORMS AND LEGAL POSITIVISM

Two important approaches to accounting for legitimacy in law are found in the theories of legal positivism developed by Hans Kelsen and H. L. A. Hart. At its most basic, the principle of legal positivism is that the term "law" describes social practice rather than a relationship between a rule and a prior, external set of norms. The positivist approach to the legitimation of law treats the idea of law itself as a descriptor of a social practice. That is, a rule-like proposition is a "law" if it is engendered in a way, and takes a form, that is recognized as authoritative in the society in which it occurs. To call a law "legitimate," in turn, does not imply any requirement that such a rule have any particular moral quality, or accord with any particular philosophical commitments, only that it be consonant with the understandings reflected in prevalent sociolegal practices in the society in which it occurs. This does not imply that law needs to be amoral, only that morality is not any essential part of law. In Frederick Schauer's words, "To the positivist, law may very well be moral, and certainly should be moral, but it is not necessarily moral" (Schauer, 1993: 801.) For a legal positivist, the assertion that a law is "legitimate" names an observed sociological fact rather than an analytic proposition.[28]

---

[28] Schauer connects the idea of legal positivism directly to the issues of completeness and exclusivity in the context of constitutional design, arguing for a "limited domain," in which "law" identifies "distinctly legal norms from among the entire universe of social (including moral) norms." Against this description, Schauer points to Ronald Dworkin's model of constitutional decision making in which law is part of a "seamless web ... of the full set of a society's public norms." Schauer is willing to concede that as an empirical description of judicial practice, this model has merit in some categories of cases. "[T]he limited domain thesis, if conceptually

Applied to constitutionalism, the parallel claim would be that to speak of a "legitimate constitutional regime" is to describe the way a system of government is prevalently perceived by its citizens. The analytical question of the conditions of possibility for constitutional legitimacy is thus translated into a proposition of the form "a constitution is legitimate if and only if all/most/some number of its citizens perceive it to be so." Converted into the Lockean constitutionalism that provides the basis for arguments of this book, the legal positivist's test for legitimacy would become something like the following: "A constitutional regime is legitimate if and only if all/most/some of its citizens accept the initial commitment to constitutional language as binding upon themselves and perceive the subsequently created constitutional order as an act of self-sovereignty exercised through inscription."

That last statement, more or less, captures the legal positivist's answer to the question "Consent How?" On closer examination, however, the various theories of legal positivism have rather more to say in response to the question "Consent to What?" and in particular to the question of the degrees of exclusivity and completeness that a constitutional language is required to have if it is to be an adequate basis for a legitimate constitutional regime. A consideration of the positivist position forces us to focus more closely on the relationship between the legitimacy of laws generally and the particular question of establishing the conditions of legitimacy for a constitution.

There are two different ways in which this formulation might inform our consideration of the content of constitutional language. On the one hand, we might revert to something like Jeremy Waldron's appeal to a thick understanding of "good faith" or other versions of an argument from culture in order to illustrate the idea that a constitutional regime is legitimate if it is regarded that way as a matter of sociological fact. In that case, the idea of constitutional

---

sound, is likely to be more true the further one moves away from the morally soaked subject of constitutional law, and the further one moves away from (even within constitutional law) the Supreme Court of the United States." (Schauer, 1993: 823–4.) From that observation, Schauer goes on to raise the question of whether constitutional adjudication either is, or should be, conceived of as resting solely on the limited domain of "law" rather than incorporating both legal and extralegal norms in the exercise of judgment, thus positing a limited domain of law that is neither complete nor exclusive. (Schauer, 1993: 827.)

language merely identifies one of the indicia of the fact of public acceptance. That is, if we find evidence to suggest a prevalent commitment to constitutional language, then we will have grounds for proposing that the constitutional regime that is constructed out of that language has a claim to be considered legitimate.

Alternatively, we may consider the possibility that the legitimation of a constitutional regime is different in kind from the legitimation of the particular laws. From this perspective, the implication of the sociolegal argument is that to be legitimate a constitutional language must be effective in *creating* the sociological fact that the acts of the constitutional regime are recognized as "law." Characteristics of exclusivity and completeness would thus be required insofar as they could be shown to be necessary for the production of legitimate law in the operation of a constitutional regime. That second inquiry is the one I will pursue. What characteristics of exclusivity and completeness is a constitutional language required to have in order that a commitment to that language provides an adequate basis for the legitimation of the lawmaking regime that it is employed to create?

Positivism begins by describing legitimacy as a sociological fact, but the nature of the relevant sociological fact is open for discussion. A commonly drawn distinction separates "hard" positivist theories of law from "soft" versions of the same theories.[29] In hard positivism, the only possible basis for the legitimacy of a legal rule is the authority of the lawmaker. To paraphrase the questions that have motivated this book, in its barest terms legal positivism is the argument that the answer to the first question, "what are the conditions for legitimate law," is "sovereignty," and the answer to the second question, "what follows about the nature of law from the answer to the first question," is "nothing." By this understanding, the justification in the preceding chapters for constitution writing as an exercise of collective self-sovereignty, if it is accepted, ends the discussion, and problems such as balancing exclusivity with

---

[29] For a review of the literature presenting these two approaches to legal positivism, along with a consideration of some philosophical problems that are raised by each approach, see Leiter, 2003.

completeness are simply pushed aside.[30] Soft positivism, by contrast, leaves open the possibility that in a given society, the tests for the legitimacy of law may relate, in part or entirely, to some underlying conceptions of what laws *ought* to be like, conceptions that members of the relevant society employ in their evaluation of the legitimacy of a legal rule.[31]

Hans Kelsen's legal positivism reflects the continuing attempt to use a general theory of law to explain the content of legitimating consent. Constitutions and laws, for Kelsen, share basic defining characteristics. Both are constitutive of the state, both are inherently normative, and both derive their character from a dynamic system of rule generation. In the process of making his argument, however, Kelsen lays the groundwork for distinguishing between constitutional and legal legitimacy in crucial ways that ultimately cast doubt on the adequacy of his positivistic account of legitimacy for a constitutional regime.

Kelsen's first crucial move is to reconsider the relationship between law and the state. Like James Wilson in the eighteenth century, Kelsen conceives of the state as a prejuridical association. All forms of law, whether constitutional, positive or customary, are created as a function of state authority expressed in the actions of a particular form of government. "The problem of the form of government as the question of the method of law creation arises, however, not only at the level of the constitution ... but at all levels of law creation." In particular, Kelsen rejects the distinction between private and public law. "The differentiation in principle between a public (or political) and a private (or unpolitical) legal sphere is designed to prevent the recognition that the 'private' right ... is just as much the theater of the political dominion as the public law created by legislation and administration." (Kelsen, 1967: 280, 293.) As a result, for example, appeal to private law concepts such as

---

[30] "[E]very positive law, or every law strictly so called is ... a direct or circuitous command of a monarch or sovereign number to a person or persons in a state of subjection to its author. And being a command (and therefore flowing from a determinate source), every positive law is a law proper, or a law properly so called." (Austin, 2000: 134.)

[31] The term "soft positivism" comes from H. L. A. Hart's "Postscript" to *The Concept of Law* (Hart, 1997: 250–54), in which he responded to challenges from Ronald Dworkin. Hart's arguments are discussed later.

"property" cannot be used to legitimate public legal actions, since both are equally contained within a political order. "[T]he state, as a meta-legal being ... is *presupposed by the law* – and at the same time, as a subject of the law, i.e., as subjected to it, obligated and authorized by it, *presupposes the law*." (Kelsen, 1967: 285.)

The artificial duality of state and law emerges with the adoption of an anthropomorphic metaphor of the state. "The state as a social order is the ... national legal order. The state as a person is the personification of that order." In a very Hobbesian moment, Kelsen attributes the personification of the state as a "juristic person" to the conflation of sign with object. "Once it is recognized that the state, as an order of human behavior, is a relatively centralized coercive order and that the state as a juristic person is the personification of this coercive order, the dualism of state and law is abolished as one of those duplications that originate when cognition hypostatizes the unity of its object (the concept of 'person' being the expression of such unity)." (Kelsen, 1967: 293, 290, 318.) The rejection of the state/law duality means that the constitutional order of the state cannot appeal for its legitimacy to a prepolitical set of "laws," whether these are conceived in terms of natural law or the fact of historical custom. "[I]t is simply impossible to justify the state through the law; just as it is impossible to justify the law through the law .... This critical abolition of the dualism of state and law ... represents the most radical annihilation of one of the most effective ideologies of legitimacy." (Kelsen, 1967: 318–19.)[32]

The deconstruction of the opposition between law and lawgiver moves us from an understanding of sovereignty over others to the idea of self-sovereignty engendered through an act of lawmaking that has been identified as the starting-point for constitutional understanding. Like Locke's sovereign, possessed of authority over the language out of which it was created, Kelsen's state is simultaneously the creator and the creation of law, unmoored to any external legal authority.

Another, perhaps less obvious, consequence of the collapse of the opposition between state and law is that the state, no less than the

---

[32] For a general summary of Kelsen's theory of the state and its relation to law, see Stewart, 1990: 291–93.

law, is an inherently normative entity. Kelsen does not argue that the legitimacy of law as a sociological fact can be separated from normative claims, only that such claims are not relevant to the definition of "law" *at the moment of state formation*. Once created, however, a state is an inherently normative entity because it carries within it the material of its creation, just as Locke's sovereign exercised its authority over a bounded system of language that was itself the material from which sovereignty arose. "The relationship designated as state power is distinguished from other power relationships by the fact that it is legally regulated ... state power has normative character." Customary law, for example, is not different from traditional legislation precisely insofar as it expresses the organizing normative commitments of the state. "[S]ince by custom, precisely as by legislation, general legal norms are created, custom could be attributed to the state just as much as legislation." (Kelsen, 1967: 289, 294–95.)

The implication is that constitutionalism of some kind is inherent to statehood. The state is a form of social organization in which coercive force is employed, but those coercive acts are those "which the legal order attaches to certain conditions stipulated by it." "As a political organization, the state is a legal order," a form of "social community [which] can be constituted only by a normative order." (Kelsen, 1967: 286–87.) The state comes into being with the creation of both constraining and effectuating mechanisms for the exercise of power, and thereafter the actions of the state take the form of power exercised through those mechanisms. This is the constitutional point of connection between the justification for the creation of lawmaking authority and the creation of laws by that authority. For a Kelsenian positivist, the term "constitutional" names the sociolegal practice of legitimating laws by testing them against constitutionally inscribed principles.

The inherent normativity, the law-like-ness of a constitution, necessarily implies a politically critical function in its relationship to juridical practice. That is, not only new but also existing juridical practices become subject to critical evaluation. The social fact of legitimacy identifies the existence of a vocabulary in terms of which actors will accept the necessity of subjecting their juridical practices to potentially transformative criticism. Kelsen's state occupies the intermediate position of a constitutional system that is simultaneously grounded in an existing normative order and establishes the terms for challenges to or affirmations of the legitimacy of that order.

The key to understanding the consequences of Kelsen's theory for a theory of constitutional language is to recognize the relationship that he draws between norms and institutions. Since the state, no less than the system of laws, is an institution for the creation of norms, the question of identifying the necessary legitimating commitments that underlie the creation of a state is the question of identifying analytically necessary foundational norms. Ultimately, for Kelsen, this becomes the search for a grounding or "basic norm" (*grundnorm*). Ordinary norms always presuppose other norms; for example, the biblical rule against murder presupposes a norm of obedience to divine law. As a result, "the quest for the reason of validity of a norm leads back not to reality, but to another norm." (Kelsen, 1945: 110.)[33] Normative systems are grounded in initial commitments from which other normative principles follow deductively. "A norm the validity of which cannot be derived from a superior norm we call a 'basic norm.' All norms whose validity may be traced back to one and the same basic norm form a system of norms, or an order." (Kelsen, 1945: 111.)

Applying this insight to the definition of "law," Kelsen concludes that the foundational basic norm of any juridical system is definitional rather than moral, focusing on the form of law-ness rather than an evaluation of a particular rule's substantive content. The

---

[33] Robert Alexy proposes that the focus on norms makes Kelsen's argument fundamentally one about metaphysics, in contrast with "reductionist" attempts to limit the description of law to social facts. Kelsen's norms are most frequently described as versions of the Kantian *a priori* commitments. Kelsen himself drew this analogy but, as critics have noted, the fit between Kantian moral commitment and Kelsen's norms is far from perfect. (Tur and Twining, 1986; Stewart, 1990.) A different approach is offered by Dhananjai Shivakumar, who conceives of Kelsenian norms as analogues to Weberian ideal types by focusing on links between Kelsen's and Weber's methods of analysis rather than on the obvious distinction between Weber's project of social description and Kelsen's search for a "pure" theory of law. (Shivakumar, 1996: 1404.) For additional connections between Weber's and Kelsen's methodologies, particularly with regard to the conditions for social knowledge, see Stewart, 1998: 184–85, 187, n. 16.) For purposes of this discussion, the focus on Kelsen's description of norms in action are more relevant than his exploration of transcendental categorical concepts.

question, in other words, is one of the validity of propositions rather than the correctness of their substantive content. "Legal norms are not valid because they themselves or the basic norm have a content the binding force of which is self-evident .... A norm is a valid legal norm by virtue of the fact that it has been created according to a definite rule and by virtue thereof only." (Kelsen, 1945: 111, 113.)

The difficulty, obviously, is the danger of infinite regress, "[f]or the higher, authorizing norm is itself the subjective meaning of an act of will directed toward others; and only if this act too is authorized by a still higher norm is [it] ... a binding, valid norm." (Kelsen, 1986: 112.) Here, Kelsen's commitment to positivism reasserts itself in the form of a presupposed tendency to accept a certain way of thinking as "normal" within a community, again emphasizing Kelsen's desire to collapse the boundaries separating law, politics, and society. Kelsen draws an analogy to a father ordering his son to go to school. In response to the question, "why should I go to school," the father responds "because God has commanded that parents be obeyed." When the son then asks why the commands of God should be obeyed, Kelsen observes, the chain of authorization has come to an end. "The only possible answer is this: because, as a believer, one presupposes that one ought to obey the commands of God. This is the statement of the validity of a norm that must be presupposed in a believer's thinking in order to ground the validity of the norms of a religious morality .... The statement is not a positive norm – that is, not a norm posited by a real act of will – but a norm presupposed in a believer's thinking." (Kelsen, 1986: 112.)

Where an appeal to God is unavailable to ground a constitutional order, the issue is the authority of the sovereign. "If we ask why the constitution is valid, perhaps we come upon an older constitution. Ultimately we reach some constitution that is the first historically .... That the first constitution is a binding legal norm is presupposed, and the formulation of the presupposition is the basic norm of this legal order." (Kelsen, 1945: 115.) In a constitutional system, the normative force of law is grounded in a *grundnorm* of commitment to constitutionalism; "one presupposes, as [a] jurist, that one ought to conduct oneself as the constitution prescribes," which means "in conformity with the subjective meaning of the act of will creating

the constitution, the commands of the creator of the constitution."
(Kelsen, 1986: 115.) The appeal to an unjustified "presupposition"
points backward in the mythical history of constitutional formation
to a point of "natural" social organization.[34]

Thus the basic norm of any juridical system becomes the definition of "law" that identifies rules as legally valid; in a constitutional
regime, this is the function of the constitution. "Validity," in this
sense, is understood as a sociolegal descriptor. The name for
legitimacy as social fact, in turn, is "efficacy. "The efficacy of the
entire legal order is a necessary condition for the validity of every
single norm of the order . . . . The efficacy of the total legal order is a
condition, not the reason for the validity of its constituent
norms . . . . The principle of legitimacy is restricted by the principle
of effectiveness." Past the point of its initial promulgation, an
individual norm depends for its validity on the fact of efficacy. "If
the norm remains permanently inefficacious, the norm is deprived
of its validity by . . . the negative legal effect of custom. A norm may
be annulled by custom, viz., by a custom contrary to the norm as well
as it may be created by custom." Such an occurrence requires time,
however. "It is only an enduring lack of efficacy that ends the
validity." (Kelsen, 1945: 119.)

Arguably, the appeal to efficacy means that laws cannot be
required, or expected, to provide a language for transformative
criticism of juridical practice, but Kelsen denies the necessity of such
a conclusion. At the same time that Kelsen insists on a connection
between legal norms of validity and sociolegal practice, he effectively insists that the identification of a legal order with a system of
norms precludes the idea of a purely preservative legal order. "[A]
certain antagonism between the normative order and the actual
human behavior to which the norms of the order refer must be
possible. Without such a possibility, a normative order would be
completely meaningless. . . . The relationship which exists between
the validity and efficacy of a legal order . . . is, so to speak, the
tension between the 'ought' and the 'is'." (Kelsen, 1945: 120.)

[34] Modern critics of Kelsen's positivism often point to the difficulty of explaining the
ground for the authority of the originary constitution as a demonstration of the
inescapability of natural law reasoning. For a sympathetic review of these
arguments, see Brand-Ballard, 1996.

What is true of a legal order is *a fortiori* true of a constitutional order system. Lawrence Lessig has identified two distinct forms of constitutionalism as "preservative" and "transformative," respectively,[35] but Kelsen's theory does not admit the former possibility. One reason is that the normative prescriptions of the constitutional text are the tests for the legitimacy of the state and its actions. In addition, however, Kelsen adds a critical observation about the way law – and, by extension, a constitution – operate in practice. Kelsen recognizes that, in practice, the processes of decision making, and hence norm-generation, occur at multiple levels. Much of the discussion thus far has taken place against an image of a single, central lawmaking entity issuing edicts that are expected to bind everyone equally. But, in practice, the processes of rule- and lawmaking look nothing at all like this. Instead, there are multiple levels of official actors who engage in a variety of kinds of rule-making at a variety of levels, and whose actions interact with one another in complex ways. The dynamic character of a legal order inheres in the formal institutional vesting of different orders of norms in different institutional settings, resulting in Kelsen's observation that "the judge is, therefore, always a legislator also in the sense that the contents of his decision never can be completely determined by the preexisting norm of substantive law." (Kelsen, 1945: 146.)

Applied to the question of the nature of constitutional language, Kelsen's argument has important implications for exclusivity and completeness. The observation that juridical practices are "dynamic" brings us back to the concepts of exclusivity and completeness. Although exclusivity is essential to Kelsen's concept of norms grounded in authority, Kelsen argued that a system of constitutional norms neither can nor should be complete. He rejected a static model of legal authority, one in which all questions of authority refer back to a single anthropomorphic "sovereign," precisely on the basis of his recognition that incompleteness is inevitable. Further, the recognition of dynamic systems of rule making means that at descending levels of norm creation, exclusivity may be sacrificed, as increasingly broad sources are drawn upon by the relevant actors. So long as constitutional norms are not

[35] Quoted at Sunstein, 2001: 67.

violated, judicial actors engaged in the promulgation of statutes or regulations are unconstrained in the range of sources on which they may draw without imperiling the legitimacy of the system.[36]

The recognition of a dynamic, multileveled system of rule generation in practice emphasizes the analytical necessity for a constitution to contain normative standards against which juridical practices can be tested. If the lower levels of lawmaking are legitimated based on the assertion of a relationship to constitutional grounding norms – if, in other words, we are talking about a constitutional regime – then ultimately all acts of lawmaking must be justified in constitutional terms. The inescapable fact of incompleteness demonstrates that a constitution stands in relation to a system of laws as the system of laws stands in relation to social practices, simultaneously dependent upon the sociological fact of legitimacy for "efficacy" and required to assert grounding norms sufficient to validate *or invalidate* subsequent acts of lawmaking. A constitution, no less than a law, is caught between an "ought" and an "is." But the relationship between efficacy and legitimation is different for a constitution than for a law, for the simple reason that whereas laws may be entirely preservative, a constitution is always at least potentially transformative.

A thought experiment illustrates the point. At the beginning of this discussion, a "constitution" was defined as a text that establishes institutionalized mechanisms for collective actions and limitations on the exercise of power that is created as a result. Imagine a

---

[36] "Thus, in the familiar case, the constitution authorises the legislature to create statutes, which authorise the higher executive organs to create regulations, which authorise lower executive organs to create lesser regulations. Expressed more precisely: each higher norm recognises the act of will of the lower organ – or recognises custom – as a 'law-creating fact'. Since there is a reference to acts, at no stage is law-creation a matter simply of logical deduction .... The organ's act of will draws on both the authorising norm and other sources, including norms drawn from morality and politics; however, the moral and political norms do not thereby become part of the legal order." (Stewart, 1990: 285.) As Stewart points out, one of the least formalistic aspects of Kelsen's theory is his description of the norm authorizing the institutional enforcement of laws as "primary," and the norm of a particular law that is being enforced as secondary. (Stewart, 1990:288.) That is, the norms that legitimate institutional arrangements precede the promulgation of juridical rules, just as in Locke's argument, the creation of the commonwealth precedes the creation of positive law, with direct consequences for the construction of key concepts such as "property."

constitution that fails to include the first element, so that the institutions of government have no connection to the constitutional system. Imagine, in other words, a constitution that addressed itself only to the description of a non-exclusive set of goals, without any mention of institutional structures to carry those goals to fruition and no assertion of authority over institutions that had been previously created. Such a constitution would not be meaningless. It would serve as a potentially useful rhetorical device, a resource of political capital available to institutional actors, but not in any way as the statement of the grounding norms of the system. But such a "constitution" would be utterly insufficient to serve as the basis for a constitutional regime, since it would not have any necessary connection to the system of laws actually being promulgated. Lawmaking would neither be legitimated by appeal to a grant of constitutional authority, nor subject to tests for constitutional validity; the grounding norms of the lawmaking system would simply exist elsewhere.

Now consider a constitution that establishes a system of institutions for collective action, but defines no limits to those actions and thus provides no basis for determining when norm-generating activities undertaken by institutional actors might be found to fail a test for legitimacy. In that situation, the constitution would provide a ground, but not a norm. In either instance, if lower-level rule makers' actions are not grounded in constitutional norms, then it is simply not the case that their actions reflect the operation of institutionalized mechanisms for collective action in the constitutional text. They may be grounded on any number of other, alternative, sources of authority, but in that situation, the constitution is only putative; it is not, in fact, the basis for the exercise of authority.

This is the reason why a genuinely constitutional regime, in which the constitutional text defines the grounding norms of legitimation for the system of laws, can never be purely preservative as a matter of definition. To the extent that a constitution is described as preservative of "longstanding practices" (Sunstein, 2001: 1967), it merely ratifies modes of interaction that exist at a particular moment of time, exerting no normative force over present practices while freezing out future modifications with no justification beyond the brute fact of contemporary prominence. After all, if the "present" practices of the moment of constitutional creation are to be preserved against all change, it can only be because those practices are defined as perfect, or because they are perfectly accepted by the members of the relevant community. Either of these conditions takes us outside the realm of liberal constitutionalism altogether.

As noted previously, the appeal to efficacy draws a connection between constitutional legitimation and prevalent juridical practice, but that connection is different from the one between efficacy and the legitimacy of ordinary law. To repeat the point, a constitution must always be transformative of juridical practice, whereas law's efficacy is greatest when it is preservative. Consequently, a constitution needs a basis for efficacy other than accordance with practice.

On the other hand, the focus on practices may be misleading. If, by contrast, a constitution is understood to be "preservative" with reference to *norms*, rather than practices, then by Kelsen's analysis the opposite proposition is obtained: A constitution that purports to be transformative of its own grounding norms is just as much a contradiction in terms as a constitution that purports to be entirely preservative. The reason, again, is that such a version of "constitutional" order violates the conditions of possibility for its legitimate foundation, and hence, once again, cannot be legitimated.

Furthermore, in practice, the fact of constitutional incompleteness imposes a limitation on the scope of its transformative effects. Should the understandings that govern areas subject to constitutional constraint become entirely incommensurate with those that prevail in extraconstitutional areas of juridical practice, the possibility of constitutional efficacy is destroyed, and with it the legitimacy of the regime. Imagine, for example, attempting to impose a new constitution designed around a state-run socialist economy on an existing system of private property ownership and American-style private law; one or the other would have to give way, and there is little doubt as to which would be the most likely choice. Thus although past practices cannot define the scope of a constitutional regime, past and present practices are never irrelevant to an assessment of its meaning and validity.

The differences in the role that efficacy plays in legal and constitutional legitimation points toward an answer to the question of how complete a constitutional language is required to be. A constitutional language must be sufficiently complete to provide the basis for the critical evaluation, and potential transformation, of all juridical practices, but sufficiently incomplete to secure efficacy through the continuing operation of juridical norms.

The consideration of efficacy also points to the connection between completeness and exclusivity. Kelsen's argument describes the operation of a language of validation that is possessed of exclusivity, in the sense that all laws subsequently promulgated are tested for their validity against a *grundnorm* that associates legitimacy with constitutionality. The norms of validity that make it possible to apply the *grundnorm* in practice, in turn, need to be sufficiently complete to define laws as constitutional or unconstitutional. Thus, where Sunstein proposed radical incompleteness combined with exclusivity in order to avoid substantive normative commitments, the incorporation of Kelsen's positivism into the arguments indicates the need for both exclusivity and completeness at the level of constitutional lawmaking, but permits considerable relaxation of both of those requirements as one moves to lower levels of rule generation.

The qualities of exclusivity and completeness of a system of constitutional language are what make it the basis for critique sufficient to challenge to the legitimacy of established practices. A moment of consent that fails to produce a system of constitutional language that is both exclusive and complete is a pretense incapable of binding the self-sovereign People, precisely because the content of what is consented to is defined outside the subject of consent. A constitution, in this view, would be an empty vessel, to be filled by past or present practices.[37] This will be recognized as the beginning of an argument about constitutional interpretation, which is only

---

[37] The empty vessel theory of constitutional language is illustrated perfectly by the opinion of Chief Justice Rehnquist in *Paul v. Davis* (1976), 424 U.S. 693, 711–12, in which he concluded that the procedural guarantees of the Due Process Clause of the Fourteenth Amendment are only triggered where a person is deprived of a liberty or property "interest" previously established in state or federal law. The result is that in states where the local law defines a "right" to one's reputation, defamation by a government official without due process is a proper basis for a claim of a constitutional violation, whereas in other states, the same conduct does

tangentially relevant to the current discussion, although it is important to recognize here that a theory of constitutional interpretation that is limited by the brute fact of past practice is the exemplar of what I earlier called "putative" constitutionalism. But what is more relevant and important to recognize for the present purpose is that the conditions of possibility for binding consent by a self-sovereign people require that the instrument that is the subject of content contain semantic as well as grammatical constraints. A "constitution" whose terms are empty vessels to be filled by historical practice fails to meet the conditions for legitimate constitutional consent, and hence cannot be legitimated.

Iain Stewart points out that there is a tension between the recognition of the fact of dynamic rule making, on the one hand, and a deductively organized system of norms, on the other. This is an important criticism, since the different roles that efficacy plays for legal and constitutional legitimacy implies that a system of constitutional rules is, in fact, deductive in a way that a system of laws need not be (and, indeed, arguably cannot be if law is to be efficacious). Essentially, Stewart argues that Kelsen fails to give adequate consideration to the consequences of his abandonment of the anthropomorphic metaphor of the state for his desire to retain the description of "law" as an act of sovereign will.[38] Kelsen's response of an appeal to "presupposed" norm of constitutionality, suggests Stewart, is unsatisfactory as an account for the operation of constitutional norms interacting with legal rules. For example, the analogy of the father's appeal to divine authority to the social experience of juridical practice is strained. "While this father knows the whole chain of validation, an official may work from a manual,

---

not give rise to such a claim. This particular form of indeterminacy does not seem to trouble the Court unduly.

[38] "Kelsen ... develop[s] an explicitly Freudian critique of State-personification, yet fails to make the link from the false objectivity of the personified State to a false objectivity of the legal norm attributed to that State-person as its author." The problem, in other words, is that the abandonment of a monarchial sovereign has not been accompanied by a willingness "to cut off the King's head" (quoting Michel Foucault), resulting in a tendency to equate "objectivity" with a top-down model of lawmaking authority that denies the dynamic element of subsequent norm generation by juridical actors at other levels of rule making. (Stewart, 1998: 192–93.)

even a leaflet, and be unable to identify a regulation, still less a statute, relevant to their decision." (Stewart, 1998: 197.)

Instead, Stewart suggests, Kelsen's account might be better understood as a description of a norm by which possible alternative rules are excluded from consideration. "Now the angle of approach has been flipped. The legal norm is to be approached not under the sign of *inclusion*, as with Kelsen's appearance of 'objectivity', but under that of *exclusion*." (Stewart, 1998: 198.) With respect to law, Stewart notes, the exclusionary function is not separately legitimate, but rather inheres in the legal form itself. "The exclusion is not effected by any supplementary norm, nor by any supplementary statement that is not a norm.... The exclusion is effected by the legal norm itself. Not, to be sure, through its content, but through its form, its legal character. If to have legal character is for a norm to be absolute, the exclusion is effected by a default." (Stewart, 1998: 199.) That is, low-level officials will understand themselves to be bound to create only law-like rules, rather than as making rules that are the direct expression of norms contained in higher-order laws.

Applied to constitutional language, Stewart's argument reaffirms the proposition that the presupposed norm is not one that binds us to the constitution-makers' subjective will expressed in a constitutional text so much as it binds us to the constitution-makers' subjective will to *constitutionalism* – in other words, to the use of constitutional language. This goes a long way toward resolving the problem of indeterminacy that results from incompleteness. If the basis for the social acceptance of the legitimacy of a legal system is acceptance of the primary norms that empower juridical actors to promulgate secondary norms, rather than acceptance of the secondary norms themselves, then there is no inherent reason why those secondary norms need to be determinate, or even that they be known to the members of the society at large at all. If the allocation of authority in primary norms is determinate, arguably it becomes the case that indeterminacy in the formulation of secondary norms is not problematic in sociolegal practice.[39]

---

[39] Drury Stevenson explores this idea in an article that proposes that positive laws should be understood as statements addressed from the politically sovereign people to the state, rather than from the state to citizens, an idea that he connects to Kelsen's description of authorizing norms as primary and behavioral norms as

Distinguishing between primary and secondary norms continues the process of separating an analysis of the conditions of legitimacy applicable to a constitutional system of primary norms from those that apply to a system of secondary norms articulated in legal rules. This is also one way of expressing the separation between a theory of constitutional legitimacy and a defense or criticism of a particular practice of constitutional interpretation: if the legitimation of the practice of constitutional interpretation is sufficiently determinate, the existence of disagreements as to its manner or outcome does not threaten the legitimacy of the constitutional order. In turn, the reconceptualization of sovereignty as an act of collective self-inscription, rather than as "an act of will directed toward others" (Kelsen, 1986: 112), relocates the validating presupposition away from legal metaphysics and toward a historically specific political understanding captured in the idea of popular sovereignty-in-action that was discussed in Chapter 3.

Suddenly, and quite unexpectedly, this analysis of the requirements of exclusivity and completeness in constitutional language leads to the case for a robust system of something like judicial review. Consider that, following Kelsen, we have posited the existence both of multiple levels of decision makers who generate rules or norms and a negative or exclusionary commitment to constitutionalism rather than a specific affirmative set of directives emanating from a single sovereign lawmaker. In that situation, the preservation of the constitutional regime requires one of two things: that all decision makers, at all levels, be both committed to and capable of restricting themselves to the deployment of constitutional language in their actions, or that there be an institutional mechanism for testing the validity of lower-order rules against grounding constitutional norms. But in order to rely on lower-order decision makers to always apply grounding constitutional norms, either those norms would have to be sufficiently complete to provide affirmative direction to all acts of norm creation, or else the official actors themselves would have to be relied upon to always enforce the

---

secondary. (Stevenson, 2003: 127.) What would separate constitutional principles from ordinary law, from this perspective, would be the fact that constitutional propositions are intended for an audience that includes all citizens: the popular sovereign capable of constitutional consent.

exclusivity of constitutional language. The latter, as Stewart points out, is the solution that responds sensibly to Kelsen's challenge, but insisting that lower-level decision makers enforce the exclusivity of constitutional language goes beyond a commitment to constitutionalism to a commitment to particular constitutional rules, with the unfortunate result that the maintenance of a constitutional regime becomes unnecessarily restrictive on legal practice. In terms of the theory of constitutional language, this becomes the situation in which *langue* strangles *parole*.

This is the critical distinction between legal and constitutional language. At the level of legal, or political, or policy discourse – that is, at the level at which lower-level decision makers operate under secondary norms: it is unnecessary and undesirable to require too strict an enforcement of exclusivity just as it is unnecessary and undesirable to curtail completeness. The reason is the same in both instances: the lower the level of decision making, the more critical it is that rules reflect sociological practices of legitimation in order to preserve their efficacy. As one moves up the discursive scale, to the level at which particular acts of rule generation are tested for validity against constitutional grounding principles, the necessity for a commitment to an exclusive constitutional language becomes greater at the same time that the necessity for completeness in that language becomes less. There are, then, only two alternatives: to ask decision makers to switch between one role and another, to employ the complete and weakly exclusive language of law in generating rules and the incomplete and more strictly exclusive language of constitutionalism to test the validity of their own actions, or else to divide these two functions between two sets of institutional actors.

Kelsen himself relied on the latter institutional arrangement. In designing the Constitution of Austria, Kelsen included the creation of a special Constitutional Court, which has become the model for similar courts throughout Europe. Unlike the American Supreme Court, whose justices are required to engage in a "now we do law, now we do constutionalism" movement back and forth between discussions, Kelsenian constitutional courts are specialized institutions created to serve as the discursively highest level of norm generation and norm application. While the American arrangement, since the days of John Marshall, is based on the assertion that a constitution is a species of law, the Kelsenian model of a constitutional court recognizes differences between constitutional and legal legitimation, differences that I have characterized in terms of the requirements of exclusivity and completeness in their respective systems of language. Regardless, whether the American or the European system of reviewing courts is being considered, it is important to recognize that such an institutional arrangement is not contrary to collective action; it is necessary for the preservation of the collective moment of consent to constitutional language that was identified as the essential answer to the question "Consent How?" in Chapter 3.

The question of what institutional arrangements are best suited to the maintenance of a constitutional regime will be the subject of further discussion. But to reiterate the argument thus far, an initial commitment to the creation of a system of constitutional language possessed of exclusivity and completeness is the first moment of constitutional consent; the second is the creation of a system of constitutional language possessed of those qualities that is also sufficiently grounded in familiar practices that its operation does not threaten the validity of the initial commitments.[40] Here is the point where issues of completeness and substance overlap. The system of constitutional signs must be sufficiently complete to establish itself as adequately grounded in sociolegal practice, but the more complete the constitutional language, the more serious the problem of possible conflicts with the substantive values of citizens.

LEGAL LEGITIMACY AND SOCIAL VALUES: H. L. A. HART'S RULES OF RECOGNITION

The problem, then, is how to describe a source for efficacy in a constitutional regime other than accordance with prevalent juridical

---

[40] Where a constitutional text is written in a way that challenges the shared understandings of the community, it is likely that the judicial interpretation of that text will restore continuity. Ran Hirschl, comparing constitutional doctrines of negative and affirmative rights in Canada, New Zealand, and Israel, concludes that preexisting conceptions of negatively defined rights effectively delimits the possibility of judicial interpretation even where textual rights language lends itself to affirmative constructions. "In sum," he concludes, "judicial interpretations of constitutional rights appear to possess a very limited capacity to advance progressive notions of social justice in arenas ... which require greater state intervention and more public expenditure." (Hirschl 2000: 1098.)

practices. The suggestion has been made that differentiating accordance with norms from accordance with practices helps avoid some of the problems that result from conflating legal and constitutional language. Ultimately, I have argued, the grounding norm for a constitutional regime is discursive, a commitment to speak constitutionally. Constitutional efficacy is therefore grounded in the social acceptance of these discursive norms, captured in a continuing acceptance of the initial commitment to language. The appeal to a theory of constitutionalism grounded in socially accepted discursive norms points in the direction of the more sociological, less philosophically formal application of legal positivism to the discussion of constitutional foundations that appears in the work of H. L. A. Hart.[41]

In his attempt to make law objective, Kelsen was willing to go very far indeed in avoiding any claim of a connection between legal validity and any substantive norms. In his most extreme moments, Kelsen imagined the possibility of a system of legal rules that lacked any coherence – any expression of an identifiable will – but which nonetheless remain legitimate as a matter of socio-legal description, so that even a self-contradictory set of norms might nonetheless constitute "law."[42] Hart, by contrast, focuses less on the abstract qualities of the system of norms and more on the experience of participation, a distinction that appears in Hart's insistence on treating "law" as a system of reasoning separate from political or social systems of authority, with a system of norms of its own. Where Kelsen's formalistic positivism led him to posit a general, basic norm

[41] There is an extensive literature documenting Hart's theories, and in particular his debates with Ronald Dworkin and (to a lesser extent) with Joseph Raz. For a summary of these debates, and a defense of the positivist project against challenges from John Finnis and other recent critics seeking to identify substantive claims of moral right as the necessary ground to any claim of legal legitimacy, see Leiter, 2003. For Finnis' response, see Finnis, 2003. Both Leiter's discussion and Finnis' response are treated at greater length in the next chapter.

[42] As Iain Stewart wryly observes, "It is not clear how something self-contradictory can have truth-value and accordingly be capable of being false. It is even less clear that, although something can be false but useful, something can be self-contradictory but useful; it might simply fail to make sense, in which case the concept is lost. And, if the concept of a basic norm is lost, that of dynamic legal order is lost and, with that, the core of the pure theory. All of Kelsen's theory-construction that is left intact is the conception of a 'normative science', which in its emphatic modernism is hardly flavour-of-the-age." (Stewart, 1998: 191.)

of authority ascertainable by an observer outside the system, Hart's positivism derives from his attempt to describe the system of juridical norms from the internalist perspective of the experience of juridical practices.[43] As a result, he is far more open to the imputation of some kind of value judgment to the social experience of legitimacy. Hart is insistent that the social experience of law *as* a normatively obligating set of rules must be taken into account in any theory of law, a suggestion that blurs the distinction between positivist and non-positivist theories.[44]

Like Kelsen, Hart rejects an Austinian command theory that defines law as simply an order issued by a sovereign and backed by force. In the first place, such an argument still requires a metarule to define an authorized lawmaker; that is, Kelsen's grounding norm of authority. But Hart goes farther than this. What is also missing, he argues, is the sense of obligation that is experienced by participants in a legal system. The concept of obligation is different from the fact of coercion. "There is a difference ... between the assertion that someone was obliged to do something and the assertion that he had an obligation to do it." (Hart, 1997: 82.) A sense of obligation

---

[43] On the first page of *Pure Theory of Law*, Kelsen explains the necessity for separating the study of law from the study of sociology, psychology, or other social sciences. The pure theory of law "undertakes to delimit the cognition of law against these disciplines, not because it ignores or denies the connection, but because it wishes to avoid the uncritical mixture of methodologically different disciplines." (Kelsen, 1945: 1.) What Hart adds to the discussion is an exploration of the social experience of legal norms, treated as an essential element of the sociolegal fact of legitimacy, thus moving away from the elements in Kelsen's argument that have been analogized to Weber's theory of ideal types, and toward an understanding that simultaneously demarcates the separate sphere of law and makes it comprehensible as an element of a more general theory of social practice. Hart, then, draws a more strict separation than does Kelsen between the study of law and other subject matters, at the same time drawing a less strict separation between the methods of study applicable to investigations of these different areas.

[44] Kent Greenawalt suggests that much of the distinction between positivist and antipositivist legal writing reflects a difference of perspective rather than genuinely opposing commitments. "[I]n so far as one can distinguish legal positivism from other theories of law, it yields an account that is much more illuminating for an 'outsider's' perspective than for the standpoint of a participant who is determining what the law provides. The determinedly 'insider' focus of most writing about law in the United States helps explain why 'legal positivism' has often been used as a term of summary condemnation by those with little patience for complex philosophic refinement." (Greenawalt, 1996: 1.) Critics of legal positivism, of course, take a somewhat different view.

implies the existence of "social rules ... making certain types of behaviour a standard." In other words, substantive as well as procedural and definitional juridical norms are required to provide a ground for efficacy that still permits transformative critiques of current practices. Defining the qualities that are required for the production of a social experience of obligation points directly toward the project of defining the necessary content of a binding act of constitutional consent, with the caveat that bending the focus of Hart's argument in this way may change its consequences.

For Hart, a rule has the quality of obligation if three conditions are met: there is sufficient "importance or seriousness of social pressure" supporting its observance; the rule is considered "necessary to the maintenance of social life or some highly prized feature of it"; and "the conduct required by these rules may, while benefiting others, conflict with what the person who owes the duty may wish to do." (Hart, 1997: 86–7.) This is a formulation that partially dissolves the distinction between fact and norm by an appeal to experience. Kelsen used a similar argument to deny the distinction between making and applying laws, insisting that both elements are always involved in any exercise of juridical authority within a constitutional system, with a similar focus on the importance of language. The effect of Hart's argument is to alter the signification involved in the use of legal language by pointing to the necessity of applying mid-level rules to reach particular conclusions in particular cases. The statement that "a person has an obligation" becomes an exercise in the application of a general rule, or norm, to a particular set of facts in a manner akin to the adjudication of a case or the drafting of statutory language.

Constitutionalism, in this view, appears as a special case of a general theory of law that extends to the limits of social obligation by the operation of a dynamic system of rule making. Hart makes this focus a key to his discussion, describing the obligatory force of law as an effect of "the whole distinctive style of human thought, speech, and action which is involved in the existence of rules and which constitutes the normative structure of society." (Hart, 1997: 88.)[45] The connection to a theory of constitutional language is

---

[45] The emphasis on the experience of a sense of obligation causes Hart to warn against the "external" view that conceives of law as merely a prediction to the effect

through the idea of completeness. The constitutional analogy to Hart's (overstated) proposition that law constitutes the normative structure of society *tout court* is the proposition that a constitutional regime defines the normative structure of that portion of society that is concerned with the exercise of juridical authority.

The categorical distinction that grounds Hart's positivism is between primary and secondary rules, which effectively inverts Kelsen's classification of primary and secondary norms. Primary rules are simple rules of conduct; secondary rules are those that legitimate primary rules. (Hart, 1997: 81.) Secondary rules lead to the creation of duties or obligations "when the general demand for conformity is insistent and the social pressure brought to bear upon those who deviate or threaten to deviate is great." When that social pressure takes the form of physical sanctions, "we shall be inclined to classify the rules as a primitive or rudimentary form of law." (Hart, 1997: 86.) Simple systems of social control, such as those characteristic of a "small community closely knit by ties of kinship, common sentiment, and belief," may be (explicitly) composed solely of primary rules. Formal secondary rules become necessary, however, in the face of diversity. (Hart, 1997: 91–2.)

In other words, like Locke and Wilson, Hart would look to ground constitutionalism in a democratic theory of self-sovereignty by shifting the moment of consent backward in time from the issuance of an order or rule to the establishment of the system of authoritative rule making. Consensual adoption of rules of conduct lead to the creation of institutional mechanisms of enforcement, leading in turn to the promulgation of new rules of conduct.

---

that "deviations from rules are generally met by hostile reactions" or the description of a psychological sense of compulsion. Such a description of social conduct "cannot be in terms of rules at all,"and thus omits the reasons for which people experience legal rules as legitimate and tailor their conduct accordingly. "What the external point of view, which limits itself to the observable regularities of behavior, cannot reproduce is the way in which the rules function as rules in the lives of those who normally are the majority of society." (Hart, 1997: 89–90.) On the other hand, however, Hart is concerned with the social fact of obedience to law as the experience of *rule-based* obligations. Thus, although the sociological element of the analysis remains at the forefront, it is cast in terms of formal categories.

The simplest and primary form of a secondary rule is a "rule of recognition," Hart's version of Kelsen's norm of validity. "This will specify some feature or features, possession of which by a suggested rule is taken as a conclusive affirmative indication that it is a rule of the group to be supported by the social pressure it exerts." Such a rule of recognition might include a requirement that a rule must be written and published, in the manner of a positive statute, but no such specific requirement is necessary for a meaningful rule of recognition. "[W]hat is crucial is the acknowledgment of reference to the writing or inscription as authoritative, i.e. as the proper way of disposing of doubts as to the existence of the rule." (Hart, 1997: 94, 95.)[46]

The introduction of rules of recognition shifts the focus away from the personified "sovereign" who promulgates the rules onto the content of the rule-like statements themselves. In addition, insofar as rules of recognition may be rules concerning the process of promulgation of laws, the focus may be further shifted onto the process of lawmaking. And a rule of recognition based on the process of becoming a legitimate lawmaker – as in a requirement that lawmakers be democratically elected – performs the same shift away from person to process in the context of popular sovereignty.

---

[46] Challenging legal positivism on its own terms, Gerald Postema criticizes the description of law as "autonomous" on the grounds that the "limited domain" over which it exercises exclusionary force is insufficient to account for the experience of a sense of obligation on the part of its subjects. "Regarding their subject-scope: presumably they [laws] are addressed to (all?) agents subject to the legal norms in question, but are they also addressed to some or all of those charged to enforce, administer, and maintain the law's domain? Similarly, regarding their *substance-scope*: do they exclude all, or only some, considerations falling outside the law's domain?" (Postema, 1996: 86.) In the case of a theory of constitutional language, the answers to these questions are (1) that constitutional norms are addressed solely to "those charged to enforce, administer, and maintain the law's domain," and (2) considerations falling outside the domain of constitutional norms are excluded insofar as they cannot be translated into constitutional language. This also answers Postema's second objection, which is that although a theory of law as autonomous may permit moral or other criticisms of legal rules, "its weakness lies ... in what it offers to structure or discipline such appeals in order to facilitate the public deliberation. Law, on this model, provides no such resources." As a result, Postema says, "we should look for a model that integrates arguments of political morality into proper legal argument and justification, starting from recognition of the reflectively self-critical character of legal practice." (Postema, 1996: 110, 111.) This argument will be taken up in the next chapter.

This is similar to the move that we observed in Chapter 3, away from reliance on an anthropomorphic "sovereign" in favor of a form of discourse that identifies the exercise of sovereignty, but Hart's treatment of the issue is one of content rather than form. That is, a law may be legitimated by virtue of meeting a set of procedural requirements, but those requirements themselves are substantive norms specified in secondary rules of recognition. In the terms of a theory of constitutional language, such norms are semantic rather than merely grammatical, while still one step removed from being determinative of substantive policy outcomes.

Positing the existence of implicit rules of recognition resolves the question of customary law in a way different from that employed by Kelsen. Where Kelsen found the state in action in the translation from custom to norm based on a grounding norm of authority, Hart finds a rule of recognition that serves the same grounding function in socio-legal practice. Speaking of custom and judicial precedent, he writes that "they owe their status of law, precarious as this may be, not to a 'tacit' exercise of legislative power but to the acceptance of a rule of recognition which accords them this independent though subordinate place." As the example of customary law demonstrates, rules of recognition are frequently not explicitly declared. "For the most part the rule of recognition is not stated, but its existence is *shown* in the way in which particular rules are identified" – that is, by juridical practice. These unstated grounding norms define the element that is missing in the purely sociological, descriptive version of positivism. "The use of unstated rules of recognition, by courts and others, in identifying particular rules of the system is characteristic of the internal point of view. Those who use them in this way thereby manifest their own acceptance of them as guiding rules and with this attitude there goes a characteristic vocabulary different from the natural expressions of the external point of view." (Hart, 1997: 101–02.) Like Wilson's society whose advancement to a level capable of law depended on the development of sophisticated language, for Hart the deployment of a specialized vocabulary to indicate the operation of rules of recognition demonstrates the existence of systemic juridical norms.

For Hart, a rule of recognition provides the supreme grounding norm for a system of norms, since the identification of valid norms logically precedes their adoption. (Hart, 1997: 107.) A rule of recognition, however, need not be a tacit background understanding; indeed such a role can be played by a formal statute or a well-understood convention. What is critical is that such a declaration of a rule of recognition be effective – that is, that it be accepted, either unanimously, or by a sufficient majority that other members of the relevant community are compelled in practice to act as if they shared in that acceptance. (Hart, 1997: 111, 104–05.) In this sense, a grounding norm comprising a rule of recognition is the initial condition of possibility for a system of laws; in its formal, positive manifestation, such a rule would satisfy the conditions that were identified at the outset as necessary for constitutional government. For Hart, finally, the existence of such rules is not a matter of speculation. Like a physicist who derives principles from the observation of phenomena that cannot be otherwise made explicable, Hart concludes that rules of recognition are analytically necessary to explain the possibility of law because they are necessary for law to be effective.

At this point, the critical distinctions between a theory of constitutional adequacy and a general theory of law become evident. Constitutional norms bind juridical actors – "officials," more often than not – whereas legal norms bind private subjects. The consequence of this is that the range of actors likely to be bound by constitutional norms, in practice, is coextensional with the range of activities to which constitutional norms apply and within which constitutional norms are required to be exclusive.

The recognition that constitutional norms operate within a more limited range of activities than legal norms, a byproduct of the recognition of dynamic systems of rule generation, helps resolve the questions of exclusivity and completeness with relation to constitutional language. Sunstein, Whittington, Kelsen, and Hart, despite other important disagreements, ultimately all lead to the same conclusion about the necessary characteristics of constitutional language. Constitutional language is required to be exclusive and incomplete for the legitimation of a constitutional regime, just as legal language is required to be complete and only weakly exclusive for the legitimation of a system of laws. Finding this conclusion in Whittington's arguments, in particular, required separating legal and constitutional legitimacy in the manner suggested by Kelsen, a move that directly connected the discussion of the necessary characteristics of constitutional language with a possible set of institutional arrangements. Sunstein's arguments, too, have undergone considerable revision in the discussions of exclusivity and completeness, as I have argued that the reliance on incompletely theorized agreements similarly makes sense at the level of legitimizing law but must give way to a quite thoroughly theorized agreement in the commitment to constitutional language that provides the grounding norms against which acts of lawmaking must be tested in any "constitutional" regime.

Combining the lessons of Kelsen's and Hart's arguments, we can state the requirements of exclusivity and completeness for a constitutional language sufficient to ground a legitimate constitutional regime. The system of constitutional language must provide a system of signs sufficient that it covers the actions of juridical norm creation, through legislation, rule making, or adjudication, applied in accordance with a principle of exclusivity that excludes any propositions that cannot be translated into formally valid and substantively sensible constitutional formulations. The requirement that constitutional language be exclusive within the scope of its application is an analytically necessary element of a "constitutional" regime of lawmaking. That language is required to be sufficiently complete to permit its efficacy in defining the socially accepted basis for the legitimation of lower-level decisions. "Efficacy" is not the source of legitimacy; it is one of the criteria or indicia of its successful establishment. The legitimacy of the constitutional regime remains grounded in the commitment to the language – Balkin's constitutional fidelity – that we have been describing all along.

Applied to a theory of constitutional language, the discussion of the distinction between primary and secondary rules suggests that the relationship between constitutional and ordinary legal rules has important parallels with the relationship between legal and moral norms in terms of the nature of the "obligation" that is the basis for efficacy in each case. "If morality is autonomous, controversy is bound to be endemic. ... one vital point of legal institutions is exactly that they exist (*inter alia*) to settle authoritatively for practical purposes what cannot be settled morally." (MacCormick, 1996: 167, 169.)

In a similar way, the generation of rules in a dynamic legal system reflects plurality among juridical institutions whose differences in structure, mission, and constituency may preclude anything like ordered systematic description, let alone agreement. (MacCormick, 1996: 180.) A constitution, in this analogy, exists to "settle" questions that, if left to the juridical process of lower-order decision making, would inevitably result in either the dissolution of the regime or the forcible subordination of some one set of rule-generating institutional actors by another. As a result, heteronomous legal rules are seen as occurring within an autonomous constitutional framework; this is the essential point to the focus on self-sovereignty that began this discussion. To serve such a function, however, constitutional norms must not only be "supreme" in cases of conflict with other juridical norms – that is, possessed of the quality of exclusivity – but also sufficiently complete to reduce the space of conflict to institutionally manageable dimensions. (MacCormick, 1996: 180–81, 190.)

In Hart's terms, exclusivity and completeness are required in order for a system of constitutional language to be efficacious in creating the special obligations that a constitutional regime requires. In Kelsen's terms, those obligations identify the commitment to constitutional language as the grounding norm for the system of laws. McCormick's gloss on autonomy and heteronomy, finally, direct our attention to the connection between institutional arrangements and the hierarchy of norms or rules. At the end of this discussion of legal positivism, we are left with the recognition that in a specifically constitutional regime, "efficacy" refers to the acceptance of a set of relationships between different levels of juridical language, reflected in stable institutional arrangements, and supported by sufficient levels of exclusivity and completeness in constitutional language.

At the same time, while constitutional language is required to be sufficiently complete to permit efficacy, it is simultaneously required to be sufficiently incomplete to allow for a relaxation of the requirement of exclusivity at the level of lawmaking and political discourse. A constitutional regime is not a totalizing system that absorbs all other forms of public interaction; it is a mechanism to secure a space for those other forms of interaction while preserving the necessary elements of self-sovereignty in the face of a plurality of value commitments. Neil MacCormick describes law as "institutional, authoritative, and heteronomous," whereas morality is "personal and controversial," "discursive," and "autonomous." (MacCormick, 1996: 164.)

Just as the consideration of exclusivity led inevitably into the question of completeness, the requirement of incompleteness leads to the question of substantive normative commitments. The supposed absence of such normative commitments is the basis for the most common, and most far-reaching, criticism of legal positivism as an approach to grounding the validity or legitimacy of a juridical order. Applied to the discussion of this book, that challenge reaches all the way back to the foundational discussion of self-sovereignty and constitutional consent. The absence of substantive normative commitments, the anti-positivist would argue, yields a version of constitutional commitment that is insufficient to satisfy the definitional requirements for a constitutional order with which we began: a stable system of formalized collective action accompanied by an institutionally enforceable rule of law.

In one sense, this criticism is simply inaccurate; it is not true that the theories described here are value-free, despite their general commitment to the separation between legal and moral reasoning. Undoubtedly, some version of the grounding norms of legal positivism or the political conditions required for deliberative democracy are necessary conditions for constitutionalism insofar as the problem of sovereignty is to be solved by an appeal to self-rule.

But even from the perspective of a methodological commitment to minimalism, a critic would argue, these proceduralist arguments are insufficient. What they lack is a description of the necessary *content* of the system of constitutional signs. Hart's ultimate rule of recognition, for example, is a secondary norm, yet he also insists that legal systems embody substantive norms, but does not explain the connection between these two levels of commitment. Sunstein's conditions of discourse provide opportunities for effective participation in a certain version of democratic constitutionalism, but he says very little about the moment when discrete groups submit their ideas for larger public approval. That is, while Sunstein is articulate and illuminating about the perils and benefits of different modes of

discourse, he says little about what any particular level of deliberation has to sound like in order to satisfy the conditions required for
constitutional democracy, let alone how those restrictions can be
explained as the result of a moment of constitutional consent. The
most powerful attempt at filling in that content was provided by
Kelsen, who illuminated the question by his characterization of legal
discourse as an event occurring "between the 'ought' and the 'is.'"
But that in-between status may be understood to require elements of
both substantive prescription and sociolegal description.

These comments introduce the question of substance that is the
basis for a continued exploration of the question "Consent to
What?" in the next chapter. What kind, and what amount, of substantive normative commitments is constitutional language required
to contain if a commitment to that language is to provide an adequate ground for a constitutional regime? In the process, we must
continue to explore the question of the relationship between the
constitutional language and other forms of discourse. The necessity
of a separation between constitutional and legal legitimacy has
already been introduced; in the idiom that was employed earlier,
this was described as the separation of constitutional *langue* from
constitutional *parole*. In turning to the question of substance, it
becomes necessary to consider the question of the degree to which
constitutional language must be similarly separated from other
forms of public discourse. Does the need for incompleteness to
preserve freedom of legal action translate into a need to avoid
substantive normative commitments?

The question of substance raises a problem that is particularly
thorny for liberal constitutionalism. Any substantive normative
commitment contained within a system of constitutional language
creates a privileged point of entry for the public discourse that most
readily accommodates that norm. If there are elements of public
discourse that are directly reflected in the system of constitutional
signs, then the rules of constitutional grammar do not require that
propositions framed in those terms undergo translation, and perspectives that can be articulated in that language occupy a privileged
position in constitutional discourse. The result is a kind of discursive
inequality, in which the burden of translation falls more heavily on
some potential participants in constitutional discourse than upon

others. The desire to avoid that kind of unequal outcome is what motivates the search for a purely proceduralist set of constitutional norms, but as the discussion of positivism and its relation to constitutional language has made clear, the problem cannot be entirely avoided. In particular, we must confront the relationship between constitutional language and the languages of religion and morality, as well as that of "law" writ large. Recognizing the unequal burdens that the requirement of translation imposes upon constitutional speakers, what kinds of substantive normative commitments is a system of constitutional language required to contain?

5

The Question of Substance

Morality, Law, and Constitutional Legitimacy

This chapter is concerned with the question of substance: Is there a minimum amount of substantive normative commitments that a system of constitutional language is required to have in order to ground a legitimate constitutional regime? As in each of the preceding discussions, the analysis in this chapter breaks down into a series of questions: What are the arguments for including normative substance in a constitutional language, and how do those arguments differ from arguments about the substantive content of "law" generally? What function does normative substance serve for constitutional language? What are the implications of identifying a necessary amount of normative substance for the design and maintenance of a legitimate constitutional regime?

In Chapter 4, an argument that constitutional language should be exclusive and incomplete was developed by engaging theories of law, particularly legal positivism. That analysis led to the recognition that constitutional and legal theories of legitimacy are separate from one another. Those arguments were not silent on the question of substance. Indeed, many of the approaches that were considered in Chapter 4 began from an assumption that the conditions of juridical discourse can, and perhaps should, be described without reference to particular normative content. Despite the inclusiveness of Kelsen's and Hart's appeals to the internal experience of normativity, positivist arguments describe tests for validity rather than tests for correctness; thus they retain the is/ought distinction that separates legal positivism from the substantive tests for legitimacy imposed by older theories of divine or human natural law. Sunstein, too, is essentially a proceduralist when it comes to the question of legitimating the moment of constitutional rule formation, although he is committed to substantive goals in the process of interpretation in the form of an "anticaste" principle of equality. (Sunstein, 1993: 155.)

In answer to the question "what substantive normative content is a constitution minimally required to contain?" these theories for the most part answer "none in particular."

But at this point we need to consider a basic challenge to the positivist argument. This challenge takes the form of a revival of something like the tradition of natural law, in which the legitimacy of a constitution depends on the correctness and completeness of its moral commitments. These arguments, like those of the legal positivists, arise originally in the context of a general theory of law, and assert some version of the claim that "law" is necessarily related to "justice." The force of that basic assertion must be granted, but its consequences require reconsideration in the context of the distinctions that were drawn between constitutional and legal theories. Accepting the necessity of an exclusive but incomplete constitutional language, are there aspects of "justice" that are necessarily involved in the system of signs that are comprised by a constitutional language, as opposed to the language of "law" generally?

The basic challenge to the idea of a substance-less constitution is that such a text may be inadequately grounded in shared social norms to establish effective grounds for a legitimate regime, a return to the concept of efficacy that was introduced in Chapter 4. A constitutional language, it was argued, needs to be incomplete so as to permit the operation of other languages at lower levels of decision making, but at the same time it must be sufficiently complete to be "efficacious," meaning that it must have sufficient scope that its grounding norms can be seen to have a connection to prevalent community norms of other kinds. The argument for the necessity of including substantive normative commitments within the incomplete scope of constitutional language is that normative substance is what provides that possibility of groundedness, and thus preserves the connection to self-sovereignty.

That connection between the production of a constitutional language and the possibility of popular-sovereignty-in-action identifies the starting point for the discussion of substance that follows. If it is the case that constitutional language is required to contain normative substance, it is because in the absence of such substance that language would not have the capacity to act as the expression of self-sovereign People, and as a result would lose its basis for the claim of legitimacy. The question of substance is the question of what kind of normative commitments is a constitutional language required to contain in order to preserve the legitimacy of its originary moment of consent.

THE QUESTION OF SUBSTANCE AND THE CHALLENGE OF MORAL CORRECTNESS

To address the question of substance, a return to first principles is required. Because the fundamental grounding norm of a constitutional regime is the consent of a self-sovereign people, democratic theory rather than theories of law provides the source material for the argument. The shift in focus from legal theories to democratic theories of constitutional legitimacy should not be surprising. The substantive normative commitments that are required of a constitutional language, after all, represent the limits to a tolerable level of value pluralism in a legitimate constitutional regime. At the stage of "Consent How?" the limit to pluralism was a universal acceptance of the requirements of constitutional language. At the stage of "Consent to What?" what additional constraints appear?

At the outset, the term "constitution" was defined as a text that describes a system for institutionalized collective action and a set of limits on such action. It is, frankly, difficult to see how the system of language created by the adoption of such a text could *fail* to define substantive normative commitments of some kind. The suggestion verges on absurdity, in the most Hobbesian sense of a "round quadrangle" or other analytical contradiction in terms. In addition, the problem of constitutional evils is quite real. Particularly given an insistence that constitutional language be incomplete, the danger that a system of constitutional language will either require or permit substantively evil actions raise an obvious challenge to the conditions of possibility for legitimacy. That challenge, moreover, cannot be answered by an appeal to constitutional politics or some other extratextual source of meaning if there exists the possibility of a different constitutional text capable of preventing or diminishing the scope of constitutional evils by virtue of a greater amount of normative substance. The problem of constitutional evils poses a challenge to the legitimacy of a constitutional text independent of its significance for our understanding of constitutional politics.

This is a difficult challenge to answer from a purely positivistic point of view. In its inclusive forms, to be sure, positivism acknowledges the possibility that rules of recognition might include substantive moral judgments. As Jules Coleman puts it, "[i]f the rule of recognition asserts that morality is a condition of legality, then morality is a condition of legality in that system .... Inclusive legal positivism is the claim that positivism allows or permits substantive or moral tests of legality; it is not the view that positivism requires such tests." But any form of legal positivism is fundamentally grounded in the proposition that "validity" is a question of "social facts – not moral argument." (Coleman, 2001: 108, 107.) This basic assumption of positivism that Coleman identifies has given rise to criticism in the form of the two challenges to substance-less constitutionalism identified above. The argument is either that positivism is morally inadequate because of its failure to specify substantive content that is required for legitimacy, or else that positivism is an inadequate description of the social experience of legitimacy and hence fails on its own terms.

The first criticism is summarized in the classical dictum, "an unjust law is not law." Robert George articulates this position when he addresses the positivist's claim that "law" implies, as a social fact, a claim of obligation. "What is interesting about human positive law, from the moral point of view, is not merely that laws enforce obligations that already exist as a matter of moral law, but that laws sometimes create moral obligations that would otherwise not exist. The moral obligation to obey the law is, however, conditional and, as such, defeasible .... Even a law enacted by impeccably democratic procedures can be unjust, and insofar as it is unjust it can fail to create an obligation to obey." (George, 2001: 316.)

George uses the example of abortion to illustrate the consequences of his reasoning. "[If] abortion is the unjust killing of innocent human beings who, as a matter of right, are entitled to the equal protection of the laws, then there is a problem for a democracy in permitting abortion .... Since it is the principle of equality that provides the moral justification for democratic rule in the first place, the denial of equality, even if effected by democratic means, is inconsistent with democratic principles." Conversely, for George, a non-democratic regime's laws may deserve obedience by virtue of their moral soundness, despite a belief in the superiority of democracy as a system of political decision making. So long as laws are morally sound, "[c]itizens of nondemocratic regimes ... have reasons for obeying the laws enacted by their rulers, serving in the military, and treating the official acts of government as politically authoritative." (George, 2001: 317–18, 322.)

In George's argument, then, the democratic source of a law has nothing whatever to do with its legitimacy, which is based solely on the degree to which that law accords with substantive moral principles. At one level, this appears to be nothing more than a revival of the religious natural law tradition (George quotes the declarations of Pope John Paul II to buttress his arguments), with all the baggage that tradition brings with it. The fundamental norm of equality to which George appeals, however, is located in the meaning of democracy, rather than in some extrapolitical concept of moral right. In the terms used in this book, George is perfectly willing to translate his moral commitments into constitutional language – he identifies the reference to "persons" in the fourteenth Amendment – but only if doing so does not have the result of diminishing the force of his position such that he might lose the subsequent argument. In other words, in his view, a norm of equality among persons, and the extension of that norm to include a fetus, are minimum substantive commitments required of any legitimate constitutional regime. The implication for the design of a constitutional language is that the inclusion of fundamental moral as well as democratic norms are *necessary*, not merely permissible, elements of any legitimate constitutional regime.

As a political matter, George's argument is deeply troubling. Effectively, he proposes that his loyalty to the constitutional regime – "fidelity," in the terms used in Chapter 4 – is dependent on satisfaction of his moral preferences on the question of abortion rights, and presumably on some other unspecified range of crucial questions, as well. "[W]e could not in conscience give our unfettered allegiance to a regime committed in its very constitution to abortion-on-demand, any more than we could give wholehearted allegiance to a regime constitutionally committed to chattel slavery." (George, 2001: 324.)[1] This is a proposition that raises especially difficult questions when one considers the question of a constitution that merely fails to prevent, rather than protects, a practice that some but not all members of a pluralistic society find anathema to their values. George bases his conclusions on the significance of the words "equality" and "person" in the Fourteenth Amendment, but of course prior to the adoption of that Amendment, the word "equality" was arguably not part of the system of constitutional signs available in the American constitutional language. To those who found slavery abhorrent, this was a good and sufficient reason to amend the Constitution, but did that fact render any regime grounded in the prior version of the language-defining text "illegitimate" in the sense of George's argument?

This rejection of value pluralism becomes particularly troublesome if it is expressed by an office holder responsible for rule-and norm generation at decision-making levels lower than that of

[1] In his essay, George argues that judicial constructions of the U. S. Constitution that find any right to abortion are simply incorrect, and frames the issue as one of "usurpation" of popular sovereignty by judges. Presumably, however, if George were persuaded that the language of a constitutional text genuinely fails to include terms necessary to express some principle central to his own moral beliefs, such as the identity of a fetus as a person possessed of rights, then he would feel no reason to be bound by the terms of that text. In this way, George's position is more radical than that of Robert Bork. "I am in complete agreement with Cardinal George that the constitutional decisions he deplores are morally abhorrent, but I do not think that their odiousness is sufficient reason to condemn them as law. They stand condemned because they are not law in any sense other than the fact that the Supreme Court decided them .... If, however, the Constitution properly interpreted required those results, I could not fault the courts." (Bork, 2003: 20.) Moreover, the problem is not solved by overturning *Roe v. Wade*. If the question of abortion rights were transferred to legislatures, and the legislature in whose jurisdiction George happens to live reaches a conclusion other than his own, he would be compelled by his logic to withdraw his "wholehearted allegiance" from the state, and if Congress failed to intervene, then he would presumably withdraw his allegiance from the United States government.

constitutional principle. Such a person is confronted by the existence of a system of constitutional language against whose grammatical rules and system of signs his own assertions will be tested for validity. If such an office holder might find that constitutional language to be deficient in that it fails to permit the articulation of his deeply held moral principles, and if such a discovery would be sufficient to render that constitutional system "illegitimate" and hence no longer properly binding, for him, then how can the rest of us trust that official to carry out his constitutional function?

The example of the office holder is a special case of the problem of value pluralism in the population at large. If a constitutional language is rendered illegitimate by its failure to include commitments to deeply held values, then those values that are included in a legitimate constitution must be universally held among officers who engage in the task of testing lower-level rules for constitutionality or else the constitutional regime has ceased to function. The shift in focus from language to substantive values, and from citizens to officials, has the effect of raising the stakes, but if we are seeking the basis for a legitimate constitutional regime, these questions must be considered.[2]

The argument from sovereignty depended on an initial moment of universal "as if" commitment to a constitutional language. With the addition of George's argument, that commitment now appears to be conditional on a prior, higher-level commitment to moral principles. The result is that "sovereignty" no longer resides in the self-authored "People" but in some other, external authority,

---

[2] Karen Orren describes a "grand unified theory" of constitutional development in terms of the shift from "officer's rights" to "citizen's rights." (Orren, 2000.) In Orren's argument, "officer's rights" are conceived broadly to include the prerogatives of private employers and heads of households over others within the domain of their legally recognized authority, whereas "citizen's rights" refers to the familiar panoply of negative individual liberties asserted in modern liberal constitutionalism. Over time, she argues, preconstitutional claims of officer's rights have given way to an ever-increasing understanding of the consequences of constitutional guarantees of citizens' rights. (Orren, 2000: 876–77.) What is of most interest for the present discussion is the role of officers after the abandonment of a theory of officers' rights. In a legitimate constitutional regime, the idea of government officials, at least, as "officers" possessed of "rights" must give way to a specifically constitutional role as discursive gatekeepers willing and able to test assertions of legally protected prerogatives against the requirements of constitutional language.

whether that authority be the Pope in Rome, the World-Spirit of Hegelian historical progress, or something else.

As a thought experiment, imagine a President who insisted on altering the constitutionally prescribed oath of office to read "I do solemnly swear that I will faithfully execute the Office of President of the United States insofar as doing so does not violate the laws of God as they are understood in my religion, and will to the best of my ability, preserve, protect, and defend those elements of the Constitution of the United States that are consistent with my moral values." Other issues aside, such an officer would not be presiding over a constitutional regime at all, but rather over a regime whose grounding norms are found in religious laws and whose constitution occupies a secondary position. Even if we were to posit the existence of a constitution whose terms never contradicted the teachings of a particular moral tradition, the question of which "law" would be supreme in the hypothetical case of a conflict remains a point of dissolution. And it is obviously the case that the problem is no less if the source of the moral commitments in question is secular rather than religious. Imagine a presidential oath that inserts the words "insofar as doing so is consistent with the highest principles of corporate capitalism," or "insofar as doing so does not violate the essential dignity of all living creatures."

Nor is the problem resolved by substituting a concept such as "justice" in place of morality. If the legitimacy of a constitutional regime depends on its complete and exhaustive declaration of a set of norms sufficient to constitute "justice," then any disagreement about the meaning of justice puts the legitimacy of the regime at stake. A complete conflation of legal, moral, and constitutional commitment makes the institutionalization of constitutional self-government literally and analytically impossible.

But the unsustainability of a complete equation of constitutional with moral commitments does not necessarily imply the opposite absolute position, that the system of signs available in a constitutional language should contain no substantive moral commitments at all. Whether one speaks in terms of "morality," "justice," "equality," or some other prior, extraconstitutional source of norms, the argument can be made that there is something that might be called principles of constitutional justice that has the same relation to "justice" writ large that constitutional language has to ordinary language, and constitutional law has to law. The limited space occupied by an incomplete constitution may required to contain certain fundamental normative principles even if others are left to be debated in conditions of value pluralism at lower levels of norm-generating discourse. A legitimate constitution might therefore be sustainable in the face of *some* degree of *permitted* constitutional evil, but not in the face of too much, and not where such evils are the specifically mandated outcome of immoral or unjust constitutional norms.

This is essentially the position of Robert Alexy's "argument from injustice," which states that, in general, "legal character is forfeited when individual norms of a legal system cross a *certain threshold* of injustice." (Alexy, 2002: 40, emphasis added.) Taking the extreme case, Alexy's criticism of legal positivism is that it does not provide a basis for declaring a Nazi legal regime illegitimate because it does not contain a reference to grounding normative commitments external to the law. In constitutional terms, this becomes an argument that proceeds as follows: a constitution is required to contain statements of substantive norms as well as linguistic principles against which laws are tested for their validity; these substantive norms must be sufficiently developed to guide the development of the law in order to ensure the continuing legitimacy of the constitutional regime; and these constitutional norms must be correct, in the absolute sense. Alexy insists that I, as an outside observer, cannot describe as "legitimate" any regime that is grounded either on inadequate or incorrect constitutional norms.[3]

---

[3] There are two problems of uncertainty associated with this proposition. In response to the concern that the meaning of "the law" becomes too uncertain where subjects deny any obligation to obey an unjust law, Alexy responds that the argument from injustice applies only in an extreme case. "[T]he more extreme the injustice, the more certain the knowledge of it. This principle connects material and epistemological considerations." He concedes that the issue is not always clear cut, but contends that the possibility of uncertainty does not diminish the validity of the use of moral criteria for judging the validity of laws. "There may well be cases, of course, in which one cannot say with complete certainty whether or not extreme injustice is at hand. This scarcely counts at all, however, when compared with the uncertainties generally attending knowledge of the law .... The value of legal certainty must be weighed against the value of material justice." (Alexy, 2002: 52.) Finally, to provide the content for "justice," Alexy appeals to the idea of a "broad

In a 2003 essay, John Finnis makes a more positivistic and analytical version of the argument when he proposes that the failure of
a positivistic descriptions of law formation – and, by extension,
constitution formation – is that it fails to make sense of "law" as that
concept is understood in actual social practice.[4] In Finnis' essentially
functionalist account, moral purposes are intrinsic to "law" in the
way that recording the passage of time is intrinsic to "clock," or the
way that logical coherence is an innate characteristic of the object
identified by the term "argument." In an argument with clear
precedents in both Hobbes' and Locke's descriptions of conventional language, Finnis argues that any (non-natural) object can be
described only in terms of its purposes. "[T]he enquiry we are
hypothesizing, the enquiry about law, starts humbly enough as: Why
have the sort of thing or things that get called the law and legal
system, legal institutions, and processes and arrangements that we
call the law of our time and town?" (Finnis, 2003: 108.)[5]

---

consensus on fundamental rights" (Alexy, 2002: 55). This, in turn, connects to one
of the requirements for a valid constitution, social efficacy, (Alexy, 2002: 102–04), a
concept that requires Hart's sense of obligation. Ultimately, then, a constitution to
be valid must accord with a prevailing moral consensus concerning the meaning of
"justice" in order to be efficacious and to avoid extreme injustice.

[4] Finnis writes in response to Brian Leiter's critiques of Finnis' 1980 book, *Natural
Law and Natural Rights*. In that book, Finnis argues that in the study of any
phenomenon that appears in a wide variety of forms, the attempt to find universally
common elements, "the lowest common denominator or highest common factor," is
a mistake. Instead, Finnis offers the recommendation that we focus on "central
cases." (Finnis, 1980: 10–11). He then propounds a complex theoretical argument
that concludes that "reciprocity" is fundamental to central cases of any system of
"law," and that as a result "the rule of law ... is always liable to reduce the efficiency
for evil of an evil government" at the same time that it promotes the common good,
and consequently incorporate a substantive conception of justice. (Finnis, 1980: 16,
266–74, 161–64.) Sounding much like Hart, Finnis argues that these descriptions
do no more than accurately capture the way law is thought about in practice by those
engaged in juridical activities, and that they therefore demonstrate the short-
comings of the positivist account. (Finnis, 1992: 356–58.) Leiter insists, however,
that Finnis has called on legal positivism to respond to a question for which the
theory never proposed an answer. "To wit, about 'the authoritativeness, for an
official's or a private citizen's conscience (ultimate rational judgment), of these
alleged and imposed [legally valid] requirements' and about 'their lack of authority
when radically unjust.'" (Leiter, 2003: 29.) The essay quoted in the text is Finnis'
response to that criticism.

[5] As an example, Finnis uses the example of the word "argument." "What is an
argument? I hear the word used in relation to statements, or connected series of
statements, asserting reasons for accepting some proposition; I learn soon enough

Following the same line, Finnis argues that the term "law" necessarily incorporates an appeal to a concept of "justice" that names the practical ends. Laws that fail to serve the general purpose of justice, in turn, have no authority and should not produce the sense of obligation that Hart identified as central to the experience of law as social practice. "Posited (enacted or judicially pronounced) rules of the latter kind are analogous to contracts which have been made in full compliance with every formality and other procedural condition specified by the law of contract but are void for illegality. Or, to take two perhaps closer analogies, they are like medicines which prove futile or lethal and are thus not medicinal at all, or like arguments whose formal elegance only masks their invalidity: no argument. Unjust laws are not laws." (Finnis, 2003: 114.) Finnis' argument, then, is that as a matter of definition, any system of constitutional signs couched in terms of "law" already includes an appeal to principles of justice, which are then available as elements of constitutional discourse in even the most strictly exclusive and complete system of constitutional language.

George, Alexy, and Finnis exemplify arguments for the necessary inclusion of substantive norms in the constitutional language of any legitimate constitutional regime: George and Alexy by focusing on the word "legitimate," and Finnis by focusing on the meaning of "law," a term implicitly at work in the deployment of the word "constitutional." But as noted in Chapter 4, "law" and "constitution" are not equivalent terms, and *a fortiori* neither are "constitution" and "morality." The differences between these concepts point to strong reasons to want to identify the minimum necessary level of

---

that some such statements or sets of statements do really give reasons for their purported conclusion, while others, intended and perhaps appearing to do so, fail, on reflection, to do so .... So I come to understand that not everything proposed and spoken of and considerable as a reason is a reason, and that not every argument is really any argument at all for what it is proposed as arguing for." (Finnis, 2003: 108.) Elsewhere, in a more sociological vein, Finnis phrases the argument in terms of collective reasons for action. "[T]he reasons people have for establishing systems of positive law (with power to override immemorial custom) ... include certain moral reasons, on which many of those people often act. And only those moral reasons suffice to explain why such people's undertaking takes the shape it does, giving legal systems the many defining features they have." (Finnis, 1996: 204.)

substantive commitments required for a constitution.[6] This is not an argument for the exclusion of moral claims from public discourse. To the contrary, as noted earlier, the requirement that constitutional language be exclusive means that limiting the substantive commitments that it contains, like limiting the scope of its completeness, leave open space for the inclusion of moral arguments at lower levels of decision making.

THE FUNCTION OF SUBSTANCE AND THE CHALLENGE OF DEMOCRATIC THEORY

In Gerald Postema's words, the difference between constitutional and legal forms of discourse appears in terms of the degree to which each is required to be "autonomous," "able to serve the tasks assigned to it because of its autonomy from moral and political reasoning," proceeding on the basis of norms "determined by criteria that make no essential reference to considerations of political morality." (Postema, 1996: 80.) Postema makes the case that, as a description of socio-legal practice, the "autonomy thesis" is incomplete without an account of moral justification for legal norms that explains their "practical force . . . relative to their moral counterparts." Postema suggests that this becomes especially problematic where one confronts the "pre-emption thesis," a version of what I

---

[6] For example, imagine a situation in which everyone shares George's insistence on making loyalty to the system depend on moral approval, and in which people disagree completely in their moral evaluation of different rules, and in which these debates are not extraordinary but rather characterize the discussion of a wide range of issues. Such a situation may simply be the defining case of the conditions of constitutional failure. In a discussion of the conditions under which constitutions fail, Mark Brandon describes "failure of constitutional discourse," which occurs "when a constitutional order is unable to speak coherently or, more seriously to sustain itself through constitutional interpretation or through discourse pertaining to its constitution." This, in turn, can ultimately lead to a "failure of constitutional order . . . the breakdown of a political regime established or authorized by a constitution." Concerning the American debate over the constitutional status of abortion rights, Brandon speculates that "either the lines of division are sufficiently complex and crosscutting that they do not threaten the failure of the order itself, or factions whose beliefs are strong enough to rationalize disruption are too weak to convulse the larger political order." (Brandon, 2001: 308, 309, 310.)

have described as the requirement of exclusivity.[7] Echoing Finnis' functionalist test, Postema insists that an adequate theory of the autonomy of legal reasoning must "not only describe *how law works*, but also, and more importantly, explain *why it is important* to have it." (Postema, 1996: 83–4, 88.)

The argument of the autonomy thesis, says Postema, is that law will rescue us from the uncertainty and conflict of unliquidated moral disagreement.[8] Since he finds that the judicial practice of case adjudication does not, in fact, reflect autonomous legal reasoning, Postema urges the abandonment of the model of autonomy as either a description or an aspiration of law.[9] In its place, he proposes an "integrated" model of legal discourse, in which justification requires "not only justifying a particular result, but also justifying the way one reaches that result to those who reason differently," thus making possible "a kind of public practical reasoning which allows different forms of argument, and different ways of making sense of the practice and its commitments, to compete on rational grounds against a background of the common practice." (Postema, 1996: 111–12.)

Postema's argument points toward the desire to accommodate constitutionalism with democratic theory, and in particular with theories of deliberative democracy that focus on reasoning and discursive practices and the processes of collective decision making as the locii for substantive norms. Jules Coleman, in his argument

---

[7] "Legal norms not only provide rational agents with positive (first-order) reasons to act in certain ways, but they also provide them with second-order reasons for *not acting* on certain other *reasons*." (Postema, 1996: 85.)

[8] The problem that plagued the formulation of a grammar for binding precommitments in Chapters 3 and 4 thus reappears at the stage of filling in the semantic content of the constitutional text produced as a result.

[9] The latter argument turns, once again, on a consideration of the conditions under which Hart's social experience of obligation is likely to occur. Postema argues that court practices influence citizens' attitudes toward law. "Legal norms have preemptive force only in so far as agents to whom they are addressed accord the norms pre-emptive force in their practical reasoning. However, I shall argue that agents will have reason to accord them that force only to the extent that they believe that *courts* reliably do so." (Postema, 1996: 100.) Concluding that courts do not, in practice, accord legal norms preemptive force over moral claims even in ordinary cases (those in which the rules of adjudication appear to be relatively determinate), Postema similarly concludes that the claim of preemption, identified in this discussion by the term "exclusivity," similarly fails. (Postema, 1996: 100–110.)

for inclusive positivism, takes a different approach. Although Coleman agrees that it is perfectly permissible for moral arguments to play a role in legal discourse, he insists that something like a rule of recognition remains necessary to identify the appropriate application of those arguments, thus preserving the autonomy of the system of legal discourse. (Coleman, 1996: 288.) But Coleman identifies this discursive rule of recognition in the phenomenon of "convergent social practice among officials" – that is, in the observation that over time, the practices of those responsible for the maintenance and enforcement of a constitutional regime tend to become the same. Coleman proposes that this definition expresses Hart's commitment to an "internal point of view," which "transforms convergent behavior into a social norm." Like Finnis and Postema, Coleman looks to the translation of norms into reasons for action, but rather than appealing to moral suasion, he finds these reasons either in an officials' self-interest in coordination with others or in the acceptance of others' judgment as a good indicator of what is right. (Coleman, 1996: 297, 299–301)[10]

Coleman's focus on describing the behavior of officials is an obvious point of distinction between his argument and that of Postema, who is concerned with identifying citizens' reasons for finding a certain model of autonomous legal reasons in the actions of those officials. In fact, viewed as attempts to illuminate different levels of decision making, the two arguments need not be read in as disagreeing at all. One might say that Coleman is correct that patterns of incorporation of moral argumentation into legal conclusions by officials demonstrate a converging practice that defines an internal rule of recognition. Simultaneously, one might also join with Postema in saying that citizens observing the operation of this discursive rule of recognition will correctly conclude that they no longer have any reason to conceive of "law" as a mode of discourse autonomous from ordinary practical or moral reasoning. But constitutional language is required to be more "autonomous" and less

---

[10] Since Coleman concerns himself only with norms generated through the convergent practices of officials, the rule of recognition for the valid application of moral principles is coextensional with the law, a point that parallels the discussion of the "addressee" of constitutional norms (see Chapter 6). (Coleman, 1996: 302.)

bound by "convergent social practices among officials" – in Postema's terms, less "integrated" – than legal language. The problem of substance in constitutional language therefore has to be analyzed separately from the parallel problem as it appears in ordinary law.

I have argued that to treat constitutional norms as coextensional with moral norms is self-defeating, in part on the basis of the arguments for incompleteness that were presented in Chapter 4. On the other hand, Alexy's objection to a constitutional language unconstrained by any substantive moral commitments has undeniable strength. And although I have previously argued that constitutional and legal legitimacy must have differing bases, certainly Finnis' argument that the connection between constitutional language and law compels a recognition that the claim of legitimacy is normatively weighted, and that the discussion of groundedness and efficacy necessitates a consideration of the meaning of that normative claim. At the same time, however, the constitutional implications of an argument that "law" definitionally refers to an appeal to "justice" has to be considered in light of the necessary separation between the requirements of constitutional and legal legitimacy.

To reiterate, if the criticisms of positivism developed by Finnis, Postema, and others are right, then a constitutional language, no less than a system of positively enacted laws, needs more than exclusivity and a limited scope of completeness; it needs some minimal level of substantive normative commitment. The initial moment of consent to a constitutional language, to be effective, must carry with it a commitment to a set of norms contained in the terms of that language. At the same time, one of the reasons for avoiding too broad a set of substantive commitments in constitutional discourse is to leave as much room as possible at lower levels of rule- and norm generation by ordinary lawmaking. This is the parallel to the point that was made with regard to completeness in Chapter 4. But whereas that argument was couched in terms of the formulation of legal arguments, and hence connected most directly to general theories of law, here the connection that is drawn is between constitutional and democratic theory.

There is a close connection between the theory of constitutional language presented in this book and theories of deliberative democracy. These are arguments that seek to ground the legitimacy of political regimes in conditions of discourse rather than in the satisfaction of aggregated interests, but to do so in a way that has substantive as well as proceduralist consequences. While the literature on deliberative democracy is extensive, and some of that literature has already appeared in the discussion, to introduce the issues that arise from a consideration of this body of arguments I will rely on three essays by Seyla Benhabib, Iris Marion Young, and Joshua Cohen, respectively (all three of which first appeared in a seminal collection edited by Benhabib).

As Benhabib describes it, the theory of deliberative democracy derives from the proposition that "legitimacy in complex democratic societies must be thought to result from the free and unconstrained public deliberation of all about matters of common concern." (Benhabib, 1996: 68.) As a result, the first critical concern of any democratic system is securing the conditions necessary for public deliberation.

Already, a significant tension is evident between the theory of constitutional language explored in this book and the project of establishing legitimacy by securing conditions of "unconstrained public deliberation." The description of constitutional language presented thus far, after all, has focused heavily on constraints on constitutional deliberation, in the form of requirements of exclusivity, on the one hand, and incompleteness, on the other. Moreover, the discussion of the problem of precommitment pointed to the fact that the legitimation of a constitutional regime necessarily involves explaining the legitimacy *of* a commitment to discursive constraints within the scope of constitutional discourse.

Benhabib's further development of the argument brings these distinctions into sharp focus. To Benhabib, the legitimation of democratic governance depends on appealing to the underlying logic of "anonymous yet intelligible collective rules, procedures, and practices that form a way of life," (Benhabib, 1996: 68–9), a Hart-like formulation close to Coleman's "convergent social practice among officials." But for Benhabib, these practices do not generate grounding norms; rather they presuppose thick shared commitments as necessary background facts preceding the exercise of deliberation. These shared background norms are constitutive of political discourse by their hermeneutic effect. "We never begin our deliberations concerning these matters at a moral ground zero. Rather, in moral theory as in everyday morality, in political theory as in everyday political discourse, we are always situated within a horizon of presuppositions, assumptions, and power relations, the totality of which can never become wholly transparent to us." These foundational shared norms are those that are required for effective deliberation, conditions of equal participation and the need for universal assent to legitimate political actions that are the defining features of deliberative democracy. "Discourse ethics in this sense presupposes the reciprocal moral recognition of one another's claims to be participants in the moral-political dialogue." (Benhabib, 1996: 79.)

Benhabib's "background norms" are not the same thing as Michelman's constitutional culture or Waldron's good faith. At times, the discourse that takes place within these hermeneutic horizons reaffirms its own legitimacy by the operation of what Benhabib calls "hermeneutic validation," an appeal to the thick deliberative norms entrenched, however unknowingly, in existing social practice. At the same time, however, such deliberation has the capacity to be transformative by virtue of the simultaneous operation of "recursive validation," through the formal definitions of "rights" and other constitutional claims that emerge from the practice of discourse. "What is distinctive about the discourse model is that although it presupposes that participants must recognize one another's entitlement to moral respect and reciprocity in some sense, the determination of the precise content and extent of these principles would be a consequence of discourses themselves." (Benhabib, 1996: 79.)

In Benhabib's understanding, constitutionalism thus becomes an acceptance of the starting set of rules of democratic discourse, the legitimacy of which is guaranteed by their grounding in the existence of thick norms of moral respect and reciprocity. "[T]he normative conditions of discourses, like basic rights and liberties, are to be viewed as rules of the game that can be contested within the game but only insofar as one first accepts to abide by them and play the game at all." The result is that the divisions between constitutionalism, law, and politics break down, except insofar as at any given moment some set of proceduralist rules are presumed to be in place until they are changed. "Conceptually as well as sociologically, models of deliberative and dualistic democracy focus on this process of 'recursive' and 'hermeneutic' interdependence between constitution-making and democratic politics." (Benhabib, 1996: 79–80.)

It is not clear, in the first instance, that this description of the relationship between constitutionalism and democracy does very much to solve the problems that were the subject of earlier chapters. Neither the fact nor even the possibility of "universal assent" is self-evidently given, and the pressure to presuppose a hermeneutically operative set of norms thick enough to produce the conditions of that possibility is consequently very great. Recognition of moral reciprocity as participants in deliberation is a starting point, to be sure, but without considerably more, it is difficult to see how that is a sufficient basis to resolve the fact of value pluralism. If Benhabib's approach is to be the basis for constitutional legitimation, the set of presupposed norms will have to be made much thicker.

Iris Marion Young makes the point that even where the question is framed in terms of conditions of deliberation, too thick a set of such commitments has an exclusionary effect on those whose core concerns do not translate well into the universalizing, homogeneous model of discourse that results. "Deliberative theorists tend to assume that bracketing political and economic power is sufficient to make speakers equal. This assumption fails to notice that the social power that can prevent people from being equal speakers derives not only from economic dependence or political domination but also from an internalized sense of the right one has to speak or not to speak, and from the devaluation of some people's style of speech and the elevation of others." (Young, 1996: 122.)

As an example, Young points out that if the goal of deliberative democracy is assumed to be a competition between programs in the manner of Holmes' famous marketplace of ideas, the result is that expression that takes the form of a clearly articulated argument is valued above other forms of expression. "Speech that is assertive and confrontational is here more valued than speech that is tentative, exploratory, or conciliatory," and the same is true of speech that follows established rules of political contest, or takes the form of a "formal and general" argument, a set of characteristics that,

Young suggests, has clear gender, class, and educational connotations. (Young, 1996: 123–4.)

Alternatively, if the goal of deliberation is presumed to be either the discovery or the manufacture of unity based on common interests, the pressure is toward homogeneity in the form of a privileged perspective that everyone is asked to assume. "When discussion participants aim at unity, the appeal to a common good in which they are all supposed to leave behind their particular experience and interests, the perspectives of the privileged are likely to dominate the definition of that common good. The less privileged are asked to put aside the expression of their experience, which may require a different idiom, or their claims of entitlement or interest must be put aside for the sake of a common good whose definition is biased against them." (Young, 1996: 126.)

In place of the deliberative model, Young proposes what she calls "communicative democracy," characterized by three fundamental norms: that the "polity consists of people who live together, who are stuck with one another"; that "members must have a commitment to equal respect . . . to say that all have a right to express their opinions and points of view, and all ought to listen"; and that there must be agreed-upon "procedural rules of fair discussion and decision-making." As Young points out, these are "much thinner conditions than those of shared understandings or the goals of finding common goods" of the kind that Benhabib assumed, and these thinner presuppositions leave open the possibility that forms of value pluralism previously conceived of as disruptive of democratic political discourse may instead come to be recognized are resources. "Within the context of this minimal unity that characterizes communicative democracy, a richer understanding of processes of democratic discussion results if we assume that differences of social position and identity perspective function as a resource for public reason rather than as divisions that public reason transcends." (Young, 1996: 126–7.)

Young's formulation of communicative democracy is motivated by the same goal that leads to the argument for a constitutional language that is characterized by incompleteness and minimal normative substance, in addition to a strong form of exclusivity. This idea was discussed earlier in terms of limiting the scope and content of constitutional decisional discourse in order to free the language of lower-level decision making. My argument in Chapter 4 was that a differentiation between constitutional and other forms of discourse is essential to ensure that ordinary legal discourse is free to draw on norms deriving from other areas of experience just as much as that differentiation is necessary to preserve constitutional language against instrusion. Benhabib effectively concedes some version of the need for differentiation between levels of language insofar as she treats constitutional rules as discourse-shaping pre-suppositions operative at any given moment, although subject to subsequent alteration through the interplay of constitutionalism, law, and politics. But Young's thinner set of substantive commitments requires that the differentiation be maintained much more sharply, so that the thick normative commitments of politics and law are not permitted to become privileged elements of constitutional language, precisely so that the possibility of Benhabib's "recursive validation" will not be foreclosed.

Joshua Cohen takes a different approach from those of Benhabib or Young, and ends with the analysis that is most directly relevant to the discussion of constitutional language. Cohen accepts the need for a relatively thick set of normative commitments, but attempts to account for the existence of such norms as the necessary consequence of the initial commitment to deliberative democracy, rather than as the precondition for that commitment. This is the political/democratic equivalent of the project of identifying substantive norms that are necessary as elements of constitutional language, such that the acceptance of that language analytically implies acceptance of substantive norms.

Cohen's basic argument begins, as always, with the fact of pluralism. Unlike Benhabib, however, he does not rely on the idea of deliberative practice to reduce that pluralism, either in terms of the definition of common interests or matters of moral values. "Apart from the sheer fact of disagreement, there is, moreover, no apparent tendency to convergence generated by the exercise of practical reason; furthermore, we have no *theory* of the operations of practical reason that would lead us to predict convergence on comprehensive moralities; nor can I think of any marginally attractive social or political mechanisms that might generate such agreement." (Cohen,

1996: 96.) Against this background of unliquidated disagreement, Cohen finds the challenge to be a justification for the preservation of Benjamin Constant's "liberties of the moderns," the kinds of freedoms of conscience, person, and property that are the traditional bases of liberal constitutionalism. His answer is that such liberties are required to prevent exclusion from the deliberative process, an outcome that would defease the justification for deliberative democracy in the first place.

Like other theorists of deliberative democracy – including Sunstein and Rawls as well as Benhabib and Young – Cohen focuses on the idea of an acceptable set of reasons, rather than on outcomes. In the terms of the argument of this book, his focus is on the range of substantive elements in the system of constitutional signs that speakers will be able to avail themselves of in translating their values and preferences into constitutional arguments. The difficulty comes in defining a range of acceptable reasons that is sufficiently broad to include the fact of value pluralism. "One must ... find reasons that are compelling to others, acknowledging those others as equals, aware that they have alternative reasonable commitments, and knowing something about the kinds of commitments that they are likely to have." The result will not be consensus, but a sufficiently inclusive language to ensure legitimacy. "[I]f there is disagreement... participants may appeal to considerations that are quite generally recognized as having considerable weight, and as a suitable basis for collective choice, even among people who disagree about the right result: when participants confine their argument to such reasons, majority support itself will commonly count as reason for accepting the decision as legitimate." (Cohen, 1996: 100.)

The requirement of unanimous "as if" consent that was identified earlier as the basis for the creation of a constitutional language thus reenters the equation in its operation, but in terms of modes of reasoning rather than in terms of collective interests. "By requiring justification on terms acceptable to others, deliberative democracy provides for a form of political autonomy: that all who are governed by collective decisions – who are expected to govern their own conduct by those decisions – must find the bases of those decisions acceptable." Cohen calls this the "principle of deliberative inclusion," and he rightly recognizes the special challenge that is posed by religion. "Religious views set demands of an especially high order – perhaps transcendent obligations – on their adherents; moreover, if we see these requirements from the believer's point of view, then we cannot think of them as self-imposed.... Religious adherents, then, cannot accept, as sufficient reasons in support of a law or system of policy, considerations that would preclude their compliance with those demands." In response to this challenge, simply treating all religious or equivalently absolute moral commitments as unreasonable violates the principle of inclusion, as does treating religious commitments as "interests" or "preferences" to be balanced against others on an equal basis. "This reductive response indicates an unwillingness to see the special role of religious convictions from the point of view of the person who has them, an unwillingness to see how the religious view, in virtue of its content, states or implies that the requirements provide especially compelling reasons." (Cohen, 1996: 102–03.)

Cohen develops his idea about the inclusion of religious voices in the context of explaining why freedom of religious practice – one of the "liberties of the moderns" – must be included in a system of deliberative democracy. His comments, however, require recognition of the challenges, posed by Benhabib and Young, of defining a constitutional language that is sufficiently grounded to be efficacious yet sufficiently modest in its substantive commitments to avoid exclusion by a too-narrow specification of a mode of constitutional reasoning. Part of the answer that appears in Cohen's discussion (again, drawing elements of his argument out of their original context) is a reliance on the multiple levels of norm generation that informed the distinction between constitutional and legal language. Cohen speaks of "associative democracy," an argument that at lower (more localized, more specific) levels of norm generation, government should give way to civil society, broadly conceived. (Cohen, 1996: 110–12.) The result of combining the principle of inclusion with the model of associative democracy is to describe a multileveled system of democratic governance in which the higher the level of decision making – that is, the more general the norm that is created by official action – the greater the requirement of inclusion, a model that has clear parallels in the idea that we ultimately arrive at an exclusive but incomplete constitutional language.

This does not, yet, get to an argument about the minimal substantive normative commitments that a constitutional language is required to have in order that consent to that language will suffice to provide a foundation for the legitimacy of the regime that is produced as a result. But the arguments of Benhabib, Young, and Cohen point toward a resolution sufficient to satisfy Finnis' or Alexy's demands for substance without falling into George's moral absolutism.

Benhabib's appeal to a background of shared values reinforces the necessity of "efficacy," the anchoring relationship between constitutional language and other, lower levels of norm generating discourse that was described in Chapter 4. Young's observation that genuine pluralism extends to discursive styles as well as of interests and values becomes the basis for an argument that normative commitments need to be limited to the point where they do not undercut the possibility of that grounded-ness by defeasing the "as if" unanimous commitment to constitutional language in the first place. The grammatical requirements of exclusivity and incompleteness necessarily involve elements of exclusion, but the substantive content of the system of constitutional signs must be sufficiently inclusive to permit identification with the linguistic community that is created by its adoption. That observation was strengthened by Cohen's observations concerning the special case of religious commitments, and gives weight to his argument that substantive commitments at the level of constitutional language should be restricted to those that follow necessarily from conditions of democratic participation. Cohen's model of "associative democracy," finally, identifies the criteria for differentiation between a whole spectrum of norm-generating authority, from the most universal (constitutional) to the most local and specific (associational), with the political regime occupying the series of spaces in between.

Theories of deliberative democracy thus mark a path between pure proceduralism and an outright conflation of democracy with morality. These theories are the political equivalents of the legal theories of inclusive positivism that were exemplified in Jules Coleman's description of law as norms engendered by "convergent social practices." But the claim remains that commitment to moral principles is an inescapable element of the initial moment of consent, whether in the form of Hart-like "rules of recognition" or Benhabib's "horizons."

It will be remembered that at the outset, the argument proceeded from the necessity for sovereignty to the discovery of the possibility that a constitutional regime's legitimacy required, at a minimum, an initial moment of unanimous consent to the adoption of a constitutional language. That move was explained as possible by virtue of its consistency with norms of self-sovereignty and government by consent, and by the relationship between language and the generation of reasons. In theories of deliberative democracy, the focus shifts from the justification for that initial commitment to its content, the language of deliberation, which is tested against norms of democratic equality and participation. The separation between the justification and the content of the moment of linguistic consent represents an attempt to separate the "ought" and the "is" by interposing the act of popular-sovereignty-in-action between them. Insofar as such a strategy is successful, it resolves the problem of legitimating the moment of creation by an appeal to postconstitutional moments of consent, and then derives a normative order of law and politics from that fact.

But the project of theories of deliberative democracy is larger than the project of this book. Applying these democratic theorists' arguments directly to the question of constitutional legitimacy represents an abandonment of the minimalist commitment to what is logically necessary, in favor of a (potentially persuasive) argument to the effect that certain forms of constitutional rule are more *desirable* than others. Thus, if the positivistic theories of law described earlier proved too little, like the appeal to moral consensus these democratic theories prove too much; they illustrate a possibly attractive version of what a successful constitutional regime might look like, but only by expanding the requirements for success to include a fairly specific model of law, politics, and morality. Cohen's focus on different levels of discursive norm generation points toward an approach to disentangling the competing claims to inclusion and groundedness, but his conclusions need to be evaluated separately for a consideration of constitutional language.

This discussion of deliberative democracy has a great deal to say about the relationship between constitutional and political legitimacy in the same way that the earlier discussion of legal positivism illuminated the relationship between constitutionalism and law. In addition, arguments based on theories of deliberative democracy are important in that they focus specifically on the idea of normative commitments contained in language, rather than on more general ideals of democratic practice. The task for a theory of constitutional language is to describe the scope and kind of normative commitments that are required to ground constitutional legitimacy without running into the Scylla of moral claims that deny the possibility of value pluralism or the Charybdis of a purely positivistic appeal to social practice that fails to provide the basis for a constitutional text's essential critical function.

LAW, DEMOCRACY, AND LANGUAGE: TOWARD A NORM OF CONSTITUTIONAL INTEGRITY

At this point, the question of substance has come clearly into focus. Incorporating the insights of the theory of deliberative democracy, the inquiry can be reformulated to something like the following: "What is the amount of normative substance that a system of constitutional language is required to contain in order to be sufficiently grounded in shared background understandings to be efficacious while at the same time minimizing the constraints on democratic participation that are imposed as a result?" In order to get to an answer, however, the arguments from democratic theory must be reconnected to the specific project of constitutionalism and law.

Ronald Dworkin, Joseph Raz, and Jürgen Habermas each provides arguments that help to illuminate this dimension of the argument. Dworkin's interpretive principle of "integrity" is a further development of the idea that the initial commitment of a constitutional order – its grounding norm – is a discursive/linguistic principle that implies the adoption of substantive norms by necessary implication. "Integrity" is a classic example of a thin but nonetheless substantive grounding norm of the kind that theorists of deliberative democracy have proposed in response to the challenge of combining constitutional legitimacy with value pluralism.

Raz' argument returns us to the question of grounding constitutional officials' claims to legitimate authority. Whether one relies on a norm of integrity or some other, similarly thin grounding norms, it is necessary to provide an explanation for the authority of officials to pursue or protect those norms in practice. Raz' argument points toward an explanation of how the initial commitment to constitutional language suffices to establish a legitimate basis for the authority that constitutional officials are required to have if the text's substantive normative commitments are to ground constitutional language.

The remaining piece of the argument emerges from consideration of Jürgen Habermas' description of the relationship between normative and juridical language systems. Reviving the hermeneutic concept of horizons that Benhabib relied on, Habermas reverses the relationship between language and norms by demonstrating that moral commitments function *as* exclusionary linguistic principles, just as much as rules of linguistic construction delimit the range of possibility for the articulation of moral positions.

Combining the insights of these three writers' proposals with the argument that has been developed thus far provides the missing elements of the theory of constitutional language: a much clearer understanding of the nature and scope of substantive normative commitments that are required for constitutional legitimacy; an explanation for the authority of officials to enforce those commitments by maintaining the requirement of translation; and an initial description of the kind of appropriately constitutional norms, as opposed to ordinary moral or legal norms, that can provide the ground for the legitimation of a regime based on an exclusive and incomplete system of constitutional language. Together, these approaches provide a standpoint from which to reply to the question "Consent to What?" in a way that takes account of the necessary distinctions between the languages of constitutionalism, law, and democracy.

We begin with Ronald Dworkin's norm of integrity. Like Cass Sunstein, Dworkin locates law as a specifically discursive practice. Dworkin, however, goes beyond Sunstein's proceduralism-plus-moral-sentiments in characterizing the grounds of juridical legitimacy in a democratic system. For Dworkin, positivistic descriptions of law as social behavior pay insufficient attention to the discursive nature of law, and to the consequences that flow from that nature. "Of course, law is a social phenomenon. But its complexity, function, and consequence all depend on one special feature of its structure. Legal practice, unlike many other social phenomena, is argumentative." (Dworkin, 1986: 13.)

As a result, extending Hart's call for an internal understanding of juridical practice, Dworkin insists on the continued relevance of formal jurisprudential analysis. "[T]he historian cannot understand the law as an argumentative social practice, even enough to reject it as deceptive, until he has a participant's understanding, until he has his own sense of what counts as a good or bad argument within that practice. We need a social theory of law, but it must be jurisprudential just for that reason." (Dworkin, 1986: 14.) Conversely, he understands the concern that drives a positivist to want to identify a clear basis for characterizing "law" as a matter of definition. The fear of legal nihilism is contained in "the argument that unless lawyers and judges share factual criteria about the grounds of law there can be no significant thought or debate about what the law is." Dworkin refers to this as "the semantic sting," (Dworkin, 1986: 44, 45), a characterization that points up the direct connection between substantive and discursive norms. The argument can be stated nicely in Hobbesian terms. If the names of abstracts such as "law" lose their secure claim on an accurate identification of shared norms, then the entirety of the discourse constructed around those signs risks becoming "absurd."

The search for a properly jurisprudential grounding norm is therefore the search for characteristics that secure both the definition of "law" and the conditions of its legitimacy. Where (some) positivists might conflate the two questions, Dworkin argues that the necessity of interpretation renders the inquiries analytically separate. The term "interpretation" does not fully capture Dworkin's specific model of juridical reading; a more descriptive term would be "extraction," a process of determining a rule from a relevant set of materials through practices of interrogation and discursive construction. This is not political discourse between interested or morally committed actors; it is the discourse between sovereign reader and the text that characterizes the processes of constitutional maintenance.[11] The nature of that process is what generates

---

[11] Sotirios A. Barber suggests that the "maintenance" of a constitutional system depends, ultimately, on a form of political public education that has the effect of

Dworkin's grounding norm of "integrity," the principle that the law should always be treated in a way that renders it internally consistent, or "coherent." Coherence is achieved when the body of legal decisions is grounded in a reference to a consistent set of substantive normative commitments, "the principles of personal and political morality the explicit decisions presuppose by way of justification." (Dworkin, 1986: 96.) In historical practice, suggests Dworkin, a working conception of integrity has guided American constitutional practice even in the absence of its explication. "Integrity," writes Dworkin, "is our Neptune," unobservable by direct means, but nonetheless identifiable by its gravitational influence over jurisprudential development. (Dworkin, 1986: 183.) Dworkin's law as integrity thus partakes of many of the characteristics of consistency and groundedness that were identified earlier as elements of law's efficacy.

Both the necessity for, and the form of, a norm of integrity derive from the discursive nature of law. Integrity is required because lawmakers and judges are required to navigate the imperfect fit between moral norms and positive rules in the process of inter-pretation/extraction. Conversely, it is because this process of navigation – whether in the form of inspiration or reconciliation – takes the form of discourse that there exists a "textual" under-standing to be made integral in the first instance. "Integrity would not be needed as a distinct political virtue in a utopian state. Coherence would be guaranteed because officials would always do what was perfectly just and fair." (Dworkin, 1986: 176.) Since jur-idical actors do not automatically and necessarily act in perfect accordance with extrinsic standards of justice, it becomes important to maintain the integrity of the applicable and enforceable standards against which their conduct is tested for its legitimacy. Moreover, "justice" is not a unitary term. In practice, the demands of substantive justice and procedural fairness often pull in opposite directions. Confronted by the need to resolve a tension between procedural and substantive standards for right outcomes, a juridical

---

"inculcating lawfulness," a formulation that draws attention to the roles of many different areas of policymaking and administrative areas of government in addition to courts or other specialized juridical institutions. (Barber, 2001: 165.)

actor requires a third principle to justify choosing between the two. (Dworkin, 1986: 177.) Dworkin proposes that integrity fits the bill

Integrity does not directly follow from democracy. One perfectly democratic alternative to a requirement of integrity would be a "checkerboard" system of laws that apply different rules to different cases, so that each moral position gets a voice in some area. As Dworkin points out, such a solution is neither obviously less fair nor obviously less just than a consistent alternative. From the perspective of fairness, a checkerboard solution maximizes the ability of differing voices to be heard and to have an effect on at least some set of particular outcomes, and from the perspective of justice any uniform solution will be less desirable than some of the outcomes produced by a checkerboard strategy even as it is more desirable than others. So, Dworkin asks, what is the "instinct" that the suggestion of a checkerboard strategy to the resolution of hotly debated questions violates? (Dworkin, 1986: 178–83.)

The answer is that such an approach violates the ideal of constitutionalism as a model of collective action. "[W]e reject a division between parties of opinion when matters of principle are at stake. We follow a different model: that each point of view must be allowed a voice in the process of deliberation but that the collective decision must nevertheless aim to settle on some coherent principle whose influence then extends to the natural limits of its authority." (Dworkin, 1986: 179.) That is, the checkerboard model violates the premise that legitimation is fundamentally a discursive process that takes the form of a narrative, which seeks coherence as a necessary condition for its legitimation in the republic of reasons.

Ultimately, a norm of integrity is both necessitated and made plausible by a set of social conditions that include persistent disagreement, and the desire for a constitutional order despite the fact of that disagreement. Part of Dworkin's argument is that a norm of legal integrity defines the scope of a political community. There is no sacrifice in integrity, after all, if different regimes have different rules, but there is if the rules apply differently within a regime. The existence of a meaningful political community is the precondition for legitimation through appeal to integrity. The adoption of a norm of integrity, in turn, is the Lockean act of constitutional consent. "[A] political society that accepts integrity as a political virtue thereby becomes a special form of community ... that promotes its moral authority to assume and deploy a monopoly of coercive force." (Dworkin, 1986: 185–86, 187–88.) The norm of integrity makes the imagined consent to the political system of decision making sensible. "[A] state that accepts integrity as a political ideal has a better case for legitimacy than one that does not." (Dworkin, 1986: 192.)

Applied to the practice of lawmaking, a strong norm of integrity creates a constructive discourse among the members of a political association. Dworkin employs the metaphor of a "chain novel," a narrative constructed over time by different writers, each adding a "chapter." The fact that the text is in the form of a narrative imposes a requirement of integrity, both by its nature and by virtue of the intent of the initiators of the project. Within the range of possible integral understandings, the writers strive to make the text "the best it can be." For this appeal to an external normative standards, Dworkin invokes a set of fundamental substantive values: justice, fairness, and procedural due process. "According to law as integrity, propositions of law are true if they figure in or follow from the principles of justice, fairness, and procedural due process that provide the best constructive interpretation of the community's legal practice." (Dworkin, 1986: 225.)

The point is made clear in Dworkin's application of his standard to the Civil War Amendments to the U.S. Constitution. What is called for in the interpretation of the Fourteenth Amendment, he says, is "to look directly to the overall structure of the post-Civil War amendments ... seen as part of the more general constitutional system they left in place, and to ask what principles of equality are *necessary to justify that structure*." (Dworkin, 1986: 363, emphasis added). This back-and-forth reversion to grammatical and substantive norms, from the requirement of integrity to the background principles that define its meaning, is the process of "law working itself pure."[12] The continued emphasis on integrity, and the

---

[12] Rawls describes a similar process of back-and-forth negotiation between sets of principles as the search for "reflective equilibrium." To get from the original position of ignorance to a working set of political principles, Rawls suggests that we begin with "provisional fixed points." "For example, we are confident that religious intolerance and racial discrimination are unjustified ... But we have

commitment to the construction over time of a coherent narrative that is informed by shared values as a critical check on integrity, make the process of constitutional interpretation an extension of the normative assumptions implied at the moment of its establishment. (Dworkin, 1986: 403.) Integrity is what is required to permit the extraction of rules from a constitutional text to take place in the space between the "is" of juridical practice and the "ought" of political aspiration.

Earlier in the discussion, the norm of integrity was invoked to decide between the competing claims of justice and fairness. But the simultaneous invocation of positivist norms of integrity and substantive, deontological norms of justice imply the possibility of an outright conflict. "If no interpretation can be found that is not flawed in that way [by violating substantive norms], then the chain novelist will not be able fully to meet his assignment; he will have to settle for an interpretation that captures most of the text, conceding that it is not wholly successful." (Dworkin, 1986: 230.) Ultimately, such a conflict may become insupportable, and the project may fail. Conversely, so long as fundamental substantive norms remain in the background – that is, so long as the constitutional order is commensurate with a shared moral consensus – Dworkin's argument is a statement about the conditions of possibility for legitimate constitutionalism.

Applied to the notion of constitutional language, what follows logically from Dworkin's analysis of textual interpretation is the proposition that only a text capable of being read integrally can legitimately function as a constitution. As a result, Dworkin's argument can be understood as the proposition that a constitutional language is required, at a minimum, to contain a degree of normative substantive sufficient to generate an integral normative

---

much less assurance as to what is the correct distribution of wealth and authority." Thereafter, we can test our provisional fixed points of understanding against the thought-experiment of the original position to arrive at a more complete set of governing principles "[b]y going back and forth, sometimes altering the conditions of the contractual circumstances, at others withdrawing our judgments." (Rawls, 1996: 628–29, 629.) In the terms of this book's discussion, the original position and the veil of ignorance can be thought of as rules of grammatical construction, while our acknowledgment of provisional fixed points of agreement identifies the substantive normative content of our constitutional language.

system. Furthermore, some of the most problematic aspects of Dworkin's account of legitimacy are greatly reduced if his argument is applied to a system of constitutional language that is incomplete, rather than trying to make legal, political, and constitutional legitimacy mutually dependent and coextensional.

"Integrity," therefore, names the first test for the minimum scope of normative substance that is required in a constitutional language. What is still lacking, however, is an account that explains *how* substantive normative content leads to integrity. Put another way, the appropriation of Dworkin's argument has led to the observation that "integrity" names a set of conditions that is required for a sufficient constitutional language, and integrity requires the specification in that language of some substantive normative commitments around which coherent meanings are to be interpreted. But in order to get from there to a serious answer to the question of what substantive commitments are required in order for integrity to be possible, the relationship between these different kinds of norms has to be explained further. An approach to that explanation is provided by Joseph Raz.

MAKING INTEGRITY WORK: THE AUTHORITY OF OFFICIALS AND THE NEED FOR HORIZONS

While Raz' writings cover a great deal of legal, moral, and political theory, I will focus on his treatment of the relationship between grounding in moral substance and legitimacy, the special importance of underdetermination, and the role and authority of "officials" that emerges as a result of his discussion of these points. The discussion of officials, in particular, continues the necessary connection between conditions of legitimacy and principles of interpretation that emerged in the discussion of Dworkin's norm of integrity. Incorporating Raz' insights on these points into the argument illuminates the function that substance serves for a system of constitutional language, and illuminates the relationship between constitutional and other forms of discourse.[13]

---

[13] Raz is a difficult writer to classify in terms of positivistic, natural law, or discourse theories. Brian Leiter classifies Raz as a leading figure in the hard positivist school.

Like Sunstein, Raz rejects the idea of legitimation by consent expressed in Hart's rule of recognition, insofar as that concept appeals solely to the maintenance of a set of social and economic conditions, on the grounds that such an argument can demonstrate the operation of a legal regime only as a "social fact," not as genuinely "legitimate." Even as a matter of socio-legal description, Raz says the assumption that the customary acceptance of a system of law reflects any version of reasoned consent to long-term constraints on short-term decision making is simply fictitious. "It assumes that the law, constitutional law at the very least, develops exclusively in response to the relatively stable aspects of the social conditions of the country to which it applies. As we know, this is far too rationalistic a view of the development of the law." (Raz, 2001: 155.)

What is true of law, generally, is equally true of constitutions. "That the adoption and development of constitutions are affected by a variety of short-term factors is no mere aberration in the life of one country or another. It is a universal feature of the political life of all countries with a constitution. Constitutional theory had better allow for that. A theory that condemns all such influences as aberrations to be avoided is too remote from this world to be much use in it." (Raz, 2001: 156.) More importantly, for Raz, consent can become the basis for legitimation only in the context of an established moral tradition. That is, the background "society" agreement

---

"According to Raz ... a legal system can only claim authority if it is possible to identify its directives without reference to the underlying ('dependent') reasons for that directive." But as Leiter notes, Raz adds additional elements to his definition of "law," exemplified in the Normal Justification Thesis discussed in this section. (Leiter, 2003: 25.) This makes the classification of Raz as a "hard positivist" problematic, at best, as Raz himself suggests. (Raz, 2003: 253.) The key point to recognize, and the point that creates this difficulty of classification, is that Raz insists on separating the question of validity from the question of authority. On the question of validity, Raz is rightly classed as an exclusive positivist, which is to say that when asked to provide a sociolegal description of the phenomenon of "law," he appeals solely to the authority granted to the source of the law and its satisfaction of formal requirements internal to the system. But where the question is under what circumstances one is justified in experiencing the claims of the law as obligation, his approach is quite different. It is Raz' contribution to this latter question that is of interest here, as it points directly to a description of the minimal level of substantive moral commitment that is required for juridical legitimacy in a way that connects moral substance directly to Dworkin's property of "integrity."

that is requires is one of substantive, not just procedural, norms, and accordance with those norms is the test for legitimacy.

Raz recognizes the force of the positivist argument that the problem of defining lawmaking sovereignty is inescapable. "Unless the authority of the constitution derives from the authority of its makers, there is no explaining the fact that it matters that it was made by one body rather than another." (Raz, 2001: 158.) In the eighteenth century, James Wilson appealed to customary law in order to identify the legitimating sovereign as the collective will of the people. Similarly, Raz situates the point of necessary consensus at the pre-juridical stage of societal development, arguing that an autonomous, technical form of legal argument emerges only after an initial moment of moral legitimation. "Legal authority is itself a form of claimed moral authority . . . . A theory of law is, therefore, and among other things, a theory of the conditions, if any, under which the law is morally legitimate and of the consequences that follow from the assumption that it is morally legitimate." (Raz, 2001: 159)

Raz's appeal to the moral authority of a legal order is neither Wilson's appeal to common law nor Michelman's constitutional culture; it is closer to Benhabib's invocation of the hermeneutic effect of shared background assumptions. The word "moral" is understood broadly, to include fundamental democratic principles in the manner of a theory of deliberative democracy as well as norms of conduct in the manner of appeals to natural law. For example, moral authority may derive from a shared fundamental political principle of self-sovereignty, which would explain why its adoption by consent matters for its legitimacy.

But while consent is relevant to legitimacy, it cannot be sufficient in and of itself. What remains necessary for Hart-style positivism is the addition of an externally grounded reason to accept a "rule of recognition" argument that is present and accepted before that argument can be articulated. That externally grounded reason requires the articulation of a moral claim. We may consent to things that we later determine to have been wrong, after all, and the possibility of that later determination keeps open the necessity for a moral argument in favor of accepting our consent as a basis for legitimation. An appeal to "consent," for Raz, is never a purely positivistic description of an historical event; rather it is always a way to get at the idea of good reasons. "Consent is given in the true belief that there is adequate belief to recognize the authority of the institutions, or principles, in question. The question arises whether these considerations are not enough to establish the authority of those bodies or principles, independently of the consent." (Raz, 2001: 163.) This is not to say that consent is irrelevant, only that its significance has been redefined. Consent is relevant insofar as it demonstrates the social fact of acceptance of moral principles, where those principles provide an adequate reason for accepting the exercise of juridical authority in the first place.

Raz uses this argument to draw the connection between the moral basis for law and the authority of officials, and consequently between the creation and the interpretation of legal rules. To draw these connections, he depends on three "theses," called preemption, dependence, and normal justification. "Preemption" refers to something like the idea of exclusivity, applied more generally to acts of officials.[14] If the creation of a law is sufficiently justified by the other two principles, that is sufficient reason for the duty to obey that law to trump competing, personally held norms. "Dependence" refers to the idea that the legitimacy of a law depends on the underlying moral principles upon which it is based.[15] The "normal justification thesis," finally, describes the idea that a person has an obligation to follow laws – that is, laws are legitimate – when doing so would result in that *person* being better able to follow the moral dictates that she already accepts as valid than if she were to rely on her own, unguided judgment.[16] The last argument, in particular,

---

[14] "[T]he fact that an authority requires performance of an action is a reason for its performance which is not to be added to all other relevant reasons when assessing what to do, but should exclude and take the place of some of them. " (Raz, 1986: 46.)

[15] "First, the arbitrator's decision is for the disputants a reason for action. They ought to do as he says because he says so. But this reason is related to the other reasons which apply to the case .... The arbitrator's decision is meant to be based on the other reasons, to sum them up and to reflect their outcome." Thus the arbitrator's decision is a reason for action, but it is a dependent reason that derives its force from the existence of other "reasons" on which it draws. "Note that a dependent reason is not one which does in fact reflect the balance of reasons in which it depends; it is one which is meant to do so." (Raz, 1986: 41.)

[16] "[T]he normal way to establish that a person has authority over another person involves showing that the alleged subject is likely better to comply with reasons which apply to him (other than the alleged authoritative directives) if he accepts

points to the source of the authority of officials, which is grounded in their expertise at devising and applying rules that, if followed, will result in our acting in accordance with fundamental normative principles. "[A]ll authoritative directives should be based on reasons which already independently apply to the subjects of the directives and are relevant to their action in the circumstances covered by the directive." (Raz, 1986: 47.) These justifications similarly operate as descriptions of the conditions for binding consent. (Green, 1989.)

By this argument, as noted earlier, "consent" cannot legitimate the exercise of authority unless there were good substantive reasons for granting consent in the first place. But law is not simply coextensional with morality. As Leslie Green puts it, "If only those requirements which there is a moral obligation to obey count as law, then the problem of legitimacy is solved by sheer definition. That implausible thesis is now rarely defended." (Green, 1989: 797.) In part, the equation of law with morality is inadequate for Raz because of the observation that while law is grounded in moral principles, morality underdetermines law's content. Law is needed to organize moral principles into rules for action by adding necessary elements. "[M]ediation through law serves the role of concretizing moral principles – that is, of giving them the concrete content they must have in order for people to be able to follow them . . . . Its point and purpose . . . is to supplement morality. To do that, its content cannot be determined by moral considerations. It must reflect social practices or traditions or some other social facts." (Raz, 2001: 172.)

The "social fact" of law is its capacity for what Raz calls "coordination," the parallel to Hart's "efficacy," the possibility of organizing collective action in terms of concretized shared moral principles. But coordination is carried out by institutional actors operating within a legal regime, not as the spontaneous effect of social practices. This is the reason why the problem of grounding

---

the directives of the alleged authority as authoritatively binding and tries to follow them, rather than by trying to follow the reasons which apply to him directly." Raz draws the analogy of advice from a friend. "The normal reason for accepting a piece of advice is that it is likely to be sound advice." That primary reason for accepting advice, in turn, may may be reinforced by secondary reasons, such as identification, the idea that "accepting the authority or leadership of a person or an institution . . . [is] a way of defining one's own identity as a member of a nation or some other group" (Raz, 1986: 53–4.)

the authority of officials is so central to the problem of defining the conditions of juridical legitimacy. In light of the necessity that law demonstrate the capacity for coordination, the critical question, clearly, is the basis for the distinction between officials and ordinary citizens: by what authority do officials exercise this authority?, *which* officials?, why these and not others?

The same questions occur at the level of constitutional, or state, coordination, as well. The underdetermination of law by morality is paralleled by the underdetermination of political arrangements by grounding political norms. "[T]here can be in principle many morally legitimate ways of organizing democratic governments: federal republics and unitary constitutional monarchies, single-member constituencies, and proportional representation systems ... Possibly, the circumstances of one country or another will make one or more of them inadequate for that country. But – that is the assumption underlying the example – such considerations will not reduce the number of acceptable systems to one." (Raz, 2001: 172.)

What is required, then, is an explanation for the legitimate authority of officials to choose among underdetermined outcomes, based on a grounding norm that is consistent with shared moral commitments and that satisfies the requirements of coordination. An example of such an explanation might be the normal justification thesis that allowing constitutional court judges to adjudicate cases results in our being more effectively able to live up to our shared norms of equality. But explaining why this should be so requires a more careful examination of the basis of officials' authority, and in particular the claim of authority grounded in expertise.

If accepting the authority of officials in a regime makes us more able to follow the dictates of our own deeply held normative commitments than we would otherwise be, it must be the case that these officials are able to do something that some of us, at least, are unable to do for ourselves. This may be because officials are uniquely virtuous persons or, more likely, it may simply be the result of a division of labor in which acting as a constitutional official is considered a specialized task requiring ability, training, and commitment to a particular way of doing things. In either case, the officials' claim to authority is legitimated by an appeal to some version of special expertise. What is that expertise? What is needed, moreover, is an answer to this question that is non-tautological. John Marshall, for example, famously answered that "it is emphatically the province of the court to say what the law is," thus appealing to an expertise in the subject of legal study as the basis for judicial authority, but that answer becomes perfectly circular once we recognize that what we are looking for is an explanation for why "law" is the relevant area of expertise in the first place.[17]

A straightforward argument that officials such as judges or legislators are simply better moral reasoners than anyone else gives rise to obvious objections similar to those that apply to the equation of morality and law. Leslie Green points out that "moral expertise" is a slippery concept at best, and that whatever that phrase connotes, it is not something that is particularly associated with government officials.[18] Jeremy Waldron makes the same case in a more pointed way. If the issue is one of expertise at answering moral questions, he asks, then why are members of Congress rather than Catholic bishops our logical candidates for official status? (Waldron, 2003: 63–4.) The issue of officials' relations to one another leads to further complications. Among officials, after all, lower official B is expected to abide by and implement the decision of higher official A even if B believes that his contrary decision is "better."

Most of all, there is the problem of efficacy. Turning Raz' commitment to positivism against him, Waldron points out that in addition to the normal justification thesis ("NJT") explaining why an official's decisions could be considered legitimate, there needs to be an explanation for the proposition that it will be so treated in practice in order for "law" to serve its coordinating function. "Maybe the normal justification of public authority, in particular, has two levels to it: the first level might be given by something like

---

[17] *Marbury v. Madison*, 5 U.S. 137, 177 (1803).

[18] "First, it is unlikely that the relevant sort of expertise is available in political affairs. Scientific experts may be authorities on what we should believe but not on what we should do. There are experts on whales but not on whether we should save the whales. Second, even if policy-relevant expertise is available, there is little reason to suppose that officials have uniquely rich reserves of it .... Finally, and this is in any case conclusive, there are profound moral objections to a society run by experts, objections which are rooted in the values of self-government and political equality." (Green, 1989: 804.)

Raz' NJT; but the second level requires in addition some sense that a large number of the people who would be governed by the putatuive authority if it were an authority do actually accept that it satisfied NJT." (Waldron, 2003: 66.)

Expressed as a purely descriptive question – "under what historical or cultural circumstances does it tend to be the case that most/all/enough people accept the authority of officials?" – Waldron's challenge addresses issues beyond the scope of this discussion. And if the implicit argument is that any time any citizens challenges the authority of an official that authority ceases to be legitimate, that argument is yet another example of a claim that proves far too much to be useful. But Waldron's challenge can be reframed in terms appropriate to the question of substance. There must be some justification for the move from a legitimate constitution to a legitimate constitutional regime, in the form of a grounding norm that justifies the authority of officials within the regime to interpret and apply a constitution. Since the premise of the discussion thus far is that the necessary conditions for the creation of a legitimate constitutional regime inhere in the consensual adoption of a constitutional language, the answer to this challenge to the authority of officials, if there is one, must be something that follows from the fact of the adoption of that language and the substance of its contents. And since "officials" include interpreters as well as makers of law, the answer must establish a connection between the creation and the interpretation of a constitution sufficient to carry the burden of legitimating the exercise of authority.

Raz' own response to Waldron's challenge is singularly unhelpful in this context: "[W]hen we deal with institutions, what they can or cannot do is determined, to a large degree by their constitution, formal or informal." But he also restates his central argument in a way that focuses attention on a critical point of unclarity: "If I would track reasons better if I followed someone's directives, then that someone has authority over me, if I can follow his or her directives. The same is true of an institution, but whether one institution can follow the directives of another depends, *inter alia*, on its constitution." (Raz, 2003: 262.) Authority generally follows from the assertion that its exercise yields a superior ability to follow reasons that are themselves accepted as valid. But the argument for incompleteness dictates that a constitution be underterminative of law just as law is underdeterminative of morality, and vice versa. In other words, in order to ground the legitimacy of a constitutional regime we need to be looking for specifically constitutional "reasons," whose efficacy is enhanced by the grant of authority to specifically constitutional officials. The need for an identification of these reasons is the first answer to the question of substance; constitutional language must contain sufficient substance to provide reasons for its own existence.

This description of the role of normative substance in constitutional language takes on special importance when we consider the distinction between new, or "originating," constitutions and those that have been in operation for a period of time. For "old" constitutions, the social fact of consent can be demonstrated through the operation of rules of recognition, thus providing a basis for a positivistic assertion of validity that weakens the is-ought distinction. "Constitutions, at least old ones, do not derive their authority from the authority of their authors. But there is no need to worry as to the source of their authority. They are self-validating. They are valid just because they are there, enshrined in the practices of their countries." (Raz, 2001: 173.) That is, the maintenance of a constitutional regime, as opposed to its creation, can be legitimated in fundamentally positivistic ways. But, as was noted earlier (in Chapter 2), there is a crucial caveat: "*As long as they remain with the boundaries set by moral principles*, [old] constitutions are self-validating .... It should be added that this conclusion follows *if morality underdetermines* the principles concerning the form of government and the content of individual rights enshrined in constitutions." (Raz, 2001: 173, emphasis in the original.) A consideration of the connection between underdetermination and "self-validating" constitutional regimes leads to a further refinement of the role of substance in constitutional language.

An established constitution is required to act as a rule of recognition for lower-order laws. But constitutionality cannot be a test for legitimacy merely by the determination that a law is consistent with its terms, if those terms have no normative content of their own. "Social facts establish existence, not legitimacy, of legal systems."

(Raz, 2001: 161–2) An appeal to constitutional validity implies an acceptance of the persuasiveness of the grounding norms of the constitution to which one refers. Therefore, to repeat the point, a constitutional rule (or set of rules) of recognition cannot be taken to exhaust the content of legitimizing juridical claims; normative substance is required.

It is important to remember that this discussion is taking place against a context of an earlier conclusion that constitutional language is required to be incomplete.[19] The need for substance exists within the incomplete scope of constitutional language, not merely to act as the source for gap-filling constructions.[20] To posit that normative claims are available to supplement constitutional principles is merely to locate moral arguments at the same level as legal and political preferences; to be employed as gap-filling mechanisms, such claims are still required to undergo the process of translation or else to be presented as an addition required for the preservation of integrity in a constitutional text working itself pure. The question is what substantive commitments occurring *within* an incomplete and underdetermining scheme of constitutional values are necessary to ground the authority of constitutional officials past the moment of constitution making? But since the possibility of constitutional amendment leaves open the possibility of future, supplemental moments of constitutional formulation, we are better

---

[19] In his general argument, Raz insists that "law" is "comprehensive," by which he means that it is at least a potentially complete system of norms, in that even constitutional limitations to lawmaking can be removed by other acts of lawmaking (amendments), so that the authority of the lawmakers implicitly extends as far as they choose to extend it. Leslie Green raises a strong challenge to this claim, both in terms of its accuracy as a description and in terms of its necessity for Raz' overall argument. "Even if every government necessarily claims the power to regulate anything that does not show that every government has such power. Law governs its own creation, but it can do so by limiting its own authority." (Green, 1989: 800.) Green's statement is a perfect illustration of the theory with which this entire discussion began, Bodin's description of the limitations on the exercise of sovereignty that inhere in the nature of the authority. Neither the sovereign lawmaker nor "the law" can act in ways that would contradict the terms of its own authority; the sovereign may not act so as to destroy his sovereignty, and "law" may not extend to the point where it loses some fundamental aspect of law-like-ness.

[20] Robert Alexy argues that since a law necessarily involves a claim of moral authority, moral arguments must be available to fill gaps in the system of laws. (Alexy, 2003: 14.)

served to say that what is needed is sufficient substance to effectively ground the authority of officials during periods of ordinary democratic rule, or sovereignty-in-reserve.

The underdetermining role of constitutional principles for law-making parallels the relationship between "thin" and "thick" values. Thick values are specific, parochial norms that derive from the perception of particular cultural understandings or social practices. Thin values, by contrast, are those generalized and hence universalizable propositions on the basis of which assertions of thick normative claims are evaluated. These are norms that Raz calls "non-parochial." Law requires grounding in norms that are not parochial if it is to be legitimate in a system of governance grounded in an ideal of self-rule. "[O]nly concepts access to which is coextensive with the capacities to have knowledge and to act intentionally are non-parochial, for only they are available to all knowers." (Raz, 2003: 258.) In terms of a theory of constitutional language, this description can be paraphrased as the proposition that "only concepts, access to which is coextensive with the capacities to express reasons in constitutional language, and to act on the basis of reasons so expressed, are non-parochial within a system of constitutional signs, for only they are available to all who speak that language."

The answer to the question of substance is beginning to come into focus in the same way that the question itself emerged at the end of the preceding section. A constitutional language must contain sufficient substance to articulate non-parochial reasons for its own existence and to ground the authority of juridical officials during periods of ordinary democratic governance. The scope of that substantive content remains bound by the requirements of incompleteness, while the strength of the claim on our loyalties that the substantive commitments of constitutional language exert is defined by the requirement of exclusivity.

Changes in the system of constitutional signs are possible through the exercise of sovereignty-in-action and a renewed act of self-inscription, but what creates the pressure for those changes is the evolution of societal norms during periods in which the constitutional language remains stable. During such periods of stability, the substantive commitments contained in constitutional language function as non-parochial thin values that provide the background understandings in terms of which thicker values may change over time. "Evolving practices give rise to new values. Commonly their emergence is recognized by subsuming them under familiar values. Thus existing values make possible the recognition of new values when encountered." Changes in prevailing thick normative commitments exert upward pressure for the modification of the non-parochial thin value commitments contained in constitutional language. "Once new subsumed values emerge reflection on them leads to a reinterpretation and a change of understanding of the more universal value concepts under which they were subsumed, thus leading to the emergence of new abstract value concepts to cover both new and old concrete values. In this way the intelligibility and the social dependence of values are reconciled." (Raz, quoted at Penner, 2003: 85–86.)

Here is the beginning of an answer to the objections to the argument that officials' authority derives from a claim of moral expertise. The expertise at issue in the resolution of constitutional questions, at least, is much more limited than that; what is being claimed is only expertise in matters of thin, universal norms inscribed in constitutional language. Constitutional officials' authority derives from the belief that following their decisions makes us better able to act in accordance with specifically constitutional reasons, not with moral, legal, or political reasons generally. Constitutional reasons are different from other kinds of reasons, and their elucidation requires different expertise. The expertise of constitutional officials lies in the application of non-parochial norms to the problem of ordering thicker norms that inform the decision- and norm-generating actions of lower-level officials, who are themselves free to draw on a much richer field of "reasons" by virtue of constitutional incompleteness.

It bears repeating here that accepting the legitimate authority of officials does not in any way involve an abandonment of deeply held normative positions. Raz proposes that over time, thick parochial norms are recognized, defined, and assimilated into existing thin universals. "[T]he dependence of our understanding of less general values on understanding more general values is an essential part of our ability to understand how values can come into being." (Raz,

2003: 258.) Over time, as new substantive moral, political, and legal concepts come to the fore – or as old ones are rediscovered – the prevailing conception of constitutional principles of "equality," "liberty," or "due process" are subjected to challenge. If these thick norms cannot be readily translated into existing constitutional language, pressure develops to expand the range of substantive normative vocabulary available in that language; in Dworkin's description, that language can be "worked pure" by mechanisms permitted by the particular rules governing collective action, which mechanisms are themselves subject to being tested against the substantive norms contained constitutional language. The authority of constitutional, as opposed to legal, officials is thus a special case of the claim of authority based on expertise, in which the expertise at issue is the ability and willingness to order values and rights claims in terms of fundamental, non-parochial constitutional norms such as principles of deliberative democratic practice.[21]

Consider the idea of constitutionally guaranteed individual rights, an example central to any discussion of constitutionalism. Here, interestingly, Raz moves away from his insistence on grounding in moral principle in favor of an explanation that relies on the existence of a legitimate regime in the first instance, and

---

[21] James Penner argues that the relationship between thin and thick norms is the reverse of that assumed by Raz and most democratic theorists. Penner argues that thin norms such as "equality" themselves rest on universally shared thick norms such as "courage" or "generosity." This does not imply that across cultures the conceptions of "courage" will be identical, but Penner argues that there are universal understandings of "paradigm cases" on the basis of which culturally specific instantiations of concepts are worked out. (Penner, 2003: 92.) In Penner's view, the authority of officials, exemplified by the case of common law judges, rests on their claim to expertise in applying thin norms to the thick concepts out of which they were generated to the first place. (Penner, 2003: 94.) In practice, Penner and Raz do not necessarily disagree. By Penner's argument, *even if* the legitimacy of law depends on its consistency with morally correct judgments, the authority of constitutional officials is not diminished because their claimed expertise resides in the area of using thin normative concepts to order true and correct thick norms. The authority of officials, in other words, is not based on a claim of superior moral judgment in the thick sense of the term, only on a claim of special ability in the application of thin, political norms. For Raz, of course, the same conclusion follows much more forthrightly. In either instance, the answer to the question of substance is restricted to the provision of thin norms available to officials, the presence of which simultaneously establishes the basis for their authority and defines its scope.

instrumental arguments in favor of rights guarantees thereafter. "[T]heir role is not in articulating fundamental moral or political principles, nor in the protection of individualistic personal interests of absolute weight. It is to maintain and protect the fundamental moral and political culture of a community through specific institutional arrangements or political conventions." (Raz, 1986: 245.) In other words, "rights" for the most part fall in the area of constitutional rules that is *not* determined by attachment to norms. It is the utility of "rights" that makes them desirable, not any notion of a direct connection to grounding norms central to the legitimacy of the constitutional regime. The reference to rights as instruments for the generation of a desired "political culture" is squarely in line with the theory of deliberative democracy in locating fundamental grounding norms in terms of public political conditions of discourse rather than private legal claims of prerogative.

Raz's description of rights fits neatly with the theory of constitutionalism articulated here. Constitutional language stands between a direct appeal to moral principle and the expression of political rights claims. Moral claims appear in the substantive content of the language, and thereafter have no additional avenue of expression in constitutional discourse. "Rights" are not morally neutral claims, but they are indirectly related to such claims, taking their moral content from the terms in which they are articulated rather than by the unmediated importation of propositions derived from extraconstitutional moral systems.

Raz also provides another, different instrumental account that reconnects the argument from expertise to the normal justification thesis by an appeal to the division of labor. "[I]n various countries, due to their circumstances and to other features of their political institutions, the best way to ensure that people act as they should, i.e. that they show due respect for these interests, is by a division of labor which restricts the right of most people and of some political institutions to judge for themselves what precise duties those interests justify. The best way to secure the proper recognition for those interests is to confine the decision about their proper weight to a few specialist institutions, whose composition and mode of operation make them most suitable for the task." (Raz, 1986: 261) This justification for guarantees of rights is connected to the conditions under which officials have legitimate authority based on principles of dependence and normal justification. "All institutional rights are subject to the mediation of an authority whose task it is, in accordance with the dependence thesis, so to act that people will conform to reasons which apply to them better than if they were to decide independently of the authority's intervention." (Raz, 1986: 261–62.)

Here we see the consequences for constitutional interpretation of decoupling rights claims from extraconstitutional moral language. Constitutional "rights" serve the same ordering function for positively guaranteed legal rights that non-parochial political norms serve for thick local norms of the kind that appear in subconstitutional discourse. "[R]ights play a central role as important ingredients in a mosaic of value-relations whose significance and implications cannot be spelled out except by reference to rights." (Raz, 1986: 255.) The inclusion of substantive normative elements in constitutional language, in other words, provides guiding principles for the interpretation of the text. Without such principles, the consequence of separating constitutional from ordinary moral discourse would be that arguments to the effect that one approach to interpretation is superior to another become literally meaningless. There is no standard against which to measure "better" and "worse" if there are no normative standards of "good" and "bad" within the system of constitutional discourse.

The consequence of standardless constitutional discourse is severe, a return to the bare competition for supremacy. The absence of substance in the constitutional text opens the door to precisely the danger that the creation of a constitutional regime grounded in language was intended to prevent – the reduction of constitutional argument to competing expressions of incommensurate, absolute preferences. In that situation, the authority of officials would have to be grounded in supposed expertise in the expression of thick, parochial normative preferences, and that authority of necessity could only be considered "legitimate" by those who both shared those moral preferences and accepted the officials' claims to expertise in their expostulation. It was to escape that situation that Jean Bodin started us down the road to search for sovereignty four centuries ago.

The complaints about the supposed "moral expertise" of legal officials are thus pulled away from application to constitutional officials in the same way that the systems of constitutional and legal language were earlier separated. Whatever the claimed expertise of common-law judges may be, for example, constitutional officials' authority rests on the supposition that they will be specially able to employ thin constitutional norms to resolve conflicts of priority among the thick parochial norms that we as individuals bring to a dispute or policy question. The officials' actions thus make us better able to act in accordance with those specifically constitutional norms by accepting their authority than we would be if we were left to our independent decisions. Turning that proposition around gives us a formulation of Raz's answer to the question of substance. A constitutional language is required to contain sufficient non-parochial normative substance so that the application of that language, by someone more expert in its terms than ourselves, enhances our ability to live in accordance with the fundamental political values that led us to consent to the creation of constitutional language in the first place. Constitutional language, in other words, must be sufficiently substantive to be self-sustaining.

The question is, how? What is it that normative substance does for constitutional language, including the non-substantive elements of the text, that creates this quality of self-sustaining justification? Dworkin's norm of "integrity" provided the beginning of an answer, that substantive norms in a constitutional language provide the material necessary for self-reference. Raz's argument went further, demonstrating that the inclusion of normative substance of a certain kind is required to ground the authority of officials in a constitutional regime. But it remains the case that the connection between substantive normative propositions and constitutional language remains unresolved.

The answers to these questions turn in large part on the role that substance plays in maintaining a constitutional language that is autonomous with relation to other forms of discourse. The inclusion of a substantive normative commitment in the system of constitutional language does not remove the language of that norm from other forms of discourse. As a result, over time the constitutional meaning of a term such as "equality" or "liberty" may – indeed, is most likely required to – grow away from the meanings attached to those terms in ordinary, legal, or religious discourse. The claim of officials' hermeneutic expertise is sensible only if it is assumed that the creation of a constitutional norm displaces extraconstitutional understandings of that same norm in other contexts, a proposition expressed in the principle of exclusivity. Consider that some definitions of "equality" will be commensurate with the goal of constitutional integrity, and some will not. Adopting Raz' arguments, constitutional officials' authority has been said to be grounded in their special expertise in ordering norms in a way commensurate with integrity. But how does this work in practice? How is the relationship between constitutional and extraconstitutional language experienced in a way that makes sense of the legitimacy of the constitutional regime and the authority of its officials to maintain its linguistic horizons?

THE AUTONOMY OF CONSTITUTIONAL LANGUAGE AND THE REQUIREMENT OF TRANSLATION

At this point, there are two remaining questions to be addressed in resolving the problem of substance: (1) how does normative substance provide constitutional language with the capacity for something like interpretive "integrity," and, (2) what is the relationship between constitutional and legal and moral language that justifies the authority of officials to interpret substantive commitments of constitutional language in ways binding on the rest of us, so that the commitment to constitutional language entails a commitment to accepting juridical authority? The theoretical explorations of Jürgen Habermas provide the material that will enable us to answer these questions.

Habermas begins with the idea of systems theory developed by Gerald Luhman. This is a theory in which different specialized areas of institutional life ("law," "politics," "economics," "education") work entirely independently of one another, each with its own internal language and mode of operation. The result is that these different systems are mutually impenetrable, rendering them entirely incapable of evaluation in terms of any set of universal norms. "The states of the system are exclusively determined by its own operations. The environment can eventually destroy the system, but it contributes neither operations nor structures." (Habermas, 1999: xxii, quoting Luhman, 1992: 1424.)[22] Habermas rejects Luhman's description, not on the basis of any commitment to metaphysically grounded morality, but on the purely positivistic grounds that it does not accurately describe what Hart called the "internal" experience of law in practice. (Habermas, 1999: 50, 52.) In practice, as many of the writers discussed here have observed, law is understood as asserting claims of legitimacy, not merely assertions of coercive power, and that fact precludes any absolute separation between "law" and other areas of life.

What is needed is an explanation that situates claims of validity in a concrete social context. Instead of being reducible to a set of systems, society is understood in Habermas' description as a "lifeworld" accompanied by a set of specialized institutions. Activities in the lifeworld are characterized by the use of "ordinary language," while specialized institutions generate their own, specific vocabularies.[23] In social practice, ordinary language provides a medium of communication that extends across all institutional discourses and provides a standpoint external to those institutional structures for political discussions. "Like that other anthropological monopoly, the hand, ordinary language ... possessed the merit of multifunctionality. With its practically unlimited capacity for interpretation and range of circulation, it is superior to special codes in that it provides a sounding board for the external costs of differentiated subsytems and thus remains sensitive to problems affecting the whole of society." (Habermas, 1999: 55.)

As a result, for Habermas ordinary language provides the basis for a normative critique of specialized practices, rather than the

---

[22] This is a logical extension of the idea of Legal Realism, which described legal rules as predictors of likely case outcomes in which normative explanations functioned essentially as a smoke screen to hide interest-driven agendas. "As so described, the meaning of legal arguments is exhausted by their function of reducing the surprise value of court decisions (which find their motivations elsewhere) ... .What counts for participants as 'justification' shrinks, from the viewpoint of the sociological observer, to necessary fictions." (Habermas, 1999: 50.)

[23] To describe the lifeworld, Habermas approvingly cites Talcott Parsons' description of a "societal community" as "the core sphere from which each differentiated social system is supposed to have developed." (Habermas, 1999: 73–4.)

other way around. A simple case illustrates the point. Accounting professionals employ a specialized and technical discourse in their work, in which terms such as "asset," and "liability" are defined. The language of accounting therefore creates its own horizons; something that is not recognized in accounting language as an "asset" cannot be expressed in accounting terms. For example, consider an assertion that a sense of moral goodness produces higher morale among executives, so that forgoing profits in order to maintain environmental standards higher than those required by law should be valued on a dollar-for-dollar basis as a company "asset," or the converse claim that the corrosive effects of a moral sense of guilt produced by "merely" complying with regulatory standards should be included as a financial liability. From the perspective of an accountant, it seems fair to say, this argument would seem not only incorrect but "absurd."

On the other hand, among economic theorists there is nothing at all absurd about a model that attempts to quantify precisely such goods. Over time, the formal description of a quantified form of "moral satisfaction" might make its way into the language of accounting and hence onto balance sheets, an example of interaction between specialized discourses sufficiently related to be mutually influential. More plausibly, from time to time, when the results of accounting practices do not accord with general understandings of "fairness," "accuracy," or "transparency," pressure from investors may lead regulators to redefine the meaning of accounting terms. Applying Habermas' terminology, the general language of the lifeworld provides the medium in which economic interests are translated into political arguments, which then become the basis for the redefinition of legal standards of language in response to what was earlier referred to as "upward pressure" within the system of juridical authority, in addition to the "downward" pressure that occurs when economic theories are incorporated into practical accounting standards.

Law plays a special role in this interaction across subsystems. Law provides instruments for the reconstruction of other institutional orders that have failed to make satisfactory responses to their own experiences of upward pressure. This is a function that cannot be served by a simple appeal to the grounds of moral critique, but rather requires a specialized institutional language capable of serving a meta-institutional, umpire-like role. "The morality that supplies the criteria for the disillusioning assessment of existing institutions does not itself offer any operative means for their reconstruction. To this end, positive law stands in reserve as an action system able to take the place of other institutions." (Habermas, 1999: 117.)

Law acts as the medium through which critiques of specialized language systems, framed in the language and within the horizons of general social experience, become the basis for a process of redefinition that alters the institutional language that is the subject of critique. In the example of revisions to the formal language of accounting, it is ultimately the creation of legal rules governing the construction of accounting language that creates change. Law, or rather the system of legal discourse, exists to maintain the connection between system-specific ethos and the morality of ordinary life. The language of law is therefore a special case. "[T]he legal code not only keeps one foot in the medium of ordinary language ... it also accepts messages that originate there and puts these into a form that is comprehensible to the special codes of the power-steered administration and the money-steered economy." (Habermas, 1999: 81.) As a result, uniquely, law provides the basis for its own critique as well as its own authority. "Law alone is reflexive in its own right; it contains secondary rules that serve the production of primary rules of behavior." (Habermas, 1999: 113.) The reference to secondary rules invokes Hart's rules of recognition; law, in other words, provides a substantive ground for critique of other systems, but is itself grounded in the acceptance of discursive norms of legitimacy.[24]

---

[24] Habermas finds the same dual pattern of mutual legitimation between law and politics that was recognized by Kelsen. "State-sanctioned law and legally exercised political power ... reciprocally require one another." (Habermas, 1999: 74.) On the other hand, like Raz, Habermas continues to find a background normative consensus of some kind to be a necessary precondition to a juridical order. The exercise of political precommitment is justified by its efficacy in achieving compliance with those norms, combined with a mechanism that explains the ability and willingness of individuals to enter into binding commitments. "What is required is a symmetrical relationship between the moral authority of existing social orders and a corresponding self-control anchored in personality systems." (Habermas, 1999: 67.) At one level, this is familiar ground. What Habermas is after

This is Habermas' version of the attempt to ground authority in sociolegal positivism, since the explanation of legitimacy turns more on the claim that a legal order authentically reflects social practice than on any genuinely grounded normative commitment.[25] At the same time, Habermas seeks to restore the internal normative dimension of legal discourse identified by Hart, without which "[w]hat is specific to legal validity, the tension between facticity and validity inhabiting law itself, does not come into view." (Habermas, 1999: 65, 64.) This is accomplished through the understanding of the special role of law as a meeting place between moral theory and political practice. "[L]egal orders are 'legitimate orders' that, although certainly not fitting ideas seamless together with interests, do interpret interests through ideas, thereby making reasons and validity claims factually effective," (Habermas, 1999: 70), a description that invokes the idea of efficacy in a way quite consistent with Raz' normal justification thesis.

Habermas' discussion emphasizes the need for a mechanism for converting normative propositions between ordinary language to specialized institutional discourses by the translation of interest-claims into ideational language, similar to Raz' ordering of thick, parochial norms by the application of thin universalizable principles. This metaphor of *translation* (a term that Habermas himself does not employ) between the language of the lifeworld and institutional forms of action is once again the crucial element in illuminating the implicit role of juridical language as the discursive prior equivalent to constitutional principles. A constitutional order

---

is an argument for the legitimation of governing systems by consent that does not depend, as an intermediate step, on the generation of a collective subject to translate popular sovereignty into lawmaking authority. Habermas hopes to find such an argument in a description of the conditions of political discourse as the expression of individual normative commitments translated into a participatory system of decision making. The problem with this description is that it does not provide any obvious basis for the exercise of sovereign lawmaking authority at all, a variation on the difficulty that was encountered in Frank Michelman's description of "Ida's Way" in Chapter 3.

[25] "The more Rawls believes he should base the theory of justice on the public support for culturally molded intuitions that none of 'us' can reasonably reject, the less clear is the boundary separating the task of philosophically justifying principles of justice ... from a particular community's enterprise of reaching a political self-understanding." (Habermas, 1999: 59–60.)

determines the acceptable manner in which interests and moral preferences can be asserted as legal claims; juridical/constitutional discourse determines the acceptable manner in which interests and moral preferences can be expressed as legal propositions.[26]

There is a provocative implication in this argument. Perhaps the problem of legitimating a moment of constitutional founding does not turn on the irreducibility of legitimation claims, perhaps those claims are in and of themselves necessary elements of constitutional language by virtue of their capacity to generate a "systemic" juridical discourse called "constitutionalism." This is not a proposition that is clearly articulated in Habermas' own writings, but it is one plausible interpretation of the consequences of his argument. The possibility of constitutional rule, in this understanding, emerges as a stage of sociolegal development differentiated from ordinary "law" by the degree of its development.

In Habermas' description, law operates to rationalize relationships between otherwise incommensurate specialized modes of discourse and the general language of the lifeworld. But as Habermas concedes, law itself requires rationalization. "The positivization of law necessarily results from the rationalization of its validity basis. As a result, modern law can stabilize behavioral expectations in a complex society with structurally differentiated lifeworlds and functionally independent subsystems only if law ... can maintain the inherited claims to solidarity in the abstract form of an acceptable claim to legitimacy." (Habermas, 1999: 76.) The "abstract form of an acceptable claim to legitimacy" is the set of non-parochial norms that is included in a system of constitutional language. We can conceive of constitutional language as the separation of crucial critical and self-critical elements of "law" writ large from its

---

[26] Penner captures this idea neatly in his description of the basis for the authority of common-law judges. "In short, an institution of moral discourse which emphasizes past assimilation of cases in which thick ethical concepts have been applied, continuing exposure to new cases as a source of knowledge, and a commitment to past 'selections' of particular values and the concepts that represent them as ones which are to serve more foundational roles in the discourse of practical reasoning, may count as a genuine case of institutionalized moral expertise." (Penner, 2003: 96–7.) Where a specialized system of language is created, the effect is to create an artificial set of horizons, a discursive "space" in which both the modes and the subjects of reference and understanding are drawn from a delimited subset of those available to members of the society at large.

mediating functions in relation to other language systems. Constitutionalism extends the rationalizing critical function to the legitimating basis of law itself, a move necessary to produce conditions in which law as a specialized language system can be the subject of critique at the same time that it provides the medium for the critique of other systems by appeal to concepts contained in general language.

This argument, which can be thought of either as a critique of or an extrapolation from Habermas' discussion, is another way of describing the dual role of constitutional language, as the foundational basis for the legitimation of the regime and as the medium for the experience of upward pressure for change, including change in the terms of that language itself. The normative commitments that led to the moment of consent to a constitutional language need not – indeed, arguably ultimately cannot – be identical to the norms contained in that language, as they do not serve the same function. The first, preconstitutional normative commitments create the conditions for legitimate regime creation. The second set of commitments, or the second version of the initial commitments as they appear in constitutional discourse, serves to legitimate the subsequent constitutional regime.

The result is that the relationship of constitutional language to ordinary discourse is quite different from that of general law. Constitutional language does not keep "one foot in the lifeworld," because it is uniquely designed for limited functions; unlike law writ large, constitutions do not mediate relations between specialized systems, nor do they assert the constructive authority that positive law exercises. This is what was meant by "incompleteness" in Chapter 4, and the consequence of that requirement of incompleteness is that, in any legitimate constitutional regime, not only "accounting" but also "law," "politics," and "morality" are all equally separated from the ground of constitutional legitimation, which rests on the relationship between those discourses and constitutional language. Law can continue to play its mediating and critical functions, but faced with a challenge to its own legitimacy it is required to undergo the difficult and sometimes exclusionary process of translation into constitutional language just like everything else.

But the answer to the question "what does substance do for a constitutional language" can only partly be derived from a consideration of the relationship between constitutional language and other modes of discourse, or the authority of constitutional officials relative to citizens. The question of substance also requires an account of the relationship between normative commitments and normatively underdetermined elements *within* a constitutional language, a relationship that establishes the connection to interpretation.

Applied to constitutional language, Habermas' description of general and specialized language systems is insufficient because it lacks this dimension. A far better description of the relationship between the elements of constitutional language, and between that language and other forms of public discourse, is provided by the metaphor of "horizons" that was an element of Benhabib's discussion of deliberative democracy. The term "horizons" comes from hermeneutics, a field that has its roots in the interpretation of religious liturgy. Fundamentally, the idea is that the interpretation of a text takes place in a bounded intellectual environment defined by the reader's organizing conceptions of the world captured in the rules of grammar and the system of signs that our language comprises. (Gadamer, 1975: xvi.) In Benjamin Cardozo's words, "we can never see with any eyes but our own," (Cardozo, 1921: 14), and the eyes through which we read a text delimit the range of possibilities for the meaning that we will find there. This is the sense in which Benhabib used the term, and she urges us to consider carefully the importance of the observation that when we engage in moral reasoning "we are always situated within a horizon of presuppositions, assumptions, and power relations, the totality of which can never become wholly transparent to us." (Benhabib, 1996: 79.)[27]

---

[27] The application of hermeneutic models to a description of law and legal regimes is associated with modern, text-based constitutionalism. In 1837, Francis Lieber published *Legal and Philosophical Hermeneutics* in response to his realization that the techniques of textual interpretation that had been developed in theological and philological contexts were directly relevant to the interpretation of a constitutional text. Lieber's version of hermeneutics emphasized "correct" understandings based on philological principles (Farr, 1992); by contrast, the modern version of hermeneutics associated with Gadamer focuses on the inescapable conditions under which understandings are necessarily constructed, and the consequences of

Artificially constructed systems of specialized language, if they are sufficiently substantive to function autonomously, create horizons of understanding of their own, narrower than and situated within the larger, more encompassing horizons that define the scope of discourse within a society. This explains the capacity of ordinary language to provide the standpoint for the critique of specialized systems. Since the more limited artificial horizons of a specialized language system occur as a delimited subset of the larger, background environment, the language of that greater environment includes perspectives external to those of the specialized language, and hence provides a standpoint from which they can be critiqued.

Incorporating the element of hermeneutic horizons into our understanding of constructed language suggests that Habermas' rejection of systems theories went too far. Following Habermas, Gregory Leyh treats translation as obligation of appellate judges to explain the meaning of legal concepts for modern social practice. (Leyh, 1992: 286.) In Leyh's version, normative constitutional provisions are measured against the infinite plurality of convictions on an infinitude of issues that appear in the lifeworld; by definition, these norms will be found wanting. The hermeneutic metaphor of horizons helps demonstrate why, in the case of constitutional language, the opposite is true; the burden of translation falls on those wishing to have their positions articulated in constitutional terms. So long as citizens profess a desire to engage in constitutional discourse, that profession necessarily implies a willingness to translate propositions developed from the horizons of their life experience into the more limited, artificial horizons created by the substantive normative content of constitutional language. This recognition, in turn, provides a way to articulate the answer to the question of substance. The consent to constitutional language is the consent to the creation of a new, artificial set of horizons, and a constitutional language, to be adequate to its task, must provide sufficient substantive basis for their creation. A constitutional language that lacks

---

the recognition of those conditions for critical analysis of different interpretations of a text. Applied to questions of law, Gadamer's approach is closer to the socio-legal efforts of the "soft" legal positivists, whereas Lieber speaks for a generation of strict doctrinalists.

sufficient substance to generate horizons of understanding is too
thin to impose a requirement of translation because it is too thin to
create a basis for constitutionalism at all; such a constitutional text
is merely a placeholder for the "real" legitimating source of the
governing regime.

The recognition that an adequate constitutional language is one
that creates horizons of understanding connects the elements of the
responses to the question of substance. In order for the fact of
consent to the creation of a constitutional language to be the basis
for the formation of a legitimate constitutional regime, that language must contain sufficient substance to constitute a set of moral
horizons. Under those circumstances, the consequences of the
argument that a legitimate constitutional regime begins with
unanimous "as if" consent to the creation of a constitutional language become clear. In any legitimate constitutional regime, to
make a valid constitutional argument one is required to ground
propositions in a simultaneously constraining and enabling set of
normative commitments defined by the horizons of the constitutional language. The requirement of translation, thus understood, is
not the result of an extended argument about useful political safeguards or conditions of deliberative democracy, it is the analytically
necessary implication of the minimum necessary ground for any
constitutional regime to come into being in the first place.

This answer to the problem of substance refocuses our attention,
or it should, on the costs of defining a limit to the pluralism of values
in constitutional discourse. Normative commitments contained in a
system of language delimit the possibility of not only what will be
expressed but also what *can* be expressed. In a theory of democracy
informed by standards of constitutionalist discourse, citizens remain
autonomous legal subjects, but at the cost of losing the freedom to
choose the language that they employ in articulating legitimating
claims to which constitutional officials are bound to listen. Citizens,
as a condition of their participation in the processes of collective
sovereignty, must "speak constitutionally," not as the result of a
second, postconstitutional act of consent but as the analytically
necessary consequence of consenting to the creation of a constitutional language sufficiently substantive to generate artificial normative horizons. Constitutional officials' authority derives from

their special expertise in helping us fulfill our commitment to the creation and maintenance of the horizons of constitutional language better than we would be able to do on our own. As Habermas writes, "as legal subjects [citizens] achieve autonomy only by both understanding themselves as, and acting as, authors of the rights they submit to as addressees. To be sure, as legal subjects, they may no longer choose the medium in which they can actualize their autonomy. They no longer have a choice about which language they might want to use. Rather, the legal code is given to legal subjects in advance as the only language in which they can express their autonomy. The idea of self-legislation must be realized in the medium of law itself." (Habermas, 1999: 126.) The result is a "circular process in which the legal code, or legal form, and the mechanism for producing legitimate law – hence the democratic principle – are co-originally constituted" at one and the same time. (Habermas, 1999: 121–22).[28]

The commitment to juridical language, like Dworkin's "integrity" and Raz's thin norms, remains underdeterminative of the content of juridical principles. It is similarly the case that both moral and ethical norms, in combination, are underdeterminative of juridical norms, which develop autonomously over time. (Habermas, 1999: 155–56.) Since juridical language defines the terms of interaction between ordinary moral language and system-specific ethical arguments, the continuing development of an autonomous system of juridical language implies the constant possibility of readjustment. The fluidity and autonomy of constitutional concepts explains the constant necessity to reformulate the translations of ordinary language propositions into constitutionally valid form. What is required to remain stable is the structural relationship between

---

[28] There is some ambiguity as to the precise significance of Ronald Dworkin's characterization of rights as "trumps" in *Taking Rights Seriously*. Jeremy Waldron read the term "trumps" to denote a set of constitutional principles that exclude improper discursive formulations of reasons for outcomes, rather than for the outcomes themselves. "[T]he 'trumping' force of rights, on Dworkin's theory, is not a way of rendering certain individual interests as such impervious to considerations of the general good . . . . Instead, the idea is that certain reasons are to be excluded from politics, and the term trumps simply expresses a determination not to let such excluded reasons back in." (Waldron, 2000:303.) For a contrary reading of Dworkin as committing himself to conceive of rights as the protection of interests against majoritarian concerns, see Pildes, 1998.

discourses. The moment of constitutional consent is the acceptance of the legitimacy of that structural relation, and carries with it a commitment to the authority of officials to exercise a role in its maintenance.

This final formulation of the answer to the question of substance makes the connections between exclusivity, incompleteness, and substance in constitutional language clear. Constitutional language is required to be autonomous from the language of the lifeworld; to a far greater degree than "law" writ large, constitutional language is a system-specific discourse. To maintain its autonomy, constitutional language must contain sufficient substance to be self-sustaining by generating its own set of hermeneutic "horizons." The norms contained in the substantive contents of constitutional law must be sufficiently thin to be non-parochial, a requirement that parallels the necessity of incompleteness in the scope of constitutional language, and they must articulate the fundamental political values that led us to consent to the creation of constitutional language in the first place. At the same time, to create conditions of democratic constitutional deliberation, the set of constitutional norms must be exclusive within their domain, a commitment that is an analytically necessary implication of the commitment to constitutional language and the first rule of constitutional grammar. Together, these requirements ground the authority of juridical officials in the necessity of translation, the obligation to convert propositions of moral or policy preference or ordinary law into constitutional language. During periods of ordinary sovereignty, we are better able to meet the obligations involved in our commitment to translation if we grant authority to juridical officials than if we try to do it ourselves. The creation of a legitimate constitutional regime depends on a prior commitment to constitutional language, and the continuing legitimacy of such a regime depends on the adequacy of that language to its task.

6

The Defense of Constitutional Language

This book began with two questions: First, under what conditions is the creation of a legitimate constitutional regime possible? Second, what must be true about a constitution if the regime that it grounds is to retain its claim to legitimacy? Both of these questions were specifically posed in the context of a liberal constitutional regime, meaning one committed to ideals of democratic self-rule and the presence of value pluralism. As a result, the questions were framed in terms of the necessity of finding a source of legitimacy in some version of consent, so that the two questions could be conveniently rephrased as "Consent How?" and "Consent to What?" The answers to these questions were pursued through the development of a theory of constitutional language. So for the purposes of the development of that theory, the questions were rephrased yet again, this time becoming "How is binding consent to a system of constitutional language possible?" and "What must be true about that system of constitutional language in order that consent to its creation and maintenance is sufficient to ground a liberal constitutional regime?" It is now possible to summarize those answers as they have appeared in the preceding five chapters.

In order to frame the question, Chapter 1 focused on the historical roots of liberal constitutionalism, from Jean Bodin's personal sovereign exercising near-absolute authority over subjects, through Thomas Hobbes' anthropomorphic commonwealth, and finally to John Locke's constitutionalism. In Locke's model, the lawmaking authority of a legislature may be legitimated by an appeal to not one but a series of moments of consent, characterized by decreasing degrees of necessary unanimity and increasingly formal and concrete arrangements. The first of these moments was the consent to the use of juridically significant language, exemplified in the acceptance of "money" and the redefinition of property. Thereafter, following the second moment of constitutional consent, the legislature was granted the authority to promulgate a new juridical language by giving critical terms new meanings different from those they had previously had or continued to have in ordinary speech. These two elements of the Lockean approach to constitutionalism – the division of consent into a series of different moments, and the identification of sovereignty over language as the beginning of constitutional self-rule – were adopted as the basis for the development of a theory of constitutional language.

The decision to proceed from a Lockean approach required an engagement with the various challenges that modern writers have raised to the idea of political legitimation by consent. In Chapter 2, I proposed that at the outset we are required to reconsider our theory of sovereignty. Theories based on the assumption of universally shared moral values, appearing in different ways in arguments raised by Randy Barnett's appeal to prior moral commitments, John Rawls' invocation of "public reason" and "constitutional essentials," and Luigi Ferrajoli's appeal to international conventions, were found to be incapable of providing a secure ground for the exercise of lawmaking. Instead, drawing on ideas suggested by writers such as William Harris, Jeb Rubenfeld, Keith Whittington and Bruce Ackerman, I proposed that what is required is a continuation of Locke's move toward an abandonment of the anthropomorphic metaphor in favor of an understanding in which "sovereignty" names a set of discursive conditions that make self-rule meaningful, and the exercise of sovereignty-in-action is a periodic occurrence rather than a description of the working of all aspects of the constitutional system. In this understanding, the People's sovereignty is understood as its authority to create and re-create itself through an act of "inscription" in a constitutional text, a capacity that itself depends upon a prior commitment to the use of a particular form of juridical language in the act of constitution making. Such a universal but highly unstructured agreement to a system of specifically constitutional language is the act that creates "sovereignty," understood as the name for the conditions of possibility of constitutional authorship.

The question "Consent How?" was not answered by this analysis, however, as it remained to be seen how such an initial commitment to constitutional language could be justified as binding future actors, a challenge associated in different ways with Larry Kramer, Jeremy Waldron, Jack Balkin and Frank Michelman. In response, I argued in Chapter 3 that what was needed was an explanation specifically suited to collective political action rather than one based on a tradition of private legally enforceable promises. To develop such an explanation, I drew on Stephen Holmes' suggestion that constitutional precommitments should be conceived of as "constitutive rules," Jon Elster's connection between the "upstream authority" of such rules and the need for a sufficient continuity of collective identity, and Christopher Eisgruber's description of institutions of constitutional review as mechanisms for specialized exercises in collective democratic action. Ultimately, I concluded that democratic consent is present in the decision not to engage in sovereignty-in-action, demonstrated by the continuing unanimous "as if" commitment to employ constitutional language. Borrowing terms from Ferdinand de Saussure's system of structural linguistics, I proposed that this approach permits the continuing dialogue concerning constitutional *parole* without the constant risk of an abandonment of the constitutional *langue*.

At this point in the discussion, the connection was drawn between a theory of constitutional legitimacy and the role of courts or other juridical institutions empowered to engage in constitutional review. Legitimate institutions of constitutional rule are essential if a theory of liberal constitutionalism is to establish the basis for binding precommitments after the abandonment of the anthropomorphic model of a self-sovereign state. I argued that binding precommitments can result from consent at the initial moment of self-sovereignty if those commitments are understood to relate to the language in terms of which subsequent arguments will be carried out in a specific institutional setting, rather than to substantive outcomes of those arguments or to the procedures of decision making.

Embodied in a set of institutional arrangements, consent to a constitutional language provides the elusive moment of consensus that is required to ground subsequent claims of legitimation.

At the end of Chapter 3, the description of the conditions of possibility for the creation of a legitimate constitutional regime – the answer to the question "Consent How?" – was complete. What is required is an initial unanimous commitment to translate moral propositions into constitutional language through institutionalized mechanisms of juridical dialogue. The initial commitment to constitutional language justifies the creation and maintenance of those institutions, and the authority of institutional actors, by virtue of the necessity of translation. And the commitment to the authority of those institutions of translation remains binding over time because it is necessary for the effective exercise of popular sovereignty through the creation of constitutional language that began the process of constitutional formation. The capacity for collective self-sovereignty begins with a commitment to language, so that the preservation of that language is the duty of self-preservation that is the inherent limitation on any sovereign's powers.

But to speak of "an initial commitment to constitutional language" tells only half the story. Chapters 4 and 5 explored the question of what must be true about a system of constitutional language if it is to do the work of justification that is required for liberal constitutionalism. In its shortened form, this was described as the question "Consent to What?" which was explored in terms of qualities of exclusivity, completeness, and substance.

Chapter 4 examined the qualities of exclusivity and completeness, leaving the question of moral substance for Chapter 5. The question of exclusivity asked whether constitutional argument must be made only and entirely in constitutional language, while a consideration of "completeness" involved asking how much of the subject matter of juridical conduct constitutional language is required to encompass, and how much can be left to extra-constitutional discourse. In the course of this chapter, I reached the conclusion that constitutional language must be both exclusive and incomplete.

To develop the argument for exclusivity as a necessary characteristic of constitutional language, I began by acknowledging the "violence" that is inherent to any claim of exclusivity, building an understanding of that term from the writings of Jacques Derrida. Derrida's simple but powerful point was that the act of linguistic construction excludes possible meanings from identification with a name or sign at the same time that it enables others. The consequences of this observation are inescapable in the context of constitutionalism: a commitment to a system of constitutional language means excluding, or at least burdening, certain classes of propositions at the same time that it relatively privileges others.

But despite the obvious salience of the challenge that is posed by the recognition of the violent effects of discursive exclusion, I argued that a requirement of exclusivity is the first necessary rule, or metarule, of constitutional grammar. In part, this argument proceeded from the straightforward observation that some degree of exclusivity is inherent in any system of meaning. More particularly, in the case of constitutional language, exclusivity followed from the earlier discussion of sovereignty. A non-exclusive constitutional language violates the commitment to constitutional language that defined the initial exercise of popular sovereignty, and thus either defeats the claim of binding constitutional commitment or else locates the possibility of sovereignty-in-action in some other, non-constitutional place. The former possibility denies the necessary conditions for constitutional legitimation, and the latter identifies a regime that is not "constitutional" at all. As a result, I concluded that constitutional language is required to be exclusive if it is to do the work of justification that a liberal constitutional regime requires.

Turning to the question of completeness, I considered different approaches, proposed by Samuel Freeman in his commentary on Rawls, Keith Whittington in his discussion of constitutional construction, and Cass Sunstein's argument in favor of "incompletely theorized" agreements, each of which presented a version of an incomplete constitutional language. To work out an argument for incompleteness as an element of a larger theory of constitutional language, however, it was necessary to consider the relationship between the legitimation of a constitutional regime and the justification for legal systems generally. To get at this relationship, I examined the theories of legal positivism proposed by Hans Kelsen and H. L. A. Hart, and some of the commentaries on those theories.

Combining the lessons of those investigations, I proposed that a system of constitutional language must be sufficiently complete to cover the actions of subconstitutional juridical norm creation, yet sufficiently incomplete to permit such lower levels of rule making to be non-exclusive and hence more directly grounded in prevalent social norms.

Thus the requirement of incompleteness followed from the earlier derived requirement of exclusivity. Constitutional language is required to be sufficiently complete to permit its efficacy in defining the socially accepted basis for the legitimation of lower-level decisions. Conversely, constitutional language is required to be sufficiently incomplete to allow for a relaxation of the requirement of exclusivity at the level of lawmaking and political discourse. To repeat a proposition from the last part of Chapter 4, a constitutional regime is not a totalizing system that absorbs all other forms of public interaction; it is a mechanism to secure a space for those other forms of interaction while preserving the necessary elements of self-sovereignty in the face of a plurality of value commitments.

Just as the consideration of exclusivity led inevitably into the question of completeness, the requirement of incompleteness led to the question of substantive normative commitments, "the question of substance," which was the subject of Chapter 5. The argument that constitutional legitimacy depends on accordance with moral correctness, which had been briefly considered in Chapter 2, reappeared here in arguments made by Robert George, Robert Alexy, and John Finnis. Conversely, arguments from democratic theory that identified norms of deliberation and discourse as the essential grounds for the legitimation of a constitutional regime were considered in the form of arguments by Seyla Benhabib, Iris Marion Young, and Joshua Cohen. The question of what degree of normative substantive commitments is required in order for a system of constitutional language to do its work of legitimation for a political regime required maneuvering between these two perspectives.

To develop a response to the question of substance, I drew on Ronald Dworkin's argument for a norm of "integrity" in constitutional interpretation, Joseph Raz' discussion of the basis for the authority of officials, and Jürgen Habermas' description of the relationship between legal and other forms of discourse. Elements drawn from these three theorists' arguments provided the pieces that were needed to complete a theory of constitutional language.

Dworkin's argument concerned the idea of textual interpretation, returning us to the consideration of the relationship between the people as sovereign authors and the constitutional text that they create. In the face of value pluralism and imperfect justice, a commitment to a norm of textual integrity was Dworkin's suggestion for the substantive content of the commitment to constitutional language. But this only reformulated the question: what level of normative substantive content is required in a constitutional language in order for its acceptance to produce a grounding norm of integrity?

Raz's analyses pointed to an answer. Like other writers concerned with questions of moral substance, Raz insists on the necessity of a background of shared normative principles as the necessary basis for popular sovereignty, and hence for legitimation by an appeal to consent. One difference was that Raz was willing to accept the adequacy of political, rather than moral, societal norms, so that a shared commitment to popular sovereignty, itself, might be sufficient to ground legitimation by consent. Such an argument provided the beginning of an explanation for the authority of officials, based on their presumed expertise in applying these shared norms.

Raz also introduced the observation that morality underdetermines law. The underdetermination of law by morality is paralleled by the underdetermination of the form of a constitutional regime by substantive normative commitments such as democratic self-rule. What was needed to ground the authority of constitutional officials, then, was an explanation for the authority of officials to choose among underdetermined outcomes, as well as an assumption of some set of shared grounding norms that legitimate the constitutional order. Like Benhabib, Young, and Cohen, Raz focused on "thin" or "non-parochial" norms to describe the kind of underdeterminative commitments that are properly the focus of constitutional language, as opposed to ordinary legal discourse.

Earlier, I proposed that a plausible justification for the exercise of authority by constitutional officials was found in the assertion of officials' linguistic expertise, which enables them to enforce the requirement of translation. Incorporating the distinction between thin and thick norms helped flesh out this argument. The authority of constitutional officials derives from the claim that they have expertise in determining whether and how claims asserting thick norms can be translated into valid constitutional propositions. As a result, while constitutional principles are, and should be, under-determinative of ordinary lawmaking, the authority of constitutional officials requires a constitutional language that contains sufficient substantive norms to account for its own legitimacy. Applying what Raz called the "normal justification thesis" to the problem completed the argument. The substantive requirements for constitutional language are a sufficient number of thin, non-parochial commitments such that the application of that language renders us better able to live in accordance with the fundamental political values that led us to consent to the creation of a constitutional language in the first place.

But the "how" of the matter remained unclear. That is, we did not yet have a description of what it was that the inclusion of a minimum amount of normative substance in a constitutional language did for the remainder of that constitutional language to carry it along to this form of justification. The difficulty became particularly acute with the recognition that the same concept may, over time, develop new meanings in the context of constitutional discourse that are inconsistent with their meanings in ordinary moral, legal, or political language. For a constitutional language to provide the basis to legitimate a constitutional regime past the moment of its creation, a fuller account of the process of translation and its relation to the system of constitutional language was required.

This fuller account was found by engaging the arguments of Jürgen Habermas. Habermas' analysis of the interaction between legal language and the language of the "lifeworld" led him to conclusions concerning the language of law that were in some ways the opposite of those that I had earlier reached concerning constitutional language. Recognizing that point of disagreement, however, sharpened the focus of the distinction between constitutional and ordinary legal language. Habermas' depiction of a system of legal language that mediates between the language of ordinary life and those specific to institutionalized systems of authority reinforced the earlier conclusion that constitutional language, with its close connection to the authority of juridical actors, derives its legitimating power precisely from the fact that it is separated from the lifeworld.

The necessity of this conclusion appeared most clearly in Habermas' deployment of the metaphor of heremeneutic horizons. Constitutional language, like any specialized language, creates a set of meaning-delimiting horizons. The imposition of a requirement of translation is necessary for constitutional language to maintain the possibility of integrity, and the authority of constitutional officials derives from the necessity of maintaining the hermeneutic horizons that are established in the adoption of a system of constitutional language. The "violence" that is experienced by those whose voices are diminished by the requirement of translation is the consequence of moving between horizons.

In summary, then, what is required for the possibility of creating a legitimate constitutional regime is a prior "as if" commitment, universally shared among citizens, to the creation and employment of a system of constitutional language. Such a commitment can be seen either as an implicit element of the creation of a written constitutional text – whether or not that text is itself the subject of unanimous consent – or, less clearly, as the consequences of conventions of constitutional discourse. Consent to language is a form of binding precommitment that is consistent with the character of a self-sovereign people yet is at the same time commensurate with conditions of value pluralism. To account for the possibility of such a moment of consent requires conceiving of such a people as engaged in an act of collective self-authorship, which creates the basis for the creation of a constitutional regime and its constituent institutions even in the absence of unanimous agreement. The requirements for such a regime to remain legitimate in its operations, in turn, fill in the qualities of exclusivity, incompleteness, and thin normative substance that a constitutional language is required to possess. A sufficient degree of normative substance is required to establish horizons of interpretation capable of encompassing all the elements of the constitutional order in the discursive norms of constitutional language. The crucial requirement of translation, finally, describes the consequences of this theory of constitutional language for the practice of constitutional discourse, and thus defines the task and authority of constitutional officials.

Throughout the discussion, I have refrained (for the most part) from drawing conclusions about the relative merits of different modes of constitutional interpretation, particular institutional arrangements, or the "right" outcomes to particular controversies in constitutional law. A reader who is concerned with those questions, at this point, may understandably be inclined to paraphrase Aesop's fable and ask "have you so labored to bring forth this mouse?" After all, the conclusion that a constitutional regime depends on a language of constitutional discourse may seem like a small point, even if it has been established by the argument presented here. But I am inclined to apply the caution of Ambrose Bierce's revised version of the fable, which goes like this: "A mountain was in labour, and the people of seven cities had assembled to watch its movements and hear its groans. While they waited in breathless expectancy, out came a Mouse. 'Oh, what a baby!' they cried in derision. 'I may be a baby,' said the Mouse, gravely, as he passed outward through the forest of shins, 'but I know tolerably well how to diagnose a volcano.'"[1]

If the arguments of this book are sensible, there are serious and important consequences for a broad range of issues of the kind that arise in more traditional discussions of constitutional law. I argued that there are substantive and demanding commitments that are analytically necessary if a constitutional regime is to maintain its legitimacy. In particular, I argued that maintaining a distinction between the norms of constitutional language and those contained in the discourses of religion, morality, and ordinary law is essential if a liberal constitutional regime is to preserve its claim to legitimacy. Here is where the ability of a mouse to diagnose a volcano comes into play. There are grounds for concern that in many places, and in many ways, these commitments are slipping, or that in the process of constitutional design, the necessity for these commitments is being overlooked. Where constitutional design is at issue, proponents of one model or another seek to incorporate thick, parochial

---

[1] The Bierce version of the fable is in the public domain. It is available on line at http://www.pacificnet.net/~johnr/cgi/aesop1.cgi?ab&TheMountainandtheMouse.

norms into putatively liberal constitutional texts. Where constitutional regimes are in place, juridical actors err both by failing to preserve the thin, non-parochial norms of constitutional language and by importing norms from ordinary law, moral preference, or religious tradition into constitutional discourse without translation.

To mention only a few examples, arguments that whatever was permitted under preconstitutional law must be similarly permitted under a constitutional regime are instances of the kind of importation that threatens the exclusivity of constitutional language. So, too, are appeals to the brute fact of historical practice or the bare social fact of majoritarian moral preference. None of these arguments is commensurate with the kind of language of constitutional discourse, and the necessary roles of institutional actors in maintaining that language, that is required for a constitutional regime to preserve its legitimacy in the face of persistent differences over questions of values.

The claim that preconstitutional legal understandings define the scope of constitutional norms is instances of the attempt to define the terms of constitutional language in terms drawn from the discourse of ordinary law. While the need to distinguish legal and constitutional discourse has been discussed previously, the implications of that argument deserve further attention. Earlier, the historical attempt to appeal to an "immemorial" legal tradition was identified as one of the early efforts to legitimate a constitutional regime by appealing to essentially positivistic facts about historical and current social practice. I argued that such an approach was incommensurate with the idea of constitutionalism as a practice of self-sovereignty, since it either treats the apparent constitutional text as a mere stand-in for an unnamed earlier set of commitments, or else it avoids the problem of defining a lawmaking authority altogether by treating "laws" as natural objects.

A different kind of problem arises, however, when an established constitution is treated as though its terms derive their meaning from usage in ordinary legal discourse, rather than generating specifically constitutional meanings. In this situation, a constitutional interpreter denies the language-generating element of constitutional creation and attempts to treat the text as simply a legal instrument occurring within the horizons of established legal discourse. This was referred to earlier as an example of the "empty vessel" theory of constitutional interpretation, in which the terms of the text have no substantive meaning of their own but are "filled" by appeals to extraconstitutional sources. The danger is that constitutional discourse becomes an exercise in sleight-of-hand whereby the apparent "text" disappears in the act of its application to reveal the system of language specific to lawyers. This is not simply a question of whether a constitutional text establishes a language characterized by thin or thick norms, it is a question of whether that system of language will be understood to generate meaning at all, or whether a constitution is merely one more text in a library of legal documents.

The relationship between constitutional and legal language takes us back to the discussions of Chapter 1. Locke recognized that the first exercise of legislative authority is the generation of juridical language, coexisting with and autonomous from ordinary or other specialized languages. Applied to constitutional creation, rather than ordinary legislation, the same argument applies; a self-sovereign people's act of constitutional creation asserts the authority to generate a new layer of language specific to its sphere, with the same metasystemic relationship to other forms of language that was observed in the relationship between law and other forms of discourse. To make legal language the source for the meaning of constitutional propositions is to invert that relationship. That reversal sacrifices all claims to legitimacy on behalf of the constitution since, as we have seen, none of the arguments for the justification of the act of creating a constitutional language applies to law generally. The language of law, to be legitimate, must be relatively complete and non-exclusive, whereas constitutional language is required to be incomplete and exclusive, not least so as to preserve its appropriate relationship with law.

Furthermore, making the meaning of constitutional propositions depend on their meaning in ordinary law is to reverse the levels of decision making and norm creation, such that lower-level juridical actors are given the authority to dictate the terms for higher-level, constitutional actors. Here, again, the claim to legitimacy is lost, as the expertise of constitutional actors was presumed to be their knowledge of constitutional language and their ability to enforce the requirements of translation. As was the case with the incorporation of religious law into constitutional law, the intrusion of ordinary legal language into constitutional discourse disrupts both the institutional and the conceptual bases for the legitimacy of a liberal constitutional regime. This is not an issue that arises with the use of law to fill textual gaps by construction; it is an issue that arises when terms of constitutional language are made subject to linguistic developments that occur in a different area rather than serving as the basis for a continuing and integral language of their own. The move to an empty-vessel theory of constitutionalism is a usurpation of the authority of the people to exercise their sovereignty by the generation of language.

Usurpations of this kind are deeply embedded in American constitutional practice. The move to an empty-vessel theory appears Wilson's equation of the Constitution with the common law, and in John Marshall's 1803 appeal to the traditional common law authority of courts to interpret laws as the explanation for judicial constitutional review.[2] More recently, as noted in the text, the attempts to define constitutional "rights" in terms of state legislation, or to define the limits of legislative authority on the basis of an extraconstitutional "bundle of rights" inherited from legal customs, arguably represent additional examples of an empty-vessel theory of constitutional language in action. There is a similar usurpation of constitutional language, although not one that is necessarily based on legal language in particular, when constitutional officials are willing to ignore the terms of the text outright in favor of some "background understanding" demonstrated by past legal practice. If the expression of these principles or purposes requires the importation of norms or concepts that do not appear in the system of constitutional language, their utilization by constitutional officials violates the fundamental principles of constitutional grammar and therefore directly threaten commitment to that language that grounds the legitimacy of the constitutional regime.

Here is where the theory of constitutional language that was developed through this book begins to have consequences for the practice of constitutional interpretation. Originalist, textualist, and progressive theories of constitutional interpretation are all

---

[2] *Marbury v. Madison*, 1 U. S. Cranch 137 (1803).

examples of languages within the language of constitutionalism; none of them threatens the integrity of the constitutional language or the continuing commitment to its maintenance. An appeal to the implications of the overall structure of a constitution may be taken as an affirmation of its linguistic integrity by appeal to its grammatical principles to determine the relative validity of proposed constitutional statements. Nor is it the case that the basis for the legitimacy of a constitutional regime is called into question when extraconstitutional discourse is employed in ordinary lawmaking, the adjudication of cases, administrative rule making, or other forms of subconstitutional juridical actions.

But the incorporation of the extraconstitutional discourse of ordinary law into the process of constitutional interpretation threatens the integrity of constitutional language. The legitimacy of a liberal constitutional regime requires, at a minimum, a commitment to the creation and preservation of a constitutional system of language. The legitimacy of binding constitutional precommitments depends on our ability to conceive of ourselves as collectively capable of generating sovereignty by the creation of such a language. And the legitimacy of constitutional officials' authority rests on our need for gatekeepers to preserve the bounds of that language, just as our continuing capacity for sovereignty-in-action rests in the possibility of the future alteration of the text in which the elements of the constitutional language are identified.

A different example of the importation of extraconstitutional norms into the language of constitutional discourse appears in the appeal to majoritarian moral preference. A law that expresses moral preferences of the community that do not appear in the substantive norms of constitutional language cannot be justified under any legitimate constitutional regime. Since only certain kinds of substantive norms are suitable for inclusion in a system of constitutional language, the implication is that the appeal to other kinds of communal moral preferences is simply not a legitimate element of constitutional discourse. Moral preferences that cannot be directly translated into the kind of non-parochial norms that are the necessary substance of constitutional language are necessarily excluded from the discourse of any legitimate constitutional regime. A law that rests for its justification entirely on thick, parochial norms, therefore, necessarily involves a violation of either the principle of exclusivity or the principle of incompleteness, without either of which the commitment to constitutional language cannot do its work of legitimation. This is yet another argument that puts the distinction between constitutional and legal language into sharp focus. In the tradition of Anglo-American common law, for example, lawmakers were understood to have a general mandate to protect the "morals" of the community. If the argument of this book is correct, that understanding cannot survive the transition to constitutional self-rule.

The importation of legal and moral norms into constitutional discourse represent examples of the failure of juridical actors to maintain the exclusivity and incompleteness of constitutional language. In the obverse case, a classic example of an insufficient commitment to the integrity of constitutionalism appears when judges take it upon themselves to diminish the completeness of constitutional language by reading clauses and concepts out of the text. These juridical officials are insufficiently committed to the maintenance of the substance of constitutional language, the non-parochial norms that provide the ground for efficacy and the basis for critical assessment of acts of lawmaking. Constitutional language must be incomplete, and the normative commitments contained in that language are required to be "thin," but the commitment to constitutional language that undergirds constitutional democracy extends to the entirety of that language, not merely to those particular elements that suit a particular reader on a particular day.

The classic example from American constitutional jurisprudence is the Ninth Amendment.[3] Regardless of one's theory of constitutional

---

[3] "The enumeration in the Constitution of certain rights, shall not be construed to deny or disparage others retained by the people." As Lawrence Sager observes, at first read the meaning of this provision seems quite straightforward. "At the conceptional level, it is easy to read this language as an indication that the liberty-bearing provisions of the Constitution are to be understood as prominent and accessible instantiations of a general sense of the proper relationship between a government and its citizens but not as a complete set of the limitations on government necessary to perfect that relationship. At the functional level, this reading has its obvious corollary: the amendment announces that there are valid claims of constitutional right that are not explicitly manifest in the liberty-bearing provisions of the Constitution but which enjoy the same status as do those made explicit in the text." As Sager notes, this "obvious interpretation" is not new. "Give or take, it was Justice Goldberg's view in

interpretation, to argue that an explicit reference to unenumerated rights can be simply ignored, read out of the constitutional text on the basis of nothing more than Robert Bork's verbal equivalent of a shrug of the shoulders,[4] is to perform an act of unauthorized violence upon constitutional language. Again, the point can be made in terms of the distinction between constitutional and legal reasoning. The fact that a right, or grant of governmental power, or any other concept or norm does not appear in the language of ordinary law cannot alter the significance of the appearance of that concept in a constitutional text. The text, to repeat, defines the set of semantic signs that provides the content for a system of constitutional language. The inclusion of a concept in the system of constitutional language means that concept is properly available for the formulation of propositions in constitutional language. The Ninth Amendment has both a semantic and a syntactic content. Semantically, the Ninth Amendment tells us that the concept of unenumerated rights is an element of the system of American constitutional language. Syntactically, the key term is "construed." The Ninth Amendment is a grammatical rule for the formulation of valid propositions; it says that it is the responsibility of juridical officials to apply the non-parochial norms and the set of signs contained in the language of the constitutional text to formulate specific unenumerated "rights." Debates over those rights, as always, must take place in the terms provided by the remainder of the constitutional language, but the authority of juridical officials to

---

Griswold v. Connecticut, 5 and it has the general support of a thin but venerable line of scholarship, running back at least as far as Justice Story. But for the most part, judges and scholars have labored against this straightforward reading. They have had to labor rather hard." (Sager, 1988: 240–41.)

[4] During his confirmation hearings on the occasion of his nomination to the United States Supreme Court, Bork famously referred to the Ninth Amendment as an "inkblot" whose meaning was so indeterminate that it could not provide the basis for judicial interpretation. (*Wall Street Journal*, Oct. 5, 1987, pg. 22, col. 1.) Later, Bork took the position that the Ninth Amendment constituted "a perfectly straightforward statement that rights already held by the people under their state charters would remain with the people and that the enumeration of rights in the federal charter did not alter that arrangement." (Bork, 1990: 185.) This latter argument is an example of the kind of empty-vessel approach to constitutional interpretation that was discussed earlier, and is no less an abdication of judges' responsibility to preserve the boundaries of constitutional language.

enforce the requirement of translation does not extend to the erasure of acts of inscription undertaken by the self-sovereign People.

These observations about the separation between moral, legal, and constitutional language are primarily addressed to problems of constitutional maintenance. Applied to the question of constitutional design in the modern world, the theory of constitutional language that has been developed here presents a particularly serious set of implications for the relationship between constitutionalism and religion. It bears repeating that the theory developed here is one of liberal constitutionalism, and that the conclusions I have just identified are specific to that topic. One need not accept the liberal premises of value pluralism and democratic self-rule. Instead, one might seek to design a constitutional regime based on religious dogma. Such a system need not relegate non-believers to the status of non-citizens; the law might simply demand outward conformity to dogma, a form of "as if" commitment that even Puritan writers recognized as the positive side of "hypocrisy."[5] The problem arises when one attempts to design a constitutional system that incorporates principles of liberal democracy and religion simultaneously.

Examples of efforts to accommodate religion and democracy in constitutional design are not hard to find. In Israel, for example, an effort is presently underway to craft a written constitution. One possibility, continuing current practices, is that certain classes of cases will be left for resolution to the authority of religious courts. Let us imagine, hypothetically, a constitution in which the decisions of such courts are not subject to constitutional review. Or imagine a constitutional provision that contains language similar to that in the draft of a constitution for Iraq that was presented to the public in September 2005:

Article (2): First, Islam is the official religion of the state and is a basic source of legislation:

a) No law can be passed that contradicts the undisputed rules of Islam.

---

[5] In 1655, John Cotton, a leading figure among Massachusetts ministers, declared, "[M]en may discover such hypocrisie as may make them unfit for the Church, but yet they may not altogether be unfit for the Commonwealth." (Quoted in Curry, 1986: 7.)

b) No law can be passed that contradicts the principles of democracy.

c) No law can be passed that contradicts the rights and basic freedoms outlined in this constitution.[6]

Certainly these provisions may be a cause for concern among secular-minded citizens of these two nations, but do they necessarily defease the basic assumptions that ground the claim to legitimacy of the constitutional regimes? Can these reservations of authority over matters of religious law be squared with the legitimating principles of "liberal" constitutionalism, or do they imply a different model grounded in a metaphysical authority rather than popular sovereignty?

The question may arise in two distinct ways, illustrated by the two examples cited here. First, a constitutional system may attempt to establish separate languages for the discussion of religious and non-religious questions. Second, a constitutional system may divide the allocation of authority to officials, so that the differentiation between religious and constitutional languages (or between secular constitutional and religious constitutional languages) follows the division in institutional structures.

To clarify the issues involved, let us treat these two possibilities separately. Consider one version that is solely concerned with the content of the relevant language of juridical discourse, and another that is solely concerned with delegation of authority among multiple sets of officials. The first example presents a case of mixed language without institutional delegation, while the second presents a case of pure institutional delegation without any supposed alteration in the meaning or effect of constitutional language. Since I propose to show that *either one* of these features necessarily defeats any claim to constitutional legitimacy, it goes without saying that a combination of the two only creates an even more troubling case.

The fundamental idea of sovereignty is that there is ultimately a single lawgiver whose authority legitimates rule making by others. In the creation of a constitution, I have argued, a people becomes sovereign in the act of creating a language for those subsequent acts

---

[6] Available on line at http://www.nytimes.com/aponline/internatioAP-Iraq-Con/AP-Iraq-Constitution-Text.html.

of legitimation. That description does not obviously result in any inherent limitation on the ways in which authority can be organized and exercised without losing its connection to the sovereignty of the people. So in the first case, the question is whether there is anything inherently, necessarily inconsistent about the idea of a constitutional text that incorporates by reference an entirely separate system of juridical discourse. And in the second case, the question is whether the situation changes with the delegation of constitutional authority to two distinct sets of officers.

At any level of decision making or rule generation below that of constitutional action, the delegation of authority to some particular agency is not inherently problematic, although it is likely the case that in practice any constitution grounded in principles of liberal democracy will limit such acts of delegation as a matter of its substantive normative content. If we imagine a new American constitution, or examine other constitutional regimes in other countries, there is no inherent reason why authority might not be delegated to religious leaders, business leaders, or scientific experts. The only limitation on such a delegation is the need for groundedness in order for legitimacy to be efficacious. So a delegation of authority to a set of constitutional officials need not delegitimate the constitutional regime so long as such delegation does not run so severely afoul of prevailing social norms as to dissolve the connection between the constitutional system and the society in which it occurs.

The difficulty arises when the delegated authority is exercised at the level of constitutional decision making, so that the delegation of authority creates separate and independent systems of constitutional officers. The temptation is to answer that there is no necessary conflict on the ground that so long as the different systems of constitutional authority – in this example, religious and civil courts – deal with entirely separate matters, there is no necessity of ever reconciling the reasoning in one arena with that in another.

There is a minor problem and a major problem with this analysis. The minor problem is that conflict is inevitable in practice by virtue of the fact that people's lives occur in all of the spheres at once. In Habermas' terms, the lifeworld extends across all specialized institutionalized modes of discourse, and the special role of a constitution is to order relations among competing discursive systems and render them subject to critique in the event of conflict. The major problem is more profound, and it too arises out of the closing discussion on the question of substance. Recall that the argument was that a constitutional language requires sufficient thin normative commitments to generated horizons of understanding, and furthermore that these commitments are subject to upward pressure for change as a result of social practices that diverge from established constitutional norms. Over time, the division of officials into separate institutional environments will produce discontinuities in the evolution of systems of constitutional *langue* by virtue of inevitable variations between systems of constitutional *parole*. Where one set of these institutions is independently grounded in a separate set of thin originary norms – whether these derive from a religion or a philosophy of scientific inquiry or a model of market conditions – the pressure for language to evolve in a particular direction is intensified. Conversely, the absence of those same pressures and the presence of others in the other system guarantees, over time, the appearance of two inconsistent systems of constitutional language.

So the problem of pure delegation dissolves into the problem of multiple modes of constitutional discourse exemplified in the provision of the Iraqi constitution that imports the body of Shari'ah as a check on lawmaking authorized by the other provisions of the constitution. By this understanding, we are assuming that the sovereign people constituted themselves by a commitment to two separate and simultaneous systems of constitutional language. Is this an analytically stable solution to the problem?

As the phrasing of the question probably suggests, the answer is "no." At the first level, this conclusion derives from the inevitability of conflict between two systems of norms, and the need for some determination of which trumps the other. This is the same problem that was discussed earlier in the case of constitutional officials who declare ultimate allegiance to the laws of their particular religion rather than to the regime they serve. Conflicting sets of normative commitments in two systems of rules point to different outcomes in practice, and consequently the necessity for choosing which set of rules to apply. Returning to the issue of delegation for a moment, if the juridical actor in question accepts that in cases of conflict constitutional principles trump the rules of Shari'ah (however those are understood), then that actor can be described as a constitutional official who also applies religious law in places where the set of norms contained in the constitutional language is incomplete. But if the opposite is the case, then the actor is a religious official, and the relationship between constitutional text and religious law is the opposite. Sovereignty, the authority to generate grounding norms with the force of law, is ultimately necessarily unitary.[7]

The impossibility of maintaining two simultaneous systems of sovereignty-expressing norms goes beyond the inevitability of conflicts in their application. The deeper problem is the inevitability of untranslatable propositions – that is, valid normative statements in one language that cannot be expressed in the other. This a difficulty that gets to the heart of the recognition that in a constitutional regime, sovereignty is exercised first over the generation of language. None of the justifications for law generally, or for constitutionalism in particular, operate in the absence of the possibility of translation, and I have argued at some length that the requirement of translation is the preeminent consequence of the theory of constitutional language. As has been repeatedly emphasized throughout the discussion, propositions that cannot be translated into constitutional language are not unconstitutional, they are extraconstitutional. To attempt, therefore, to simultaneously maintain two separate linguistic bases for a constitutional regime is to maintain two incommensurate systems of sovereignty in two unconnected systems of discourse. The "people" in such a scenario have constituted themselves into a sovereign with a split personality.

The problem can be escaped, of course, merely by eschewing the assumption of popular self-sovereignty that is the identifying characteristic of liberal constitutionalism. If there is a divine lawgiver whose authority is accepted as paramount, then any act of apparent constitution making is in reality a lower-order exercise of norm generation subject to being overruled by the higher-level legislator. And in the absence of value pluralism – in the hypothesized case, if

---

[7] It is worth noting that this is not an argument that invalidates the American idea of dual sovereignty, since the supremacy of federal and constitutional law over state law has been recognized by courts, at least since the late 1700s. See *Ware v. Hylton*, 3 U.S. 199 (1796).

everyone accepts the same authoritative version of religious law; there is no risk of conflict with societal norms that might threaten the groundedness of the religious system of laws, which is the nation's true "constitution." But in a liberal constitutional system, committed to self-sovereignty and value pluralism, the inclusion in a constitutional text of provisions that import an incommensurate language for the formulation of constitutional propositions is a contradiction in terms." (There is a danger, of course, that the declaration that a nation contains no plurality of values or of religious traditions will turn out to be incorrect, in which case the legitimacy of a constitutional commitment to religious law is called into question.)

The discussion of Iraq's draft constitution is an illustration of the point that was repeatedly made earlier, about the necessary "pulling away" of constitutional norms from moral and religious norms. The same point was made with regard to the relationship between constitutional and ordinary legal language and the claims that ground the legitimacy of each. Similar problematic outcomes would result from the intrusion of scientific, economic, or other specialized language systems into the realm of constitutional discourse. The impossibility of complete translation between these and constitutional languages makes their employment in constitutional discourse inconsistent with the thin normative commitments that make the initial commitment to constitutional language a basis for government by consent. In the sphere of juridical action, either propositions are required to undergo the violent process of translation into constitutional language, despite the loss of the original sense that such a process might entail, or else the system is not genuinely constitutionally grounded.

The theory of constitutional language has consequences for constitutional design and practice beyond the requirements of exclusivity, incompleteness, and substance. For one thing, the theory of constitutional language is a cautionary argument against the temptations of departmentalism, the idea that various sets of institutional actors contained in the several branches of government should be conceived of as equally able and equally authorized to engage in constitutional interpretation. The temptations of such an argument are the same as those that were presented by the democratic challenges to constitutional language. It is, after all, discomfiting to democratic sensibilities to embrace the idea that some particular set of institutional actors such as judges possess a special expertise that makes them better able than elected representatives or the citizenry at large to comprehend and apply the provisions of a constitutional text to questions of constitutional law. But this is the inescapable consequence of recognizing the fundamental distinction between constitutional and legal language.

It is not impossible, of course, for officials other than judges to move between forms of discourse; indeed, in the American system, judges are asked to do just that as they alternately adjudicate legal claims and evaluate the constitutionality of governing laws. But the difficulty inherent in moving between sets of horizons, and the challenge of keeping a clear grasp of different and possibly incommensurate systems of language, provide strong arguments in favor of the creation of specialized institutions akin to Kelsenian constitutional courts for the all-important task of preserving the boundaries of constitutional language.

Efforts to introduce religious or moral principles into constitutional meaning, efforts to convert constitutional signs into empty vessels to be filled by ordinary law, and challenges to institutional arrangements designed to further the maintenance of a system of constitutional language are not the only threats to which the integrity of constitutional language is vulnerable. There are, for example, other specialized languages that compete for inclusion in constitutional discourse. As noted earlier, at various times and in various ways constitutional actors may be tempted to import the languages of science and social science, ordinary politics, historiography, or philosophy in ways that threaten the autonomy of constitutional language and consequently the integrity of the constitutional regime. But perhaps the most important issue is not the content of the extraconstitutional language that is introduced into constitutional discourse, but rather the circumstances that are appealed to in order to justify the act of incorporation. By far the most destructive degradation of constitutional language is that which occurs by the invocation of an emergency.

A constitutional text may provide, as the U. S. Constitution provides, that certain rules are altered in the case of an emergency.

There is nothing about a proposition of that form that threatens the commitment to constitutional language. There may be violent disagreements about what empirical set of facts are required to trigger emergency provisions, and about the meaning of the particular terms involved, but so long as these arguments are carried out in terms that are provided in the system of constitutional language contained in the text, they do not threaten the prior commitment to constitutional language. These debates may be described as arguments over "constitutional emergencies," in which the term "emergency" is understood to have a meaning in the system of constitutional language that is separate and potentially different from its meaning in ordinary speech. There are two situations, however, in which the commitment to constitutional language is threatened. One has to do with the way in which constitutional emergencies are defined, and the other has to do with the idea of an extraconstitutional emergency that is said to justify suspension of constitutional discourse altogether.

The problem of defining a constitutional emergency is a strong illustration of the argument that was presented in Chapter 5 in response to the question of substance. Imagine a constitutional provision that simply grants unfettered discretion to a Prime Minister to determine the existence of an emergency, and to suspend the operation of any and all other constitutional provisions for its duration. Such a provision is obviously unwise; in Justice Robert Jackson's memorable words, "emergency powers tend to kindle emergencies."[8] But that observation does not establish whether a provision of this kind can be an element of a legitimate constitutional system. The theory of constitutional language helps explain why it cannot.

The hypothetical constitutional provision described here fails the requirements for legitimate constitutional rule on essentially all possible grounds, but its flaws can be most succinctly described by the idea of abdication. Such a provision represents an abdication of the commitment to constitutional language, both in its abandonment of the constitutional language itself and in its destruction of the authority of constitutional officials whose authority is grounded

---

[8] *Youngstown Sheet & Tube Co. v. Sawyer*, 343 U. S. 579, 650 (1952).

in their constitutional linguistic expertise. The hypothetical Prime Minister has no binding commitment to constitutional language, and other constitutional officials have no ground for their authority at all. The prime minister's actions may accord perfectly with prevalent sociolegal norms, and they may even reflect a legitimate exercise of legal authority, but they cannot involve the assertion of *constitutional* authority because they occur outside the system of constitutional discourse.

When the Prime Minister invokes "emergency" under the provision described above, he or she is no longer bound by the restrictions of constitutional language, which means that he or she is no longer speaking in that language. It is possible, to be sure, that such an official would continue to use terms familiar from that system of discourse, but the meanings of those terms in their emergency usage would be linguistically autonomous from the system of constitutional signs and unbounded by the rules of constitutional grammar. Nothing about this analysis is changed if the Prime Minister declares, "we are in a state of emergency and the constitutionally guaranteed protections of due process shall continue to be operative," because the phrase "constitutionally guaranteed protections of due process" is no longer the same phrase it was when used in constitutional discourse.

Recognizing that a constitution operates as a language system entails recognizing the connections that bind the system of language together; to take a phrase of that language and employ it in extraconstitutional discourse involves an act of translation precisely akin to the act of translation that was involved in bringing legal or philosophical language into constitutional discourse. The hypothetical Prime Minister is authorized to abandon the system of constitutional language by the the translation of constitutional terms into something else. At that point, the legitimacy of the constitutional regime as a whole is called into question; it cannot be grounded in a commitment to constitutional language, since there is no such binding commitment but only an agreement of convenience. The legitimacy of the regime now depends on demonstrating an independent, extraconstitutional ground for the emergency authority of the Prime Minister, from which the authority for the operation of constitutional government derives as an exception.

To put the matter another way, the statement "The Constitution shall operate during periods that are not emergencies declared by the Prime Minister" is as accurate a description of the imagined constitutional system as the statement "The Constitution shall operate except during emergencies declared by the Prime Minister," and the relationship between those two statements cannot be resolved within the system of constitutional language. Some set of extraconstitutional principles of legitimation would be required to justify both the operations of the ordinary constitutional regime and the exercise of authority during emergencies. Those principles, in turn, cannot be expressed in the language of the constitution, and so the regime is not in any meaningful sense "constitutional." The term "abdication" here refers to a failure in constitutional design, in which the acting sovereign People fail to maintain the commitment that was the precondition for a legitimate act of constitutional creation.

The second version of the "emergency" argument occurs in the operation of an existing constitutional regime, and takes the form of an act of usurpation. Imagine that the question at hand has nothing to do with the phrasing of a constitutional provision. In such a situation, the existence or non-existence of "emergency powers" as an element of constitutional language is irrelevant. Imagine, instead, that a constitutional actor – a judge, perhaps, a sitting President, or an Attorney General – declares that he or she will act outside the scope of the existing constitutional text in order to respond to a specific set of circumstances, and that such an action has widespread popular support. Such a situation need not be restricted to war or violent conflict; there can be political and economic "emergencies," or even simply a perceived "emergency" need to resolve an issue. What then?

What occurs in the situation described here is the usurpation of popular sovereignty by the abandonment of the commitment to constitutional language. A judge who declares that he or she will not apply constitutional principles on the grounds that there is an emergency has abandoned the legitimate basis for judicial authority. In doing so, he or she has claimed instead the authority to contradict prior acts of popular sovereignty-in-action. This is not the situation where a judge simply invokes a constitutional provision that defines an emergency, nor when a judge's determination is subject to dispute. An incorrect invocation of a constitutional emergency powers provision may reflect a failure of performance on the part of a constitutional officer, but it does not call into question the continuing validity of the office. The situation that I describe as a usurpation occurs only when a judge asserts the authority to determine *whether* the provisions of the constitution dictate his actions; that is, whether a justification couched in the terms of constitutional language is required at all.

The point is not simply that the judge has acted in a way that exceeds his or her proper authority, it is much more specific than that. By assuming the authority to determine whether the decision-making process requires justification in the language of the constitutional regime, the judge usurps the sovereign authority of the people to establish that regime in the first place. The minimum initial commitment that made constitutional sovereignty-in-action possible resulted in the creation of a constitutional language, and a judge is a constitutional officer whose brief is framed in terms of that language, and whose authority derives from a presumption of expertise in that language. For such an officer to appeal to an authority that supercedes the commitment to constitutional language by appealing to an extraconstitutional concept of "emergency" is to assert authority to replace the sovereign people with a sovereign individual ruling over subjects, a reversion to the pre-Lockean form of sovereignty and a complete dissolution of the premises of constitutional rule.

The issue is far more starkly framed in the case of a judge than for any other actor. The concept of extraconstitutional emergency judicial powers is an Hobbesian absurdity, a concatenation of incommensurate terms. As in the earlier case of a substance-less textual provision, from the perspective of ordinary law the problem is far less grave. In the Anglo-American legal tradition, in particular, decision making is ultimately grounded in the irreducible exercise of human judgment. But where the issue is a constitutional one, specifically, then any simple appeal to individual judgment becomes an act either of abdication or usurpation.

The case of a different category of constitutional official is only somewhat different. Consider an official who appeals to the inherent powers of the office to justify an act that is otherwise unsupportable in the constitutional text. Such an official may be making one of two claims: that the name of the office in the Constitution includes this inherent authority, or that the office carries with it the authority to appeal to considerations that cannot be articulated in the language of constitutional discourse, and on that basis he is permitted to ignore constitutional limitations that would otherwise apply. The first argument is highly contestable but not subversive of the legitimacy of the constitutional regime; the second, by contrast, is an overt act of usurpation. Nor can such an argument be rescued by virtue of the imprimatur of a judge's decision; the judge's authority is based on a claim of expertise with respect to constitutional language, not authority to choose when constitutional and other forms of language should be employed.

Most of all, the idea of judicial emergency powers – that a constitutionally empowered *judge* could assert the existence of an emergency as the basis for engaging in some kind of extraconstitutional review of laws or government actions – is an absurdity. It is the literal and precise equivalent of declaring an intention to utter in English a proposition that cannot be expressed in the English language. A judge who employs extraconstitutional criteria to determine the application of constitutional principles has entirely dissolved the basis of her authority. Naturally, any judicial ruling of which one disapproves may be accused of straying beyond the bounds of constitutional language; such an accusation is nothing more than the tired assertion of "judicial activism" that is heard any time a court's ruling fails to accord with the policy preferences of the speaker. But that is quite different from a judge who affirmatively declares that propositions that have not been or cannot be translated into constitutional language are the determinants of her ruling.

The arguments in the past few paragraphs are readily identified with particular controversies and cases in recent American history, and a reader will have little difficulty in identifying moments that present troubling concerns. I have refrained from entering into those specific debates, however, because my purpose in this concluding discussion is not to present an accusation but to sound a caution. This book has presented an argument for the legitimacy of a regime grounded in principles of liberal constitutionalism. The conditions of possibility for such a legitimate regime are stringent, and the preservation of those conditions is simultaneously the duty and the source of the authority of constitutional officers. If it is the case that those actors allow those conditions to be compromised, then their own authority may be only the first of a series of institutional arrangements whose legitimacy can no longer be presumed. And if the constitutional regime is to be not only legitimate but also successful, then not only officials but all citizens must be willing and able to reaffirm a commitment to speak in the terms of an established constitutional language, or to argue for its revision. That is the challenge and the promise of liberal constitutionalism.

Bibliography

Aarsleff, Hans. *From Locke to Saussure: Essays on the Study of Language in Intellectual History*. London, 1982.

Aarsleff, Hans. "The State of Nature and the Nature of Man in Locke." In *John Locke: Problems and Perspectives*, ed. John Yolton. Cambridge, 1969: 99–136.

Ackerman, Bruce. *We the People: Tranformations*. Cambridge, MA, 1992.

Ackerman, Bruce. *We The People: Foundations*. Cambridge, MA, 1993.

Adler, Matthew D. "Expressive Theories of Law: A Skeptical Overview." *University of Pennsylvania Law Review* 148 (2000): 1363–1450.

Aeschylus. *The Oresteia*, Robert Fagles, trans. New York, 1977.

Alexander, Lawrence, ed. *Constitutionalism*. Cambridge, 2001.

Alexy, Robert. "The Nature of Arguments About the Nature of Law." In *Rights, Culture, and the Law: Themes from the Legal and Political Philosophy of Joseph Raz*, eds. Lukas H. Meyer, Stanley L. Paulson, and Thomas W. Pogge. Oxford, 2003: 3–16.

Alexy, Robert. *The Argument From Injustice: A Reply to Legal Positivism*. Oxford, 2002.

Amar, Akhil Reed. *America's Constitution: A Biography*. New York, 2005.

Amar, Akhil Reed. "Popular Sovereignty and Constitutional Amendment." In *Responding to Imperfection: The Theory and Practice of Constitutional Amendment*, ed. Sanford Levinson. Princeton, 1995a: 89–115.

Amar, Akhil Reed. "Presidents, Vice-Presidents, and Death: Closing the Constitution's Succession Gap." *Arkansas Law Review* 48 (1995b): 215–38.

Amar, Akhil Reed. "The Consent of the Governed: Constitutional Amendment Outside Article V." *Columbia Law Review* 94 (1994): 457–508.

Amar, Akhil Reed. "Philadelphia Revisited: Amending the Constitution Outside Article V." *University of Chicago Law Review* 55 (1988): 1043–1103.

Ames, William. *Conscience With the Power and Cases Therof*. London, 1639.

Anderson, Elizabeth S., and Richard H. Pildes. "Expressive Theories of Law: A General Restatement." *University of Pennsylvania Law Review* 148 (2000): 1503–75.

Appleby, Joyce. "Locke, Liberalism and the Natural Law of Money." *Past and Present* 71 (1976): 43–69.

Aristotle. *The Politics and the Constitution of Athens*, ed. Stephen Everson, trans. Benjamin Jowett. Cambridge, 2004.

Ashcraft, Richard, ed. *John Locke: Critical Assessments*, 4 vols. New York, 1991.

Ashcraft, Richard. "Revolutionary Politics and Locke's Two Treatises of Government: Radicalism and Lockean Political Theory." *Political Theory* 8 (November 1980): 429–86.

Ashworth, E. J. "Locke on Language," 14 *Canadian Journal of Philosophy"* 14 (1984): 45–73. Reprinted in *John Locke: Critical Assessments*, ed. Richard Ashcraft, vol. 1. New York, 1991:235–59.

Austin, John. *The Province of Jurisprudence Determined*. New York, 2000.

Ayoub, M. "Translating the Meaning of the Quran: Traditional Opinions and Modern Debates." *Afkar Inquiry* 3 (May 1986): 34–9.

Balkin, Jack. "Fidelity in Constitutional Theory: Does the Constitution Deserve Our Fidelity?: Agreements with Hell and Other Objects of Our Faith." *Fordham Law Review* 65 (1997): 1703–38.

Barber, Sotirios A. "Notes on Constitutional Maintenance." In *Constitutional Politics: Essays on Constitution Making, Maintenance, and Change*, eds. Sotiros A. Barber and Robert P. George. Princeton, 2001: 162–66.

Barber, Sotirios A. *On What the Constitution Means*. Baltimore, 1984.

Barnett, Randy E. "Constitutional Legitimacy." *Columbia Law Review* 103 (2003): 111–48.

Beardsworth, Richard. *Derrida and the Political*. London, 1996.

Bellamy, Richard. "The Political Form of the Constitution: The Separation of Powers, Rights and Representative Democracy." In *Constitutions in Transformation: European and Theoretical Perspectives*, eds. Richard Bellamy and Dario Castiglione. Oxford, 1996: 24–44.

Benhabib, Seyla. "Toward a Deliberative Model of Democratic Legitimacy." In *Democracy and Difference: Contesting the Boundaries of the Political*, ed. Benhabib. Princeton, 1996: 3–18.

Berlin, Isaiah. *Liberty*. Oxford, 2002.

Berman, Harold J. "The Origins of Historical Jurisprudence: Coke, Selden, Hale." *Yale Law Journal* 103 (1994): 1651–1738.

Bickel, Alexander M. *The Least Dangerous Branch: The Supreme Court at the Bar of Politics*. New Haven, 1986.

Blackstone, William. *Commentaries on the Laws of England*, 4 vols, facs. ed. Stanley N. Katz. Chicago, 1979.

Bobbitt, Phillip. *Constitutional Interpretation*. Oxford, 1991.

Bobbitt, Phillip. *Constitutional Fate*. Oxford, 1982.

Bodin, Jean. *The Six Books of a Commonwealth* [1606], ed. Kenneth Douglas McRae, facs. of trans. Richard Knolles. Cambridge, MA, 1962.

Bork, Robert. "The Judge's Role in Law and Culture." *Ave Maria Law Review* 1 (2003): 19–29.

Bork, Robert. *The Tempting of America: the Political Seduction of the Law*. New York, 1990.

Boyd, Richard. "The Calvinist Origins of Lockean Political Economy." *History of Political Thought* 23 (2002): 30–60.

Brand-Ballard, Jeffrey. "Kelsen's Unstable Alternative to Natural Law: Recent Critiques." *American Journal of Jurisprudence* 41 (1996): 133–64.

Brandon, Mark E. "Constitutionalism and Constitutional Failure." In *Constitutional Politics: Essays on Constitution Making, Maintenance, and Change*, eds. Sotirios A. Barber and Robert P. George. Princeton, 2001: 298–313.

Brandon, Mark E. *Free in the World: American Slavery and Constitutional Failure*. Princeton, 1998.

Browne, Thomas. *Religio Medici*. London, 1643.

Brewer, David J. "An Independent Judiciary as the Salvation of the Nation," (1893). Reprinted in *The Annals of America: Agrarianism and Urbanization 1884–1894*, vol. 11 (Chicago, 1968: 423–30).

Byrne, James. "The Basis of Natural Law in Locke's Philosophy." *Catholic Lawyer* 10 (1964): 55–63. Reprinted in *John Locke: Critical Assessments*, vol. 2, ed. Richard Ashcraft. New York, 1991: 52–62.

Cardozo, Benjamin. *The Nature of the Judicial Process*. Boston, 1921.

Castiglione, Dario. "The Political Theory of the Constitution." In *The Constitution in Transformation: European and Theoretical Perspectives*, eds. Richard Bellamy and Castiglione. Oxford, 1996: 417–35

Carroll, Lewis. *Alice in Wonderland*.

Cohen, Joshua. "Procedure and Substance in Deliberative Democracy." In *Democracy and Difference: Contesting the Boundaries of the Political*, ed. Benhabib. Princeton, 1996: 95–119.

Cohen, Barak. "Empowering Constitutionalism with Text from an Israeli Perspective." *American University International Law Review* 18 (2003): 585–650.

Cohen, Joshua. "Structure, Choice and Legitimacy: Locke's Theory of the State." *Philosophy and Public Affairs* 15 (1986): 301–24.

Coleman, Jules. *The Practice of Principle: In Defense of a Pragmatist Approach to Legal Theory*. Oxford, 2001.

Coleman, Jules. "Authority and Reason." In *The Autonomy of Law: Essays on Legal Positivism*, ed. Robert P. George. Oxford, 1996: 287–319.

Coleman, Jules, and Brian Leiter. "Determinacy, Objectivity, and Authority." *University of Pennsylvania Law Review* 142 (1993): 549–637.

Cover, Robert. "Violence and the Word." *Yale Law Journal* 95 (1986): 1601–29.

Cover, Robert. "The Supreme Court, 1982 Term – Foreword: Nomos and Narrative." *Harvard. Law Review* 97 (1983): 4–68.

Cover, Robert. *Justice Accused: Antislavery and the Judicial Process*. New Haven, 1975.

Croly, Stephen, P. "The Majoritarian Difficulty: Elective Judiciaries and the Rule of Law." *University of Chicago Law Review* 62 (1995): 689–791.

Culler, Jonathan. *On Deconstruction: Theory and Criticism After Structuralism*. Ithaca, NY, 1982.

Curry, Thomas J. *The First Freedoms*. Oxford, 1986.

Dawson, Hannah, "Locke on Private Language," *British Journal for the History of Philosophy* 11 (2003): 609–38.

Denning, Brian. "Means to Amend: Theories of Constitutional Change." *Tennessee Law Review* 65 (1997): 155–244.

Derrida, Jacques. "The Force of Law: The 'Mystical Foundation of Authority.'" *Cardozo Law Review* (1990): 920–1045.

Derrida, Jacques. *Writing and Difference*. Chicago, 1978.

Derrida, Jacques. *Of Grammatology*, trans. Gayatri Spivak. Baltimore, 1974.

Dewey, John. "Substance, Power and Quality in Locke." *Philosophical Reviews* 35 (1926): 22–38.

Dicey, A. B. *Introduction to the Study of the Law of the Constitution*, 7th ed. London, 1908.

Dorf, Michael C. "Legal Indeterminacy and Institutional Design." *New York University Law Review* 78 (2003): 875–981.

Dow, David R. "The Plain Meaning of Article V." In *Responding to Imperfection: The Theory and Practice of Constitutional Amendment*, ed. Sanford Levinson. Princeton, 1995: 117–44.

Dow, David R. "When Words Mean What We Believe They Say: The Case of Article V." *Iowa Law Review* 76 (1990): 1–66.

Dunn, John. *The Political Thought of John Locke: An Historical Account of the Argument of the Two Treatises of Government*. Cambridge, 1982.

Dunn, John. "Consent in the Political Theory of John Locke," *Historical Journal* 10 (1967): 153–82.

Dworkin, Ronald. *Law's Empire*. Cambridge, MA, 1986.

Dworkin, Ronald. *Taking Rights Seriously*. Cambridge, MA, 1977.

Eisgruber, Christopher. *Constitutional Self-Government*. Cambridge, MA, 2001.

Eisgruber, Christopher. "Judicial Supremacy and Constitutional Distortion." In *Constitutional Politics: Essays on Constitution Making, Maintenance, and Change*, eds. Sotirios A. Barber and Robert P. George. Princeton, 2001: 70–90.

Eisgruber, Christopher L., and Lawrence G. Sager. "Why the Religious Freedom Restoration Act Is Unconstitutional." *New York University Law Review* 69 (1994): 437–76.

Eleftheriadis, Pavlos. "The European Constitution and Cosmopolitan Ideals." 7 *Columbia Journal of European Law* (2001): 21–39.

Elster, John. *Ulysses Unbound: Studies in Rationality, Precommitments, and Constraints*. Cambridge, 2000.

Elster, John. *Ulysses and the Sirens*. Cambridge, 1984.

Erikson, Erik Oddvar, and Jon Fossum. "Europe in Search of Legitimacy: Strategies of Legitimation Assessed." *International Political Science Review* 25 (2004): 435–59.

Farber, Daniel A., and Suzanna Sherry. *Desparately Seeking Certainty: the Misguided Quest for Constitutional Foundations*. Chicago, 2004.

Farr, James. "The Americanization of Hermeneutics: Francis Lieber's Legal and Political Hermeneutics." In *Legal Hermeneutics:History, Theory, and Practice*, ed. Gregory Leyh. Berkeley, 1992: 83–102.

Ferrajoli, Luigi. "Beyond Sovereignty and Citizenship: A Global Constitutionalism." In *Constitutionalism, Democracy and Sovereignty: American and European Perspectives*, ed. Richard Bellamy. Aldershot, 1997: 151–59.

Fineman, Martha Albertson. "Cracking the Foundational Myths: Independence, Autonomy, and Self-Sufficiency." *American University Journal of Gender, Society, Politics and Law* 8 (2000): 13–29.

Finn, John E. "The Civic Constitution: Some Preliminaries." In *Constitutional Politics: Essays on Constitution Making, Maintenance, and Change*, eds. Sotirios A. Barber and Robert P. George. Princeton, 2001: 41–69.

Finnis, John. "Law and What I Truly Should Decide." *American Journal of Jurisprudence* 48 (2003): 107–29.

Finnis, John. "The Truth of Legal Positivism." In *The Autonomy of Law: Essays on Legal Positivism*, ed. Robert P. George. Oxford, 1996: 195–214.

Finnis, John. *Natural Law and Natural Rights*. Oxford, 1980.

Fish, Stanley. *There's No Such Thing as Free Speech, and it's a Good Thing, Too*. Oxford, 1994.

Fisher, Louis. *Religious Liberty in America: Political Safeguards*. Lawrence, KA, 2002.

Franklin, Julian H. "Introduction." Jean Bodin, *On Sovereignty*. Cambridge, 2003: ix–xxvi.

Freeman, Samuel. "The Idea of Public Reason Revisited: Public Reason and Political Justifications." *Fordham Law Review* 72 (2004): 2021–72.

Fuller, Lon L. *The Morality of Law*. Cambridge, MA: 1969.

Gadamer, Hans-Georg. *Truth and Method*. Cambridge, MA, 1975.

Gauthier, David. "Hobbes' Social Contract." *Noûs* 22 (1988): 71–82.

Gauthier, David. "Thomas Hobbes: Moral Theorist." *Journal of Philosophy* 76 (1979): 547–59.

George, Robert P. "Justice, Legitimacy, and Allegiance: 'The End of Democracy?' Symposium Revisited." In *Constitutional Politics:Essays on Constitution Making, Maintenance, and Change*, eds. Sotirios A. Barber and Robert P. George. Princeton, 2001: 314–28.

Goldie, Mark, "Introduction." In John Locke, *Political Essays*, ed. Goldie. Cambridge, 1997: xi–xxvii.

Goldstein, Leslie. "Popular Sovereignty, The Origins of Judicial Review, and the Revival of Unwritten Law." *Journal of Politics* 48 (1986): 51–71.

Graber, Mark. *Dred Scott and the Problem of Constitutional Evil* (unpublished ms., Cambridge University Press, forthcoming).

Grant, Ruth. *John Locke's Liberalism*. Chicago, 1987.

Green, Leslie. "Law, Legitimacy and Consent," *Southern California Law Review* 62 (1989): 795–825.

Greenawalt, Kent. "Too Thin and Too Rich, Distinguishing Features of Legal Positivism." In *The Autonomy of Law: Essays on Legal Positivism*, ed. Robert P. George. Oxford, 1996: 1–30.

Greenawalt, Kent. "The Religious Voice in the Public Square: Religious Expression in the Public Square – The Building Blocks for an Intermediate Position." *Loyola Law Review* 29 (1996): 1411–20.

Greenawalt, Kent. "Religious Convictions and Lawmaking." *Michigan Law Review* 84 (1985): 352–404.

Griffin, Stephen M. "Constitutionalism in the United States: From Theory to Politics." In *Responding to Imperfection: the Theory and Practice of Constitutional Amendment*, ed. Sanford Levinson. Princeton, 1995: 37–61.

Griffin, Stephen, M. "The Nominee is ... Article V." *Constitutional Commentary* 12 (1995): 171–73.

Habermas, Jürgen. *The Inclusion of the Other: Studies in Political Theory*, eds. Ciaran Cronin and Pablo De Greiff. Cambridge, MA, 2000.

Habermas, Jürgen. *Between Facts and Norms*, trans. William Rehg. Cambridge, MA, 1999.

Habermas, Jürgen. *Knowledge and Human Interests*. Boston, 1972.

Harris, William F., II. *The Interpretable Constitution*. Baltimore, 1993.

Harris, William F., II. "Bonding Word and Polity: The Logic of American Constitutionalism." *American Political Science Review* 76 (1982): 34–45.

Hart, H. L. A. *The Concept of Law*, 2nd ed. Oxford, 1997.

Hayek, Frierich A. *The Constitution of Liberty*. Chicago, 1978.

Hayes, Peter. "Hobbes's Silent Fool: A Response to Hoekstra." *Political Theory* 27 (1999): 225–29.

Hirschl, Ran. "'Negative' Rights Versus 'Positive' Entitlements: A Comparative Study of Judicial Interpretations of Rights in an Emerging Neo-Liberal Economic Order." *Human Rights Quarterly* 22 (2000): 1060–98.

Hirschmann, Albert. *The Passions and the Interests : Political Arguments for Capitalism Before Its Triumph*. Princeton, 1977.

Hobbes, Thomas. *On the Citizen* [1642], eds. Richard Tuck and Michael Silverthorne. Cambridge, 1998.

Hobbes, Thomas. *Leviathan* [1651], ed. Richard Tuck. Cambridge, 1996.

Hoekstra, Kinch. "Nothing to Declare?: Hobbes and the Advocate of Injustice." *Political Theory* 27 (1999): 230–35.

Hoekstra, Kinch. "Hobbes and the Fool." *Political Theory* 25 (1997): 620–54.

Holmes, Stephen. *Passions and Constraint: On the Theory of Liberal Democracy*. Chicago, 1995.

Jyranki, Antero. "Transferring Powers of a Nation State to International Organisations: The Doctrine of Sovereignty Revisited." In *National Constitutions in the Era of Integration*, ed. Jyranki. The Hague, 1999: 61–81.

Kahn, Paul. *Legitimacy and History : Self-Government in American Constitutional Theory*. New Haven, 1995.

Katz, Elai. "On Amending Constitutions: The Legality and Legitimacy of Constitutional Entrenchment." *Columbia Journal of Law and Social Problems* 29 (1996): 251–92.

Kavka, Gregory. *Hobbesian Moral and Political Theory*. Princeton, 1986.
Kay, Richard S. "American Constitutionalism." *Constitutionalism*, ed. Larry Alexander. Cambridge, 2001: 16–63.
Keller, Evelyn Fox and Helen E. Longino, eds. *Feminism and Science*. Oxford, 1999.
Kelsen, Hans. "The Function of a Constitution," trans. Iain Stewart. *Essays on Kelsen*, eds. Richard Tur and William Twining. Oxford, 1986: 109–19.
Kelsen, Hans. *Pure Theory of Law*, trans. Max Knight. Berkeley, 1967.
Kelsen, Hans. *General Theory of Law and State*, trans. Anders Wedberg. Cambridge, MA, 1945.
Kennedy, Duncan. 'A Semiotics of Critique." 22 *Cardozo Law Review* (2001): 1147–86.
Kennedy, Duncan. *A Critique of Adjudication (Fin de Siècle)*. Cambridge, MA, 1998.
Kenyon, J. P., *Stuart England*. London, 1985.
Kerber, Linda. *No Constitutional Right to be Ladies: Women and the Obligations of Citizenship*. New York, 1999.
Kerber, Linda K. *No Constitutional Right to be Ladies: Women and the Obligations of Citizenship*. New York, 1998.
King, Brett. "Wild Political Dreaming: Historical Context, Popular Sovereignty, and Supermajority Rules." *University of Pennsylvania Journal of Constitutional Law* 2 (2000): 609–61.
Klarman, Michael. "Majoritarian Judicial Review: The Entrenchment Problem." *Georgetown Law Journal* 85 (1997): 491–553.
Kokott, Juliane. "Federal States in Federal Europe: The German Lander and Problems of European Integration." *National Constitutions in the Era of Integration*, ed. Antero Jyranki. The Hague, 1999: 175–200.
Kramer, Larry. *The People Themselves: Popular Constitutionalism and Judicial Review*. Oxford, 2004a.
Kramer, Larry. "Popular Constitutionalism, circa 2004." *California Law Review* 92 (2004b): 959–1011.
Kramer, Matthew. *John Locke and the Origins of Private Property:Philosophical Explorations of Individualism, Community, and Equality*. Cambridge, 1997.
Kramnick, Isaac. *Bolingbroke and His Circle: The Politics of Nostalgia in the Age of Walpole*. Cambridge, MA, 1968.
Lamprecht, Sterling, "Locke's attack upon innate ideas," 36 *Philosophical Review* (1927): 145–65.
Laslett, Peter. "Introduction." In *Locke: Two Treatises on Government*, ed. Laslett. Cambridge, 1988: 3–126.
Laslett, Peter. "The English Revolution and Locke's Two Treatises of Government. *Cambridge Historical Journal* 12 (1956): 40–55.
Leiter, Brian. "Beyond the Hart/Dworkin Debate: The Methodology Problem in Jurisprudence." *American Journal of Jurisprudence* 48 (2003): 17–51.

Lessig, Lawrence. "The Regulation of Social Meaning." *University of Chicago Law Review* 62 (1995): 943–1045.

Levinson, Sanford. "The Political Implications of Amending Clauses." *Constitutional Commentary* 13 (1996): 107–23.

Levinson, Sanford. "How Many Times Has the United States Constitution Been Amended? (A) <26; (B) 26; C) 27; (D) > 27: Accounting for Constitutional Change." In *Responding to Imperfection: The Theory and Practice of Constitutional Amendment*, ed. Levinson. Princeton, 1995: 13–36.

Leyden, William von. "John Locke and Natural Law." *Philosophy* 21 (1956): 23–35.

Leyh, Gregory. "Legal Education and the Public Life." In *Legal Hermeneutics: History, Theory and Practice*, ed. Leyh. Berkeley, 1992: 269–94.

Li, Andrew I-kang. 2002. "A prototype simulated interactive shape grammar." In *Design e-ducation: connecting the real and the virtual. Proceedings of the 20th conference on education in computer aided architectural design in Europe*, eds. Krzysztof Koszewski and Stefan Wrona. Warsaw, 2002: 314–17.

Li, Andrew I-kang. "Why do Chinese buildings have curved roofs? A first look at intellectual bias in the study of Chinese architecture. (Revised version.)" In *Conference proceedings: Architecture, (Post)modernity, and Difference*. Singapore, 1993: 48–51.

Lieber, Francis. *Legal and Philosophical Hermeneutics: Principles of Interpretation and Construction in Law and Politics*. New York, 1837.

Locke, John. *Two Treatises of Government* [1689], ed. Peter Laslett. Cambridge, 1988.

Locke, John. *An Essay Concerning Human Understanding* [1689], ed. Peter H. Nidditch. Oxford, 1982.

Locke, John. "Essays on the Law of Nature [circa 1664]." In *Locke, Political Essays*, ed. Mark Goldie. Cambridge, 1997: 79–133.

Luhmann, Gerald. "Operational Closure and Structural Coupling: The Differentiation of a Legal System." *Cardozo Law Review* 13 (1992): 1419–41.

MacCormick, Neil. *Questioning Sovereignty: Law, State and Nation in the European Commonwealth*. Oxford, 1999.

MacCormick, Neil. "The Concept of Law and *The Concept of Law*." In *The Autonomy of Law: Essays on Legal Positivism*, ed. Robert P. George. Oxford, 1996: 163–94.

Madigan, James. "The Idea of Public Reason Resuscitated." *William and Mary Bill of Rights Journal* 10 (2002): 719–78.

Madison, James, Alexander Hamilton, and John Jay. *The Federalist Papers*, ed. Isaac Kramnick. New York, 1788/1987.

Magarian, Gregory P. "How to Apply the Religious Freedom Restoration Act to Federal Law Without Violating the Constitution." *Michigan Law Review* 99 (2001): 1903–98.

Mancini, Judge G. F. *Democracy and Constitutionalism in the European Union: Collected Essays*. Oxford, 2000.

Mara, Gerald M. "Hobbes's Counsel to Sovereigns." *Journal of Politics* 50 (1988): 390–411.

McCloskey, Robert G., *The American Supreme Court* (Chicago, 1967).

McCrae, Kenneth. "Introduction." In Jean Bodin, *The Six Bookes of a Commonweale* [1606], ed. McRae, trans. Richard Knolles. Cambridge, MA, 1962: i–xii, A1–A103.

McIlwain, Charles Howard. *Constitutionalism Ancient and Modern*. Ithaca, NY: 1940.

Michelman, Frank. "The Constitutional Essentials of Political Liberalism: Justice as Fairness, Legitimacy, and the Question of Judicial Review." *Fordham Law Review* 72 (2004): 1407–20.

Michelman, Frank. "Ida's Way: Constructing the Respect-Worthy Governmental System." *Fordham Law Review* 72 (2003): 345–65.

Michelman, Frank. "Constitutional Authorship." In *Constitutionalism*, ed. Larry Alexander. Cambridge, 2001: 64–98.

Michelman, Frank. "Courts and Constitutions: Thirteeen Easy Pieces." *Michigan Law Review* 93 (1995): 1297–1332.

Mitchell, Joshua. "Hobbes and the Equality of All Under the One." *Political Theory* 21 (1993): 78–100.

Mulligan, Lotte, Judith Richards, and John K. Graham. "A Concern for Understanding: A Case of Locke's Precepts and Practice." *Historical Journal* 25 (1982): 841–57. Reprinted in *John Locke:Critical Assessments*, ed. Richard Ashcraft: vol. 4. New York, 1991: 670–89.

Murphy, Walter F. "Merlin's Memory: The Past and Future Imperfect of the Once and Future Polity." In *Responding to Imperfection:The Theory and Practice of Constitutional Amendment*, ed. Sanford Levinson. Princeton, 1995: 163–90.

Murphy, Walter F. "An Ordering of Constitutional Values." *Southern California Law Review* 53 (1980): 703–60.

Noonan, John T., Jr. *Narrowing the Nation's Power: The Supreme Court Sides with the States*. Berkeley, 2002.

Norton, Ann. "Transubstantiation: The Dialectic of Constitutional Authority." *University of Chicago Law Review* 55 (1988): 458–72.

Novak, William J. *The People's Welfare: Law and Regulation in Nineteenth-Century America*. Chapel Hill, NC, 1996.

Oakeshott, Michael, *Rationalism in Politics*. 1991, Liberty Press, Indianapolis, 1991.

Oakley, Francis, and Elliott W. Urdang. "Locke, Natural Law, and God." *Natural Law Forum* 11 (1966): 92–109.

Odegard, Douglas. "Locke as an Empiricist," *Philosophy* 40 (1965):185–96. Reprinted in *John Locke: Critical Assessments*, ed. Richard Ashcraft. New York, 1991: vol. 4, 1–12.

Olivecrona, Karl. "Locke's Theory of Appropriation." *Philosophical Quarterly* 24 (1974): 220–34. Reprinted in *John Locke: Critical Assessments*, ed. Richard Ashcraft. New York, 1991: vol. 1, 327–42.

Olivecrona, Karl. "Appropriation in the State of Nature: Locke on the Origin of Property." *Journal of the History of Ideas* 35 (1974): 211–30.

Orren, Karen. "Officer's Rights: Toward a Unified Field Theory of Constitutional Development." *Law & Society Review* 34 (2000): 837–909.

Parrish, Richard. *Aporias of Justice*. Ph.D. thesis, University of Wisconsin-Madison, 2004.

Pateman, Carole. *The Sexual Contract*. Stanford, 1988.

Penner, J. E. "Legal Reasoning and the Authority of Law." In *Rights, Culture, and the Law: Themes from the Legal and Political Philosophy of Joseph Raz*, eds. Lukas H. Meyer, Stanley L. Paulson, and Thomas W. Pogge. Oxford, 2003: 71–98.

Pildes, Richard H. "Why Rights Are Not Trumps: Social Meanings, Expressive Harms, and Constitutionalism." *Journal of Legal Studies* 27 (1998): 725–63.

Pitkin, Hannah, *The Concept of Representation*. Berkeley, 1972.

Pocock, J. A. G., *The Machiavellian Moment* (Princeton, 1975).

Post, Robert. Who's Afraid of Jurispathic Courts?: Violence and Public Reason in Nomos and Narrative." *Yale Journal of Law and Humanities* 17 (2005): 9–16.

Postema, Gerald. "Law's Autonomy and Public Practical Reason." In *The Autonomy of Law: Essays on Legal Positivism*, ed. Robert P. George. Oxford, 1996: 79–118.

Powell, H. Jefferson. "Symposium on Philip Bobbitt's Constitutional Interpretation: Constitutional Investigations." *Texas Law Review* 72 (1994): 1731–51.

Preuss, Ulrich, "The Political Meaning of Constitutionalism." In *Constitutionalism, Democracy and Sovereignty: American and European Perspectives*, ed. Richarl Bellamy. Aldershot, 1997: 11–150.

Rawls, John. *Justice as Fairness: A Restatement*. Cambridge, MA: 2001.

Rawls, John. *Political Liberalism*. New York, 1996.

Raz, Joseph. "Comments and Responses." In *Rights, Culture, and the Law: Themes from the Legal and Political Philosophy of Joseph Raz*, eds. Lukas H. Meyer, Stanley L. Paulson, and Thomas W. Pogge. Oxford, 2003: 253–73.

Raz, Joseph. "On the Authority and Interpretation of Constitutions: Some Preliminaries." In *Constitutionalism*, ed. Larry Alexander. Cambridge, 2001: 152–93.

Raz, Joseph. *The Morality of Freedom*. Oxford, 1986.

Riley, Patrick. "On Finding and Equilibrium between Consent and Natural Law in Locke's Political Philosophy." *Political Studies* 22 (1974): 432–52.

Rubenfeld, Jed. *Freedom and Time: A Theory of Constitunal Self-Government*. New Haven, 2001a.

Rubenfeld, Jed. "Legitimacy and Interpretation." In *Constitutionalism: Philosophical Foundations*, ed. Larry Alexander. Cambridge, 2001b: 194–243.

Rubin, Edward L. *Beyond Camelot: Rethinking Politics and Law for the Modern State*. Princeton, 2005.

Sager, Lawrence. "The Constitutional Essentials of Political Liberalism: The Why of Constitutional Essentials." *Fordham Law Review* 72 (2004): 1421–33.

Sager, Lawrence, "The Domain of Constitutional Justice." In *Constitutionalism: Philosophical Foundations*, ed. Larry Alexander. Cambridge, 1998.

Sager, Lawrence. "You Can Raise the First, Hide Behind the Fourth, and Plead the Fifth. But What On Earth Can You Do With The Ninth Amendment?" *Chicago-Kent Law Review* 64 (1988): 239–64.

Saussure, Ferdinand de. *Course in General Linguistics*. New York, 1966.

Schauer, Frederick. "Judicial Supremacy and the Modest Constitution." *California Law Review* 92 (2004): 1045–67.

Schauer, Frederick. "Precedent and the Necessary Externality of Constitutional Norms." *Harvard Journal of Law and Public Policy* 17 (1994): 45–56.

Schauer, Frederick. "Constitutional Positivism." *Connecticut Law Review* 25 (1993): 797–828.

Schweber, Howard. *The Creation of American Common Law, 1850–1880: Technology, Politics, and the Construction of Citizenship in Illinois and Virginia*. Cambridge 2004.

Seminole Tribe of Florida v. Florida, 517 U.S. 44 (1995).

Shapin, Steven, and Simon Schaeffer. *Leviathan and the Air-pump: Hobbes, Boyle, and the Experimental Life*. Princeton, 1989.

Shivakumar, Dhananjai. "The Pure Theory as Ideal Type: Defending Kelsen on the Basis of Weberian Methodology." *Yale Law Journal* 105 (1996): 1383–1414.

Skinner, Quentin. *Foundations of Modern Political Thought*, 2 vols. Cambridge, 1978.

Smith, Steven D. "Expressivist Jurisprudence and the Depletion of Meaning." *Maryland Law Review* 60 (2001): 506–77.

Soles, David E. "Intellectualism and Natural Law in Locke's *Second Treatise*." *History of Political Thought* 8 (1977): 63–81.

Stevenson, Drury. "To Whom Is the Law Addressed?" *Yale Law and Policy Review* 21 (2003): 105–67.

Stewart, Iain. "Kelsen Tomorrow." *Current Legal Problems* 51 (1998): 181–204.

Stewart, Iain. 'The Critical Legal Science of Hans Kelsen." *Journal of Law and Society* 17 (1990): 273–308.

Stoner, James R., Jr. *Common-Law Liberty: Rethinking American Constitutionalism*. Lawrence, 2003.

Strauss, David A. "Common Law Constitutional Interpretation." *University of Chicago Law Review* 63 (1996): 877–935.

Sunstein, Cass R. *Designing Democracy: What Constitutions Do*. Oxford, 2001.

Sunstein, Cass R. "On the Expressive Function of Law." *University of Pennsylvania Law Review* 144 (1996): 2021–53.

Sunstein, Cass R. *The Partial Constitution*. Cambridge, MA, 1993.

Tomlins, Christopher. *Law, Labor and Ideology in the Early American Republic*. Cambridge, 1983.

Trenchard, John, and Thomas Gordon. *Cato's Letters: or, Essays on Liberty, Civil and Religious, and other Important Subjects*, ed. Ronald Hamowy, 2 vols. Indianapolis, 1995.

Tribe, Lawrence. *Constitutional Choices*. Cambridge, MA, 1985.

Tuck, Richard. "Introduction." In Thomas Hobbes, *On The Citizen*, eds. Richard Tuck and Michael Silverthorne. Cambridge, 2002: viii–xxxiii.

Tuck, Richard, "Introduction." Thomas Hobbes *Leviathan*, ed. Tuck. Cambridge, 1996: ix–xlv.

Tully, James. *A Discourse on Property: John Locke and His Adversaries*. Cambridge, 1980.

Tur, Richard, and William Twining, eds. *Essays on Kelsen*. Oxford, 1986.

Tushnet, Mark. *Taking the Constitution Away from the Courts*. Princeton, 2000.

Tushnet, Mark. *The American Law of Slavery, 1810–1860: Considerations of Humanity and Interest*. Princeton, 1981.

Venter, Francois. "Constitution Making and the Legitimacy of the Constitution." In *National Constitutions in the Era of Integration*, ed. Antero Jyranki. The Hague, 1999: 9–29.

Verhoeven, Amaryllis. *The European Union in Search of a Democratic and Constitutional Theory*. The Hague, 2003.

Waldron, Jeremy. "Authority for Officials." In *Rights, Culture, and the Law: Themes from the Legal and Political Philosophy of Joseph Raz*, eds. Lukas H. Meyer, Stanley L. Paulson, and Thomas W. Pogge. Oxford, 2003: 45–69.

Waldron, Jeremy. *God, Locke and Equality: Christian Foundations in Locke's Political Thought*. Cambridge, 2002a.

Waldron, Jeremy. "Christopher L. Eisgruber's Constitutional Self-Government: Eisgruber's House of Lords." *University of San Francisco Law Review* 37 (2002b): 89–114.

Waldron, Jeremy. "Precommitment and Disagreement." In *Contitutionalism: Philosophical Foundations*, ed. Larry Alexander. Cambridge, 2001: 271–99.

Waldron, Jeremy. "Pildes on Dworkin's Theory of Rights." *Journal of Legal Studies* 29 (2000): 301–07.

Waldron, Jeremy. "What is a Human Right? Universals and the Challenge of Cultural Relativism." *Pace International Law Review* 11 (1999): 129–38.

Walsh, Katherine Cramer. *Talking About Politics*. Chicago, 2003.

Weiler, Joseph H. *The Constitution of Europe: Do the New Clothes Have an Emperor? and Other Essays on European Integration*. Cambridge, 1999.

White, James Boyd. *Justice as Translation: An Essay in Cultural and Legal Criticism*. Chicago, 1990.

Whittington, Keith. *Constitutional Interpretation: Textual Meaning, Original Intent, and Judicial Review*. Lawrence, KA, 1999a.

Whittington, Keith. *Constitutional Construction: Divided Powers and Constitutional Meaning*. Cambridge, MA, 1999b.

Wilson, James. *The Works of James Wilson*, ed. Robert Green McCloskey, 2 vols. Cambridge, MA, 1967.

Wood, Gordon. *The Creation of the American Republic, 1776–1787*. Chapel Hill, 1969.

Yolton, John. "Locke on the Law of Nature." *Philosophical Review* 67 (1958): 477–98.

Young, Iris Marion. "Communication and the Other: Beyond Deliberative Democracy." In *Democracy and Difference: Contesting the Boundaries of the Political*, ed. Seyla Benhabib. Princeton, 1996: 120–35.

Zuckert, Michael. *Launching Liberalism: On Lockean Political Philosophy*. Lawrence, KA: 2002.

Index